1560

GENEVA BIBLE
New Testament

The bible of the pilgrims and the reformers

This book belongs to the Saints of God

Published by Wisdom Books, USA, 2018
wisdombooks.faith

TO OUR BELOVED IN THE LORD,

The brethren of England, Scotland, Ireland, &c.

Grace, mercy and peace, through Christ Jesus.

Besides the manifold and continual benefits which almighty God bestoweth upon us, both corporal and spiritual, we are especially bound (dear brethren) to give him thanks without ceasing for his great grace and unspeakable mercies, in that it hath pleased him to call us unto this marvelous light of his Gospel, and mercifully to regard us after so horrible backsliding and falling away from Christ to Antichrist, from light to darkness, from the living God to dumb and dead idols, and that after so cruel murder of God's saints, as alas, hath been among us, we are not altogether cast off, as were the Israelites, and many others for the like, or not so manifest wickedness, but received again to grace with most evident signs and tokens of God's especial love and favour. To the intent therefore that we may not be unmindful of these great mercies, but seek by all means (according to our duty) to be thankful for the same, it behoveth us so to walk in his fear and love, that all the days of our life we may procure the glory of his holy name. Now forasmuch as this thing chiefly is attained by the knowledge and practicing of the word of God (which is the light to our paths, the key of the kingdom of heaven, our comfort in affliction, our shield and sword against Satan, the school of all wisdom, the glass wherein we behold God's face, the testimony of his favour, and the only food and nourishment of our souls) we thought that we should bestow our labours and study in nothing which could be more acceptable to God and comfortable to his Church than in the translating of the Holy Scriptures into our native tongue; the which thing, albeit that divers heretofore have endeavored to achieve, yet considering the infancy of those times and imperfect knowledge of the tongues, in respect of this ripe age and clear light which God hath now revealed, the translations required greatly to be perused and reformed. Not that we vindicate anything to ourselves above the least of our brethren (for God knoweth with what fear and trembling we have been now, for the space of two years and more day and night occupied herein) but being earnestly desired, and by divers, whose learning and godliness we reverence, exhorted, and also encouraged by the ready wills of such, whose hearts God likewise touched, not to spare any charges for the furtherance of such a benefit and favour of God toward his Church (though the time then was most dangerous and the persecution sharp and furious) we submitted ourselves at length to their godly judgments, and seeing the great opportunity and occasions, which God presented unto us in his Church, by reason of so many godly and learned men, and such diversities of translations in divers tongues, we undertook this great and wonderful work (with all reverence, as in the presence of God, as intreating the word of God, whereunto we think ourselves insufficient) which now God according to his divine providence and mercy hath directed to a most prosperous end. And this we may with good conscience protest, that we have in every point and word, according to the measure of that knowledge which it pleased almighty God to give us, faithfully rendered the text, and in all hard places most sincerely expounded the same. For God is our witness that we have by all means endeavored to set forth the purity of the word and right sense of the Holy Ghost for the edifying of the brethren in faith and charity.

Now as we have chiefly observed the sense, and labored always to restore it to all integrity, so have we most reverently kept the propriety of the words, considering that the Apostles who spake and wrote to the Gentiles in the Greek tongue, rather constrained them to the lively phrase of the Hebrew than enterprised far by mollifying their language to speak as the Gentiles did. And for this and other causes we have in many places reserved the Hebrew phrases, notwithstanding that they may seem somewhat hard in their ears that are not well practiced and also delight in the sweet-sounding phrases of the Holy Scriptures. Yet lest either the simple should be discouraged, or the malicious have any occasion of just cavillation, seeing some translations read after one sort, and some after another, whereas all may serve to good purpose and edification, we have in the margent noted that diversity of speech or reading which may also seem agreeable to the mind of the Holy Ghost and proper for our language with this mark « .

Again where as the Hebrew speech seemed hardly to agree with ours, we have noted it in the margent after this sort » , using that which was more intelligible. And albeit that many of the Hebrew names be altered from the old text, and restored to the true writing and first original, whereof they have their signification, yet in the usual names little is changed for fear of troubling the simple readers. Moreover whereas the necessity of the sentence required anything to be added (for such is the grace and propriety of the Hebrew and Greek tongues, that it cannot but either by circumlocution, or by adding the verb or some word be understand of them that are not well practiced therein) we have put it in the text with another kind of letter, that it may easily be discerned from the common letter. As touching the division of the verses, we have followed the Hebrew examples, which have so even from the beginning distinct them. Which thing as it is most profitable for memory; so doth it agree with the best translations, &c., is most easy to find out both by the best concordances, and also by the quotations which we have diligently herein perused and set forth by this star *. Besides this the principal matters are noted and distincted by this mark ¶. Yea and the arguments both for the book and for the chapters with the number of the verse are added, that by all means the reader might be holpen. For the which cause also we have set over the head of every page some notable word or sentence which may greatly further as well for memory, as for the chief point of the page. And considering how hard a thing it is to understand the holy Scriptures, and what errors, sects, and heresies grow daily for lack of the true knowledge thereof, and how many are discouraged (as they pretend) because they cannot attain to the true and simple meaning of the same, we have also endeavored both by the diligent reading of the best commentaries, and also by the conference with the godly and learned brethren, to gather brief annotations upon all the hard places, as well for the understanding of such words as are obscure, and for the declaration of the text, as for the application of the same as may most appertain to God's glory and the edification of his Church. Furthermore whereas certain places in the books of Moses, of the Kings and Ezekiel seemed so dark that by no description they could be made easy to the simple reader, we have so set them forth with figures and notes for the full declaration thereof, that they which cannot by judgment, being holpen by the annotations noted by the letters a b c, &c. attain thereunto, yet by the perspective, and as it were by the eye may sufficiently know the true meaning of all such places. Whereunto also we have added certain maps of cosmography which necessarily serve for the perfect understanding and memory of divers places and countries, partly described, and partly by occasion touched, both in the Old and New Testament. Finally that nothing might lack which might be bought by labors, for the increase of knowledge and furtherance of God's glory, we have adjoined two most profitable tables, the one serving for the interpretation of the Hebrew names, and the other containing all the chief and principal matters of the whole Bible; so that nothing (as we trust) that any could justly desire, is omitted. Therefore, as brethren that are partakers of the same hope and salvation with us, we beseech you, that this rich pearl and inestimable treasure may not be offered in vain, but as sent from God to the people of God, for the increase of his kingdom, the comfort of his Church, and discharge of our conscience, whom it hath pleased him to raise up for this purpose, so you would willingly receive the word of God, earnestly study it and in your life practice it, that you may now appear in deed to be the people of God, not walking any more according to this world, but in the fruits of the Spirit; that God in us may be fully glorified through Christ Jesus our Lord, who liveth and reigneth for ever. Amen.

From Geneva, 10 April 1560

ORDER OF BOOKS

TO OUR BELOVED IN THE LORD,

New Testament

NEW TESTAMENT

THE HOLY GOSPEL OF JESUS CHRIST, ACCORDING TO MATTHEW

Matthew Chapter 1

1 The book of the generation of JESUS CHRIST the son of David, the son of Abraham.

2 Abraham begat Isaac. And Isaac begat Jacob. And Jacob begat Judas and his brethren.

3 And Judas begat Phares. And Zara of Thamar. And Phares begat Esrom. And Esrom begat Aram.

4 And Aram begat Aminadab. And Aminadab begat Naasson. And Naasson begat Salmon.

5 And Salmon begat Boaz of Rachab. And Boaz begat Obed of Ruth. And Obed begat Jesse.

6 And Jesse begat David the King. And David the King Begat Solomon of her that was the wife of Urias.

7 And Solomon begat Roboam. And Roboam begat Abia. And Abia begat Asa.

8 And Asa begat Josaphat. And Josaphat begat Joram. And Joram begat Ozias.

9 And Ozias begat Joatham. And Joatham begat Achaz. And Achaz begat Ezekias.

10 And Ezekias begat Manasses. And Manasses begat Amon. And Amon begat Josias.

11 And Josias begat Jakim. And Jakim begat Jechonias and his brethren about the time they were carried away to Babylon.

12 And after they were carried away into Babylon, Jechonias begat Salathiel. And Salathiel begat Zorobabel.

13 And Zorobabel begat Abiud. And Abiud begat Eliakim. And Eliakim begat Azor.

14 And Azor begat Sadoc. And Sadoc begat Achim. And Achim begat Eliud.

15 And Eliud begat Eleazar. And Eleazar begat Matthan. And Matthan begat Jacob.

16 And Jacob begat Joseph the husband of Mary, of whom was born JESUS, that is called Christ.

17 So all the generations from Abraham to David, are fourteen generations. And from David until they were carried away into Babylon, fourteen generations: and after they were carried away into Babylon until Christ, fourteen generations.

18 Now the birth of JESUS Christ was thus, When as his mother Mary was betrothed to Joseph, before they came together, she was found with child of the Holy Ghost.

19 Then Joseph her husband being a just man, and not willing to make her a public example, was minded to put her away secretly.

20 But while he thought these things, behold, the Angel of the Lord appeared unto him in a dream, saying, Joseph, the son of David, fear not to take Mary for thy wife: for that which is conceived in her, is of the Holy Ghost.

21 And she shall bring forth a son, and thou shalt call his name JESUS: for he shall save his people from their sins.

22 And all this was done that it might be fulfilled, which was spoken of the Lord by the Prophet, saying,

23 Behold, a virgin shall be with child, and shall bear a son, and they shall call his name Emmanuel, which is by interpretation, God with us.

24 Then Joseph, being raised from sleep, did as the Angel of the Lord had enjoined him, and took his wife.

25 But he knew her not, till she had brought forth her first born son, and he called his name JESUS.

Matthew Chapter 2

1 When JESUS then was born at Bethlehem in Judea, in the days of Herod the King, behold, there came Wisemen from the East to Jerusalem,

2 Saying, Where is the King of the Jews that is born? for we have seen his star in the East, and are come to worship him.

3 When King Herod heard this, he was troubled, and all Jerusalem with him.

4 And gathering together all the chief Priests and Scribes of the people, he asked of them, where Christ should be born.

5 And they said unto him, At Bethlehem in Judea: for so it is written by the Prophet,

6 And thou Bethlehem in the land of Judah, art not the least among the Princes of Judah: For out of thee shall come the governor that shall feed my people Israel.

7 Then Herod privily called the Wisemen, and diligently inquired of them the time of the star that appeared,

8 And sent them to Bethlehem, saying, Go, and search diligently for the babe: and when ye have found him, bring me word again, that I may come also, and worship him.

9 So when they had heard the King, they departed: and lo, the star which they had seen in the East, went before them, till it came, and stood over the place where the babe was.

10 And when they saw the star, they rejoiced with an exceeding great joy,

11 And went into the house, and found the babe with Mary his mother, and fell down, and worshipped him, and opened their treasures, and presented unto him gifts, even gold, and frankincense, and myrrh.

12 And after they were warned of God in a dream, that they should not go again to Herod, they returned into their country another way.

13 After their departure, behold the Angel of the Lord appeareth to Joseph in a dream, saying, Arise, and take the babe and his mother, and flee into Egypt, and be there till I bring thee word: for Herod will seek the babe, to destroy him.

14 So he arose and took the babe and his mother by night, and departed into Egypt,

15 And was there unto the death of Herod, that it might be fulfilled, which was spoken of the Lord by the Prophet, saying, Out of Egypt have I called my son.

16 Then Herod, seeing that he was mocked of the Wisemen, was exceeding wroth, and sent forth, and slew all the male children that were in Bethlehem, and in all the coasts thereof, from two year old and under, according to the time which he had diligently searched out of the Wisemen.

17 Then was that fulfilled which was spoken by the Prophet Jeremiah, saying,

18 In Ramah was a voice heard, mourning, and weeping and great lamentation: Rachel weeping for her children, and would not be comforted, because they were not.

19 And when Herod was dead, behold, an Angel of the Lord appeared in a dream to Joseph in Egypt,

20 Saying, Arise, and take the babe and his mother, and go into the land of Israel: for they are dead which sought the babes life.

21 Then he arose up, and took the babe and his mother, and came into the land of Israel.

22 But when he heard that Archelaus did reign in Judea instead of his father Herod, he was afraid to go thither: yet after he was warned of God in a dream, he turned aside into the parts of Galilee,

23 And went and dwelt in a city called Nazareth, that it might be fulfilled which was spoken by the Prophets, which was, That he should be called a Nazarite.

Matthew Chapter 3

1 And in those days, John the Baptist came and preached in the wilderness of Judea,

2 And said, Repent: for the kingdom of heaven is at hand.

3 For this is he of whom it is spoken by the Prophet Isaiah, saying, The voice of him that cryeth in the wilderness, Prepare ye the way of the Lord: make his paths straight.

4 And this John had his garment of camels hair, and a girdle of a skin about his loins: his meat was also locusts and wild honey.

5 Then went out to him Jerusalem and all Judea, and all the region round about Jordan.

6 And they were baptized of him in Jordan, confessing their sins.

7 Now when he saw many of the Pharisees, and of the Sadducees come to his baptism, he said unto them, O generations of vipers, who hath forewarned you to flee from the anger to come?

8 Bring forth therefore fruits worthy amendment of life.

9 And think not to say with yourselves, We have Abraham to our father: for I say unto you, that God is able of these stones to raise up children unto Abraham.

10 And now also is the axe put to the root of the trees: therefore every tree, which bringeth not forth good fruit, is hewn down, and cast into the fire.

11 Indeed I baptize you with water to amendment of life, but he that cometh after me, is mightier than I, whose shoes I am not worthy to bear: he will baptize you with the Holy Ghost, and with fire.

12 Which hath his fan in his hand, and will make clean his floor, and gather his wheat into his garner , but will burn up the chaff with unquenchable fire.

13 Then came Jesus from Galilee to Jordan unto John, to be baptized of him.

14 But John put him back, saying, I have need to be baptized of thee, and comest thou to me?

15 Then Jesus answering, said to him, Let be now: for thus it becometh us to fulfill all righteousness. So he suffered him.

16 And Jesus when he was baptized, came straight out of the water. And lo, the heavens were opened unto him, and John saw the Spirit of God descending like a dove, and lighting upon him.

17 And lo, a voice came from heaven, saying, This is my beloved Son, in whom I am well pleased.

Matthew Chapter 4

1 Then was Jesus led aside of the Spirit into the wilderness, to be tempted of the devil.

2 And when he had fasted forty days, and forty nights, he was afterward hungry.

3 Then came to him the tempter, and said, If thou be the Son of God, command that these stones be made bread.

4 But he answering, said, It is written, Man shall not live by bread only, but by every word that proceedeth out of the mouth of God.

5 Then the devil took him up into the Holy City, and set him on a pinnacle of the temple,

6 And said unto him, If thou be the Son of God, cast thyself down: for it is written, that he will give his Angels charge over thee, and with their hands they shall lift thee up, lest at any time you shouldest dash thy foot against a stone.

7 Jesus said unto him, It is written again, Thou shalt not tempt the Lord thy God.

8 Again the devil took him up into an exceeding high mountain, and showed him all the kingdoms of the world, and the glory of them,

9 And said to him, All these will I give thee, if thou wilt fall down, and worship me.

10 Then said Jesus unto him, Avoid Satan: for it is written, Thou shalt worship the Lord thy God, and him only shalt thou serve.

11 Then the devil left him: and behold, the Angels came, and ministered unto him.

12 And when Jesus had heard that John was delivered up, he returned into Galilee.

13 And leaving Nazareth, went and dwelt in Capernaum, which is near the sea in the borders of Zebulon and Naphtali,

14 That it might be fulfilled which was spoken by Isaiah the Prophet, saying,

15 The land of Zebulon, and the land of Naphtali by the way of the sea, beyond Jordan, Galilee of the Gentiles:

16 The people which sat in darkness, saw great light: and to them which sat in the region and shadow of death, light is risen up.

17 From that time Jesus began to preach, and to say, Amend your lives: for the kingdom of heaven is at hand.

18 And Jesus walking by the sea of Galilee, saw two brethren, Simon, which was called Peter, and Andrew his brother, casting a net into the sea (for they were fishers.)

19 And he said unto them, Follow me, and I will make you fishers of men.

20 And they straightway leaving the nets, followed him.

21 And when he was gone forth from thence, he saw two other brethren, James the son of Zebedee, and John his brother in a ship with Zebedee their father, mending their nets, and he called them.

22 And they without tarrying, leaving the ship and their father, followed him.

23 So Jesus went about all Galilee, teaching in their Synagogues, and preaching the Gospel of the kingdom, and healing every sickness and every disease among the people.

24 And his fame spread abroad through all Syria: and they brought unto him all sick people, that were taken with divers diseases and gripings, and them that were possessed with devils, and those which were lunatic, and those that had the palsy: and he healed them.

25 And there followed him great multitudes out of Galilee, and Decapolis , and Jerusalem, and Judea, and from beyond Jordan.

Matthew Chapter 5

1 And when he saw the multitude, he went up into a mountain: and when he was set, his disciples came to him.

2 And he opened his mouth and taught them, saying,

3 Blessed are the poor in spirit, for theirs is the kingdom of heaven.

4 Blessed are they that mourn: for they shall be comforted. 5 Blessed are the meek: for they shall inherit the earth.

6 Blessed are they which hunger and thirst for righteousness: for they shall be filled.

7 Blessed are the merciful: for they shall obtain mercy.

8 Blessed are the pure in heart: for they shall see God.

9 Blessed are the peacemakers: for they shall be called the children of God.

10 Blessed are they which suffer persecution for righteousness sake: for theirs is the kingdom of heaven.

11 Blessed are ye when men revile you, and persecute you, and say all manner of evil against you for my sake, falsely.

12 Rejoice and be glad, for great is your reward in heaven: for so persecuted they the Prophets which were before you.

13 Ye are the salt of the earth: but if the salt have lost his savor, wherewith shall it be salted? It is thenceforth good for nothing, but to be cast out, and to be trodden under foot of men.

14 Ye are the light of the world. A city that is set on a hill, cannot be hid.

15 Neither do men light a candle, and put it under a bushel, but on a candlestick, and it giveth light unto all that are in the house.

16 Let your light so shine before men, that they may see your good works, and glorify your Father which is in heaven.

17 Think not that I am come to destroy the Law, or the Prophets. I am not come to destroy them, but to fulfill them.

18 For Truly I say unto you, Till heaven, and earth perish, one iota, or one tittle of the Law shall not escape, till all things be fulfilled.

19 Whosoever therefore shall break one of these least commandments, and teach men so, he shall be called the least in the kingdom of heaven: but whosoever shall observe and teach them, the same shall be called great in the kingdom of heaven.

20 For I say unto you, except your righteousness exceed the righteousness of the Scribes and Pharisees, ye shall not enter into the kingdom of heaven.

21 Ye have heard that it was said unto them of the old time, Thou shalt not kill: for whosoever killeth, shall be culpable of judgment.

22 But I say unto you, whosoever is angry with his brother unadvisedly, shall be culpable of judgment. And whosoever saith unto his brother, Raca, shall be worthy to be punished by the Council. And whosoever shall say, Fool, shall be worthy to be punished with hell fire.

23 If then thou bring thy gift to the altar, and there rememberest that thy brother hath ought against thee,

24 Leave there thine offering before the altar, and go thy way: first be reconciled to thy brother, and then come and offer thy gift.

25 Agree with thine adversary quickly, whiles thou art in the way with him, lest thine adversary deliver thee to the Judge, and the Judge deliver thee to the sergeant, and thou be cast into prison.

26 Verily I say unto thee, Thou shalt not come out thence, till thou hast paid the utmost farthing.

27 Ye have heard that it was said to them of old time, Thou shalt not commit adultery.

28 But I say unto you, that whosoever looketh on a woman to lust after her, hath committed adultery with her already in his heart.

29 Wherefore if thy right eye cause thee to offend, pluck it out, and cast it from thee: for better it is for thee, that one of thy members perish, then that thy whole body should be cast into hell.

30 Also if thy right hand make thee to offend, cut it off, and cast it from thee: for better it is for thee that one of thy members perish, then that thy whole body should be cast into hell.

31 It hath been said also, Whosoever shall put away his wife, let him give her a testimonial of divorcement.

32 But I say unto you, whosoever shall put away his wife (except it be for fornication) causeth her to commit adultery: and whosoever shall marry her that is divorced, committeth adultery.

33 Again, ye have heard that it was said to them of old time, Thou shalt not forswear thyself, but shalt perform thine oaths to the Lord.

34 But I say unto you, Swear not at all, neither by heaven, for it is the throne of God:

35 Nor yet by the earth: for it is his footstool: neither by Jerusalem: for it is the city of the great King.

36 Neither shalt thou swear by thine head, because thou canst not make one hair white or black.

37 But let your communication be Yea, yea: Nay, nay. For whatsoever is more than these, cometh of evil.

38 Ye have heard that it hath been said, An eye for an eye, and a tooth for a tooth.

39 But I say unto you, Resist not evil: but whosoever shall smite thee on thy right cheek, turn to him the other also.

40 And if any man will sue thee at the law, and take away thy coat, let him have thy cloak also.

41 And whosoever will compel thee to go a mile, go with him twain.

42 Give to him that asketh, and from him that would borrow of thee, turn not away.

43 Ye have heard that it hath been said, Thou shalt love thy neighbor, and hate thine enemy.

44 But I say unto you, Love your enemies: bless them that curse you: do good to them that hate you, and pray for them which hurt you, and persecute you,

45 That ye may be the children of your father that is in heaven: for he maketh his sun to arise on the evil, and the good, and sendeth rain on the just, and unjust.

46 For if ye love them, which love you, what reward shall you have? Do not the Publicans even the same?

47 And if ye be friendly to your brethren only, what singular thing do ye? do not even the Publicans likewise?

48 Ye shall therefore be perfect, as your Father which is in heaven, is perfect.

Matthew Chapter 6

1 Take heed that ye give not your alms before men, to be seen of them, or else ye shall have no reward of your Father which is in heaven.

2 Therefore when thou givest thine alms, thou shalt not make a trumpet to be blown before thee, as the hypocrites do in the Synagoguesand in the streets, to be praised of men. Verily I say unto you, they have their reward.

3 But when thou doest thine alms, let not thy left hand know what thy right hand doeth,

4 That thine alms may be in secret, and thy Father that seeth in secret, he will reward thee openly.

5 And when thou prayest, be not as the hypocrites: for they love to stand, and pray in the Synagogues, and in the corners of the streets, because they would be seen of men. Verily I say unto you, they have their reward.

6 But when thou prayest, enter into thy chamber and when thou hast shut thy door, pray unto thy Father which is in secret, and thy Father which seeth in secret, shall reward thee openly.

7 Also when ye pray, use no vain repetitions as the heathen: for they think to be heard for their much babbling.

8 Be ye not like them therefore: for your Father knoweth whereof ye have need, before ye ask of him.

9 After this manner therefore pray ye, Our father which art in heaven, hallowed be thy Name.

10 Thy Kingdom come. Thy will be done even in earth, as it is in heaven.

11 Give us this day our daily bread.

12 And forgive us our debts, as we also forgive our debtors.

13 And lead us not into temptation, but deliver us from evil: for thine is the kingdom, and the power, and the glory forever, Amen.

14 For if ye do forgive men their trespasses, your heavenly Father will also forgive you.

15 But if ye do not forgive men their trespasses, no more will your father forgive you your trespass.

16 Moreover, when ye fast, look not sour as the hypocrites: for they disfigure their faces, that they might seem unto men to fast. Verily I say unto you, that they have their reward.

17 But when thou fastest, anoint thine head, and wash thy face,

18 That thou seem not unto men to fast, but unto thy Father which is in secret: and thy Father which seeth in secret, will reward thee openly.

19 Lay not up treasures for yourselves upon the earth, where the moth and canker corrupt, and where thieves dig through, and steal.

20 But lay up treasures for yourselves in heaven, where neither the moth nor canker corrupteth, and where thieves neither dig through, nor steal.
21 For where your treasure is, there will your heart be also.
22 The light of the body is the eye: if then thine eye be single, thy whole body shall be light.
23 But if thine eye be wicked, then all thy body shall be dark. Wherefore if the light that is in thee, be darkness, how great is that darkness?
24 No man can serve two masters: for either he shall hate the one, and love the other, or else he shall lean to the one, and despise the other. Ye cannot serve God and riches.
25 Therefore I say unto you, be not careful for your life, what ye shall eat, or what ye shall drink: nor yet for your body, what ye shall put on. Is not the life more worth than meat? and the body than raiment?
26 Behold the fowls of the heaven: for they sow not, neither reap, nor carry into the barns: yet your heavenly Father feedeth them. Are ye not much better than they?
27 Which of you by taking care, is able to add one cubit unto his stature?
28 And why care ye for raiment? Learn, how the lilies of the field do grow: they labor not, neither spin:
29 Yet I say unto you, that even Solomon in all his glory was not arrayed like one of these.
30 Wherefore if God so clothe the grass of the field which is today, and tomorrow is cast into the oven, shall he not do much more unto you, O ye of little faith?
31 Therefore take no thought, saying, What shall we eat? or what shall we drink? or where with shall we be clothed?
32 (For after all these things seek the Gentiles) for your heavenly Father knoweth, that ye have need of all these things.
33 But seek ye first the kingdom of God, and his righteousness, and all these things shall be ministered unto you.
34 Care not then for the morrow: for the morrow shall care for itself: the day hath enough with his own grief.

Matthew Chapter 7

1 Judge not, that ye be not judged.
2 For with what judgment ye judge, ye shall be judged, and with what measure ye mete, it shall be measured to you again.
3 And why seest thou the mote, that is in thy brothers eye, and perceivest not the beam that is in thine own eye?
4 Or how sayest thou to thy brother, Suffer me to cast out the mote out of thine eye, and behold a beam is in thine own eye?
5 Hypocrite, first cast out the beam out of thine own eye, and then shalt thou see clearly to cast out the mote out of thy brothers eye.
6 Give ye not that which is Holy, to dogs, neither cast ye your pearls before swine, lest they tread them under their feet, and turning again, all to rent you.
7 Ask, and it shall be given you: seek, and ye shall find: knock, and it shall be opened unto you.
8 For whosoever asketh, receiveth: and he, that seeketh, findeth: and to him that knocketh, it shall be opened.
9 For what man is there among you, which if his son ask him bread, would give him a stone?
10 Or if he ask fish, will he give him a serpent?
11 If ye then, which are evil, can give to your children good gifts, how much more shall your Father which is in heaven, give good things to them that ask him?

12 Therefore whatsoever ye would that men should do to you, even so do ye to them: for this is the Law and the Prophets.

13 Enter in at the straight gate: for it is the wide gate, and broad way that leadeth to destruction: and many there be which go in thereat,

14 Because the gate is straight, and the way narrow that leadeth unto life, and few there be that find it.

15 Beware of false prophets, which come to you in sheep's clothing, but inwardly they are ravening wolves.

16 Ye shall know them by their fruits. Do men gather grapes of thorns? or figs of thistles?

17 So every good tree bringeth forth good fruit, and a corrupt tree bringeth forth evil fruit.

18 A good tree cannot bring forth evil fruit: neither can a corrupt tree bring forth good fruit.

19 Every tree that bringeth not forth good fruit, is hewn down, and cast into the fire.

20 Therefore by their fruits ye shall know them.

21 Not every one that saith unto me, Lord, Lord, shall enter into the kingdom of heaven, but he that doeth my Fathers will which is in heaven.

22 Many will say to me in that day, Lord, Lord, have we not by thy Name prophesied? and by thy name cast out devils? and by thy name done many great works?

23 And then will I profess to them, I never knew you: depart from me, ye that work iniquity.

24 Whosoever then heareth of me these words, and doeth the same, I will liken him to a wise man, which hath builded his house on a rock:

25 And the rain fell, and the floods came, and the winds blew, and beat upon that house, and it fell not: for it was grounded on a rock.

26 But whosoever heareth these my words, and doeth them not, shall be likened unto a foolish man, which hath builded his house upon the sand:

27 And the rain fell, and the floods came, and the winds blew, and beat upon that house, and it fell, and the fall thereof was great.

28 And it came to pass, when Jesus had ended these words, the people were astonished at his doctrine.

29 For he taught them as one having authority, and not as the Scribes.

Matthew Chapter 8

1 Now when he was come down from the mountain, great multitudes followed him.

2 And lo, there came a Leper and worshipped him, saying, Master, if thou wilt, thou canst make me clean.

3 And Jesus putting forth his hand, touched him, saying, I will, be thou clean: and immediately his leprosy was cleansed.

4 Then Jesus said unto him, See thou tell no man, but go, and show thyself unto the Priest, and offer the gift that Moses commanded, for a witness to them.

5 When Jesus was entered into Capernahum, there came unto him a Centurion, beseeching him,

6 And said, Master, my servant lieth sick at home of the palsy, and is grievously pained.

7 And Jesus said unto him, I will come and heal him.

8 But the Centurion answered, saying, Master, I am not worthy that thou shouldest come under my roof: but speak the word only, and my servant shall be healed.

9 For I am a man also under the authority of another, and have soldiers under me: and I say to one, Go: and he goeth, and to another, Come: and he cometh, and to my servant, Do this, and he doeth it.

10 When Jesus heard that, he marveled, and said to them that followed him, Verily, I say unto you, I have not found so great faith, even in Israel.

11 But I say unto you, that many shall come from the East and West, and shall sit down with Abraham, and Isaac, and Jacob in the kingdom of heaven.

12 And the children of the kingdom shall be cast out into utter darkness: there shall be weeping and gnashing of teeth.

13 Then Jesus said unto the Centurion, Go thy way, and as thou hast believed, so be it unto thee. And his servant was healed the same hour.

14 And when Jesus came to Peters house, he saw his wife's mother laid down, and sick of a fever.

15 And he touched her hand, and the fever left her: so she arose, and ministered unto them.

16 When the Even was come, they brought unto him many that were possessed with devils: and he cast out the spirits with his word, and healed all that were sick,

17 That it might be fulfilled, which was spoken by Isaiah the Prophet, saying, He took our infirmities, and bare our sicknesses.

18 And when Jesus saw great multitudes of people about him, he commanded them to go over the water.

19 Then came there a certain Scribe, and said unto him, Master, I will follow thee whethersoever thou goest.

20 But Jesus said unto him, The foxes have holes, and the birds of the heaven have nests, but the Son of man hath not whereon to rest his head.

21 And another of his disciples said unto him, Master, suffer me first to go, and bury my father.

22 But Jesus said unto him, Follow me, and let the dead bury their dead.

23 And when he was entered into the ship, his disciples followed him.

24 And behold, there arose a great tempest in the sea, so that the ship was covered with waves: but he was asleep.

25 Then his disciples came, and awoke him, saying, Master, save us: we perish.

26 And he said unto them, Why are ye fearful, O ye of little faith? Then he arose, and rebuked the winds and the sea: and so there was a great calm.

27 And the men marveled, saying, What man is this, that both the winds and the sea obey him!

28 And when he was come to the other side, into the country of the Gerasenes, there met him two possessed with devils, which came out of the graves very fierce, so that no man might go by that way.

29 And behold, they cried out, saying, Jesus the Son of God, what have we to do with thee? Art thou come hither to torment us before the time?

30 Now there was afar off from them, a great heard of swine feeding.

31 And the devils besought him, saying, If thou cast us out, suffer us to go into the herd of swine.

32 And he said unto them, Go. So they went out, and departed into the herd of swine: and behold, the whole herd of swine was carried with violence from a steep down place in the sea, and died in the water.

33 Then the herdsmen fled: and when they were come into the city, they told all things, and what was become of them that were possessed with the devils.

34 And behold all the city came out, to meet Jesus: and when they saw him, they besought him to depart out of their coasts.

Matthew Chapter 9

1 Then he entered into a ship, and passed over, and came into his own city.

2 And lo, they brought to him a man sick of the palsy, lying on a bed. And Jesus seeing their faith, said to the sick of the palsy, Son, be of good comfort: thy sins are forgiven thee.

3 And behold, certain of the Scribes said with themselves, This man blasphemeth.

4 But when Jesus saw their thoughts, he said, Wherefore think ye evil things in your hearts?

5 For whether is it easier to say, Thy sins are forgiven thee, or to say, Arise, and walk?

6 And that ye may know that the Son of man hath authority in earth to forgive sins, (then said he unto the sick of the palsy,) Arise, take up thy bed, and go to thine house.

7 And he arose, and departed to his own house.

8 So when the multitude saw it, they marveled, and glorified God, which had given such authority to men.

9 And as Jesus passed forth from thence, he saw a man sitting at the receipt of custom named Matthew, and said to him, Follow me. And he arose, and followed him.

10 And it came to pass, as Jesus sat at meat in his house, behold, many Publicans and sinners, that came thither, sat down at the table with Jesus and his disciples.

11 And when the Pharisees saw that, they said to his disciples, Why eateth your master with Publicans and sinners?

12 Now when Jesus heard it, he said unto them, The whole need not a Physician, but they that are sick.

13 But go ye and learn what this is, I will have mercy, and not sacrifice: for I am not come to call the righteous, but the sinners to repentance.

14 Then came the disciples of John to him, saying, Why do we and the Pharisees fast oft, and thy disciples fast not?

15 And Jesus said unto them, Can the children of the marriage chamber mourn as long as the bridegroom is with them? But the days will come, when the bridegroom shall be taken from them, and then shall they fast.

16 Moreover no man pieceth an old garment with a piece of new cloth: for that that should fill it up, taketh away from the garment, and the breach is worse.

17 Neither do they put new wine into old vessels: for then the vessels would break, and the wine would be spilled, and the vessels should perish: but they put new wine into new vessels, and so are both preserved.

18 While he thus spake unto them, behold, there came a certain ruler, and worshipped him, saying, My daughter is now deceased, but come and lay thine hand on her, and she shall live.

19 And Jesus arose and followed him with his disciples.

20 (And behold a woman which was diseased with an issue of blood twelve years, came behind him, and touched the hem of his garment.

21 For she said in herself, If I may touch but his garment only, I shall be whole.

22 Then Jesus turned himself about, and seeing her, did say, Daughter, be of good comfort: thy faith hath made thee whole. And the woman was made whole at that hour.)

23 Now when Jesus came into the Rulers house, and saw the minstrels and the multitude making noise,

24 He said unto them, Get you hence: for the maid is not dead, but sleepeth. And they laughed him to scorn.

25 And when the multitude were put forth, he went in and took her by the hand, and the maid arose.

26 And this bruit went throughout all that land.

27 And as Jesus departed thence, two blind men followed him, crying, and saying, O son of David, have mercy upon us.

28 And when he was come into the house, the blind came to him, and Jesus said unto them, Believe ye that I am able to do this? And they said unto him, Yea, Lord.

29 Then touched he their eyes, saying, According to your faith be it unto you.

30 And their eyes were opened, and Jesus charged them, saying, See that no man know it.

31 But when they were departed, they spread abroad his fame throughout all that land.

32 And as they went out, behold, they brought to him a dumb man possessed with a devil.

33 And when the devil was cast out, the dumb spake: then the multitude marveled, saying, The like was never seen in Israel.

34 But the Pharisees said, He casteth out devils, through the prince of devils.

35 And Jesus went about all cities and towns, teaching in their Synagogues, and preaching the Gospel of the kingdom, and healing every sickness and every disease among the people.

36 But when he saw the multitude, he had compassion upon them, because they were dispersed, and scattered abroad, as sheep having no shepherd.

37 Then said he to his disciples, Surely the harvest is great, but the laborers are few.

38 Wherefore pray the Lord of the harvest, that he would send forth laborers into his harvest.

Matthew Chapter 10

1 And he called his twelve disciples unto him, and gave them power against unclean spirits, to cast them out, and to heal every sickness, and every disease.

2 Now the names of the twelve Apostles are these. The first is Simon, called Peter, and Andrew his brother: James the son of Zebedee, and John his brother.

3 Philip and Bartholomew: Thomas, and Matthew that Publican: James the son of Alphaeus, and Lebbaeus whose surname was Thaddaeus:

4 Simon the Canaanite, and Judas Iscariot, who also betrayed him.

5 These twelve did Jesus send forth, and commanded them, saying, Go not into the way of the Gentiles, and into the cities of the Samaritans enter ye not:

6 But go rather to the lost sheep of the house of Israel.

7 And as ye go, preach, saying, The kingdom of heaven is at hand.

8 Heal the sick: cleanse the lepers: raise up the dead: cast out the devils. Freely ye have received, freely give.

9 Possess not gold, nor silver, nor money in your girdles,

10 Nor a script for the journey, neither two coats, neither shoes, nor a staff: for the workman is worthy of his meat.

11 And into whatsoever city or town ye shall come, inquire who is worthy in it, and there abide till ye go thence.

12 And when ye come into a house, salute the same.

13 And if the house be worthy, let your peace come upon it: but if it be not worthy, let your peace return to you.

14 And whosoever shall not receive you, nor hear your words, when ye depart out of that house, or that city, shake off the dust of your feet.

15 Truly I say unto you, it shall be easier for them of the land of Sodom and Gomorrah in the Day of Judgment, then for that city.

16 Behold, I send you as sheep in the midst of wolves: be ye therefore wise as serpents, and innocent as doves.

17 But beware of men, for they will deliver you up to the Councils, and will scourge you in their Synagogues.

18 And ye shall be brought to the governors and Kings for my sake, in witness to them, and to the Gentiles.

19 But when they deliver you up, take no thought how or what ye shall speak: for it shall be given you in that hour, what ye shall say.

20 For it is not ye that speak, but the spirit of your father which speaketh in you.

21 And the brother shall betray the brother to death, and the father the son, and the children shall rise against their parents, and shall cause them to die.

22 And ye shall be hated of all men for my Name: but he that endureth to the end, he shall be saved.

23 And when they persecute you in this city, flee into another: for verily I say unto you, ye shall not finish all the cities of Israel, till the Son of man be come.

24 The disciple is not above his master, nor the servant above his Lord.

25 It is enough for the disciple to be as his master is, and the servant as his Lord. If they have called the master of the house Beelzebub, how much more them of his household?

26 Fear them not therefore: for there is nothing covered, that shall not be disclosed, nor hid, that shall not be known.

27 What I tell you in darkness, that speak ye in light: and what ye hear in the ear, that preach ye on the houses.

28 And fear ye not them which kill the body, but are not able to kill the soul: but rather fear him, which is able to destroy both soul and body in hell.

29 Are not two sparrows sold for a farthing, and one of them shall not fall on the ground without your Father?

30 Yea, and all the hairs of your head are numbered.

31 Fear ye not therefore, ye are of more value than many sparrows.

32 Whosoever therefore shall confess me before men, him will I confess also before my Father, which is in heaven.

33 But whosoever shall deny me before me, him will I also deny before my Father, which is in heaven.

34 Think not that I am come to send peace into the earth: I came not to send peace, but the sword.

35 For I am come to set a man at variance against his father, and the daughter against her mother, and the daughter in law against her mother in law.

36 And a mans enemies shall be they of his own household.

37 He that loveth father or mother more than me, is not worthy of me. And he that loveth son, or daughter more than me, is not worthy of me.

38 And he that taketh not his cross, and followeth after me, is not worthy of me.

39 He that will save his life, shall lose it, and he that loseth his life for my sake, shall save it.

40 He that receiveth you, receiveth me: and he that receiveth me, receiveth him that hath sent me.

41 He that receiveth a Prophet in the name of a Prophet, shall receive a Prophets reward: and he that receiveth a righteous man, in the name of a righteous man, shall receive the reward of a righteous man.

42 And whosoever shall give unto one of these little ones to drink a cup of cold water only, in the name of a Disciple, verily I say unto you, he shall not lose his reward.

Matthew Chapter 11

1 And it came to pass that when Jesus had made an end of commanding his twelve disciples, he departed thence to teach and to preach in their cities.

2 And when John heard in the prison the works of Christ, he sent two of his disciples, and said unto him,

3 Art thou he that should come, or shall we look for another?

4 And Jesus answering, said unto them, Go, and show John, what things ye have heard and seen.

5 The blind receive sight, and the halt go: the lepers are cleansed, and the deaf hear: the dead are raised up, and the poor receive the Gospel.

6 And blessed is he that shall not be offended in me.

7 And as they departed, Jesus began to speak unto the multitude, of John, What went ye out into the wilderness to see? A reed shaken with the wind?

8 But what went ye out to see? A man clothed in soft raiment? Behold, they that wear soft clothing, are in Kings houses.

9 But what went ye out to see? A Prophet? Yea, I say unto you, and more than a Prophet.

10 For this is he of whom it is written, Behold, I send my messenger before thy face, which shall prepare thy way before thee.

11 Verily I say unto you, among them which are begotten of women, arose there not a greater than John Baptist: notwithstanding, he that is the least in the kingdom of heaven, is greater than he.

12 And from the time of John Baptist hither to, the kingdom of heaven suffereth violence, and the violent take it by force.

13 For all the Prophets and the Law prophesied unto John.

14 And if ye will receive it, this is Elijah, which was to come.

15 He that hath ears to hear, let him hear.

16 But whereunto shall I liken this generation? It is like unto little children which sit in the markets, and call unto their fellows,

17 And say, We have piped unto you, and ye have not danced, we have mourned unto you, and ye have not lamented.

18 For John came neither eating nor drinking, and they say, He hath a devil.

19 The son of man came eating and drinking, and they say, Behold a glutton and a drinker of wine, a friend unto Publicans and sinners: but wisdom is justified of her children.

20 Then began he to upbraid the cities, wherein most of his great works were done, because they repented not.

21 Woe be to thee, Chorazin: Woe be to thee, Bethsaida: for if the great works, which were done in you, had been done in Tyre and Sidon, they had repented long ago in sackcloth and ashes.

22 But I say to you, It shall be easier for Tyre and Sidon at the Day of Judgment, than for you.

23 And thou, Capernaum, which art lifted up unto heaven, shalt be brought down to hell: for if the great works, which have been done in thee, had been done among them of Sodom, they had remained to this day.

24 But I say unto you, that it shall be easier for them of the land of Sodom in the Day of Judgment, than for thee.

25 At that time Jesus answered, and said, I give thee thanks, O Father, Lord of heaven and earth, because thou hast hid these things from the wise and men of understanding, and hast opened them unto babes.

26 It is so, O Father, because thy good pleasure was such.

27 All things are given unto me of my Father: and no man knoweth the Son, but the Father: neither knoweth any man the Father, but the Son, and he to whom the Son will reveal him.

28 Come unto me, all ye that are weary and laden, and I will ease you.

29 Take my yoke on you, and learn of me, that I am meek and lowly in heart: and ye shall find rest unto your souls.

30 For my yoke is easy, and my burden light.

Matthew Chapter 12

1 At that time Jesus went on a Sabbath day through the corn, and his disciples were an hungred, and began to pluck the ears of corn and to eat.

2 And when the Pharisees saw it, they said unto him, Behold, thy disciples do that which is not lawful to do upon the Sabbath.

3 But he said unto them, Have ye not read what David did when he was an hungred, and they that were with him?

4 How he entered into the house of God, and ate the showbread, which was not lawful for him to eat, neither for them which were with him, but only for the Priests?

5 Or have ye not read in the Law, how that on the Sabbath days the Priests in the Temple break the Sabbath, and are blameless?

6 But I say unto you, that here is one greater than the Temple.

7 Wherefore if ye knew what this is, I will have mercy and not sacrifice, ye would not have condemned the innocents.

8 For the son of man is Lord, even of the Sabbath.

9 And he departed thence, and went into their Synagogue:

10 And behold, there was a man which had his hand dried up. And they asked him, saying, Is it lawful to heal upon a Sabbath day? that they might accuse him.

11 And he said unto them, What man shall there be among you, that shall have a sheep, and if it fall on a Sabbath day into a pit, will he not take it and lift it out?

12 How much more then is a man better than a sheep? therefore, it is lawful to do well on a Sabbath day.

13 Then said he to the man, Stretch forth thine hand. And he stretched it forth, and it was made whole as the other.

14 Then the Pharisees went out, and consulted against him, how they might destroy him.

15 But when Jesus knew it, he departed thence, and great multitudes followed him, and he healed them all,

16 And charged them that they should not make him known,

17 That it might be fulfilled, which was spoken by Isaiah the Prophet, saying,

18 Behold my servant whom I have chosen, my beloved in whom my soul delighteth: I will put my Spirit on him, and he shall show judgment to the Gentiles.

19 He shall not strive, nor cry, neither shall any man hear his voice in the streets.

20 A bruised reed shall he not break, and smoking flax shall he not quench, till he bring forth judgment unto victory.

21 And in his Name shall the Gentiles trust.

22 Then was brought to him one, possessed with a devil, both blind, and dumb, and he healed him, so that he which was blind and dumb, both spake and saw.

23 And all the people were amazed, and said, Is not this the son of David?

24 But when the Pharisees heard it, they said, This man casteth the devils no otherwise out, but through Beelzebub the prince of devils.

25 But Jesus knew their thoughts, and said to them, Every kingdom divided against itself, shall be brought to naught: and every city or house, divided against itself, shall not stand.

26 So if Satan cast out Satan, he is divided against himself: how shall then his kingdom endure?

27 Also if I through Beelzebub cast out devils, by whom do your children cast them out? Therefore they shall be your judges.

28 But if I cast out devils by the Spirit of God, then is the kingdom of God come unto you.

29 Else how can a man enter into a strong mans house and spoil his goods, except he first bind the strong man, and then spoil his house.

30 He that is not with me, is against me: and he that gathereth not with me, scattereth.

31 Wherefore I say unto you, every sin and blasphemy shall be forgiven unto men: but the blasphemy against the Holy Ghost shall not be forgiven unto men.

32 And whosoever shall speak a word against the Son of man, it shall be forgiven him: but whosoever shall speak against the Holy Ghost, it shall not be forgiven him, neither in this world nor in the world to come.

33 Either make the tree good, and his fruit good: or else make the tree evil, and his fruit evil: for the tree is known by the fruit.

34 O generations of vipers, how can you speak good things, when ye are evil? For of the abundance of the heart the mouth speaketh.

35 A good man out of the good treasure of his heart bringeth forth good things: and an evil man out of an evil treasure, bringeth forth evil things.

36 But I say unto you, that of every idle word that men shall speak, they shall give account thereof at the Day of Judgment.

37 For by thy words thou shalt be justified, and by thy words thou shalt be condemned.

38 Then answered certain of the Scribes and of the Pharisees, saying, Master, we would see a sign of thee.

39 But he answered, and said to them, An evil and adulterous generation seeketh a sign, but no sign shall be given unto it, save the sign of the Prophet Jonah.

40 For as Jonah was three days, and three nights in the whales belly: so shall the Son of man be three days and three nights in the heart of the earth.

41 The men of Nineveh shall rise in judgment with this generation, and condemn it: for they repented at the preaching of Jonah: and behold, a greater than Jonah is here.

42 The Queen of the South shall rise in judgment with this generation, and shall condemn it: for she came from the utmost parts of the earth to hear the Wisdom of Solomon: and behold a greater than Solomon is here.

43 Now when the unclean spirit is gone out of a man, he walketh throughout dry places, seeking rest, and findeth none.

44 Then he saith, I will return into mine house, from whence I came: and when he is come, he findeth it empty, swept and garnished.

45 Then he goeth, and taketh unto him seven other spirits worse than himself, and they enter in, and dwell there: and the end of that man is worse than the beginning. Even so shall it be with this wicked generation.

46 While he yet spake to the multitude, behold, his mother, and his brethren stood without, desiring to speak with him.

47 Then one said unto him, Behold, thy mother and thy brethren stand without, desiring to speak with thee.

48 But he answered, and said to him that told him, Who is my mother? and who are my brethren?

49 And he stretched forth his hand toward his disciples, and said, Behold my mother and my brethren.

50 For whosoever shall do my Fathers will which is in heaven, the same is my brother and sister and mother.

Matthew Chapter 13

1 The same day went Jesus out of the house, and sat by the seaside.

2 And great multitudes resorted unto him, so that he went into a ship, and sat down: and the whole multitude stood on the shore.

3 Then he spake many things to them in parables, saying, Behold, a sower went forth to sow.

4 And as he sowed, some fell by the wayside, and the fowls came and devoured them up.

5 And some fell upon stony ground, where they had not much earth, and soon they sprung up, because they had no depth of earth.

6 And when the sun rose up, they were parched, and for lack of rooting, withered away.

7 And some fell among thorns, and the thorns sprung up, and choked them.

8 Some again fell in good ground, and brought forth fruit, one corn an hundred fold, some sixty fold, and another thirty fold.

9 He that hath ears to hear, let him hear.

10 Then the disciples came, and said to him, Why speakest thou to them in parables?

11 And he answered and said unto them, Because it is given unto you, to know the secrets of the kingdom of heaven, but to them it is not given.

12 For whosoever hath, to him shall be given, and he shall have abundance: but whosoever hath not, from him shall be taken away, even that he hath.

13 Therefore speak I to them in parables, because they seeing, do not see: and hearing, they hear not, neither understand.

14 So in them is fulfilled the prophecy of Isaiah, which prophecy saith, By hearing, ye shall hear, and shall not understand, and seeing ye shall see, and shall not perceive.

15 For this peoples heart is waxed fat, and their ears are dull of hearing, and with their eyes they have winked, lest they should see with their eyes, and hear with their ears, and should understand with their hearts, and should return, that I might heal them.

16 But blessed are your eyes, for they see: and your ears, for they hear.

17 For verily I say unto you, that many Prophets, and righteous men have desired to see those things which ye see, and have not seen them, and to hear those things which ye hear, and have not heard them.

18 Hear ye therefore the parable of the sower.

19 Whensoever a man heareth the word of the kingdom, and understandeth it not, the evil one cometh, and catcheth away that which was sown in his heart: and this is he which hath received the seed by the way side.

20 And he that received seed in the stony ground, is he which heareth the word, and incontinently with joy receiveth it,

21 Yet hath he no root in himself, and endureth but a season: for as soon as tribulation or persecution cometh because of the word, by and by he is offended.

22 And he that receiveth the seed among thorns, is he that heareth the word: but the care of this world, and the deceitfulness of riches choke the word, and he is made unfruitful.

23 But he that receiveth the seed in the good ground, is he that heareth the word, and understandeth it, which also beareth fruit, and bringeth forth, some an hundred fold, some sixty fold, and some thirty fold.

24 Another parable put he forth unto them, saying, The kingdom of heaven is like unto a man which sowed good seed in his field.

25 But while men slept, there came his enemy, and sowed tares among the wheat, and went his way.

26 And when the blade was sprung up, and brought forth fruit, then appeared the tares also.

27 Then came the servants of the householder, and said unto him, Master, sowest not thou good seed in thy field? from whence then hath it tares?

28 And he said to them, The envious man hath done this. Then the servants said unto him, Wilt thou then that we go and gather them up?

29 But he said, Nay, lest while ye go about to gather the tares, ye pluck up also with them the wheat.

30 Let both grow together until the harvest, and in time of harvest I will say to the reapers, Gather ye first the tares, and bind them in sheaves to burn them: but gather the wheat into my barn.

31 Another parable he put forth unto them, saying, The kingdom of heaven is like unto a grain of mustard seed, which a man taketh and soweth in his field:

32 Which indeed is the least of all seeds: but when it is grown, it is the greatest among herbs, and it is a tree, so that the birds of heaven come and build in the branches thereof.

33 Another parable spake he to them, The kingdom of heaven is like unto leaven, which a woman taketh and hideth in three pecks of meal, till all be leavened.
34 All these things spake Jesus unto the multitude in parables, and without parables spake he not to them,
35 That it might be fulfilled, which was spoken by the Prophet, saying, I will open my mouth in parables, and will utter the things which have been kept secret from the foundation of the world.
36 Then sent Jesus the multitude away, and went into the house. And his disciples came unto him, saying, Declare unto us the parable of the tares of the field.
37 Then answered he, and said to them, He that soweth the good seed, is the Son of man.
38 And the field is the world, and the good seed, they are the children of the kingdom, and the tares are the children of the wicked,
39 And the enemy that soweth them, is the devil, and the harvest is the end of the world, and the reapers be the Angels.
40 As then the tares are gathered and burned in the fire, so shall it be in the end of this world.
41 The Son of man shall send forth his Angels, and they shall gather out of his kingdom all things that offend, and them which do iniquity,
42 And shall cast them into a furnace of fire. There shall be wailing and gnashing of teeth.
43 Then shall the just men shine as the sun in the kingdom of their Father. He that hath ears to hear, let him hear.
44 Again, the kingdom of heaven is like unto a treasure hid in the field, which when a man hath found, he hideth it, and for joy thereof departeth and selleth all that he hath, and buyeth that field.
45 Again the kingdom of heaven is like to a merchant man, that seeketh good pearls,
46 Who having found a pearl of great price, went and sold all that he had, and bought it.
47 Again the kingdom of heaven is like unto a drawnet cast into the sea, that gathereth of all kinds of things.
48 Which, when it is full, men draw to land, and sit and gather the good into vessels, and cast the bad away.
49 So shall it be at the end of the world. The Angels shall go forth, and sever the bad from among the just,
50 And shall cast them into a furnace of fire: there shall be wailing, and gnashing of teeth.
51 Jesus said unto them, Understand ye all these things? They said unto him, Yea, Lord.
52 Then said he unto them, Therefore every Scribe which is taught unto the kingdom of heaven, is like unto an householder, which bringeth forth out of his treasure things both new and old.
53 And it came to pass, that when Jesus had ended these parables, he departed thence,
54 And came into his own country, and taught them in their Synagogue, so that they were astonished, and said, Whence cometh this wisdom and great works unto this man?
55 Is not this the carpenters son? Is not his mother called Mary, and his brethren James and Joseph, and Simon and Judas?
56 And are not his sisters all with us? Whence then hath he all these things?
57 And they were offended with him. Then Jesus said to them, A Prophet is not without honor, save in his own country, and in his own house.
58 And he did not many great works there, for their unbeliefs sake.

Matthew Chapter 14

1 At that time Herod the Tetrarch heard of the fame of Jesus,

2 And said unto his servants, This is John Baptist. He is risen again from the dead, and therefore great works are wrought by him.

3 For Herod had taken John, and bound him, and put him in prison for Herodias sake, his brother Philips wife.

4 For John said unto him, It is not lawful for thee to have her.

5 And when he would have put him to death, he feared the multitude, because they counted him as a Prophet.

6 But when Herod's birthday was kept, the daughter of Herodias danced before them, and pleased Herod.

7 Wherefore he promised with an oath, that he would give her whatsoever she would ask.

8 And she being before instructed of her mother, said, Give me here John Baptists head in a platter.

9 And the King was sorry: nevertheless because of the oath, and them that sat with him at the table, he commanded it to be given her,

10 And sent, and beheaded John in the prison.

11 And his head was brought in a platter, and given to the maid, and she brought it unto her mother.

12 And his disciples came, and took up his body, and buried it, and went, and told Jesus.

13 And when Jesus heard it, he departed thence by ship into a desert place apart. And when the multitude had heard it, they followed him a foot out of the cities.

14 And Jesus went forth and saw a great multitude, and was moved with compassion toward them, and he healed their sick.

15 And when even was come, his disciples came to him, saying, This is a desert place, and the hour is already past: let the multitude depart, that they may go into the towns, and buy them vitals.

16 But Jesus said to them, They have no need to go away: give ye them to eat.

17 Then said they unto him, We have here but five loaves, and two fishes.

18 And he said, Bring them thither to me.

19 And he commanded the multitude to sit down on the grass, and took the five loaves and the two fishes, and looked up to heaven and blessed, and brake, and gave the loaves to his disciples, and the disciples to the multitude.

20 And they did all eat, and were sufficed, and they took up of the fragments that remained, twelve baskets full.

21 And they that had eaten, were about five thousand men, beside women and little children.

22 And straightway Jesus compelled his disciples to enter into a ship, and to go over before him, while he sent the multitude away.

23 And as soon as he had sent the multitude away, he went up into a mountain alone to pray: and when the evening was come, he was there alone.

24 And the ship was now in the midst of the sea, and was tossed with waves: for it was a contrary wind.

25 And in the fourth watch of the night, Jesus went unto them, walking on the sea.

26 And when his disciples saw him walking on the sea, they were troubled, saying, It is a spirit, and cried out for fear.

27 But straight way Jesus spake unto them, saying, Be of good comfort. It is I: be not afraid.

28 Then Peter answered him, and said, Master, if it be thou, bid me come unto thee on the water.

29 And he said, Come. And when Peter was come down out of the ship, he walked on the water, to go to Jesus.

30 But when he saw a mighty wind, he was afraid: and as he began to sink, he cried, saying, Master, save me.

31 So immediately Jesus stretched forth his hand, and caught him, and said to him, O thou of little faith, wherefore didst thou doubt?

32 And as soon as they were come into the ship, the wind ceased.

33 Then they that were in the ship, came and worshipped him, saying, Of a truth thou art the Son of God.

34 And when they were come over, they came into the land of Gennesaret.

35 And when the men of that place knew him, they sent out into all that country round about, and brought unto him all that were sick,

36 And besought him, that they might touch the hem of his garment only: and as many as touched it, were made whole.

Matthew Chapter 15

1 Then came to Jesus the Scribes and Pharisees, which were of Jerusalem, saying,

2 Why do thy disciples transgress the tradition of the Elders? for they wash not their hands when they eat bread.

3 But he answered and said unto them, Why do ye also transgress the commandment of God by your tradition?

4 For God hath commanded, saying, Honor thy father and mother: and he that curseth father or mother, let him die the death.

5 But ye say, Whosoever shall say to father or mother, By the gift that is offered by me, thou mayest have profit,

6 Though he honor not his father, or his mother, shall be free: thus have ye made the commandment of God of no authority by your tradition.

7 O hypocrites, Isaiah prophesied well of you, saying,

8 This people draweth near unto me with their mouth, and honoreth me with the lips, but their heart is far off from me.

9 But in vain they worship me, teaching for doctrines, mens precepts.

10 Then he called the multitude unto him, and said to them, Hear and understand.

11 That which goeth into the mouth, defileth not the man, but that which cometh out of the mouth, that defileth the man.

12 Then came his disciples, and said unto him, Perceivest thou not, that the Pharisees are offended in hearing this saying?

13 But he answered and said, Every plant which mine heavenly Father hath not planted, shall be rooted up.

14 Let them alone, they be the blind leaders of the blind: and if the blind lead you blind, both shall fall into the ditch.

15 Then answered Peter, and said to him, Declare unto us this parable.

16 Then said Jesus, Are ye yet without understanding?

17 Perceive ye not yet, that whatsoever entereth into the mouth, goeth into the belly, and is cast out into the draught?

18 But those things which proceed out of the mouth, come from the heart, and they defile the man.

19 For out of the heart come evil thoughts, murders, adulteries, fornications, thefts, false testimonies, slanders.

20 These are the things, which defile the man: but to eat with unwashen hands, defileth not the man.

21 And Jesus went thence, and departed into the coasts of Tyre and Sidon.

22 And behold, a woman a Canaanite came out of the same coasts, and cried, saying unto him, Have mercy on me, O Lord, the son of David: my daughter is miserably vexed with a devil.

23 But he answered her not a word. Then came to him his disciples, and besought him, saying, Send her away, for she cryeth after us.

24 But he answered, and said, I am not sent, but unto the lost sheep of the house of Israel.

25 Yet she came and worshipped him, saying, Lord, help me.

26 And he answered, and said, It is not good to take the childrens bread, and to cast it to whelps.

27 But she said, Truth, Lord: yet indeed the whelps eat of the crumbs, which fall from their master's table.

28 Then Jesus answered, and said unto her, O woman, great is thy faith: be it to thee, as thou desirest. And her daughter was made whole at that hour.

29 So Jesus went away from thence, and came near unto the sea of Galilee, and went up into a mountain and sat down there.

30 And great multitudes came unto him, having with them, halt, blind, dumb, maimed and many other, and cast them down at Jesus feet, and he healed them.

31 In so much that the multitude wondered, to see the dumb speak, the maimed whole, the halt to go, and the blind to see: and they glorified the God of Israel.

32 Then Jesus called his disciples unto him, and said, I have compassion on this multitude, because they have continued with me already three days, and have nothing to eat: and I will not let them depart fasting, lest they faint in the way.

33 And his disciples said unto him, Whence should we get so much bread in the wilderness, as should suffice so great a multitude!

34 And Jesus said unto them, How many loaves have ye? And they said, Seven, and a few little fishes.

35 Then he commanded the multitude to sit down on the ground,

36 And took the seven loaves, and the fishes, and gave thanks, and break them, and gave to his disciples, and the disciples to the multitude.

37 And they did all eat, and were sufficed: and they took up of the fragments that remained, seven baskets full.

38 And they that had eaten, were four thousand men, beside women, and little children.

39 Then Jesus sent away the multitude, and took ship, and came into the parts of Magdala.

Matthew Chapter 16

1 Then came the Pharisees and Sadducees, and did tempt him, desiring him to show them a sign from heaven.

2 But he answered, and said unto them, When it is evening, ye say, Fair weather: for the sky is red.

3 And in the morning ye say, Today shall be a tempest: for the sky is red and glowing. O hypocrites, ye can discern the face of the sky, and can ye not discern the signs of the times?

4 The wicked generation, and adulterous seeketh a sign, and there shall no sign be given it, but the sign of the Prophet Jonah: so he left them, and departed.

5 And when his disciples were come to the other side, they had forgotten to take bread with them.

6 Then Jesus said unto them, Take heed and beware of the leaven of the Pharisees and Sadducees.

7 And they thought in themselves, saying, It is because we have brought no bread.

8 But Jesus knowing it, said unto them, O ye of little faith, why think you thus in yourselves, because ye have brought no bread?

9 Do ye not yet perceive, neither remember the five loaves, when there were five thousand men, and how many baskets took ye up?

10 Neither the seven loaves when there were four thousand men, and how many baskets took ye up?

11 Why perceive ye not that I said not unto you concerning bread, that ye should beware of the leaven of the Pharisees and Sadducees?

12 Then understood they that he had not said that they should beware of the leaven of bread, but of the doctrine of the Pharisees, and Sadducee s.

13 Now when Jesus came into the coasts of Caesarea Philippi, he asked his disciples, saying, Whom do men say that I, the Son of man am?

14 And they said, Some say, John Baptist: and some, Elijah: and others, Jeremiah, or one of the Prophets.

15 He said unto them, But who say ye that I am?

16 Then Simon Peter answered, and said, Thou art the Christ the Son of the living God.

17 And Jesus answered, and said to him, Blessed art thou, Simon, the son of Jonah: for flesh and blood hath not revealed it unto thee, but my Father which is in heaven.

18 And I say also unto thee, that thou art Peter, and upon this rock I will build my Church: and the gates of hell shall not overcome it.

19 And I will give unto thee the keys of the kingdom of heaven, and whatsoever thou shalt bind upon earth, shall be bound in heaven: and whatsoever thou shalt loose on earth, shall be loosed in heaven.

20 Then he charged his disciples, that they should tell no man that he was Jesus the Christ.

21 From that time forth Jesus began to show unto his disciples, that he must go unto Jerusalem, and suffer many things of the Elders, and of the high Priests, and Scribes, and be slain, and rise again the third day.

22 Then Peter took him aside, and began to rebuke him, saying, Master, pity thyself: this shall not be unto thee.

23 Then he turned back, and said unto Peter, Get thee behind me, Satan: thou art an offence unto me, because thou understandest not the things that are of God, but the things that are of men.

24 Jesus then said to his disciples, If any man will follow me, let him forsake himself: and take up his cross, and follow me.

25 For whosoever will save his life, shall lose it: and whosoever shall lose his life for my sake, shall find it.

26 For what shall it profit a man though he should win the whole world, if he lose his own soul? or what shall a man give for recompense of his soul?

27 For the Son of man shall come in the glory of his Father with his Angels, and then shall he give to every man according to his deeds.

28 Verily I say unto you, there be some of them that stand here, which shall not taste of death, till they have seen the Son of man come in his kingdom.

Matthew Chapter 17

1 And after six days, Jesus took Peter, and James, and John his brother, and brought them up into an high mountain apart,

2 And was transfigured before them: and his face did shine as the sun, and his clothes were as white as the light.

3 And behold, there appeared unto them Moses, and Elijah, talking with him.

4 Then answered Peter, and said to Jesus, Master, it is good for us to be here: if thou wilt, let us make here three tabernacles, one for thee, and one for Moses, and one for Elijah.

5 While he yet spake, behold, a bright cloud shadowed them: and behold, there came a voice out of the cloud, saying, This is my beloved Son, in whom I am well pleased: hear him.

6 And when the disciples heard that, they fell on their faces and were sore afraid.

7 Then Jesus came and touched them, and said, Arise, and be not afraid.

8 And when they lifted up their eyes, they saw no man, save Jesus only.

9 And as they came down from the mountain, Jesus charged them, saying, Show the vision to no man, until the Son of man rise again from the dead.

10 And his disciples asked him, saying, Why then say the Scribes that Elijah must first come?

11 And Jesus answered, and said unto them, Certainly Elijah must first come, and restore all things.

12 But I say unto you, that Elijah is come already, and they knew him not, but have done unto him whatsoever they would: likewise shall also the Son of man suffer of them.

13 Then the disciples perceived that he spake unto them of John Baptist.

14 And when they were come to the multitude, there came to him a certain man, and kneeled down to him.

15 And said, Master, have pity on my son: for he is lunatic, and is sore vexed: for oft times he falleth into the fire, and oft times into the water.

16 And I brought him to thy disciples, and they could not heal him.

17 Then Jesus answered, and said, O generation, faithless, and crooked, how long now shall I be with you! how long now shall I suffer you! bring him thither to me.

18 And Jesus rebuked the devil, and he went out of him: and the child was healed at that hour.

19 Then came the disciples to Jesus apart, and said, Why could not we cast him out?

20 And Jesus said unto them, Because of your unbelief: for Verily I say unto you, if ye have faith as much as is a grain of mustard seed, ye shall say unto this mountain, Remove hence to yonder place, and it shall remove: and nothing shall be impossible unto you.

21 Howbeit this kind goeth not out, but by prayer and fasting.

22 And as they abode in Galilee, Jesus said unto them, The Son of man shall be delivered into the hands of men,

23 And they shall kill him, but the third day shall he rise again: and they were very sorry.

24 And when they were come to Capernaum, they that received poll money, came to Peter, and said, Doth not your Master pay tribute?

25 He said, Yes. And when he was come into the house, Jesus prevented him, saying, What thinkest thou, Simon? Of whom do the Kings of the earth take tribute, or poll money? of their children, or of strangers?

26 Peter said unto him, Of strangers. Then said Jesus unto him, Then are the children free.

27 Nevertheless, lest we should offend them: go to the sea, and cast in an angle, and take the first fish that cometh up, and when you hast opened his mouth, thou shalt find a piece of twenty pence: that take, and give it unto them for me and thee.

Matthew Chapter 18

1 The same time the disciples came unto Jesus, saying, Who is the greatest in the kingdom of heaven?

2 And Jesus called a little child unto him, and set him in the midst of them,

3 And said, Verily I say unto you, except ye be converted, and become as little children, ye shall not enter into the kingdom of heaven.

4 Whosoever therefore shall humble himself as this little child, the same is the greatest in the kingdom of heaven.

5 And whosoever shall receive such little child in my Name, receiveth me.

6 But whosoever shall offend one of these little ones which believe in me, it were better for him, that a millstone were hanged about his neck, and that he were drowned in the depth of the sea.

7 Woe be unto the world because of offences: for it must needs be that offences shall come, but woe be to that man, by whom the offence cometh.

8 Wherefore, if thine hand or thy foot cause thee to offend, cut them off, and cast them from thee: it is better for thee to enter into life, halt, or maimed, than having two hands, or two feet, to be cast into everlasting fire.

9 And if thine eye cause thee to offend, pluck it out, and cast it from thee: it is better for thee to enter into life with one eye, then having two eyes, to be cast into hell fire.

10 See that ye despise not one of these little ones: for I say unto you, that in heaven their Angels always behold the face of my Father which is in heaven.

11 For the Son of man is come to save that which was lost.

12 How think ye? If a man have an hundred sheep, and one of them be gone astray, doth he not leave ninety and nine, and go into the mountains, and seek that which is gone astray?

13 And if so be that he find it, verily I say unto you, he rejoiceth more of that sheep, then of the ninety and nine which went not astray:

14 So is it not the will of your Father which is in heaven, that one of these little ones should perish.

15 Moreover, if thy brother trespass against thee, go and tell him his fault between thee and him alone: if he hear thee, thou hast won thy brother.

16 But if he hear thee not, take yet with thee one or two, that by the mouth of two or three witnesses every word may be confirmed.

17 And if he will not vouchsafe to hear them, tell it unto the Church: and if he refuse to hear the Church also, let him be unto thee as an heathen man, and a Publican.

18 Verily I say unto you, Whatsoever ye bind on earth, shall be bound in heaven: and whatsoever ye loose on earth, shall be loosed in heaven.

19 Again, verily I say unto you, that if two of you shall agree in earth upon anything, whatsoever they shall desire, it shall be given them of my Father which is in heaven.

20 For where two or three are gathered together in my Name, there am I in the midst of them.

21 Then came Peter to him, and said, Master, how oft shall my brother sin against me, and I shall forgive him? unto seven times?

22 Jesus said unto him, I say not to thee, unto seven times, but unto seventy times seven times.

23 Therefore is the kingdom of heaven likened unto a certain King, which would take an account of his servants.

24 And when he had begun to reckon, one was brought unto him, which ought him ten thousand talents.

25 And because he had nothing to pay, his master commanded him to be sold, and his wife, and his children, and all that he had, and the debt to be paid.

26 The servant therefore fell down, and besought him, saying, Master, appease thine anger toward me, and I will pay thee all.

27 Then that servants master had compassion, and loosed him, and forgave him the debt.

28 But when the servant was departed, he found one of his fellows, which ought him an hundred pence, and he laid hands on him, and took him by the throat, saying, Pay me that thou owest.

29 Then his fellow fell down at his feet, and besought him, saying, Appease thine anger towards me, and I will pay thee all.

30 Yet he would not, but went and cast him into prison, till he should pay the debt.

31 And when his other fellows saw what was done, they were very sorry, and came, and declared unto their master all that was done.

32 Then his master called him, and said to him, O evil servant, I forgave thee all that debt, because thou prayest me.

33 Ought not thou also to have had pity on thy fellow, even as I had pity on thee?

34 So his master was wroth, and delivered him to the jailors, till he should pay all that was due to him.

35 So likewise shall mine heavenly Father do unto you, except ye forgive from your hearts, each one to his brother their trespasses.

Matthew Chapter 19

1 And it came to pass, that when Jesus had finished those sayings, he departed from Galilee, and came into the coasts of Judea beyond Jordan.

2 And great multitudes followed him, and he healed them there.

3 Then came unto him the Pharisees tempting him, and saying to him, Is it lawful for a man to put away his wife for every fault?

4 And he answered and said unto them, Have ye not read, that he which made them at the beginning, made them male and female,

5 And said, For this cause, shall a man leave father and mother, and cleave unto his wife, and they twain shall be one flesh.

6 Wherefore they are no more twain, but one flesh. Let not man therefore put asunder that, which God hath coupled together.

7 They said to him, Why did then Moses command to give a bill of divorcement, and to put her away?

8 He said unto them, Moses, because of the hardness of your heart, suffered you to put away your wives: but from the beginning it was not so.

9 I say therefore unto you, that whosoever shall put away his wife, except it be for whoredom, and marry another, committeth adultery: and whosoever marrieth her which is divorced, doth commit adultery.

10 Then, said his disciples to him, If the matter be so between man and wife, it is not good to marry.

11 But he said unto them, All men cannot receive this thing, save they to whom it is given.

12 For there are some chaste, which were so born of their mothers belly: and there be some chaste, which be made chaste by men: and there be some chaste, which have made themselves chaste for the kingdom of heaven. He that is able to receive this, let him receive it.

13 Then were brought to him little children, that he should put his hands on them, and pray: and the disciples rebuked them.

14 But Jesus said, Suffer the little children, and forbid them not to come to me: for of such is the kingdom of heaven.

15 And when he had put his hands on them, he departed thence.

16 And behold one came, and said unto him, Good Master, what good thing shall I do, that I may have eternal life?

17 And he said unto him, Why callest thou me good? there is none good but one, even God: but if thou wilt enter into life, keep the commandments.

18 He said to him, Which? And Jesus said, These, Thou shalt not kill: Thou shalt not commit adultery: Thou shalt not steal: Thou shalt not bear false witness.

19 Honor thy father and mother: and thou shalt love thy neighbor as thyself.

20 The young man said unto him, I have observed all these things from my youth: what lack I yet?

21 Jesus said unto him, If thou wilt be perfect, go, sell that thou hast, and give it to the poor, and thou shalt have treasure in heaven, and come and follow me.

22 And when the young man heard that saying, he went away sorrowful: for he had great possessions.

23 Then Jesus said unto his disciples, Verily I say unto you, that a rich man shall hardly enter into the kingdom of heaven.

24 And again I say unto you, It is easier for a camel to go through the eye of a needle, than for a rich man to enter into the kingdom of God.

25 And when his disciples heard it, they were exceedingly amazed, saying, Who then can be saved?

26 And Jesus beheld them, and said unto them, With men this is impossible, but with God all things are possible.

27 Then answered Peter, and said to him, Behold, we have forsaken all, and followed thee: what shall we have?

28 And Jesus said unto them, Verily I say to you, that when the Son of man shall sit in the throne of his majesty, ye which followed me in the regeneration, shall sit also upon twelve thrones, and judge the twelve tribes of Israel.

29 And whosoever shall forsake houses, or brethren, or sisters, or father, or mother, or wife, or children, or lands, for my Names sake, he shall receive an hundred fold more, and shall inherit everlasting life.

30 But many that are first, shall be last, and the last shall be first.

Matthew Chapter 20

1 For the kingdom of heaven is like unto a certain householder, which went out at the dawning of the day to hire laborers into his vineyard.

2 And he agreed with the laborers for a penny a day, and sent them into his vineyard.

3 And he went out about the third hour, and saw others standing idle in the market place,

4 And said unto them, Go ye also into my vineyard, and whatsoever is right, I will give you: and they went their way.

5 Again he went out about the sixth and ninth hour, and did likewise.

6 And he went about the eleventh hour, and found other standing idle, and said unto them, Why stand ye here all the day idle?

7 They said unto him, Because no man hath hired us. He said to them, Go ye also into my vineyard, and whatsoever is right, that shall ye receive.

8 And when even was come, the master of the vineyard said unto his steward, Call the laborers, and give them their hire, beginning at the last, till thou come to the first.

9 And they which were hired about the eleventh hour, came and received every man a penny.

10 Now when the first came, they supposed that they should receive more, but they likewise received every man a penny.

11 And when they had received it, they murmured against the master of the house,

12 Saying, These last have wrought but one hour, and thou hast made them equal unto us, which have born the burden, and heat of the day.

13 And he answered one of them, saying, Friend, I do thee no wrong: didst thou not agree with me for a penny?

14 Take that which is thine own, and go thy way: I will give unto this last, as much as to thee.

15 Is it not lawful for me to do as I will with mine own? Is thine eye evil because I am good?

16 So the last shall be first, and the first last: for many are called, but few chosen.

17 And Jesus went up to Jerusalem, and took the twelve disciples apart in the way, and said unto them,

18 Behold, we go up to Jerusalem, and the Son of man shall be delivered unto the chief Priests, and unto the Scribes, and they shall condemn him to death,

19 And shall deliver him to the Gentiles, to mock, and to scourge, and to crucify him: but the third day he shall rise again.

20 Then came to him the mother of Zebedees children with her sons, worshipping him, and desiring a certain thing of him.

21 And he said unto her, What wouldest thou? She said to him, Grant that these my two sons may sit, the one at thy right hand, and the other at thy left hand in thy kingdom.

22 And Jesus answered and said, Ye know not what ye ask. Are ye able to drink of the cup that I shall drink of, and to be baptized with the baptism that I shall be baptized with? They said to him, We are able.

23 And he said unto them, Ye shall drink indeed of my cup, and shall be baptized with the baptism, that I am baptized with, but to sit at my right hand, and at my left hand, is not mine to give: but it shall be given to them for whom it is prepared of my Father.

24 And when the other ten heard this, they disdained at the two brethren.

25 Therefore Jesus called them unto him, and said, Ye know that the lords of the Gentiles have domination over them, and they that are great, exercise authority over them.

26 But it shall not be so among you: but whosoever will be great among you, let him be your servant.

27 And whosoever will be chief among you, let him be your servant.

28 Even as the Son of man came not to be served, but to serve, and to give his life for the ransom of many.

29 And as they departed from Jericho, a great multitude followed him.

30 And behold, two blind men, sitting by the wayside, when they heard that Jesus passed by, cried saying, O Lord, the Son of David, have mercy on us.

31 And the multitude rebuked them, because they should hold their peace: but they cried the more, saying, O Lord, the Son of David, have mercy on us.

32 Then Jesus stood still, and called them, and said, What will ye that I should do to you?

33 They said to him, Lord, that our eyes may be opened.

34 And Jesus moved with compassion touched their eyes, and immediately their eyes received sight, and they followed him.

Matthew Chapter 21

1 And when they drew near to Jerusalem, and were come to Bethphage, unto the Mount of the Olives, then sent Jesus two disciples,

2 Saying to them, Go into the town that is over against you, and soon ye shall find an ass bound, and a colt with her: loose them, and bring them unto me.

3 And if any man say ought unto you, say ye, that the Lord hath need of them, and straightway he will let them go.

4 All this was done that it might be fulfilled, which was spoken by the Prophet, saying,

5 Tell ye the daughter of Zion, Behold, thy King cometh unto thee, meek and sitting upon an ass, and a colt, the foal of an ass used to the yoke.

6 So the disciples went, and did as Jesus had commanded them,

7 And brought the ass and the colt, and put on them their clothes, and set him thereon.

8 And a great multitude spread their garments in the way: and other cut down branches from the trees, and strawed them in the way.

9 Moreover, the people that went before, and they also that followed, cried, saying, Hosanna to the Son of David, Blessed be he that cometh in the Name of the Lord, Hosanna thou which art in the highest heavens.

10 And when he was come into Jerusalem, all the city was moved, saying, Who is this?

11 And the people said, This is Jesus the Prophet of Nazareth in Galilee.

12 And Jesus went into the Temple of God, and cast out all them that sold and bought in the Temple, and overthrew the tables of the money changers, and the seats of them that sold doves,

13 And said to them, It is written, Mine house shall be called the house of prayer: but ye have made it a den of thieves.

14 Then the blind, and the halt came to him in the Temple, and he healed them.

15 But when the chief Priests and Scribes saw the marvels that he did, and the children crying in the Temple, and saying, Hosanna the Son of David, they disdained,

16 And said unto him, Hearest thou what these say? And Jesus said unto them, Yea: read ye never, By the mouth of babes and sucklings thou hast made perfect the praise?

17 So he left them, and went out of the city unto Bethany, and lodged there.

18 And in the morning as he returned into the city, he was hungry,

19 And seeing a fig tree in the way, he came to it, and found nothing thereon, but leaves only, and said to it, Never fruit grow on thee hence forwards. And soon the fig tree withered.

20 And when his disciples saw it, they marveled, saying, How soon is the fig tree withered!

21 And Jesus answered and said unto them, Verily I say unto you, if ye have faith, and doubt not, ye shall not only do that, which I have done to the fig tree, but also if ye say unto this mountain, Take thyself away, and cast thyself into the sea, it shall be done.

22 And whatsoever ye shall ask in prayer, if ye believe, ye shall receive it.

23 And when he was come into the Temple, the chief Priests, and the Elders of the people came unto him, as he was teaching, and said, By what authority doest thou these things? and who gave thee this authority?

24 Then Jesus answered and said unto them, I also will ask of you a certain thing, which if ye tell me, I likewise will tell you by what authority I do these things.

25 The baptism of John, whence was it? from heaven, or of men? Then they reasoned among themselves, saying, If we shall say from heaven, he will say unto us, Why did ye not then believe him?

26 And if we say, Of men, we fear the people: for all hold John as a Prophet.

27 Then they answered Jesus, and said, We cannot tell. And he said unto them, Neither tell I you by what authority I do these things.

28 But what think ye? A certain man had two sons, and came to the elder, and said, Son, go and work today in my vineyard.

29 But he answered and said, I will not: yet afterward he repented himself, and went.

30 Then came he to the second, and said likewise. And he answered, and said, I will, Sir: yet he went not.

31 Whether of them twain did the will of the father? They said unto him, The first. Jesus said unto them, Verily I say unto you, that the Publicans and the harlots shall go before you into the kingdom of God.

32 For John came unto you in the way of righteousness, and ye believed him not: but the Publicans, and the harlots believed him, and ye, though ye saw it, were not moved with repentance afterward, that ye might believe him.

33 Hear another parable, There was a certain householder, which planted a vineyard, and hedged it round about, and made a winepress therein, and built a tower, and let it out to husbandmen, and went into a strange country.

34 And when the time of the fruit drew near, he sent his servants to the husbandmen to receive the fruits thereof.

35 And the husbandmen took his servants and beat one, and killed another, and stoned another.

36 Again he sent other servants, more than the first: and they did the like unto them.

37 But last of all he sent unto them his own son, saying, They will reverence my son.

38 But when the husbandmen saw the son, they said among themselves, This is the heir: come, let us kill him, and let us take his inheritance.

39 So they took him, and cast him out of the vineyard, and slew him.

40 When therefore the Lord of the vineyard shall come, what will he do to those husbandmen?

41 They said unto him, He will cruelly destroy those wicked men, and will let out his vineyard unto other husbandmen, which shall deliver him the fruits in their seasons.

42 Jesus said unto them, Read ye never in the Scriptures, The stone which the builders refused, the same is made the head of the corner? This was the Lords doing, and it is marvelous in our eyes.

43 Therefore say I unto you, The kingdom of God shall be taken from you, and shall be given to a nation, which shall bring forth the fruits thereof.

44 And whosoever shall fall on this stone, he shall be broken: but on whomsoever it shall fall, it will grind him into powder.

45 And when the chief Priests and Pharisees had heard his parables, they perceived that he spake of them.

46 And they seeking to lay hands on him, feared the people, because they took him as a Prophet.

Matthew Chapter 22

1 Then Jesus answered, and spake unto them again in parables, saying,

2 The kingdom of heaven is like unto a certain King which married his son,

3 And sent forth his servants, to call them that were bid to the wedding, but they would not come.

4 Again he sent forth other servants, saying, Tell them which are bidden, Behold, I have prepared my dinner: mine oxen and my fatlings are killed, and all things are ready: come unto the marriage.

5 But they made light of it, and went their ways, one to his farm, and another about his merchandise.

6 And the remnant took his servants, and entreated them sharply, and slew them.

7 But when the King heard it, he was wroth, and sent forth his warriors, and destroyed those murderers, and burned up their city.

8 Then said he to his servants, Truly the wedding is prepared but they which were bidden, were not worthy.

9 Go ye therefore out into the highways, and as many as ye find, bid them to the marriage.

10 So those servants went out into the high ways and gathered together all that ever they found, both good and bad: so the wedding was furnished with guests.

11 Then the King came in, to see the guests, and saw there a man which had not on a wedding garment.

12 And he said unto him, Friend, how camest thou in hither, and hast not on a wedding garment? And he was speechless.

13 Then said the King to the servants, Bind him hand and foot: take him away, and cast him into utter darkness: there shall be weeping and gnashing of teeth.

14 For many are called, but few chosen.

15 Then went the Pharisees and took counsel how they might tangle him in talk.

16 And they sent unto him their disciples with the Herodians, saying, Master, we know that thou art true, and teachest the way of God truly, neither carest for any man: for thou considerest not the person of men.

17 Tell us therefore, how thinkest thou? Is it lawful to give tribute unto Caesar, or not?

18 But Jesus perceived their wickedness, and said, Why tempt ye me, ye hypocrites?

19 Show me the tribute money. And they brought him a penny.

20 And he said unto them, Whose is this image and superscription?

21 They said unto him, Caesar's. Then said he unto them, Give therefore to Caesar, the things which are Caesar's, and give unto God, those things which are Gods.

22 And when they heard it, they marveled, and left him, and went their way.

23 The same day the Sadducees came to him (which say that there is no resurrection) and asked him,

24 Saying, Master, Moses said, If a man die, having no children, let his brother marry his wife, and raise up seed unto his brother.

25 Now there were with us seven brethren, and the first married a wife, and deceased: and having none issue, left his wife unto his brother.

26 Likewise also the second, and the third, unto the seventh.

27 And last of all the woman died also.

28 Therefore in the resurrection, whose wife shall she be of the seven? for all had her.

29 Then Jesus answered, and said unto them, Ye are deceived, not knowing the Scriptures, nor the power of God.

30 For in the resurrection they neither marry wives, nor wives are bestowed in marriage, but are as the Angels of God in heaven.

31 And concerning the resurrection of the dead, have ye not read what is spoken unto you of God, saying,

32 I am the God of Abraham, and the God of Isaac, and the God of Jacob? God is not the God of the dead, but of the living.

33 And when the people heard it, they were astonished at his doctrine.

34 But when the Pharisees had heard, that he had put the Sadducees to silence, they assembled together.

35 And one of them, which was an expounder of the Law, asked him a question, tempting him, and saying,

36 Master, which is the great commandment in the Law?

37 Jesus said to him, Thou shalt love the Lord thy God with all thine heart, with all thy soul, and with all thy mind.

38 This is the first and the great commandment.

39 And the second is like unto this, Thou shalt love thy neighbor as thyself.

40 On these two commandments hangeth the whole Law, and the Prophets.

41 While the Pharisees were gathered together, Jesus asked them,

42 Saying, What think ye of Christ? whose son is he? They said unto him, Davids.

43 He said unto them, How then doth David in spirit call him Lord, saying,

44 The Lord said to my Lord, Sit at my right hand, till I make thine enemies thy footstool?

45 If then David call him Lord, how is he his son?

46 And none could answer him a word, neither durst any from that day forth ask him any more questions.

Matthew Chapter 23

1 Then spake Jesus to the multitude, and to his disciples,

2 Saying, The Scribes and the Pharisees sit in Moses seat.

3 All therefore whatsoever they bid you observe, that observe and do: but after their works do not: for they say, and do not.

4 For they bind heavy burdens, and grievous to be born, and lay them on mens shoulders, but they themselves will not move them with one of their fingers.

5 All their works they do for to be seen of men: for they make their phylacteries broad, and make long the fringes of their garments,

6 And love the chief place at feasts, and to have the chief seats in the assemblies,

7 And greetings in the markets, and to be called of men, Rabbi, Rabbi.

8 But be not ye called, Rabbi: for one is your doctor, to wit, Christ, and all ye are brethren.

9 And call no man your father upon the earth: for there is but one, your Father which is in heaven.

10 Be not called doctors: for one is your doctor, even Christ.

11 But he that is greatest among you, let him be your servant.

12 For whosoever will exalt himself, shall be brought low: and whosoever will humble himself, shall be exalted.

13 Woe therefore be unto you Scribes and Pharisees, hypocrites, because ye shut up the kingdom of heaven before men: for ye yourselves go not in, neither suffer ye them that would enter, to come in.

14 Woe be unto you Scribes and Pharisees, hypocrites: for ye devour widow's houses, even under a color of long prayers: wherefore ye shall receive the greater damnation.

15 Woe be unto you, Scribes and Pharisees, hypocrites: for ye compass sea and land to make one of your profession: and when he is made, ye make him two fold more the child of hell, than you yourselves.

16 Woe be unto you blind guides, which say, Whosoever sweareth by the Temple, it is nothing: but whosoever sweareth by the gold of the Temple, he offendeth.

17 Ye fools and blind, whether is greater, the gold, or the Temple that sanctifieth the gold?

18 And whosoever sweareth by the altar, it is nothing: but whosoever sweareth by the offering that is upon it, offendeth.

19 Ye fools and blind, whether is greater, the offering, or the altar which sanctifieth the offering?

20 Whosoever therefore sweareth by the altar, sweareth by it, and by all things thereon.

21 And whosoever sweareth by the Temple, sweareth by it, and by him that dwelleth therein.

22 And he that sweareth by heaven, sweareth by the throne of God, and by him that sitteth thereon.

23 Woe be to you, Scribes and Pharisees, hypocrites: for ye tithe mint, and anise, and cumin, and leave the weightier matters of the law, as judgment, and mercy, and fidelity. These ought ye to have done, and not to have left the other.

24 Ye blind guides, which strain out a gnat, and swallow a camel.

25 Woe be to you, Scribes and Pharisees, hypocrites: for ye make clean the utter side of the cup, and of the platter: but within they are full of bribery and excess.

26 Thou blind Pharisee, cleanse first the inside of the cup and platter, that the outside of them may be clean also.

27 Woe be to you, Scribes and Pharisees, hypocrites: for ye are like unto whited tombs, which appear beautiful outward, but are within full of dead mens bones, and of all filthiness.

28 So are ye also: for outward ye appear righteous unto men, but within ye are full of hypocrisy and iniquity.

29 Woe be unto you, Scribes and Pharisees, hypocrites: for ye build the tombs of the Prophets, and garnish the sepulchers of the righteous,

30 And say, If we had been in the days of our fathers, we would not have been partners with them in the blood of the Prophets.

31 So then ye be witnesses unto yourselves, that ye are the children of them that murdered the Prophets.

32 Fulfill ye also the measure of your fathers.

33 O serpents, the generation of vipers, how should ye escape the damnation of hell!

34 Wherefore behold, I send unto you Prophets, and wise men, and Scribes, and of them ye shall kill and crucify: and of them shall ye scourge in your Synagogues, and persecute from city to city,

35 That upon you may come all the righteous blood that was shed upon the earth, from the blood of Abel the righteous, unto the blood of Zecharias the son of Berachias, whom ye slew between the Temple and the altar.

36 Verily I say unto you, all these things shall come upon this generation.

37 Jerusalem, Jerusalem, which killest the Prophets, and stonest them which are sent to thee, how often would I have gathered thy children together, as the hen gathereth her chickens under her wings, and ye would not!

38 Behold, your habitation shall be left unto you desolate,

39 For I say unto you, ye shall not see me henceforth till that ye say, Blessed is he that cometh in the Name of the Lord.

Matthew Chapter 24

1 And Jesus went out, and departed from the Temple, and his disciples came to him, to show him the building of the Temple.

2 And Jesus said unto them, See ye not all these things? Verily I say unto you, there shall not be here left a stone upon a stone, that shall not be cast down.

3 And as he sat upon the mount of Olives, his disciples came unto him apart, saying, Tell us when these things shall be, and what sign shall be of thy coming, and of the end of the world.

4 And Jesus answered, and said unto them, Take heed that no man deceive you.

5 For many shall come in my name, saying, I am Christ, and shall deceive many.

6 And ye shall hear of wars, and rumors of wars: see that ye be not troubled: for all these things must come to pass, but the end is not yet.

7 For nation shall rise against nation, and realm against realm, and there shall be pestilence, and famine, and earthquakes in divers places.

8 All these are but the beginning of sorrows.

9 Then shall they deliver you up to be afflicted, and shall kill you, and ye shall be hated of all nations for my Names sake.

10 And then shall many be offended, and shall betray one another, and shall hate one another.

11 And many false prophets shall arise, and shall deceive many.

12 And because iniquity shall be increased, the love of many shall be cold.

13 But he that endureth to the end, he shall be saved.

14 And this Gospel of the kingdom shall be preached through the whole world for a witness unto all nations, and then shall the end come.

15 When ye therefore shall see the abomination of desolation spoken of by Daniel the Prophet, standing in the Holy place, (let him that readeth consider it.)

16 Then let them which be in Judea, flee into the mountains.

17 Let him which is on the house top, not come down to fetch anything out of his house.

18 And he that is in the field, let not him return back to fetch his clothes.

19 And woe shall be to them that are with child, and to them that give suck in those days.

20 But pray that your flight be not in the winter, neither on the Sabbath day.

21 For then shall be great tribulation, such as was not from the beginning of the world to this time, nor shall be.

22 And except those days should be shortened, there should no flesh be saved: but for the elects sake those days shall be shortened.

23 Then if any shall say unto you, Lo, here is Christ, or there, believe it not.

24 For there shall arise false Christs, and false prophets, and shall show great signs and wonders, so that if it were possible, they should deceive the very elect.

25 Behold, I have told you before.

26 Wherefore if they shall say unto you, Behold, he is in the desert, go not forth: Behold, he is in the secret places, believe it not.

27 For as the lightning cometh out of the East, and shineth into the West, so shall also the coming of the Son of man be.

28 For wheresoever a dead carcass is, thither will the Eagles resort.

29 And immediately after the tribulations of those days, shall the sun be darkened, and the moon shall not give her light, and the stars shall fall from heaven, and the powers of heaven shall be shaken.

30 And then shall appear the sign of the Son of man in heaven: and then shall all the kinreds of the earth mourn, and they shall see the Son of man come in the clouds of heaven with power and great glory.

31 And he shall send his Angels with a great sound of a trumpet, and they shall gather together his elect, from the four winds, and from the one end of the heaven unto the other.

32 Now learn the parable of the fig tree: when her bough is yet tender, and it bringeth forth leaves, ye know that summer is near.

33 So likewise ye, when ye see all these things, know that the kingdom of God is near, even at the doors.

34 Verily I say unto you, this generation shall not pass, till all these things be done.

35 Heaven and earth shall pass away: but my words shall not pass away.

36 But of that day and hour knoweth no man, no not the Angels of heaven, but my father only.

37 But as the days of Noah were, so likewise shall the coming of the Son of man be.

38 For as in the days before the flood they did eat and drink, marry, and give in marriage, unto the day that Noah entered into the Ark,

39 And knew nothing, till the flood came and took them all away, so shall also the coming of the Son of man be.

40 Then two men shall be in the fields, the one shall be received, and the other shall be refused.

41 Two women shall be grinding at the mill: the one shall be received, and the other shall be refused.

42 Wake therefore: for ye know not what hour your master will come.

43 Of this be sure, that if the good man of the house knew at what watch the thief would come, he would surely watch, and not suffer his house to be digged through.

44 Therefore be ye also ready: for in the hour that ye think not, will the Son of man come.

45 Who then is a faithful servant and wise, whom his master hath made ruler over his household, to give them meat in season?

46 Blessed is that servant whom his master, when he cometh, shall find so doing.

47 Verily I say unto you, he shall make him ruler over all his goods.

48 But if that evil servant shall say in his heart, My master doth defer his coming,

49 And begin to smite his fellows, and to eat and to drink with the drunken,

50 That servants master will come in a day, when he looketh not for him, and in an hour that he is not ware of,

51 And will cut him off, and give him his portion with hypocrites: there shall be weeping, and gnashing of teeth.

Matthew Chapter 25

1 Then the kingdom of heaven shall be likened unto ten virgins, which took their lamps, and went to meet the bridegroom.

2 And five of them were wise, and five foolish.

3 The foolish took their lamps, but took none oil with them.

4 But the wise took oil in their vessels with their lamps.

5 Now while the bridegroom tarried long, all slumbered and slept.

6 And at midnight there was a cry made, Behold, the bridegroom cometh: go out to meet him.

7 Then all those virgins arose, and trimmed their lamps.

8 And the foolish said to the wise, Give us of your oil, for our lamps are out. 9 But the wise answered, saying, We fear lest there will not be enough for us and you: but go ye rather to them that sell, and buy for yourselves. 10 And while they went to buy, the bridegroom came: and they that were ready, went in with him to the wedding, and the gate was shut.

11 Afterwards came also the other virgins, saying, Lord, Lord, open to us.

12 But he answered, and said, Verily I say unto you, I know you not.

13 Watch therefore: for ye know neither the day, nor the hour, when the son of man will come.

14 For the kingdom of heaven is as a man that going into a strange country, called his servants, and delivered to them his goods.

15 And unto one he gave five talents, and to another two, and to another one, to every man after his own ability, and straightway went from home.

16 Then he that had received the five talents, went and occupied with them, and gained other five talents.

17 Likewise also, he that received two, he also gained other two.

18 But he that received that one, went and digged it in the earth, and hid his masters money.

19 But after a long season, the master of those servants came, and reckoned with them.

20 Then came he that had received five talents, and brought other five talents, saying, Master, thou deliverest unto me five talents: behold, I have gained with them other five talents.

21 Then his master said unto him, It is well done good servant and faithful, Thou hast been faithful in little, I will make thee ruler over much: enter into thy masters joy.

22 Also he that had received two talents, came and said, Master, thou deliverest unto me two talents: behold, I have gained two other talents with them.

23 His master said unto him, It is well done good servant, and faithful, Thou hast been faithful in little, I will make thee ruler over much: enter into thy masters joy.

24 Then he which had received the one talent, came and said, Master, I knew that thou wast an hard man, which reapest where thou sowedst not, and gatherest where thou strawedst not:

25 I was therefore afraid, and went and hid thy talent in the earth: behold, thou hast thine own.

26 And his master answered, and said unto him, Thou evil servant, and slothful, thou knewest that I reap where I sowed not, and gather where I strawed not.

27 Thou oughtest therefore to have put my money to the exchangers, and then at my coming should I have received mine own with vantage.

28 Take therefore the talent from him, and give it unto him which hath ten talents.

29 For unto every man that hath, it shall be given, and he shall have abundance, and from him that hath not, even that he hath, shall be taken away.

30 Cast therefore that unprofitable servant into utter darkness: there shall be weeping and gnashing of teeth.

31 And when the Son of man cometh in his glory, and all the Holy Angels with him, then shall he sit upon the throne of his glory,

32 And before him shall be gathered all nations, and he shall separate them one from another, as a shepherd separateth the sheep from the goats.

33 And he shall set the sheep on his right hand, and the goats on the left.

34 Then shall the king say to them on his right hand, Come ye blessed of my father: inherit ye the kingdom prepared for you from the foundation of the world.

35 For I was hungred, and ye gave me meat: I thirsted, and ye gave me drink: I was a stranger, and ye lodged me.

36 I was naked, and ye clothed me, I was sick, and ye visited me: I was in prison, and ye came unto me.

37 Then shall the righteous answer him, saying, Lord, when saw we thee hungred, and fed thee? or a thirst, and gave thee drink?

38 And when saw we thee a stranger, and lodged thee? or naked, and clothed thee?

39 Or when saw we thee sick, or in prison, and came unto thee?

40 And the King shall answer, and say unto them, Verily I say unto you, in as much as ye have done it unto one of the least of these my brethren, ye have done it to me.

41 Then shall he say unto them on the left hand, Depart from me ye cursed, into everlasting fire, which is prepared for the devil and his angels.

42 For I was an hungred, and ye gave me no meat: I thirsted, and ye gave me no drink:

43 I was a stranger, and ye lodged me not: I was naked, and ye clothed me not: sick, and in prison, and ye visited me not.

44 Then shall they also answer him, saying, Lord, when saw we thee an hungred, or a thirst, or a stranger, or naked, or sick, or in prison, and did not minister unto thee?

45 Then shall he answer them, and say, Verily I say unto you, in as much as ye did it not to one of the least of these, ye did it not to me.

46 And these shall go into everlasting pain, and the righteous into life eternal.

Matthew Chapter 26

1 And it came to pass, when Jesus had finished all these sayings, he said unto his disciples,

2 Ye know that within two days is the Passover, and the Son of man shall be delivered to be crucified.

3 Then assembled together the chief Priests and the Scribes, and the Elders of the people into the hall of the high Priest, called Caiaphas:

4 And consulted how they might take Jesus by subtlety, and kill him.

5 But they said, Not on the feast day, lest any uproar be among the people.

6 And when Jesus was in Bethany, in the house of Simon the leper,

7 There came unto him a woman, which had a box of very costly ointment, and poured it on his head, as he sat at the table.

8 And when his disciples saw it, they had indignation, saying, What needed this waste?

9 For this ointment might have been sold for much, and been given to the poor.

10 And Jesus knowing it, said unto them, Why trouble ye the woman? for she hath wrought a good work upon me.

11 For ye have the poor always with you, but me shall ye not have always.

12 For in that she poured this ointment on my body, she did it to bury me.

13 Verily I say unto you, Wheresoever this Gospel shall be preached throughout all the world, there shall also this that she hath done, be spoken of for a memorial of her.

14 Then one of the twelve, called Judas Iscariot, went unto the chief Priests,

15 And said, What will ye give me, and I will deliver him unto you? and they appointed unto him thirty pieces of silver.

16 And from that time, he sought opportunity to betray him.

17 Now on the first day of the feast of unleavened bread the disciples came to Jesus, saying unto him, Where wilt thou that we prepare for thee to eat the Passover?

18 And he said, Go you into the city to such a man, and say to him, The master saith, My time is at hand: I will keep the Passover at thine house with my disciples.

19 And the disciples did as Jesus had given them charge, and made ready the Passover.

20 So when the Even was come, he sat down with the twelve.

21 And as they did eat, he said, Verily I say unto you, that one of you shall betray me.

22 And they were exceeding sorrowful, and began every one of them to say unto him, Is it I, Master?

23 And he answered and said, He that dippeth his hand with me in the dish, he shall betray me.

24 Surely the Son of man goeth his way, as it is written of him: but woe be to that man, by whom the Son of man is betrayed: it had been good for that man, if he had never been born.

25 Then Judas which betrayed him, answered and said, Is it I, Master? He said unto him, Thou hast said it.

26 And as they did eat, Jesus took the bread: and when he had given thanks, he break it, and gave it to the disciples, and said, Take, eat: this is my body.

27 Also he took the cup, and when he had given thanks, he gave it them, saying, Drink ye all of it.

28 For this is my blood of the New Testament, that is shed for many, for the remission of sins.

29 I say unto you, that I will not drink henceforth of this fruit of the vine until that day, when I shall drink it new with you in my Fathers kingdom.

30 And when they had sung a Psalm, they went out into the Mount of Olives.

31 Then said Jesus unto them, All ye shall be offended by me this night: for it is written, I will smite the shepherd, and the sheep of the flock shall be scattered.

32 But after I am risen again, I will go before you into Galilee.

33 But Peter answered, and said unto him, Though that all men should be offended by thee, yet will I never be offended.

34 Jesus said unto him, Verily I say unto thee, that this night, before the cock crow, thou shalt deny me thrice.

35 Peter said unto him, Though I should die with thee, yet will I not deny thee. Likewise also said all the disciples.

36 Then went Jesus with them into a place which is called Gethsemane, and said unto his disciples, Sit ye here, while I go and pray yonder.

37 And he took Peter, and the two sons of Zebedee, and began to wax sorrowful, and grievously troubled.

38 Then said Jesus unto them, My soul is very heavy, even unto the death: tarry ye here, and watch with me.

39 So he went a little further, and fell on his face, and prayed, saying, O my Father, if it be possible, let this cup pass from me: nevertheless, not as I will, but as thou wilt.

40 After he came unto the disciples, and found them asleep, and said to Peter, What? could ye not watch with me one hour?

41 Watch, and pray, that ye enter not into temptation: the spirit indeed is ready, but the flesh is weak.

42 Again he went away the second time and prayed, saying, O my Father, if this cup cannot pass away from me, but that I must drink it, thy will be done.

43 And he came, and found them a sleep again, for their eyes were heavy.

44 So he left them and went away again, and prayed the third time, saying the same words.

45 Then came he to his disciples, and said unto them, Sleep henceforth, and take your rest: behold, the hour is at hand, and the Son of man is given into the hands of sinners.

46 Rise, let us go: behold, he is at hand that betrayeth me.

47 And while he yet spake, lo, Judas, one of the twelve, came, and with him a great multitude with swords and staves, from the high Priests and Elders of the people.

48 Now he that betrayed him, had given them a token, saying, Whomsoever I shall kiss, that is he, lay hold on him.

49 And forthwith he came to Jesus, and said, God save thee, Master, and kissed him.

50 Then Jesus said unto him, Friend, wherefore art thou come? Then came they, and laid hands on Jesus, and took him.

51 And behold, one of them which were with Jesus, stretched out his hand, and drew his sword, and struck a servant of the high Priest, and smote off his ear.

52 Then said Jesus unto him, Put up thy sword into his place: for all that take the sword, shall perish with the sword.

53 Either thinkest thou, that I cannot now pray to my Father, and he will give me more than twelve legions of Angels?

54 How then should the Scriptures be fulfilled, which say, that it must be so?

55 The same hour said Jesus to the multitude, Ye be come out as it were against a thief, with swords and staves, to take me: I sat daily teaching in the Temple among you, and ye took me not.

56 But all this was done, that the Scriptures of the Prophets might be fulfilled. Then all the disciples forsook him, and fled.

57 And they took Jesus, and led him to Caiaphas the high Priest, where the Scribes and the Elders were assembled.

58 And Peter followed him a far off unto the high Priests hall, and went in, and sat with the servants to see the end.

59 Now the chief Priests and the Elders, and all the whole council sought false witness against Jesus, to put him to death.

60 But they found none, and though many false witnesses came, yet found they none: but at the last came two false witnesses,

61 And said, This man said, I can destroy the Temple of God, and build it in three days.

62 Then the chief Priest arose, and said to him, Answerest thou nothing? What is the matter that these men witness against thee?

63 But Jesus held his peace. Then the chief Priest answered, and said to him, I charge thee by the living God, that thou tell us, if thou be the Christ the Son of God.

64 Jesus said to him, Thou hast said it: nevertheless I say unto you, hereafter shall ye see the Son of man, sitting at the right hand of the power of God, and come in the clouds of the heaven.

65 Then the high Priest rent his clothes, saying, He hath blasphemed, what have we any more need of witnesses? Behold, now ye have heard his blasphemy.

66 What think ye? They answered, and said, He is worthy to die.

67 Then spat they in his face, and buffeted him, and other smote him with their rods,

68 Saying, Prophecy to us, O Christ, Who is he that smote thee?

69 Peter sat without in the hall: and a maid came to him, saying, Thou also wast with Jesus of Galilee:

70 But he denied before them all, saying, I wot not what thou sayest.

71 And when he went out into the porch, another maid saw him, and said unto them that were there, This man was also with Jesus of Nazareth.

72 And again he denied with an oath, saying, I know not the man.

73 So after a while, came unto him they that stood by, and said unto Peter, Surely thou art also one of them: for even thy speech betrayeth thee.

74 Then began he to curse himself, and to swear, saying, I know not the man. And immediately the cock crew.

75 Then Peter remembered the words of Jesus, which had said unto him, Before the cock crow, thou shalt deny me thrice. So he went out, and wept bitterly.

Matthew Chapter 27

1 When the morning was come, all the chief Priests, and the Elders of the people took counsel against Jesus, to put him to death,

2 And led him away bound, and delivered him unto Pontius Pilate the governor.

3 Then when Judas which betrayed him, saw that he was condemned, he repented himself, and brought again the thirty pieces of silver to the chief Priests, and Elders,

4 Saying, I have sinned betraying the innocent blood. But they said, What is that to us? see thou to it.

5 And when he had cast down the silver pieces in the Temple, he departed, and went, and hanged himself.

6 And the chief Priests took the silver pieces, and said, It is not lawful for us to put them into the treasure, because it is the price of blood.

7 And they took counsel, and bought with them a potters field, for the burial of strangers.

8 Wherefore that field is called, the field of blood, until this day.

9 (Then was fulfilled that which was spoken by Jeremiah the Prophet, saying, And they took thirty silver pieces, the price of him that was valued, whom they of the children of Israel valued.

10 And they gave them for the potters field, as the Lord appointed me.)

11 And Jesus stood before the governor, and the governor asked him, saying, Art thou the King of the Jews? Jesus said unto him, Thou sayest it.

12 And when he was accused of the chief Priests and Elders, he answered nothing.

13 Then said Pilate unto him, Hearest thou not how many things they lay against thee?

14 But he answered him not to one word, in so much that the governor marveled greatly.

15 Now at the feast, the governor was wont to deliver unto the people a prisoner whom they would.

16 And they had then a notable prisoner, called Barabbas.

17 When they were then gathered together, Pilate said unto them, Whether will ye that I let loose unto you Barabbas, or Jesus which is called Christ?

18 (For he knew well, that for envy they had delivered him.

19 Also when he was set down upon the judgment seat, his wife sent to him, saying, Have thou nothing to do with that just man: for I have suffered many things this day in a dream by reason of him.)

20 But the chief Priests and the Elders had persuaded the people that they should ask Barabbas, and should destroy Jesus.

21 Then the governor answered, and said unto them, Whether of the twain will ye that I let loose unto you? And they said, Barabbas.

22 Pilate said unto them, What shall I do then with Jesus which is called Christ? They all said to him, Let him be crucified.

23 Then said the governor, But what evil hath he done? Then they cried the more, saying, Let him be crucified.

24 When Pilate saw that he availed nothing, but that more tumult was made, he took water and washed his hands before the multitude, saying, I am innocent of the blood of this just man: look you to it.

25 Then answered all the people, and said, His blood be on us, and on our children.

26 Thus let he Barabbas loose unto them, and scourged Jesus, and delivered him to be crucified.

27 Then the soldiers of the governor took Jesus into the common hall, and gathered about him the whole band,

28 And they stripped him, and put upon him a scarlet robe,

29 And platted a crown of thorns, and put it upon his head, and a reed in his right hand, and bowed their knees before him, and mocked him, saying, God save thee King of the Jews,

30 And spitted upon him, and took a reed, and smote him on the head.

31 Thus when they had mocked him, they took the robe from him, and put his own raiment on him, and led him away to crucify him.

32 And as they came out, they found a man of Cyrene, named Simon: him they compelled to bear his cross.

33 And when they came unto the place called Golgotha, (that is to say, the place of dead mens skulls.)

34 They gave him vinegar to drink, mingled with gall: and when he had tasted thereof, he would not drink.

35 And when they had crucified him, they parted his garments, and did cast lots, that it might be fulfilled, which was spoken by the Prophet, They divided my garments among them, and upon my vesture did cast lots.

36 And they sat, and watched him there.

37 They set up also over his head his cause written, THIS IS JESUS THE KING OF THE JEWS.

38 And there were two thieves crucified with him, one on the right hand, and another on the left.

39 And they that passed by, reviled him, wagging their heads,

40 And saying, Thou that destroyest the Temple, and buildest it in three days, save thyself: if thou be the Son of God, come down from the cross.

41 Likewise also the high Priests mocking him, with the Scribes, and Elders, and Pharisees, said,

42 He saved others, but he cannot save himself: if he be the King of Israel, let him now come down from the cross, and we will believe him.

43 He trusteth in God, let him deliver him now, if he will have him: for he said, I am the Son of God.

44 That same also the thieves which were crucified with him, cast in his teeth.

45 Now from the sixth hour was there darkness over all the land, unto the ninth hour.

46 And about the ninth hour Jesus cried with a loud voice, saying, Eli, Eli, lama sabachthani? that is, My God, my God, why hast thou forsaken me?

47 And some of them that stood there, when they heard it, said, This man calleth Elijah.

48 And straightway one of them ran, and took a sponge, and filled it with vinegar, and put it on a reed, and gave him to drink.

49 Other said, Let be: let us see, if Elijah will come and save him.

50 Then Jesus cried again with a loud voice, and yielded up the ghost.

51 And behold, the veil of the Temple was rent in twain, from the top to the bottom, and the earth did quake, and the stones were cloven.

52 And the graves did open themselves, and many bodies of the Saints which slept, arose,

53 And came out of the graves after his resurrection, and went into the Holy city, and appeared unto many.

54 When the Centurion, and they that were with him watching Jesus, saw the earthquake, and the things that were done, they feared greatly, saying, Truly this was the Son of God.
55 And many women were there, beholding him a far off, which had followed Jesus from Galilee, ministering unto him.
56 Among whom were Mary Magdalene, and Mary the mother of James and Joseph, and the mother of Zebedees sons.
57 And when the even was come, there came a rich man of Arimathea, named Joseph, who had also himself been Jesus disciple.
58 He went to Pilate, and asked the body of Jesus. Then Pilate commanded the body to be delivered.
59 So Joseph took the body, and wrapped it in a clean linen cloth,
60 And put it in his new tomb, which he had hewn out in a rock, and rolled a great stone to the door of the sepulcher, and departed.
61 And there was Mary Magdalene, and the other Mary sitting over against the sepulcher.
62 Now the next day that followed the Preparation of the Sabbath, the high Priests and Pharisees assembled to Pilate,
63 And said, Sir, we remember that that deceiver said, while he was yet alive, Within three days I will rise.
64 Command therefore, that the sepulcher be made sure until the third day, lest his disciples come by night, and steal him away, and say unto the people, He is risen from the dead: so shall the last error be worse then the first.
65 Then Pilate said unto them, Ye have a watch: go, and make it sure as ye know.
66 And they went, and made the sepulcher sure with the watch, and sealed the stone.

Matthew Chapter 28

1 Now in the end of the Sabbath, when the first day of the week began to dawn, Mary Magdalene, and the other Mary came to see the sepulcher,
2 And behold, there was a great earthquake: for the Angel of the Lord descended from heaven, and came and rolled back the stone from the door, and sat upon it.
3 And his countenance was like lightning, and his raiment white as snow. 4 And for fear of him, the keepers were astonished, and became as dead men.
5 But the Angel answered, and said to the women, Fear ye not: for I know that ye seek Jesus which was crucified:
6 He is not here, for he is risen; as he said: come, see the place where the Lord was laid,
7 And go quickly, and tell his disciples that he is risen from the dead: and behold, he goeth before you into Galilee: there ye shall see him: lo, I have told you.
8 So they departed quickly from the sepulcher, with fear and great joy, and did run to bring his disciples word.
9 And as they went to tell his disciples, behold, Jesus also met them, saying, God save you. And they came, and took him by the feet, and worshipped him.
10 Then said Jesus unto them, Be not afraid. Go, and tell my brethren, that they go into Galilee, and there shall they see me.
11 Now when they were gone, behold, some of the watch came into the city, and showed unto the high Priests all the things that were done.
12 And they gathered them together with the Elders, and took counsel, and gave large money unto the soldiers,
13 Saying, Say, His disciples came by night and stole him away while we slept.

14 And if the governor hear of this, we will persuade him, and save you harmless.

15 So they took the money, and did as they were taught: and this saying is noised among the Jews unto this day.

16 Then the eleven disciples went into Galilee, into a mountain, where Jesus had appointed them.

17 And when they saw him, they worshipped him: but some doubted.

18 And Jesus came, and spake unto them, saying, All power is given unto me in heaven, and in earth.

19 Go therefore, and teach all nations, baptizing them in the Name of the Father, and the Son, and the Holy Ghost,

20 Teaching them to observe all things, whatsoever I have commanded you: and lo, I am with you alway, until the end of the world, Amen.

THE HOLY GOSPEL OF JESUS CHRIST, ACCORDING TO MARK

Mark Chapter 1

1 The beginning of the Gospel of Jesus Christ, the Son of God:

2 As it is written in the Prophets, Behold, I send my messenger before thy face, which shall prepare thy way before thee.

3 The voice of him that cryeth in the wilderness is, Prepare the way of the Lord: make his paths straight.

4 John did baptize in the wilderness, and preach the baptism of amendment of life, for remission of sins.

5 And all the country of Judea, and they of Jerusalem went out unto him, and were all baptized of him in the river Jordan, confessing their sins.

6 Now John was clothed with camels hair, and with a girdle of a skin about his loins: and he did eat locusts and wild honey,

7 And preached, saying, A stronger than I, cometh after me, whose shoes latchet I am not worthy to stoop down, and unloose.

8 Truth it is, I have baptized you with water: but he will baptize you with the Holy Ghost.

9 And it came to pass in those days, that Jesus came from Nazareth, a city of Galilee, and was baptized of John in Jordan.

10 And as soon as he was come out of the water, John saw the heavens cloven in twain, and the Holy Ghost descending upon him like a dove.

11 Then there was a voice from heaven, saying, Thou art my beloved Son, in whom I am well pleased.

12 And immediately the Spirit driveth him into the wilderness.

13 And he was there in the wilderness forty days, and was tempted of Satan: he was also with the wild beasts, and the Angels ministered unto him.

14 Now after that John was committed to prison, Jesus came into Galilee, preaching the Gospel of the Kingdom of God,

15 And saying, The time is fulfilled, and the Kingdom of God is at hand: repent and believe the Gospel.

16 And as he walked by the Sea of Galilee, he saw Simon, and Andrew his brother, casting a net into the sea, (for they were fishers.)

17 Then Jesus said unto them, Follow me, and I will make you to be fishers of men.

18 And straightway they forsook their nets, and followed him.

19 And when he had gone a little further thence, he saw James the son of Zebedee, and John his brother, as they were in the ship, mending their nets.

20 And soon he called them: and they left their father Zebedee in the ship with his hired servants, and went their way after him.

21 So they entered into Capernaum, and straightway on the Sabbath day he entered into the Synagogue and taught.

22 And they were astonished at his doctrine: for he taught them as one that had authority, and not as the Scribes.

23 And there was in their Synagogue a man which had an unclean spirit, and he cried,

24 Saying, Ah, what have we to do with thee, O Jesus of Nazareth? Art thou come to destroy us? I know thee what thou art, even that Holy one of God. 25 And Jesus rebuked him, saying, Hold thy peace, and come out of him.

26 And the unclean spirit tare him, and cried with a loud voice, and came out of him.

27 And they were all amazed, so that they demanded one of another, saying, What thing is this? what new doctrine is this? for he command the foul spirits with authority, and they obey him.

28 And immediately his fame spread abroad throughout all the region bordering on Galilee.

29 And as soon as they were come out of the Synagogue, they entered into the house of Simon and Andrew, with James and John.

30 And Simon's wife's mother-in-law lay sick of a fever, and anon they told him of her.

31 And he came and took her by the hand, and lift her up, and the fever forsook her by and by, and she ministered unto them.

32 And when even was come, and the sun was down, they brought to him all that were diseased, and them that were possessed with devils.

33 And the whole city was gathered together at the door.

34 And he healed many that were sick of divers diseases: and he cast out many devils, and suffered not the devils to say that they knew him.

35 And in the morning very early, before day Jesus arose and went out into a solitary place, and there prayed.

36 And Simon, and they that were with him, followed after him.

37 And when they had found him, they said unto him, All men seek for thee.

38 Then he said unto them, Let us go into the next towns, that I may preach there also: for I came out for that purpose.

39 And he preached in their Synagogues, throughout all Galilee, and cast the devils out.

40 And there came a leper to him, beseeching him, and kneeled down unto him, and said to him, If thou wilt, thou canst make me clean.

41 And Jesus had compassion, and put forth his hand, and touched him, and said to him, I will: be thou clean.

42 And as soon as he had spoken, immediately the leprosy departed from him, and he was made clean.

43 And after he had gave him a straight commandment, he sent him away forthwith,

44 And said unto him, See thou say nothing to any man, but get thee hence, and show thyself to the Priest, and offer for thy cleansing those things, which Moses commanded, for a testimonial unto them.

45 But when he was departed, he began to tell many things, and to publish the matter: so that Jesus could no more openly enter into the city, but was without in desert places: and they came to him from every quarter.

Mark Chapter 2

1 After a few days, he entered into Capernaum again, and it was noised that he was in the house.

2 And anon, many gathered together, in so much that the places about the door could not receive any more: and he preached the word unto them.

3 And there came unto him, that brought one sick of the palsy, borne of four men.

4 And because they could not come near unto him for the multitude, they uncovered the roof of the house where he was: and when they had broken it open, they let down the bed, wherein the sick of the palsy lay.

5 Now when Jesus saw their faith, he said to the sick of the palsy, Son, thy sins are forgiven thee.

6 And there were certain of the Scribes, sitting there, and reasoning in their hearts,

7 Why doth this man speak such blasphemies? who can forgive sins, but God only?

8 And immediately when Jesus perceived in his spirit, that thus they thought with themselves, he said unto them, Why reason ye these things in your hearts?

9 Whether is it easier to say to the sick of the palsy, Thy sins are forgiven thee? or to say, Arise, and take up thy bed, and walk?

10 And that ye may know, that the Son of man hath authority in earth to forgive sins, (he said unto the sick of the palsy.)

11 I say unto thee, Arise and take up thy bed, and get thee hence into thine own house.

12 And by and by he arose, and took up his bed, and went forth before them all, in so much that they were all amazed, and glorified God, saying, We never saw such a thing.

13 Then he went again toward the sea, and all the people resorted unto him, and he taught them.

14 And as Jesus passed by, he saw Levi the son of Alphaeus sit at the receipt of custom, and said unto him, Follow me. And he arose and followed him.

15 And it came to pass, as Jesus sat at table in his house, many Publicans and sinners sat at table also with Jesus, and his disciples: for there were many that followed him.

16 And when the Scribes and Pharisees saw him eat with the Publicans and sinners, they said unto his disciples, How is it, that he eateth and drinketh with Publicans and sinners?

17 Now when Jesus heard it, he said unto them, The whole have no need of the physician, but the sick. I came not to call the righteous, but the sinners to repentance.

18 And the disciples of John, and the Pharisees did fast, and came and said unto him, Why do the disciples of John and of the Pharisees fast, and thy disciples fast not?

19 And Jesus said unto them, Can the children of the marriage chamber fast, while the bridegroom is with them? as long as they have the bridegroom with them, they cannot fast.

20 But the days will come, when the bridegroom shall be taken from them, and then shall they fast in those days.

21 Also no man soweth a piece of new cloth in an old garment: for else the new piece taketh away the filling up from the old, and the breach is worse.

22 Likewise, no man putteth new wine into old vessels: for else the new wine breaketh the vessels, and the wine runneth out, and the vessels are lost: but new wine must be put into new vessels.

23 And it came to pass as he went through the corn on the Sabbath day, that his disciples, as they went on their way, began to pluck the ears of corn.

24 And the Pharisees said unto him, Behold, why do they on the Sabbath day, that which is not lawful?

25 And he said to them, Have ye never read what David did, when he had need, and was an hungered, both he, and they that were with him?

26 How he went into the house of God, in the days of Abiathar the high Priest, and did eat the show bread, which were not lawful to eat, but for the Priests, and gave also to them which were with him?

27 And he said to them, The Sabbath was made for man, and not man for the Sabbath.

28 Wherefore the Son of man is Lord, even of the Sabbath.

Mark Chapter 3

1 And he entered again into the Synagogue, and there was a man which had a withered hand.

2 And they watched him, whether he would heal him on the Sabbath day, that they might accuse him.

3 Then he said unto the man which had the withered hand, Arise: stand forth in the midst.

4 And he said to them, Is it lawful to do a good deed on the Sabbath day, or to do evil? to save the life, or to kill? But they held their peace.

5 Then he looked round about on them angrily, mourning also for the hardness of their hearts, and said to the man, Stretch forth thine hand. And he stretched it out: and his hand was restored, as whole as the other.

6 And the Pharisees departed, and straightway gathered a council with the Herodians against him, that they might destroy him.

7 But Jesus avoided with his disciples to the sea: and a great multitude followed him from Galilee, and from Judea,

8 And from Jerusalem, and from Idumaea, and beyond Jordan: and they that dwelled about Tyre and Sidon, when they had heard what great things he did, came unto him in great number.

9 And he commanded his disciples, that a ship should wait for him, because of the multitude, lest they should throng him.

10 For he had healed many, in so much that they pressed upon him, to touch him as many as had plagues.

11 And when the unclean spirits saw him, they fell down before him, and cried, saying, Thou art the Son of God.

12 And he sharply rebuked them, to the end they should not utter him.

13 Then he went up into a mountain, and called unto him whom he would, and they came unto him.

14 And he appointed twelve that they should be with him, and that he might send them to preach,

15 And that they might have power to heal sicknesses, and to cast out devils.

16 And the first was Simon, and he named Simon, Peter,

17 Then James the son of Zebedee, and John, James brother (and named them Boanerges, which is the sons of thunder,)

18 And Andrew, and Philip, and Bartholomew, and Matthew, and Thomas, and James, the son of Alphaeus, and Thaddaeus, and Simon the Canaanite,

19 And Judas Iscariot, who also betrayed him, and they came home.

20 And the multitude assembled again, so that they could not so much as eat bread.

21 And when his kinfolks heard of it, they went out to lay hold on him: for they thought he had been beside himself.

22 And the Scribes which came from Jerusalem, said, He hath Beelzebub, and through the prince of the devils he casteth out devils.

23 But he called them unto him, and said unto them in parables, How can Satan drive out Satan?

24 For if a Kingdom be divided against itself, that Kingdom cannot stand.

25 Or if a house be divided against itself, that house cannot continue.

26 So if Satan make insurrection against himself, and be divided, he cannot endure, but is at an end.

27 No man can enter into a strong mans house, and take away his goods, except he first bind that strong man, and then spoil his house.

28 Verily I say unto you, all sins shall be forgiven unto the children of men, and blasphemies, wherewith they blaspheme:

29 But he that blasphemeth against the Holy Ghost, shall never have forgiveness, but is culpable of eternal damnation.

30 Because they said, He had an unclean spirit.

31 Then came his brethren and mother, and stood without, and sent unto him, and called him.

32 And the people sat about him, and they said unto him, Behold, thy mother, and thy brethren seek for thee without.

33 But he answered them, saying, Who is my mother and my brethren?

34 And he looked round about on them, which sat in compass about him, and said, Behold my mother and my brethren.

35 For whosoever doeth the will of God, he is my brother, and my sister, and mother.

Mark Chapter 4

1 And he began again to teach by the sea side, and there gathered unto him a great multitude, so that he entered into a ship, and sat in the sea, and all the people was by the sea side on the land.
2 And he taught them many things in parables, and said unto them in his doctrine,
3 Hearken: Behold, there went out a sower to sow.
4 And it came to pass as he sowed, that some fell by the way side, and the fouls of the heaven came and devoured it up.
5 And some fell on stony ground, where it had not much earth, and by and by sprang up, because it had not depth of earth.
6 But as soon as the sun was up, it caught heat, and because it had not root, it withered away.
7 And some fell among the thorns, and the thorns grew up and choked it, so that it gave no fruit.
8 Some again fell in good ground, and did yield fruit that sprung up, and grew, and it brought forth, some thirty fold, some sixty fold, and some an hundred fold.
9 Then he said unto them, He that hath ears to hear, let him hear.
10 And when he was alone, they that were about him with the twelve, asked him of the parable.
11 And he said unto them, To you it is given to know the mystery of the Kingdom of God: but unto them that are without, all things be done in parables,
12 That they seeing, may see, and not discern: and they hearing, may hear, and not understand, lest at any time they should turn, and their sins should be forgiven them.
13 Again he said unto them, Perceive ye not this parable? how then should ye understand all other parables?
14 The sower soweth the word.
15 And these are they that receive the seed by the wayside, in whom the word is sown: but when they have heard it, Satan cometh immediately, and taketh away the word that was sown in their hearts.
16 And likewise they that receive the seed in stony ground, are they, which when they have heard the word, straightway receive it with gladness.
17 Yet have they no root in themselves, and endure but a time: for when trouble and persecution ariseth for the word, immediately they be offended.
18 Also they that receive the seed among the thorns, are such as hear the word:
19 But the cares of this world, and the deceitfulness of riches, and the lusts of other things enter in, and choke the word, and it is unfruitful.
20 But they that have received seed in good ground, are they that hear the word and receive it, and bring forth fruit: one corn thirty, another sixty, and some an hundred.
21 Also he said unto them, Is the candle light to be put under a bushel, or under the table, and not to be put on a candlestick?
22 For there is nothing hid, that shall not be opened: neither is there a secret, but that it shall come to light.
23 If any man have ears to hear, let him hear.
24 And he said unto them, Take heed what ye hear. With what measure ye mete, it shall be measured unto you: and unto you that hear, shall more be given.
25 For unto him that hath, shall it be given, and from him that hath not, shall be taken away, even that he hath.
26 Also he said, So is the Kingdom of God, as if a man should cast seed in the ground,
27 And should sleep, and rise up night and day, and the seed should spring and grow up, he not knowing how.

28 For the earth bringeth forth fruit of herself, first the blade, then the ears, after that full corn in the ears.

29 And as anon as the fruit showeth itself, soon he putteth in the sickle, because the harvest is come.

30 He said moreover, Whereunto shall we liken the Kingdom of God? or with what comparison shall we compare it?

31 It is like a grain of mustard seed, which when it is sown in the earth, is the least of all seeds that be in the earth:

32 But after that it is sown, it groweth up, and is greatest of all herbs, and beareth great branches, so that the fouls of heaven may build under the shadow of it.

33 And with many such parables he preached the word unto them, as they were able to hear it.

34 And without parables spake he nothing unto them: but he expounded all things to his disciples apart.

35 Now the same day when even was come, he said unto them, Let us pass over unto the other side.

36 And they left the multitude, and took him as he was in the ship: and there were also with him other ships.

37 And there arose a great storm of wind, and the waves dashed into the ship, so that it was now full.

38 And he was in the stern asleep on a pillow: and they awoke him, and said to him, Master, careth thou not that we perish?

39 And he rose up, and rebuked the wind, and said unto the sea, Peace, and be still. So the wind ceased, and it was a great calm.

40 Then he said unto them, Why are ye so fearful? how is it that ye have no faith?

41 And they feared exceedingly, and said one to another, Who is this, that both the wind and sea obey him?

Mark Chapter 5

1 And they came over to the other side of the sea into the country of the Gadarenes.

2 And when he was come out of the ship, there met him incontinently out of the graves, a man which had an unclean spirit:

3 Who had his abiding among the graves, and no man could bind him, no not with chains:

4 Because that when he was often bound with fetters and chains, he plucked the chains asunder, and break the fetters in pieces, neither could any man tame him.

5 And always both night and day he cried in the mountains, and in the graves, and struck himself with stones.

6 And when he saw Jesus afar off, he ran, and worshipped him,

7 And cried with a loud voice, and said, What have I to do with thee, Jesus the Son of the most high God? I charge thee by God, that thou torment me not.

8 (For he said unto him, Come out of the man, thou unclean spirit.)

9 And he asked him, What is thy name? and he answered, saying, My name is Legion: for we are many.

10 And he prayed him instantly, that he would not send them away out of the country.

11 Now there was there in the mountains a great herd of swine, feeding.

12 And all the devils besought him, saying, Send us into the swine, that we may enter into them.

13 And incontinently Jesus gave them leave. Then the unclean spirits went out and entered into the swine, and the herd ran headlong from the high bank into the sea, (and there were about two thousand swine) and they were drowned in the sea.

14 And the swineherds fled, and told it in the city, and in the country, and they came out to see what it was that was done.

15 And they came to Jesus, and saw him that had been possessed with the devil, and had the legion, sit both clothed, and in his right mind: and they were afraid.

16 And they that saw it, told them, what was done to him that was possessed with the devil, and concerning the swine.

17 Then they began to pray him, that he would depart from their coasts.

18 And when he was come into the ship, he that had been possessed with the devil, prayed him that he might be with him.

19 Howbeit, Jesus would not suffer him, but said unto him, Go thy way home to thy friends, and show them what great things the Lord hath done unto thee, and how he hath had compassion on thee.

20 So he departed, and began to publish in Decapolis, what great things Jesus had done unto him: and all men did marvel.

21 And when Jesus was come over again by ship unto the other side, a great multitude gathered to him, and he was near unto the sea.

22 And behold, there came one of the rulers of the Synagogue, whose name was Jairus: and when he saw him, he fell down at his feet,

23 And besought him instantly, saying, My little daughter lieth at point of death: I pray thee that thou wouldest come and lay thine hands on her, that she may be healed, and live.

24 Then he went with him, and a great multitude followed him, and thronged him.

25 (And there was a certain woman, which was diseased with an issue of blood twelve years,

26 And had suffered many things of many physicians, and had spent all that she had, and it availed her nothing, but she became much worse.

27 When she had heard of Jesus, she came in the press behind, and touched his garment.

28 For she said, If I may but touch his clothes, I shall be whole.

29 And straightway the course of her blood was dried up, and she felt in her body, that she was healed of that plague.

30 And immediately when Jesus did know in himself the virtue that went out of him, he turned him round about in the press, and said, Who hath touched my clothes?

31 And his disciples said unto him, Thou seest the multitude throng thee, and sayest thou, Who did touch me?

32 And he looked round about, to see her that had done that.

33 And the woman feared and trembled: for she knew what was done in her, and she came and fell down before him, and told him the whole truth.

34 And he said to her, Daughter, thy faith hath made thee whole: go in peace, and be whole of thy plague.)

35 While he yet spake, there came from the same ruler of the Synagogues house certain which said, Thy daughter is dead: why diseasest thou the Master any further?

36 As soon as Jesus heard that word spoken, he said unto the ruler of the Synagogue, Be not afraid: only believe.

37 And he suffered no man to follow him, save Peter and James, and John the brother of James.

38 So he came unto the house of the ruler of the Synagogue, and saw the tumult, and them that wept and wailed greatly.

39 And he went in, and said unto them, Why make ye this trouble, and weep? the child is not dead, but sleepeth.

40 And they laughed him to scorn: but he put them all out, and took the father, and the mother of the child, and them that were with him, and entered in where the child lay,

41 And took the child by the hand, and said unto her, Talitha cumi, which is by interpretation, Maiden, I say unto thee, arise.

42 And straightway the maiden arose, and walked: for she was of the age of twelve years, and they were astonished out of measure.

43 And he charged them straightly that no man should know of it, and commanded to give her meat.

Mark Chapter 6

1 Afterward he departed thence, and came into his own country, and his disciples followed him.

2 And when the Sabbath was come, he began to teach in the Synagogue, and many that heard him, were astonished, and said, From whence hath he these things? and what wisdom is this that is given unto him, that even such great works are done by his hands?

3 Is not this the carpenter Mary's son, the brother of James and Joseph, and of Judah and Simon? and are not his sisters here with us? And they were offended in him.

4 Then Jesus said unto them, A Prophet is not without honor, but in his own country, and among his own kindred, and in his own house.

5 And he could there do no great works save that he laid his hands upon a few sick folk, and healed them,

6 And he marveled at their unbelief, and went about by the towns on every side, teaching.

7 And he called the twelve, and began to send them two and two, and gave them power over unclean spirits,

8 And commanded them, that they should take nothing for their journey, save a staff only: neither scrip, neither bread, neither money in their girdles,

9 But that they should be shod with sandals, and that they should not put on two coats.

10 And he said unto them, Wheresoever ye shall enter into a house, there abide till ye depart thence.

11 And whosoever shall not receive you, nor hear you, when ye depart thence, shake off the dust that is under your feet, for a witness unto them. Verily I say unto you, It shall be easier for Sodom, or Gomorrha at the Day of Judgment, than for that city.

12 And they went out and preached, that men should amend their lives.

13 And they cast out many devils: and they anointed many that were sick, with oil, and healed them.

14 Then King Herod heard of him (for his name was spread abroad) and said, John Baptist is risen again from the dead, and therefore great works are wrought by him.

15 Other said, It is Elijah: and some said, It is a Prophet, or as one of the Prophets.

16 So when Herod heard it, he said, It is John whom I beheaded: he is risen from the dead.

17 For Herod himself had sent forth, and had taken John, and bound him in prison for Herodias sake, which was his brother Philips wife, because he had married her.

18 For John said unto Herod, It is not lawful for thee to have thy brothers wife.

19 Therefore Herodias had a quarrel against him, and would have killed him, but she could not:

20 For Herod feared John, knowing that he was a just man, and an holy, and reverenced him, and when he heard him, he did many things, and heard him gladly.

21 But the time being convenient, when Herod on his birthday made a banquet to his princes and captains, and chief estates of Galilee:

22 And the daughter of the same Herodias came in and danced, and pleased Herod and them that sat at table together, the King said unto the maid, Ask of me what thou wilt, and I will gave it thee.

23 And he swear unto her, Whatsoever thou shalt ask of me, I will gave it thee, even unto the half of my Kingdom.

24 So she went forth, and said to her mother, What shall I ask? And she said, John Baptist's head.

25 Then she came in straightway with haste unto the King, and asked, saying, I would that thou shouldest gave me even now in a charger the head of John Baptist.

26 Then the King was very sorry: yet for his oaths sake, and for their sakes which sat at table with him, he would not refuse her.

27 And immediately the King sent the hangman, and gave charge that his head should be brought. So he went and beheaded him in the prison,

28 And brought his head in a charger, and gave it to the maid, and the maid gave it to her mother.

29 And when his disciples heard it, they came and took up his body, and put it in a tomb.

30 And the Apostles gathered themselves together to Jesus, and told him all things, both what they had done, and what they had taught.

31 And he said unto them, Come ye apart into the wilderness, and rest a while: for there were many comers and goers, that they had not leisure to eat.

32 So they went by ship out of the way into a desert place.

33 But the people saw them when they departed, and many knew him, and ran a foot thither out of all cities, and came thither before them, and assembled unto him.

34 Then Jesus went out, and saw a great multitude, and had compassion on them, because they were like sheep which had no shepherd: and he began to teach them many things.

35 And when the day was now far spent, his disciples came unto him, saying, This is a desert place, and now the day is far passed.

36 Let them depart, that they may go into the villages and towns about, and buy them bread: for they have nothing to eat?

37 But he answered, and said unto them, Give ye them to eat. And they said unto him, Shall we go and buy two hundred penny worth of bread, and gave them to eat?

38 Then he said unto them, How many loaves have ye? go and look. And when they knew it, they said, Five, and two fishes.

39 So he commanded them, to make them all sit down by companies upon the green grass.

40 Then they sat down by rows, by hundreds, and by fifties.

41 And he took the five loaves, and the two fishes, and looked up to heaven, and gave thanks and brakes the loaves, and gave them to his disciples to set before them, and the two fishes he divided among them all.

42 So they did all eat, and were satisfied.

43 And they took up twelve baskets full of the fragments, and of the fishes. 44 And they that had eaten, were about five thousand men.

45 And straightway he caused his disciples to go into the ship, and to go before unto the other side unto Bethsaida, while he sent away the people.

46 Then as soon as he had sent them away, he departed into a mountain to pray.

47 And when even was come, the ship was in the midst of the sea, and he alone on the land.

48 And he saw them troubled in rowing, (for the wind was contrary unto them) and about the fourth watch of the night, he came unto them, walking upon the sea, and would have passed by them.

49 And when they saw him walking upon the sea, they supposed it had been a spirit, and cried out.

50 For they all saw him, and were sore afraid: but anon he talked with them, and said unto them, Be of good comfort: it is I, be not afraid.

51 Then he went up unto them into the ship, and the wind ceased, and they were sore amazed in themselves beyond measure, and marveled.

52 For they had not considered the matter of the loaves, because their hearts were hardened.

53 And they came over, and went into the land of Gennesaret, and arrived.

54 So when they were come out of the ship, straightway they knew him,

55 And ran about throughout all that region round about, and began to carry hither and thither in beds all that were sick, where they heard that he was.

56 And whithersoever he entered into towns, or cities, or villages, they laid their sick in the streets, and prayed him that they might touch at the least the edge of his garment. And as many as touched him, were made whole.

Mark Chapter 7

1 Then gathered unto him the Pharisees, and certain of the Scribes which came from Jerusalem.

2 And when they saw some of his disciples eat meat with common hands, (that is to say, unwashen) they complained.

3 (For the Pharisees, and all the Jews, except they wash their hands oft, eat not, holding the tradition of the Elders.

4 And when they come from the market, except they wash, they eat not: and many other things there be, which they have taken upon them to observe, as the washing of cups, and pots, and of brazen vessels, and of tables.)

5 Then asked him the Pharisees and Scribes, Why walk not thy disciples according to the tradition of the Elders, but eat meat with unwashen hands?

6 Then he answered and said unto them, Surely Isaiah hath prophesied well of you, hypocrites, as it is written, This people honoreth me with their lips, but their heart is far away from me.

7 But they worship me in vain, teaching for doctrines the commandments of men.

8 For ye lay the commandment of God apart, and observe the tradition of men, as the washing of pots and of cups, and many other such like things ye do.

9 And he said unto them, Well, ye reject the commandment of God that ye may observe your own tradition.

10 For Moses said, Honor thy father, and thy mother: and, Whosoever shall curse father or mother, let him die the death.

11 But ye say, If a man say to father or mother, Corban, that is, By the gift that is offered by me, thou mayest have profit, he shall be free.

12 So ye suffer him no more to do any thing for his father, or his mother,

13 Making the word of God of none authority, by your tradition which ye have ordained: and ye do many such like things.

14 Then he called the whole multitude unto him, and said unto them, Hearken you all unto me, and understand.

15 There is nothing without a man, that can defile him, when it entereth into him: but the things which proceed out of him, are they which defile the man.

16 If any have ears to hear, let him hear.

17 And when he came into an house away from the people, his disciples asked him concerning the parable.

18 And he said unto them, What? are ye without understanding also? Do ye not know that whatsoever thing from without entereth into a man, cannot defile him,

19 Because it entereth not into his heart, but into the belly, and goeth out into the draught which is the purging of all meats?

20 Then he said, That which cometh out of man, that defileth man.

21 For from within, even out of the heart of men, proceed evil thoughts, adulteries, fornications, murders,

22 Thefts, covetousness, wickedness, deceit, uncleanness, a wicked eye, backbiting, pride, foolishness.

23 All these evil things come from within, and defile a man.

24 And from thence he rose, and went into the borders of Tyre and Sidon, and entered into an house, and would that no man should have known: but he could not be hid.

25 For a certain woman, whose little daughter had an unclean spirit, heard of him, and came, and fell at his feet,

26 (And the woman was a Greek, a Syrophenician by nation) and she besought him that he would cast out the devil out of her daughter.

27 But Jesus said unto her, Let the children first be fed: for it is not good to take the childrens bread, and to cast it unto whelps.

28 Then she answered, and said unto him, Truth, Lord: yet in deed the whelps eat under the table of the childrens crumbs.

29 Then he said unto her, For this saying go thy way: the devil is gone out of thy daughter.

30 And when she was come home to her house, she found the devil departed, and her daughter lying on the bed.

31 And he departed again from the coasts of Tyre and Sidon, and came unto the Sea of Galilee, through the midst of the coasts of Decapolis.

32 And they brought unto him one that was deaf, and stammered in his speech, and prayed him to put his hand upon him.

33 Then he took him aside from the multitude, and put his fingers in his ears, and did spit, and touched his tongue.

34 And looking up to heaven, he sighed, and said unto him, Ephphatha, that is, Be opened.

35 And straightway his ears were opened, and the string of his tongue was loosed, and he spake plain.

36 And he commanded them, that they should tell no man: but how much so ever he forbad them, the more a great deal they published it,

37 And were beyond measure astonied, saying, He hath done all things well: he maketh both the deaf to hear, and the dumb to speak.

Mark Chapter 8

1 In those days, when there was a very great multitude, and had nothing to eat, Jesus called his disciples to him, and said unto them,

2 I have compassion on the multitude, because they have now continued with me three days, and have nothing to eat.

3 And if I send them away fasting to their own houses, they would faint by the way: for some of them came from far.

4 Then his disciples answered him, How can a man satisfy these with bread here in the wilderness?

5 And he asked them, How many loaves have ye? And they said, Seven.

6 Then he commanded the multitude to sit down on the ground: and he took the seven loaves, and gave thanks, brake them, and gave to his disciples to set before them, and they did set them before the people.

7 They had also a few small fishes: and when he had given thanks, he commanded them also to be set before them.

8 So they did eat, and were sufficed, and they took up of the broken meat that was left, seven baskets full.

9 (And they that had eaten, were about four thousand) so he sent them away.

10 And anon he entered into a ship with his disciples, and came into the parties of Dalmanutha.

11 And the Pharisees came forth, and began to dispute with him, seeking of him a sign from heaven, and tempting him.

12 Then he sighed deeply in his spirit, and said, Why doth this generation seek a sign? Verily I say unto you, a sign shall not be given unto this generation.

13 So he left them, and went into the ship again, and departed to the other side.

14 And they had forgotten to take bread, neither had they in the ship with them, but one loaf.

15 And he charged them, saying, Take heed, and beware of the leaven of the Pharisees, and of the leaven of Herod.

16 And they thought among themselves, saying, It is, because we have no bread.

17 And when Jesus knew it, he said unto them, Why reason you thus because ye have no bread? perceive ye not yet, neither understand? have ye your hearts yet hardened?

18 Have ye eyes, and see not? and have ye ears, and hear not? and do ye not remember?

19 When I break the five loaves among five thousand, how many baskets full of broken meat took ye up? They said unto him, Twelve.

20 And when I break seven among four thousand, how many baskets of the leavings of broken meat took ye up? And they said, Seven.

21 Then he said unto them, How is it that ye understand not?

22 And he came to Bethsaida, and they brought a blind man unto him, and desired him to touch him.

23 Then he took the blind by the hand, and led him out of the town, and spit in his eyes, and put his hands upon him, and asked him, if he saw ought.

24 And he looked up, and said, I see men: for I see them walking like trees.

25 After that, he put his hands again upon his eyes, and made him look again. And he was restored to his sight, and saw every man a far off clearly.

26 And he sent him home to his house, saying, Neither go into the town, nor tell it to any in the town.

27 And Jesus went out, and his disciples into the towns of Caesarea Philippi. And by the way he asked his disciples, saying unto them, Whom do men say that I am?

28 And they answered, Some say, John Baptist: and some, Elijah: and some, one of the Prophets.

29 And he said unto them, But whom say ye that I am? Then Peter answered and said unto him, Thou art the Christ.

30 And he sharply charged them that concerning him they should tell no man.

31 Then he began to teach them that the Son of man must suffer many things, and should be reproved of the Elders, and of the high Priests, and of the Scribes, and be slain, and within three days rise again.

32 And he spake that thing plainly. Then Peter took him aside, and began to rebuke him.

33 Then he turned back, and looked on his disciples, and rebuked Peter, saying, Get thee behind me, Satan: for thou understandest not the things that are of God, but the things that are of men.

34 And he called the people unto him with his disciples, and said unto them, Whosoever will follow me, let him forsake himself, and take up his cross, and follow me.

35 For whosoever will save his life, shall lose it: but whosoever shall lose his life for my sake and the Gospels, he shall save it.

36 For what shall it profit a man, though he should win the whole world, if he lose his soul?

37 Or what shall a man give for recompense of his soul?

38 For whosoever shall be ashamed of me, and of my words among this adulterous and sinful generation, of him shall the Son of man be ashamed also, when he cometh in the glory of his Father with the Holy Angels.

Mark Chapter 9

1 And he said unto them, Verily I say unto you, that there be some of them that stand here, which shall not taste of death, till they have seen the Kingdom of God come with power.
2 And six days after Jesus took Peter, and James, and John, and brought them up into an high mountain out of the way alone, and he was transfigured before them.
3 And his raiment did shine, and was very white, as snow, so white as no fuller can make upon the earth.
4 And there appeared unto them Elijah with Moses, and they were talking with Jesus.
5 Then Peter answered, and said to Jesus, Master, it is good for us to be here: let us make also three tabernacles, one for thee, and one for Moses, and one for Elijah.
6 Yet he knew not what he said: for they were afraid.
7 And there was a cloud that shadowed them, and a voice came out of the cloud, saying, This is my beloved Son: hear him.
8 And suddenly they looked round about, and saw no more any man save Jesus only with them.
9 And as they came down from the mountain, he charged them that they should tell no man what they had seen save when the Son of man were risen from the dead again.
10 So they kept that matter to themselves, and demanded one of another, what the rising from the dead again should mean?
11 Also they asked him, saying, Why say the Scribes, that Elijah must first come?
12 And he answered, and said unto them, Elijah verily shall first come and restore all things: and as it is written of the Son of man, he must suffer many things, and be set at naught.
13 But I say unto you, that Elijah is come, (and they have done unto him whatsoever they would) as it is written of him.
14 And when he came to his disciples, he saw a great multitude about them, and the Scribes disputing with them.
15 And straightway all the people, when they beheld him, were amazed, and ran to him, and saluted him.
16 Then he asked the Scribes, What dispute you among yourselves?
17 And one of the company answered, and said, Master, I have brought my son unto thee, which hath a dumb spirit:
18 And wheresoever he taketh him, he teareth him, and he foameth, and gnasheth his teeth, and pineth away: and I spake to thy disciples, that they should cast him out, and they could not.
19 Then he answered him, and said, O faithless generation, how long now shall I be with you! how long now shall I suffer you! Bring him unto me.
20 So they brought him unto him: and as soon as the spirit saw him, he tare him, and he fell down on the ground, wallowing and foaming.
21 Then he asked his father, How long time is it since he hath been thus? And he said, Of a child.
22 And oft times he casteth him into the fire, and into the water to destroy him: but if thou canst do any thing, help us, and have compassion upon us.
23 And Jesus said unto him, If thou canst believe it, all things are possible to him that believeth.

24 And straightway the father of the child crying with tears, said, Lord, I believe: help my unbelief.

25 When Jesus saw that the people came running together, he rebuked the unclean spirit, saying unto him, Thou dumb and deaf spirit, I charge thee, come out of him, and enter no more into him.

26 Then the spirit cried, and rent him sore, and came out, and he was as one dead, in so much that many said, He is dead.

27 But Jesus took his hand, and lift him up, and he rose.

28 And when he was come into the house, his disciples asked him secretly, Why could not we cast him out?

29 And he said unto them, This kind can by no other means come forth, but by prayer, and fasting.

30 And they departed thence, and went through Galilee, and he would not that any should have known it.

31 For he taught his disciples, and said unto them, The Son of man shall be delivered into the hands of men, and they shall kill him, but after that he is killed, he shall rise again the third day.

32 But they understood not that saying, and were afraid to ask him.

33 After, he came to Capernaum: and when he was in the house, he asked them, What was it that ye disputed among you by the way?

34 And they held their peace: for by the way they reasoned among themselves, who should be the chiefest.

35 And he sat down, and called the twelve, and said to them, If any man desire to be first, the same shall be last of all, and servant unto all.

36 And he took a little child and set him in the midst of them, and took him in his arms, and said unto them,

37 Whosoever shall receive one of such little children in my Name, receiveth me: and whosoever receiveth me, receiveth not me, but him that sent me.

38 Then John answered him, saying, Master, we saw one casting out devils by thy Name, which followeth not us, and we forbade him, because he followeth us not.

39 But Jesus said, Forbid him not: for there is no man that can do a miracle by my Name, that can lightly speak evil of me.

40 For whosoever is not against us, is on our part.

41 And whosoever shall gave you a cup of water to drink for my Names sake, because ye belong to Christ, verily I say unto you, he shall not lose his reward.

42 And whosoever shall offend one of these little ones, that believe in me, it were better for him rather, that a millstone were hanged about his neck, and that he were cast into the sea.

43 Wherefore if thine hand cause thee to offend, cut it off: it is better for thee to enter into life, maimed, then having two hands, to go into hell into the fire that never shall be quenched,

44 Where their worm dieth not, and the fire never goeth out.

45 Likewise, if thy foot cause thee to offend, cut it off: it is better for thee to go halt into life, then having two feet to be cast into hell into the fire that never shall be quenched,

46 Where their worm dieth not, and the fire never goeth out.

47 And if thine eye cause thee to offend, pluck it out: it is better for thee to go into the Kingdom of God with one eye, than having two eyes, to be cast into hell fire,

48 Where their worm dieth not, and the fire never goeth out.

49 For every man shall be salted with fire: and every sacrifice shall be salted with salt.

50 Salt is good: but if the salt be unsavory, wherewith shall it be seasoned? Have salt in yourselves, and have peace, one with another.

Mark Chapter 10

1 And he arose from thence and went into the coasts of Judea by the far side of Jordan, and the people resorted unto him again, and as he was wont, he taught them again.
2 Then the Pharisees came and asked him, if it were lawful for a man to put away his wife, and tempted him.
3 And he answered, and said unto them, What did Moses command you?
4 And they said, Moses suffered to write a bill of divorcement, and to put her away.
5 Then Jesus answered, and said unto them, For the hardness of your heart he wrote this precept unto you.
6 But at the beginning of the creation God made them male and female:
7 For this cause shall man leave his father and mother, and cleave unto his wife.
8 And they twain shall be one flesh: so that they are no more twain, but one flesh.
9 Therefore, what God hath coupled together, let not man separate.
10 And in the house his disciples asked him again of that matter.
11 And he said unto them, Whosoever shall put away his wife and marry another, committeth adultery against her.
12 And if a woman put away her husband, and be married to another, she committeth adultery.
13 Then they brought little children to him that he should touch them: and his disciples rebuked those that brought them.
14 But when Jesus saw it, he was displeased, and said to them, Suffer the little children to come unto me, and forbid them not: for of such is the Kingdom of God.
15 Verily I say unto you, Whosoever shall not receive the Kingdom of God as a little child, he shall not enter therein.
16 And he took them up in his arms, and put his hands upon them, and blessed them.
17 And when he was gone out on the way, there came one running, and kneeled to him, and asked him, Good Master, what shall I do, that I may possess eternal life?
18 Jesus said to him, Why callest thou me good? there is none good but one, even God.
19 You knowest the commandments, Thou shalt not commit adultery. Thou shalt not kill. Thou shalt not steal. Thou shalt not bear false witness. Thou shalt hurt no man. Honor thy father and mother.
20 Then he answered, and said to him, Master, all these things I have observed from my youth.
21 And Jesus beheld him, and loved him, and said unto him, One thing is lacking unto thee. Go and sell all that thou hast, and give to the poor, and thou shalt have treasure in heaven, and come, follow me, and take up the cross.
22 But he was sad at that saying, and went away sorrowful: for he had great possessions.
23 And Jesus looked round about, and said unto his disciples, How hardly do they that have riches, enter into the Kingdom of God!
24 And his disciples were astonished at his words. But Jesus answered again, and said unto them, Children, how hard is it for them that trust in riches, to enter into the Kingdom of God!
25 It is easier for a camel to go through the eye of a needle, than for a rich man to enter into the Kingdom of God.
26 And they were much more astonished, saying with themselves, Who then can be saved?
27 But Jesus looked upon them, and said, With men it is impossible, but not with God: for with God all things are possible.
28 Then Peter began to say unto him, Lo, we have forsaken all, and have followed thee.

29 Jesus answered, and said, Verily I say unto you, there is no man that hath forsaken house or brethren or sisters, or father or mother, or wife, or children, or lands for my sake and the Gospels,

30 But he shall receive an hundred fold now at this present, houses, and brethren, and sisters, and mothers, and children, and lands with persecutions, and in the world to come, eternal life.

31 But many that are first, shall be last, and the last, first.

32 And they were in the way going up to Jerusalem, and Jesus went before them, and they were amazed, and as they followed, they were afraid, and Jesus took the twelve again, and began to tell them what things should come unto him,

33 Saying, Behold, we go up to Jerusalem, and the Son of man shall be delivered unto the high Priests, and to the Scribes, and they shall condemn him to death, and shall deliver him to the Gentiles.

34 And they shall mock him, and scourge him, and spit upon him, and kill him: but the third day he shall rise again.

35 Then James and John the sons of Zebedee came unto him, saying, Master, we would that thou shouldest do for us that that we desire.

36 And he said unto them, What would ye I should do for you?

37 And they said to him, Grant unto us, that we may sit one at thy right hand, and the other at thy left hand in thy glory.

38 But Jesus said unto them, Ye know not what ye ask. Can ye drink of the cup that I shall drink of, and be baptized with the baptism that I shall be baptized with?

39 And they said unto him, We can. But Jesus said unto them, Ye shall drink in deed of the cup that I shall drink of, and be baptized with the baptism wherewith I shall be baptized:

40 But to sit at my right hand and at my left, is not mine to give, but it shall be given to them for whom it is prepared.

41 And when the ten heard that, they began to disdain at James and John.

42 But Jesus called them unto him, and said to them, Ye know that they which delight to bear rule among the Gentiles, have domination over them, and they that be great among them, exercise authority over them.

43 But it shall not be so among you: but whosoever will be great among you, shall be your servant.

44 And whosoever will be chief of you, shall be the servant of all.

45 For even the Son of man came not to be served, but to serve, and to gave his life for the ransom of many.

46 Then they came to Jericho: and as he went out of Jericho with his disciples, and a great multitude, Bartimaeus the son of Timaeus a blind man, sat by the wayside begging.

47 And when he heard that it was Jesus of Nazareth, he began to cry and to say, Jesus the Son of David, have mercy on me.

48 And many rebuked him, because he should hold his peace: but he cried much more, O Son of David, have mercy on me.

49 Then Jesus stood still, and commanded him to be called: and they called the blind, saying unto him, Be of good comfort: arise, he calleth thee. 50 So he threw away his cloak, and rose and came to Jesus.

51 And Jesus answered, and said unto him, What wilt thou that I do unto thee? And the blind said unto him, Lord, that I may receive sight.

52 Then Jesus said unto him, Go thy way: thy faith hath saved thee. And by and by, he received his sight, and followed Jesus in the way.

Mark Chapter 11

1 And when they came near to Jerusalem, to Bethphage and Bethany unto the Mount of Olives, he sent forth two of his disciples,

2 And said unto them, Go your way into that town that is over against you, and as soon as ye shall enter into it, ye shall find a colt bound, whereon never man sat: loose him and bring him.

3 And if any man says unto you, Why do ye this? Say that the Lord hath need of him, and straightway he will send him hither.

4 And they went their way and found a colt tied by the door without, in a place where two ways met, and they loosed him.

5 Then certain of them, that stood there, said unto them, What do ye loosing the colt?

6 And they said unto them, as Jesus had commanded them. So they let them go.

7 And they brought the colt to Jesus, and cast their garments on him, and he sat upon him.

8 And many spread their garments in the way: other cut down branches off the trees and strawed them in the way.

9 And they that went before, and they that followed, cried, saying, Hosanna: blessed be he that cometh in the Name of the Lord.

10 Blessed be the Kingdom that cometh in the Name of the Lord of our father David: Hosanna, O thou which art in the highest heavens.

11 So Jesus entered into Jerusalem, and into the Temple: and when he had looked about on all things, and now it was evening, he went forth unto Bethany with the twelve.

12 And on the morrow when they were come out from Bethany, he was hungry.

13 And seeing a fig tree afar off, that had leaves, he went to see if he might find any thing thereon: but when he came unto it, he found nothing but leaves: for the time of figs was not yet.

14 Then Jesus answered, and said to it, Never man eat fruit of thee hereafter while the world standeth: and his disciples heard it.

15 And they came to Jerusalem, and Jesus went into the Temple, and began to cast out them that sold and bought in the Temple, and overthrew the tables of the money changers, and the seats of them that sold doves.

16 Neither would he suffer that any man should carry a vessel through the Temple.

17 And he taught, saying unto them, Is it not written, Mine House shall be called the House of prayer unto all nations? but you have made it a den of thieves.

18 And the Scribes and high Priests heard it, and sought how to destroy him: for they feared him, because the whole multitude was astonished at his doctrine.

19 But when even was come, Jesus went out of the city.

20 And in the morning as they passed by, they saw the fig tree dried up from the roots.

21 Then Peter remembered, and said unto him, Master, behold, the fig tree which thou cursed, is withered.

22 And Jesus answered, and said unto them, Have faith in God.

23 For verily I say unto you, that whosoever shall say unto this mountain, Take thyself away, and cast thyself into the sea, and shall not waver in his heart, but shall believe that those things which he saith, shall come to pass, whatsoever he saith, shall be done to him.

24 Therefore I say unto you, Whatsoever ye desire when ye pray, believe that ye shall have it, and it shall be done unto you.

25 But when ye shall stand, and pray, forgive, if ye have any thing against any man, that your Father also which is in heaven, may forgive you your trespasses.

26 For if you will not forgive, your Father which is in heaven, will not pardon you your trespasses.

27 Then they came again to Jerusalem: and as he walked in the Temple, there came to him the high Priests, and the Scribes, and the Elders,

28 And said unto him, By what authority doest thou these things? and who gave thee this authority, that thou shouldest do these things?

29 Then Jesus answered, and said unto them, I will also ask of you a certain thing, and answer ye me, and I will tell you by what authority I do these things.

30 The baptism of John, was it from heaven, or of men? answer me.

31 And they thought with themselves, saying, If we shall say, from heaven, he will say, Why then did ye not believe him?

32 But if we say of men, we fear the people: for all men counted John, that he had been a very Prophet.

33 Then they answered, and said unto Jesus, We cannot tell. And Jesus answered, and said unto them, Neither will I tell you by what authority I do these things.

Mark Chapter 12

1 And he began to speak unto them in parables, A certain man planted a vineyard, and compassed it with a hedge, and digged a pit for the winepress, and built a tower in it, and let it out to husbandmen, and went into a strange country.

2 And at a time, he sent to the husbandmen a servant, that he might receive of the husbandmen of the fruit of the vineyard.

3 But they took him, and beat him, and sent him away empty.

4 And again, he sent unto them another servant, and at him they cast stones, and break his head, and sent him away shamefully handled.

5 And again he sent another, and him they slew, and many other, beating some, and killing some.

6 Yet had he one son, his dear beloved: him also he sent the last unto them, saying, They will reverence my son.

7 But the husbandmen said among themselves, This is the heir: come, let us kill him, and the inheritance shall be ours.

8 So they took him, and killed him, and cast him out of the vineyard.

9 What shall then the Lord of the vineyard do? He will come and destroy these husbandmen, and give the vineyard to others.

10 Have ye not read so much as this Scripture? The stone which the builders did refuse, is made the head of the corner.

11 This was done of the Lord, and it is marvelous in our eyes.

12 Then they went about to take him, but they feared the people: for they perceived that he spake that parable against them: therefore they left him, and went their way.

13 And they sent unto him certain of the Pharisees, and of the Herodians that they might take him in his talk.

14 And when they came, they said unto him, Master, we know that thou art true, and carest for no man: for thou considerest not the person of men, but teachest the way of God truly, Is it lawful to gave tribute to Caesar, or not?

15 Should we give it, or should we not give it? But he knew their hypocrisy, and said unto them, Why tempt ye me? Bring me a penny, that I may see it.

16 So they brought it, and he said unto them, Whose is this image and superscription? and they said unto him, Caesar's.

17 Then Jesus answered, and said unto them, Give to Caesar the things that are Caesars, and to God, those that are Gods: and they marveled at him.

18 Then came the Sadducees unto him, (which say, there is no resurrection) and they asked him, saying,

19 Master, Moses wrote unto us, If any mans brother die, and leave his wife, and leave no children, that his brother should take his wife, and raise up seed unto his brother.

20 There were seven brethren, and the first took a wife, and when he died, left no issue.

21 Then the second took her, and he died, neither did he yet leave issue, and the third likewise.

22 So seven had her, and left no issue: last of all the wife died also.

23 In the resurrection then, when they shall rise again, whose wife shall she be of them? for seven had her to wife.

24 Then Jesus answered, and said unto them, Are ye not therefore deceived, because ye know not the Scriptures, neither the power of God?

25 For when they shall rise again from the dead, neither men marry, nor wives are married, but are as the Angels which are in heaven.

26 And as touching the dead, that they shall rise again, have ye not read in the book of Moses, how in the bush God spake unto him, saying, I am the God of Abraham, and the God of Isaac, and the God of Jacob?

27 He is not the God of the dead, but the God of the living. Ye are therefore greatly deceived.

28 Then came one of the Scribes that had heard them disputing together, and perceiving that he had answered them well, he asked him, Which is the first commandment of all?

29 Jesus answered him, The first of all the commandments is, Hear, Israel, The Lord our God is the only Lord.

30 Thou shalt therefore love the Lord thy God with all thine heart, and with all thy soul, and with all thy mind, and with all thy strength: this is the first commandment.

31 And the second is like, that is, Thou shalt love thy neighbor as thyself. There is none other commandment greater then these.

32 Then the Scribe said unto him, Well Master, thou hast said the truth, that there is one God, and that there is none but he,

33 And to love him with all the heart, and with all the understanding, and with all the soul, and with all the strength, and to love his neighbor as himself, is more then all burnt offerings and sacrifices.

34 Then, when Jesus saw that he answered discretely, he said unto him, Thou art not far from the Kingdom of God. And no man after that durst ask him any question.

35 And Jesus answered and said teaching in the Temple, How say the Scribes that Christ is the son of David?

36 For David himself said by the Holy Ghost, The lord said to my lord, Sit at my right hand, till I make thine enemies thy footstool.

37 Then David himself calleth him lord: by what means is he then his son? and much people heard him gladly.

38 Moreover he said unto them in his doctrine, Beware of the Scribes which love to go in long robes, and love salutations in the markets,

39 And the chief seats in the Synagogues, and the first rooms at feasts,

40 Which devour widows houses, even under a color of long prayers. These shall receive the greater damnation.

41 And as Jesus sat over against the treasury, he beheld how the people cast money into the treasury, and many rich men cast in much.

42 And there came a certain poor widow, and she threw in two mites, which make a quadrin.

43 Then he called unto him his disciples, and said unto them, Verily I say unto you, that this poor widow hath cast more in, then all they which have cast into the treasury.

44 For they all did cast in of their superfluity: but she of her poverty did cast in all that she had, even all her living.

Mark Chapter 13

1 And as he went out of the Temple, one of his disciples said unto him, Master, see what stones, and what buildings are here.

2 Then Jesus answered and said unto him, Seest thou these great buildings? there shall not be left one stone upon a stone, that shall not be thrown down.
3 And as he sat on the Mount of Olives, over against the Temple, Peter, and James, and John, and Andrew asked him secretly,
4 Tell us, when shall these things be? and what shall be the sign when all these things shall be fulfilled?
5 And Jesus answered them, and began to say, Take heed lest any man deceive you.
6 For many shall come in my Name, saying, I am Christ, and shall deceive many.
7 Furthermore when ye shall hear, of wars and rumors of wars, be ye not troubled: for such things must needs be: but the end shall not be yet.
8 For nation shall rise against nation, and Kingdom against Kingdom, and there shall be earthquakes in divers quarters, and there shall be famine and troubles: these are the beginnings of sorrows.
9 But take ye heed to yourselves: for they shall deliver you up to the Councils, and to the Synagogues: ye shall be beaten, and brought before rulers and Kings for my sake for a testimonial unto them.
10 And the Gospel must first be published among all nations.
11 But when they lead you, and deliver you up, take ye no thought afore, neither premeditate what ye shall say: but whatsoever is given you at the same time, that speak: for it is not ye that speak, but the Holy Ghost.
12 Yea, and the brother shall deliver the brother to death, and the father the son, and the children shall rise against their parents, and shall cause them to die.
13 And ye shall be hated of all men for my Names sake: but whosoever shall endure unto the end, he shall be saved.
14 Moreover, when ye shall see the abomination of desolation (spoken of by Daniel the Prophet) standing where it ought not, (let him that readeth, consider it) then let them that be in Judea, flee into the mountains,
15 And let him that is upon the house, not come down into the house, neither enter therein, to fetch anything out of his house.
16 And let him that is in the field, not turn back again unto the things which he left behind him, to take his clothes.
17 Then woe shall be to them that are with child, and to them that give suck in those days.
18 Pray therefore that your flight be not in the winter.
19 For there shall be in those days such tribulation, as was not from the beginning of the creation which God created unto this time, neither shall be.
20 And except that the Lord had shortened those days, no flesh should be saved: but for the elects sake, which he hath chosen, he hath shortened those days.
21 Then if any man say to you, Lo, here is Christ, or, lo, he is there, believe it not.
22 For false Christs shall rise, and false prophets, and shall show signs and wonders, to deceive if it were possible, the very elect.
23 But take ye heed: behold, I have showed you all things before.
24 Moreover in those days, after that tribulation the sun shall wax dark, and the moon shall not give her light,
25 And the stars of heaven shall fall: and the powers which are in heaven, shall shake.
26 And then shall they see the Son of man coming in the clouds, with great power and glory.
27 And he shall then send his Angels, and shall gather together his elect from the four winds, and from the utmost part of the earth to the utmost part of heaven.
28 Now learn a parable of the fig tree. When her bough is yet tender, and it bringeth forth leaves, ye know that summer is near.

29 So in like manner, when ye see these things come to pass, know that the kingdom of God is near, even at the doors.

30 Verily I say unto you, that this generation shall not pass, till all these things be done.

31 Heaven and earth shall pass away, but my words shall not pass away.

32 But of that day and hour knoweth no man, no, not the Angels which are in heaven, neither the Son himself, save the Father.

33 Take heed: watch, and pray: for ye know not when the time is.

34 For the Son of man is as a man going into a strange country, and leaveth his house, and giveth authority to his servants, and to every man his work, and commandeth the porter to watch.

35 Watch therefore, (for ye know not when the master of the house will come, at even, or at midnight, at the cock crowing, or in the dawning,)

36 Lest if he come suddenly, he should find you sleeping.

37 And those things that I say unto you, I say unto all men, Watch.

Mark Chapter 14

1 And two days after followed the feast of the Passover, and of unleavened bread: and the high Priests, and Scribes sought how they might take him by craft, and put him to death.

2 But they said, Not in the feast day, lest there be any tumult among the people.

3 And when he was in Bethany in the house of Simon the leper, as he sat at table, there came a woman having a box of ointment of spikenard, very costly, and she break the box, and poured it on his head.

4 Therefore some disdained among themselves, and said, To what end is this waste of ointment?

5 For it might have been sold for more then three hundred pence, and been given unto the poor, and they grudged against her.

6 But Jesus said, Let her alone: why trouble ye her? she hath wrought a good work on me.

7 For ye have the poor with you always, and when ye will ye may do them good, but me ye shall not have always.

8 She hath done that she could: she came afore hand to anoint my body to the burying.

9 Verily I say unto you, wheresoever this Gospel shall be preached throughout the whole world, this also that she hath done, shall be spoken of in remembrance of her.

10 Then Judas Iscariot, one of the twelve went away unto the high Priests, to betray him unto them.

11 And when they heard it, they were glad, and promised that they would give him money: therefore he sought how he might conveniently betray him.

12 Now the first day of unleavened bread, when they sacrificed the Passover, his disciples said unto him, Where wilt thou that we go and prepare, that thou mayest eat the Passover?

13 Then he sent forth two of his disciples, and said unto them, Go ye into the city, and there shall a man meet you bearing a pitcher of water: follow him.

14 And whithersoever he goeth in, say ye to the good man of the house, The Master saith, Where is the lodging where I shall eat the Passover with my disciples?

15 And he will show you an upper chamber which is large, trimmed and prepared: there make it ready for us.

16 So his disciples went forth, and came to the city, and found as he had said unto them, and made ready the Passover.

17 And at even he came with the twelve.

18 And as they sat at table and did eat, Jesus said, Verily I say unto you, that one of you shall betray me, which eateth with me.

19 Then they began to be sorrowful and to say to him one by one, Is it I? And another, Is it I?

20 And he answered and said unto them, It is one of the twelve that dippeth with me in the platter.

21 Truly the Son of man goeth his way, as it is written of him: but woe be to that man, by whom the Son of man is betrayed: it had been good for that man, if he had never been born.

22 And as they did eat, Jesus took the bread, and when he had given thanks, he break it and gave it to them, and said, Take, eat, this is my body.

23 Also he took the cup, and when he had given thanks, gave it to them: and they all drank of it.

24 And he said unto them, This is my blood of the New Testament, which is shed for many.

25 Verily I say unto you, I will drink no more of the fruit of the vine, until that day, that I drink it new in the Kingdom of God.

26 And when they had sung a Psalm, they went out to the Mount of Olives.

27 Then Jesus said unto them, All ye shall be offended by me this night: for it is written, I will smite the shepherd, and the sheep shall be scattered.

28 But after that I am risen, I will go into Galilee before you.

29 And Peter said unto him, Although all men should be offended, yet would not I.

30 Then Jesus said unto him, Verily I say unto thee, this day, even in this night, before the cock crow twice, thou shalt deny me thrice.

31 But he said more earnestly. If I should die with thee, I will not deny thee: likewise also said they all.

32 After they came into a place named Gethsemane: then he said to his disciples, Sit ye here, till I have prayed.

33 And he took with him Peter, and James, and John, and he began to be afraid, and in great heaviness,

34 And said unto them, My soul is very heavy, even unto the death: tarry here and watch.

35 So he went forward a little, and fell down on the ground, and prayed, that if it were possible, that hour might pass from him.

36 And he said, Abba, Father, all things are possible unto thee: take away this cup from me: nevertheless not that I will, but that thou wilt, be done.

37 Then he came and found them sleeping, and said to Peter, Simon, sleepest thou? couldest not thou watch one hour?

38 Watch ye, and pray, that ye enter not into temptation: the spirit indeed is ready, but the flesh is weak.

39 And again he went away, and prayed, and spake the same words.

40 And he returned, and found them asleep again: for their eyes were heavy: neither knew they what they should answer him.

41 And he came the third time, and said unto them, Sleep henceforth, and take your rest: it is enough: the hour is come: behold, the Son of man is delivered into the hands of sinners.

42 Rise up: let us go: lo, he that betrayeth me, is at hand.

43 And immediately while he yet spake, came Judas that was one of the twelve, and with him a great multitude with swords and staves from the high Priests, and Scribes and Elders.

44 And he that betrayed him, had given them a token, saying, Whomsoever I shall kiss, he it is: take him and lead him away safely.

45 And as soon as he was come, he went straightway to him, and said, Master, Master, and kissed him.

46 Then they laid there hands on him, and took him.

47 And one of them that stood by, drew out a sword, and smote a servant of the high Priest, and cut off his ear.

48 And Jesus answered and said to them, Ye be come out as unto a thief with swords and with staves, to take me.

49 I was daily with you teaching in the Temple, and ye took me not: but this is done that the Scriptures should be fulfilled.

50 Then they all forsook him, and fled.

51 And there followed him a certain young man, clothed in linen upon his bare body, and the young men caught him.

52 But he left his linen cloth, and fled from them naked.

53 So they led Jesus away to the high Priest, and to him came all the high Priests, and the Elders, and the Scribes.

54 And Peter followed him afar off, even into the hall of the high Priest, and sat with the servants, and warmed himself at the fire.

55 And the high Priests, and all the Council sought for witness against Jesus, to put him to death, but found none.

56 For many bear false witness against him, but their witness agreed not together.

57 Then there arose certain, and bare false witness against him, saying,

58 We heard him say, I will destroy this Temple made with hands, and within three days I will build another, made without hands.

59 But their witness yet agreed not together.

60 Then the high Priest stood up among them, and asked Jesus, saying, Answerest thou nothing? what is the matter that these bear witness against thee?

61 But he held his peace, and answered nothing. Again the high Priest asked him, and said unto him, Art thou Christ the Son of the Blessed?

62 And Jesus said, I am he, and ye shall see the Son of man sit at the right hand of the power of God, and come in the clouds of heaven.

63 Then the high Priest rent his clothes and said, What have we any more need of witnesses?

64 Ye have heard the blasphemy: what think ye? And they all condemned him to be worthy of death.

65 And some began to spit at him, and to cover his face, and to beat him with fists, and to say unto him, Prophesy. And the sergeants smote him with their rods.

66 And as Peter was beneath in the hall, there came one of the maids of the high Priest.

67 And when she saw Peter warming himself, she looked on him, and said, Thou wast also with Jesus of Nazareth.

68 But he denied it, saying, I know him not, neither wot I what thou sayest. Then he went out into the porch, and the cock crew.

69 Then a maid saw him again, and began to say to them that stood by, This is one of them.

70 But he denied it again: and anon after, they that stood by, said again to Peter, Surely thou art one of them: for thou art of Galilee, and thy speech is like.

71 And he began to curse, and swear, saying, I know not this man of whom ye speak.

72 Then the second time the cock crew, and Peter remembered the word that Jesus had said unto him, Before the cock crow twice, thou shalt deny me thrice, and waying that with himself, he wept.

Mark Chapter 15

1 And anon in the dawning, the high Priests held a Council with the Elders, and the Scribes, and the whole Council, and bound Jesus, and led him away, and delivered him to Pilate.

2 Then Pilate asked him, Art thou the King of the Jews? And he answered, and said unto him, Thou sayest it.

3 And the high Priests accused him of many things.

4 Wherefore Pilate asked him again, saying, Answerest thou nothing? behold how many things they witness against thee.

5 But Jesus answered no more at all, so that Pilate marveled.

6 Now at the feast Pilate did deliver a prisoner unto them, whomsoever they would desire.

7 Then there was one named Barabbas, which was bound with his fellows, that had made insurrection, who in the insurrection had committed murder.

8 And the people cried aloud, and began to desire that he would do as he had ever done unto them.

9 Then Pilate answered them, and said, Will ye that I let loose unto you the King of the Jews?

10 For he knew that the high Priests had delivered him of envy.

11 But the high Priests had moved the people to desire that he would rather deliver Barabbas unto them.

12 And Pilate answered, and said again unto them, What will ye then that I do with him, whom ye call the King of the Jews?

13 And they cried again, Crucify him.

14 Then Pilate said unto them, But what evil hath he done? And they cried the more fervently, Crucify him.

15 So Pilate willing to content the people, loosed them Barabbas, and delivered Jesus when he had scourged him, that he might be crucified.

16 Then the soldiers led him away into the hall, which is the common hall, and called together the whole band,

17 And clad him with purple, and platted a crown of thorns, and put it about his head,

18 And began to salute him, saying, Hail, King of the Jews.

19 And they smote him on the head with a reed, and spat upon him, and bowed the knees, and did him reverence.

20 And when they had mocked him, they took the purple off him, and put his own clothes on him, and led him out to crucify him.

21 And they compelled one that passed by, called Simon of Cyrene (which came out of the country, and was father of Alexander and Rufus) to bear his cross.

22 And they brought him to a place named Golgotha, which is by interpretation, the place of dead mens skulls.

23 And they gave him to drink wine mingled with myrrh: but he received it not.

24 And when they had crucified him, they parted his garments, casting lots for them, what every man should have.

25 And it was the third hour, when they crucified him.

26 And the title of his cause was written above, THE KING OF THE JEWS.

27 They crucified also with him two thieves, the one on the right hand, and the other on his left.

28 Thus the Scripture was fulfilled, which says, And he was counted among the wicked.

29 And they that went by, railed on him, wagging their heads, and saying, Hey, thou that destroyest the Temple, and buildest it in three days,

30 Save thyself, and come down from the cross.

31 Likewise also even the high Priests mocking, said among themselves with the Scribes, He saved other men, himself he cannot save.

32 Let Christ the King of Israel now come down from the cross, that we may see, and believe. They also that were crucified with him, reviled him.

33 Now when the sixth hour was come, darkness arose over all the land until the ninth hour.

34 And at the ninth hour Jesus cried with a loud voice, saying, Eloi, Eloi, lama sabachthani? which is by interpretation, My God, my God, why hast thou forsaken me?

35 And some of them that stood by, when they heard it, said, Behold, he calleth Elijah.

36 And one ran, and filled a sponge full of vinegar, and put it on a reed, and gave him to drink, saying, Let him alone: let us see if Elijah will come and take him down.

37 And Jesus cried with a loud voice, and gave up the ghost.

38 And the vail of the Temple was rent in twain, from the top to the bottom.

39 Now when the Centurion, which stood over against him, saw that he thus crying gave up the ghost, he said, Truly this man was the Son of God.

40 There were also women, which beheld afar off, among whom was Mary Magdalene, and Mary (the mother of James the Less, and of Joseph) and Salome,

41 Which also when he was in Galilee, followed him and ministered unto him, and many other women which came up with him unto Jerusalem.

42 And now when night was come (because it was the day of the preparation that is before the Sabbath)

43 Joseph of Arimathea, an honorable Counselor, which also looked for the Kingdom of God, came, and went in boldly unto Pilate, and asked the body of Jesus.

44 And Pilate marveled, if he were already dead, and called unto him the Centurion, and asked of him whether he had been any while dead.

45 And when he knew the truth of the Centurion, he gave the body to Joseph,

46 Who bought a linen cloth, and took him down, and wrapped him in the linen cloth, and laid him in a tomb that was hewn out of a rock, and rolled a stone unto the door of the sepulcher:

47 And Mary Magdalene, and Mary Josephs mother beheld where he should be laid.

Mark Chapter 16

1 And when the Sabbath day was past, Mary Magdalene, and Mary the mother of James, and Salome, bought sweet ointments that they might come, and embalm him.

2 Therefore early in the morning, the first day of the week, they came unto the sepulcher, when the Sun was yet rising.

3 And they said one to another, Who shall roll us away the stone from the door of the sepulcher?

4 And when they looked, they saw that the stone was rolled away (for it was a very great one.)

5 So they went into the sepulcher, and saw a young man sitting at the right side, clothed in a long white robe: and they were afraid.

6 But he said unto them, Be not afraid: ye seek Jesus of Nazareth, which hath been crucified: he is risen, he is not here: behold the place, where they put him.

7 But go your way, and tell his disciples, and Peter, that he will go before you into Galilee: there shall ye see him, as he said unto you.

8 And they went out quickly and fled from the sepulcher: for they trembled and were amazed: neither said they anything to any man: for they were afraid.

9 And when Jesus was risen again, in the morrow (which was the first day of the week) he appeared first to Mary Magdalene, out of whom he had cast seven devils.

10 And she went and told them that had been with him, which mourned and wept.

11 And when they heard that he was alive, and had appeared to her, they believed it not.

12 After that, he appeared unto two of them in another form, as they walked and went into the country.

13 And they went and told it to the remnant, but they believed them not.

14 Finally, he appeared unto the eleven as they sat together, and reproved them of their unbelief and hardness of heart, because they believed not them which had seen him, being risen up again.

15 And he said unto them, Go ye into all the world, and preach the Gospel to every creature.

16 He that shall believe and be baptized, shall be saved: but he that will not believe, shall be damned.

17 And these tokens shall follow them that believe, In my Name they shall cast out devils, and shall speak with new tongues,

18 And shall take away serpents, and if they shall drink any deadly thing, it shall not hurt them: they shall lay their hands on the sick, and they shall recover.

19 So after the Lord had spoken unto them, he was received into heaven, and sat at the right hand of God.

20 And they went forth, and preached everywhere. And the Lord wrought with them, and confirmed the word with signs that followed, Amen.

THE HOLY GOSPEL OF JESUS CHRIST, ACCORDING TO LUKE

Luke Chapter 1

1 Forasmuch as many have taken in hand to set forth the story of those things, whereof we are fully persuaded,

2 As they have delivered them unto us, which from the beginning saw them their selves, and were ministers of the word,

3 It seemed good also to me (most noble Theophilus) as soon as I had searched out perfectly all things from the beginning, to write unto thee thereof from point to point,

4 That thou mightest acknowledge the certainty of those things, whereof thou hast been instructed.

5 In the time of Herod King of Judea, there was a certain Priest named Zacharias, of the course of Abijah: and his wife was of the daughters of Aaron, and her name was Elizabeth.

6 Both were just before God, and walked in all the commandments and ordinances of the Lord, without reproof.

7 And they had no child, because that Elizabeth was barren: and both were well stricken in age.

8 And it came to pass, as he executed the Priest's office before God, as his course came in order,

9 According to the custom of the Priest's office, his lot was to burn incense, when he went into the Temple of the Lord.

10 And the whole multitude of the people were without in prayer, while the incense was burning.

11 Then appeared unto him an Angel of the Lord standing at the right side of the altar of incense.

12 And when Zacharias saw him, he was troubled, and fear fell upon him.

13 But the Angel said unto him, Fear not, Zacharias: for thy prayer is heard, and thy wife Elizabeth shall bear thee a son, and thou shalt call his name John.

14 And thou shalt have joy and gladness, and many shall rejoice at his birth.

15 For he shall be great in the sight of the Lord, and shall neither drink wine, nor strong drink: and he shall be filled with the Holy Ghost, even from his mother's womb.

16 And many of the children of Israel shall he turn to their Lord God.

17 For he shall go before him in the spirit and power of Elijah, to turn the hearts of the fathers to the children, and the disobedient to the wisdom of the just men, to make ready a people prepared for the Lord.

18 Then Zacharias said unto the Angel, Whereby shall I know this? for I am an old man, and my wife is of a great age.

19 And the Angel answered, and said unto him, I am Gabriel that stand in the presence of God, and am sent to speak unto thee, and to show thee these good tidings.

20 And behold, thou shalt be dumb, and not be able to speak, until the day that these things be done, because thou believest not my words, which shall be fulfilled in their season.

21 Now the people waited for Zacharias, and marveled that he tarried so long in the Temple.

22 And when he came out, he could not speak unto them: then they perceived that he had seen a vision in the Temple: for he made signs unto them, and remained dumb.

23 And it came to pass, when the days of his office were fulfilled, that he departed to his own house.

24 And after those days, his wife Elizabeth conceived, and hid herself five months, saying,

25 Thus hath the Lord dealt with me, in the days wherein he looked on me, to take from me my rebuke among men.

26 And in the sixth month, the Angel Gabriel was sent from God unto a city of Galilee, named Nazareth,

27 To a virgin affianced to a man whose name was Joseph, of the house of David, and the virgin's name was Mary.

28 And the Angel went in unto her, and said, Hail thou that art freely beloved: the Lord is with thee: blessed art thou among women.

29 And when she saw him, she was troubled at his saying, and thought what manner of salutation that should be.

30 Then the Angel said unto her, Fear not, Mary: for thou hast found favor with God.

31 For lo, thou shalt conceive in thy womb, and bear a son, and shalt call his name JESUS.

32 He shall be great, and shall be called the Son of the most High, and the Lord God shall give unto him the throne of his father David.

33 And he shall reign over the house of Jacob forever, and of his kingdom shall be none end.

34 Then said Mary unto the Angel, How shall this be, seeing I know no man?

35 And the Angel answered, and said unto her, The Holy Ghost shall come upon thee, and the power of the most High shall overshadow thee: therefore also that Holy thing which shall be born of thee, shall be called the Son of God.

36 And behold, thy cousin Elizabeth, she hath also conceived a son in her old age: and this is her sixth month, which was called barren.

37 For with God shall nothing be impossible.

38 Then Mary said, Behold the servant of the Lord: be it unto me according to thy word. So the Angel departed from her.

39 And Mary arose in those days, and went into the hill country with haste to a city of Judah,

40 And entered into the house of Zacharias, and saluted Elizabeth.

41 And it came to pass, as Elizabeth heard the salutation of Mary, the babe sprang in her belly, and Elizabeth was filled with the Holy Ghost.

42 And she cried with a loud voice, and said, Blessed art thou among women, because the fruit of thy womb is blessed .

43 And whence cometh this to me that the mother of my Lord should come to me?

44 For lo, as soon as the voice of thy salutation sounded in mine ears, the babe sprang in my belly for joy.

45 And blessed is she that believed: for those things shall be performed, which were told her from the Lord.

46 Then Mary said, My soul magnifieth the Lord,

47 And my spirit rejoiceth in God my Savior.

48 For he hath looked on the poor degree of his servant: for behold, from henceforth shall all ages call me blessed,

49 Because he that is mighty, hath done for me great things, and Holy is his Name.

50 And his mercy is from generation to generation on them that fear him.

51 He hath showed strength with his arm: He hath scattered the proud in the imagination of their hearts.

52 He hath put down the mighty from their seats, and exalted them of low degree.

53 He hath filled the hungry with good things, and sent away the rich empty.

54 He hath upholden Israel his servant being mindful of his mercy

55 (As he hath spoken to our fathers, to wit, to Abraham, and his seed) forever.

56 And Mary abode with her about three months: after, she returned to her own house.

57 Now Elizabeth's time was fulfilled, that she should be delivered, and she brought forth a son.

58 And her neighbors, and cousins heard tell how the Lord had showed his great mercy upon her, and they rejoiced with her.

59 And it was so that on the eighth day they came to circumcise the babe, and called him Zacharias after the name of his father.

60 But his mother answered, and said, Not so, but he shall be called John.

61 And they said unto her, There is none of thy kindred, that is named with this name.

62 Then they made signs to his father, how he would have him called.

63 So he asked for writing tables, and wrote, saying, His name is John, and they marveled all.

64 And his mouth was opened immediately, and his tongue loosed, and he spake and praised God.

65 And fear came on all them that dwelt near unto them, and all these words were noised abroad throughout all the hill country of Judea.

66 And all they that heard them, laid them up in their hearts, saying, What manner child shall this be! and the hand of the Lord was with him.

67 Then his father Zacharias was filled with the Holy Ghost, and prophesied, saying,

68 Blessed be the Lord God of Israel, because he hath visited and redeemed his people,

69 And hath raised up the horn of salvation unto us, in the house of his servant David,

70 As he spake by the mouth of his Holy Prophets, which were since the world began, saying,

71 That he would send us deliverance from our enemies, and from the hands of all that hate us,

72 That he would show mercy towards our fathers, and remember his Holy covenant,

73 And the oath which he sware to our father Abraham:

74 Which was, that he would grant unto us, that we being delivered out of the hands of our enemies, should serve him without fear,

75 All the days of our life, in holiness and righteousness before him.

76 And thou, babe, shalt be called the Prophet of the most High: for thou shalt go before the face of the Lord, to prepare his ways,

77 And to give knowledge of salvation unto his people, by the remission of their sins,

78 Through the tender mercy of our God, whereby the day spring from an high hath visited us ,

79 To give light to them that sit in darkness, and in the shadow of death, and to guide our feet into the way of peace.

80 And the child grew and waxed strong in spirit, and was in the wildernesses, till the day came, that he should show himself unto Israel.

Luke Chapter 2

1 And it came to pass in those days, that there came a commandment from Augustus Caesar, that all the world should be taxed.

2 (This first taxing was made when Quirinius was governor of Syr ia.)

3 Therefore went all to be taxed every man to his own City.

4 And Joseph also went up from Galilee out of a city called Nazareth, into Judea, unto the city of David, which is called Bethlehem (because he was of the house and linage of David,)

5 To be taxed with Mary that was given him to wife, which was with child.

6 And so it was, that while they were there, the days were accomplished that she should be delivered.

7 And she brought forth her first begotten son, and wrapped him in swaddling clothes and laid him in a creche, because there was no room for them in the inn.

8 And there were in the same country shepherds, abiding in the field, and keeping watch by night because of their flock.

9 And lo, the Angel of the Lord came upon them, and the glory of the Lord shone about them, and they were sore afraid.

10 Then the Angel said unto them, Be not afraid: for behold, I bring you tidings of great joy, that shall be to all the people:

11 That is, that unto you is born this day in the city of David, a Savior, which is Christ the Lord.

12 And this shall be a sign to you, Ye shall find the child swaddled, and laid in a creche.

13 And straightway there was with the Angel a multitude of heavenly soldiers, praying God, and saying,

14 Glory be to God in the high heavens, and peace in earth, and towards men good will.

15 And it came to pass when the Angels were gone away from them into heaven, that the shepherds said one to another, Let us go then unto Bethlehem, and see this thing that is come to pass, which the Lord hath showed unto us.

16 So they came with haste, and found both Mary and Joseph, and the babe laid in the creche.

17 And when they had seen it, they published abroad the thing, which was told them of that child.

18 And all that heard it, wondered at the things which were told them of the shepherds.

19 But Mary kept all those sayings and pondered them in her heart.

20 And the shepherds returned, glorifying and praising God, for all that they had heard and seen, as it was spoken unto them.

21 And when the eight days were accomplished, that they should circumcise the child, his name was then called JESUS, which was named of the Angel, before he was conceived in the womb.

22 And when the days of her purification after the Law of Moses were accomplished, they brought him to Jerusalem, to present him to the Lord,

23 (As it is written in the Law of the Lord, Every man child that first openeth the womb, shall be called Holy to the Lord:)

24 And to give an oblation, as it is commanded in the Law of the Lord, a pair of turtle doves, or two young pigeons.

25 And behold, there was a man in Jerusalem, whose name was Simeon: this man was just, and feared God, and waited for the consolation of Israel, and the Holy Ghost was upon him.

26 And a revelation was given him of the Holy Ghost, that he should not see death, before he had seen the Lord's Christ.

27 And he came by the motion of the spirit into the Temple, and when the parents brought in the child Jesus, to do for him after the custom of the Law,

28 Then he took him in his arms, and praised God, and said,

29 Lord, now lettest thou thy servant depart in peace, according to thy word.

30 For mine eyes have seen thy salvation,

31 Which thou hast prepared before the face of all people:

32 A light to be revealed to the Gentiles, and the glory of thy people Israel.

33 And Joseph and his mother marveled at those things, which were spoken touching him.

34 And Simeon blessed them, and said unto Mary his mother, Behold, this child is appointed for the fall and rising again of many in Israel, and for a sign which shall be spoken against,

35 (Yea and a sword shall pierce through thy soul) that the thoughts of many hearts may be opened.

36 And there was a Prophetess, one Anna the daughter of Phanuel, of the tribe of Asher, which was of a great age, and had lived with an husband seven years from her virginity.

37 And she was widow about four score, and four years, and went not out of the Temple, but served God with fastings and prayers, night and day.

38 She then coming at the same instant upon them, confessed likewise the Lord, and spake of him to all that looked for redemption in Jerusalem.

39 And when they had performed all things according to the law of the Lord, they returned into Galilee to their own city Nazareth.

40 And the child grew, and waxed strong in Spirit, and was filled with wisdom, and the grace of God was with him.

41 Now his parents went to Jerusalem every year, at the feast of the Passover.

42 And when he was twelve year old, and they were come up to Jerusalem, after the custom of the feast,

43 And had finished the days thereof, as they returned, the child Jesus remained in Jerusalem, and Joseph knew not nor his mother,

44 But they supposing, that he had been in the company, went a day's journey, and sought him among their kinsfolk, and acquaintance.

45 And when they found him not, they turned back to Jerusalem, and sought him.

46 And it came to pass three days after, that they found him in the Temple, sitting in the midst of the doctors, both hearing them, and asking them questions.

47 And all that heard him, were astonished at his understanding, and answers.

48 So when they saw him, they were amazed, and his mother said unto him, Son, why hast thou thus dealt with us? behold, thy father and I have sought thee with heavy hearts.

49 Then said he unto them, How is it that ye sought me? knew ye not that I must go about my Father's business?

50 But they understood not the word that he spake to them.

51 Then he went down with them, and came to Nazareth, and was subject to them: and his mother kept all these sayings in her heart.

52 And Jesus increased in wisdom, and stature, and in favor with God and men.

Luke Chapter 3

1 Now in the fifteenth year of the reign of Tiberius Caesar, Pontius Pilate being governor of Judea, and Herod being Tetrarch of Galilee, and his brother Philip Tetrarch of Ituraea, and of the country of Trachonitis, and Lysanias the Tetrarch of Galilee,

2 (When Annas and Caiaphas were the high Priests) the word of God came unto John, the son of Zacharias in the wilderness.

3 And he came into all the coasts about Jordan, preaching the baptism of repentance for the remission of sins,

4 As it is written in the book of the sayings of Isaiah the Prophet, which saith, The voice of him that crieth in the wilderness is, Prepare ye the way of the Lord: make his paths straight.

5 Every valley shall be filled, and every mountain and hill shall be brought low, and crooked things shall be made straight, and the rough ways shall be made smooth.

6 And all flesh shall see the salvation of God.

7 Then said he to the people that were come out to be baptized of him, O generations of vipers, who hath forewarned you to flee from the wrath to come?

8 Bring forth therefore fruits worthy amendment of life, and begin not to say with yourselves, We have Abraham to our father: for I say unto you, that God is able of these stones to raise up children unto Abraham.

9 Now also is the ax laid unto the root of the trees: therefore every tree which bringeth not forth good fruit, shall be hewn down and cast into the fire.

10 Then the people asked him, saying, What shall we do then?

11 And he answered, and said unto them, He that hath two coats, let him part with him that hath none: and he that hath meat, let him do likewise.

12 Then came their Publicans also to be baptized, and said unto him, Master, what shall we do?

13 And he said unto them, Require no more than that which is appointed unto you.

14 The soldiers likewise demanded of him, saying, and what shall we do? And he said unto them, Do violence to no man, neither accuse any falsely, and be content with your wages.

15 As the people waited, and all men mused in their hearts of John, if he were not the Christ,

16 John answered, and said to them all, Indeed I baptize you with water, but one stronger than I, cometh, whose shoes latchet I am not worthy to unloose: he will baptize you with the Holy Ghost, and with fire.

17 Whose fan is in his hand, and he will make clean his floor, and will gather the wheat into his garner, but the chaff will he burn up with fire that never shall be quenched.

18 Thus then exhorting with many other things, he preached unto the people.

19 But when Herod the Tetrarch was rebuked of him for Herodias his brother Philip's wife, and for all the evils which Herod had done,

20 He added yet this above all, that he shut up John in prison.

21 Now it came to pass, as all the people were baptized, and that Jesus was baptized and did pray, that the heaven was opened:

22 And the Holy Ghost came down in a bodily shape like a dove, upon him, and there was a voice from heaven, saying, Thou art my beloved Son: in thee I am well pleased.

23 And Jesus himself began to be about thirty year of age, being as men supposed the son of Joseph, which was the son of Eli,

24 The son of Matthan, the son of Levi, the son of Melchi, the son of Jannai, the son of Joseph,

25 The son of Mattathias, the son of Amos, the son of Nahum, the son of Hesli, the son of Naggai,

26 The son of Maath, the son of Mattathias, the son of Semein, the son of Josech, the son of Joda,

27 The son of Joanan, the son of Rhesa, the son of Zerubbabel, the son of Shealtiel, the son of Neri,

28 The son of Melchi, the son of Addi, the son of Cosam, the son of Elmadam, the son of Er,

29 The son of Joshua, the son of Eliezer, the son of Jorim, the son of Matthan, the son of Levi,

30 The son of Simeon, the son of Judah, the son of Joseph, the son of Jonam, the son of Eliakim,

31 The son of Melea, the son of Menna, the son of Mattatha, the son of Nathan, the son of David,

32 The son of Jesse, the son of Obed, the son of Boaz, the son of Salmon, the son of Nahshon,

33 The son of Amminadab, the son of Ram, the son of Herzen, the son of Perez, the son of Judah,

34 The son of Jacob, the son of Isaac, the son of Abraham, the son of Terah, the son of Nahor,

35 The son of Serug, the son of Reu, the son of Peleg, the son of Heber, the son of Shelah,

36 The son of Cainan, the son of Arphaxad, the son of Shem, the son of Noah, the son of Lamech,
37 The son of Methuselah, the son of Enoch, the son of Jared, the son of Mahalaleel, the son of Cainan,
38 The son of Enosh, the son of Seth, the son of Adam, the son of God.

Luke Chapter 4

1 And Jesus full of the Holy Ghost returned from Jordan, and was led by the Spirit into the wilderness,
2 And was there forty days tempted of the devil, and in those days he did eat nothing: but when they were ended, he afterward was hungry.
3 Then the devil said unto him, If thou be the Son of God, command this stone that it be made bread.
4 But Jesus answered him, saying , It is written, That man shall not live by bread only, but by every word of God.
5 Then the devil took him up into an high mountain, and showed him all the kingdoms of the world, in the twinkling of an eye.
6 And the devil said unto him, All this power will I give thee, and the glory of those kingdoms: for that is delivered to me: and to whomsoever I will, I give it.
7 If thou therefore wilt worship me, they shall be all thine.
8 But Jesus answered him, and said, Hence from me, Satan: for it is written, Thou shalt worship the Lord thy God, and him alone thou shalt serve.
9 Then he brought him to Jerusalem, and set him on a pinnacle of the Temple, and said unto him, If thou be the Son of God, cast thyself down from hence,
10 For it is written, That he will give his Angels charge over thee to keep thee:
11 And with their hands they shall lift thee up, lest at any time thou shouldest dash thy foot against a stone.
12 And Jesus answered, and said unto him, It is said, Thou shalt not tempt the Lord thy God.
13 And when the devil had ended all the temptation, he departed from him for a season.
14 And Jesus returned by the power of the Spirit into Galilee: and there went a fame of him throughout all the region round about.
15 For he taught in their Synagogues, and was honored of all men.
16 And he came to Nazareth where he had been brought up, and (as his custom was) went into the Synagogue on the Sabbath day, and stood up to read.
17 And there was delivered unto him the book of the Prophet Isaiah: and when he had opened the book, he found the place, where it was written,
18 The Spirit of the Lord is upon me, because he hath anointed me, that I should preach the Gospel to the poor: he hath sent me, that I should heal the broken hearted, that I should preach deliverance to the captives, and recovering of sight to the blind, that I should set at liberty them that are bruised,
19 And that I should preach the acceptable year of the Lord.
20 And he closed the book, and gave it again to the minister, and sat down: and the eyes of all that were in the Synagogue were fastened on him.
21 Then he began to say unto them, This day is this Scripture fulfilled in your ears.
22 And all bare him witness, and wondered at the gracious words, which proceeded out of his mouth, and said, Is not this Joseph's son?
23 Then he said unto them, Ye will surely say unto me this proverb, Physician, heal thyself: whatsoever we have heard done in Capernaum, do it here likewise in thine own country.
24 And he said, Verily I say unto you, No Prophet is accepted in his own country.

25 But I tell you of a truth, many widows were in Israel in the days of Elijah, when heaven was shut three years and six months, when great famine was throughout all the land,

26 But unto none of them was Elijah sent, save into Zarephath, a city of Sidon, unto a certain widow.

27 Also many lepers were in Israel, in the time of Elisha the Prophet: yet none of them was made clean, saving Naaman the Syrian.

28 Then all that were in the Synagogue, when they heard it, were filled with wrath,

29 And rose up, and thrust him out of the city, and led him unto the edge of the hill, whereon their city was built, to cast him down headlong.

30 But he passed through the midst of them, and went his way,

31 And came down into Capernaum a city of Galilee, and there taught them on the Sabbath days.

32 And they were astonished at his doctrine: for his word was with authority.

33 And in the Synagogue there was a man which had a spirit of an unclean devil, which cried with a loud voice,

34 Saying, Oh, what have we to do with thee, thou Jesus of Nazareth? art thou come to destroy us? I know who thou art, even the Holy one of God.

35 And Jesus rebuked him, saying, Hold thy peace, and come out of him. Then the devil throwing him in the midst of them, came out of him, and hurt him not.

36 So fear came on them all, and they spake among themselves, saying, What thing is this? for with authority and power he commandeth the foul spirits, and they come out?

37 And the fame of him spread abroad throughout all the places of the country round about.

38 And he rose up, and came out of the Synagogue, and entered into Simon's house. And Simon's wife's mother was taken with a great fever, and they required him for her.

39 Then he stood over her, and rebuked the fever, and it left her: and immediately she arose, and ministered unto them.

40 Now when the sun was down, all they that had sick folks of diverse diseases, brought them unto him, and he laid his hands on every one of them, and healed them.

41 And devils also came out of many, crying, and saying, Thou art the Christ the Son of God: but he rebuked them, and suffered them not to say that they knew him to be the Christ.

42 And when it was day, he departed and went forth into a desert place, and the people sought him, and came to him, and kept him that he should not depart from them.

43 But he said unto them, Surely I must also preach the kingdom of God to other cities: for therefore am I sent.

44 And he preached in the Synagogues of Galilee.

Luke Chapter 5

1 Then it came to pass, as the people pressed upon him to hear the word of God, that he stood by the lake of Gennesaret,

2 And saw two ships stand by the lake side, but the fishermen were gone out of them, and were washing their nets.

3 And he entered into one of the ships, which was Simon's, and required him that he would thrust off a little from the land: and he sat down, and taught the people out of the ship.

4 Now when he had left speaking, he said unto Simon, Launch out into the deep, and let down your nets to make a draught.

5 Then Simon answered, and said unto him, Master, we have travailed all night, and have taken nothing: nevertheless at thy word I will let down the net.

6 And when they had so done, they enclosed a great multitude of fishes, so that their net break.

7 And they beckoned to their partners, which were in the other ship, that they should come and help them, who came then, and filled both the ships, that they did sink.

8 Now when Simon Peter saw it, he fell down at Jesus' knees, saying, Lord, go from me: for I am a sinful man.

9 For he was utterly astonished, and all that were with him, for the draught of fishes, which they took.

10 And so was also James and John the sons of Zebedee, which were companions with Simon. Then Jesus said unto Simon, Fear not: from henceforth thou shalt catch men.

11 And when they had brought the ships to land, they forsook all, and followed him.

12 Now it came to pass, as he was in a certain city, behold, there was a man full of leprosy, and when he saw Jesus, he fell on his face, and besought him, saying, Lord if thou wilt, thou canst make me clean.

13 So he stretched forth his hand, and touched him, saying, I will, be thou clean. And immediately the leprosy departed from him.

14 And he commanded him that he should tell it no man: but Go, saith he, and show thyself to the Priest, and offer for thy cleansing, as Moses hath commanded, for a witness unto them.

15 But so much more went there a fame abroad of him, and great multitudes came together to hear, and to be healed of him of their infirmities.

16 But he kept himself apart in the wilderness, and prayed.

17 And it came to pass, on a certain day, as he was teaching, that the Pharisees and doctors of the Law sat by, which were come out of every town of Galilee, and Judea, and Jerusalem, and the power of the Lord was in him to heal them.

18 Then behold, men brought a man lying in a bed, which was taken with a palsy, and they sought means to bring him in, and to lay him before him.

19 And when they could not find by what way they might bring him in, because of the press, they went up on the house, and let him down through the tiling, bed and all, in the midst before Jesus.

20 And when he saw their faith, he said unto him, Man, thy sins are forgiven thee.

21 Then the Scribes and the Pharisees began to think, saying, Who is this that speaketh blasphemies? Who can forgive sins, but God only?

22 But when Jesus perceived their thoughts, he answered, and said unto them, What think ye in your hearts?

23 Whether is easier to say, Thy sins are forgiven thee, or to say, Rise and walk?

24 But that ye may know that the Son of man hath authority to forgive sins in earth, (he said unto the sick of the palsy) I say to thee, Arise: take up thy bed, and go to thine house.

25 And immediately he rose up before them, and took up his bed whereon he lay, and departed to his own house, praising God.

26 And they were all amazed, and praised God, and were filled with fear, saying, Doubtless we have seen strange things today.

27 And after that, he went forth and saw a Publican named Levi, sitting at the receipt of custom, and said unto him, Follow me.

28 And he left all, rose up, and followed him.

29 Then Levi made him a great feast in his own house, where there was a great company of Publicans, and of other that sat at table with them.

30 But they that were Scribes and Pharisees among them, murmured against his disciples, saying, Why eat ye and drink ye with Publicans and sinners?

31 Then Jesus answered, and said unto them, They that are whole, need not the Physician, but they that are sick.

32 I came not to call the righteous, but sinners to repentance.

33 Then they said unto him, Why do the disciples of John fast often, and pray, and the disciples of the Pharisees also, but thine eat and drink?

34 And he said unto them, Can ye make the children of the wedding chamber to fast, as long as the bridegroom is with them?

35 But the days will come, even when the bridegroom shall be taken away from them: then shall they fast in those days.

36 Again he spake also unto them a parable, No man putteth a piece of a new garment into an old vesture: for then the new renteth it, and the piece taken out of the new, agreeth not with the old.

37 Also no man poureth new wine into old vessels: for then the new wine will break the vessels, and it will run out, and the vessels will perish.

38 But new wine must be poured into new vessels: so both are preserved.

39 Also no man that drinketh old wine, straightway desireth new: for he saith, the old is better.

Luke Chapter 6

1 And it came to pass on the second Sabbath after the first, that he went through the corn fields, and his disciples plucked the ears of corn, and did eat, and rub them in their hands.

2 And certain of the Pharisees said unto them, Why do ye that which is not lawful to do on the Sabbath days?

3 Then Jesus answered them, and said, Have ye not read this, that David did when he himself was an hungered, and they which were with him,

4 How he went into the house of God, and took, and ate the showbread, and gave also to them which were with him, which was not lawful to eat, but for the Priests only?

5 And he said unto them, The Son of man is Lord also of the Sabbath day.

6 It came to pass also on another Sabbath, that he entered into the Synagogue and taught, and there was a man, whose right hand was dried up.

7 And the Scribes and Pharisees watched him, whether he would heal on the Sabbath day, that they might find an accusation against him.

8 But he knew their thoughts, and said to the man which had the withered hand, Arise, and stand up in the midst. And he arose, and stood up.

9 Then said Jesus unto them, I will ask you a question, Whether is it lawful on the Sabbath day to do good, or to do evil? To save life, or to destroy it?

10 And he beheld them all in compass, and said unto the man, Stretch forth thine hand. And he did so, and his hand was restored again, as whole as the other.

11 Then they were filled full of madness, and communed one with another, what they might do to Jesus.

12 And it came to pass in those days, that he went into a mountain to pray, and spent the night in prayer to God.

13 And when it was day, he called his disciples, and of them he chose twelve, which also he called Apostles.

14 (Simon whom he named also Peter, and Andrew his brother, James and John, Philip, and Bartholomew:

15 Matthew, and Thomas: James the son of Alphaeus, and Simon called Zealot,

16 Judas, James brother, and Judas Iscariot, which also was the traitor.)

17 Then he came down with them, and stood in a plain place, with the company of his disciples, and a great multitude of people out of all Judea, and Jerusalem, and from the sea coast of Tyre and Sidon, which came to hear him, and to be healed of their diseases:

18 And they that were vexed with foul spirits, and they were healed.

19 And the whole multitude sought to touch him: for there went virtue out of him, and healed them all.

20 And he lifted up his eyes upon his disciples, and said, Blessed be ye poor: for yours is the kingdom of God.

21 Blessed are ye that hunger now: for ye shall be satisfied: blessed are ye that weep now: for ye shall laugh.

22 Blessed are ye when men hate you, and when they separate you, and revile you, and put out your name as evil, for the Son of man's sake.

23 Rejoice ye in that day, and be glad: for behold, your reward is great in heaven: for after this manner their fathers did to the Prophets.

24 But woe be to you that are rich: for ye have received your consolation.

25 Woe be to you that are full: for ye shall hunger. Woe be to you that now laugh: for ye shall wail and weep.

26 Woe be to you when all men speak well of you: for so did their fathers to the false prophets.

27 But I say unto you which hear, love your enemies: do well to them which hate you.

28 Bless them that curse you, and pray for them which hurt you.

29 And unto him that smiteth thee on the one cheek, offer also the other: and him that taketh away thy cloak, forbid not to take thy coat also.

30 Give to every man that asketh of thee: and of him that taketh away thy goods, ask them not again.

31 And as ye would that men should do to you, so do ye to them likewise.

32 For if ye love them which love you, what thank shall ye have? for even the sinners love those that love them.

33 And if ye do good for them which do good for you, what thank shall ye have? for even the sinners do the same.

34 And if ye lend to them of whom ye hope to receive, what thank shall ye have? for even the sinners lend to sinners, to receive the like.

35 Wherefore love ye your enemies, and do good, and lend, looking for nothing again, and your reward shall be great, and ye shall be the children of the most High: for he is kind unto the unkind, and to the evil.

36 Be ye therefore merciful, as your Father also is merciful.

37 Judge not, and ye shall not be judged: condemn not, and ye shall not be condemned: forgive, and ye shall be forgiven.

38 Give, and it shall be given unto you: a good measure, pressed down, shaken together and running over shall men give into your bosom: for with what measure ye mete, with the same shall men mete to you again.

39 And he spake a parable unto them, Can the blind lead the blind? Shall they not both fall into the ditch?

40 The disciple is not above his master: but whosoever will be a perfect disciple, shall be as his master.

41 And why seest thou a mote in thy brother's eye, and considerest not the beam, that is in thine own eye?

42 Either how canst thou say to thy brother, Brother, let me pull out the mote that is in thine eye, when thou seest not the beam that is in thine own eye? Hypocrite, cast out the beam out of thine own eye first, and then shalt thou see perfectly, to pull out the mote that is in thy brother's eye.

43 For it is not a good tree that bringeth forth evil fruit: neither an evil tree, that bringeth forth good fruit.

44 For every tree is known by his own fruit: for neither of thorns gather men figs, nor of bushes gather they grapes.

45 A good man out of the good treasure of his heart bringeth forth good, and an evil man out of the evil treasure of his heart bringeth forth evil: for of the abundance of the heart his mouth speaketh.

46 But why call ye me Master, Master, and do not the things that I speak?

47 Whosoever cometh to me, and heareth my words, and doeth the same, I will show you to whom he is like:

48 He is like a man which built an house, and digged deep, and laid the foundation on a rock: and when the waters arose, the flood beat upon that house, and could not shake it: for it was grounded upon a rock.

49 But he that heareth and doeth not, is like a man that built an house upon the earth without foundation, against which the flood did beat, and it fell by and by: and the fall of that house was great.

Luke Chapter 7

1 When he had ended all his sayings in the audience of the people, he entered into Capernaum.

2 And a certain Centurion's servant was sick and ready to die, which was dear unto him.

3 And when he heard of Jesus, he sent unto him the Elders of the Jews, beseeching him that he would come and heal his servant.

4 So they came to Jesus, and besought him instantly, saying that he was worthy that he should do this for him.

5 For he loveth, said they, our nation, and he hath built us a Synagogue.

6 Then Jesus went with them: but when he was now not far from the house, the Centurion sent friends to him, saying unto him, Lord, trouble not thyself: for I am not worthy that thou shouldest enter under my roof.

7 Wherefore I thought not myself worthy to come unto thee: but say the word, and my servant shall be whole.

8 For I likewise am a man set under authority, and have under me soldiers, and I say unto one, Go, and he goeth, and to another, Come, and he cometh, and to my servant, Do this, and he doeth it.

9 When Jesus heard these things, he marveled at him, and turned him, and said to the people, that followed him, I say unto you, I have not found so great faith, no not in Israel.

10 And when they that were sent, turned back to the house, they found the servant that was sick, whole.

11 And it came to pass the day after, that he went into a city called Nain, and many of his disciples went with him, and a great multitude.

12 Now when he came near to the gate of the city, behold, there was a dead man carried out, who was the only begotten son of his mother, which was a widow, and much people of the city was with her.

13 And when the Lord saw her, he had compassion on her, and said unto her, Weep not.

14 And he went and touched the coffin (and they that bare him, stood still) and he said, Young man, I say unto thee, Arise.

15 And he that was dead, sat up, and began to speak, and he delivered him to his mother.

16 Then there came a fear on them all, and they glorified God, saying, A great Prophet is raised up among us, and God hath visited his people.

17 And this rumor of him went forth throughout all Judea, and throughout all the region round about.

18 And the disciples of John showed him of all these things.

19 So John called unto him two certain men of his disciples, and sent them to Jesus, saying, Art thou he that should come, or shall we wait for another?

20 And when the men were come unto him, they said, John Baptist hath sent us unto thee, saying, Art thou he that should come, or shall we wait for another?

21 And at that time, he cured many of their sicknesses, and plagues, and of evil spirits, and unto many blind men he gave sight.

22 And Jesus answered, and said unto them, Go your ways and show John, what things ye have seen and heard: that the blind see, the halt go, the lepers are cleansed, the deaf hear, the dead rise again, and the poor receive the Gospel.

23 And blessed is he, that shall not be offended in me.

24 And when the messengers of John were departed, he began to speak unto the people of John, What went ye out into the wilderness to see? A reed shaken with the wind?

25 But what went ye out to see? A man clothed in soft raiment? behold, they which are gorgeously appareled, and live delicately, are in Kings' courts.

26 But what went ye forth to see? A Prophet? Yea, I say to you, and greater than a Prophet.

27 This is he of whom it is written, Behold, I send my messenger before thy face, which shall prepare thy way before thee.

28 For I say unto you, there is no greater Prophet than John, among them that are begotten of women: nevertheless, he that is the least in the kingdom of God is greater than he.

29 Then all the people that heard, and the Publicans justified God, being baptized with the baptism of John.

30 But the Pharisees and the expounders of the Law despised the counsel of God against themselves, and were not baptized of him.

31 And the Lord said, Whereunto shall I liken the men of this generation? And what thing are they like unto?

32 They are like unto children sitting in the market place, and crying one to another, and saying, We have piped unto you, and ye have not danced: we have mourned to you, and ye have not wept.

33 For John Baptist came, neither eating bread, nor drinking wine: and ye say, He hath the devil.

34 The Son of man is come, and eateth and drinketh: and ye say, Behold, a man which is a glutton, and a drinker of wine, a friend of Publicans and sinners.

35 But wisdom is justified of all her children.

36 And one of the Pharisees desired him that he would eat with him: and he went into the Pharisee's house, and sat down at table.

37 And behold, a woman in the city, which was a sinner, when she knew that Jesus sat at table in the Pharisee's house, she brought a box of ointment.

38 And she stood at his feet behind him weeping, and began to wash his feet with tears, and did wipe them with the hairs of her head, and kissed his feet, and anointed them with the ointment.

39 Now when the Pharisee which bade him, saw it, he spake within himself, saying, If this man were a Prophet, he would surely have known who, and what manner of woman this is which toucheth him: for she is a sinner.

40 And Jesus answered, and said unto him, Simon, I have somewhat to say unto thee. And he said, Master, say on.

41 There was a certain lender which had two debtors: the one owed five hundred pence, and the other fifty.

42 When they had nothing to pay, he forgave them both. Which of them therefore, tell me, will love him most?

43 Simon answered, and said, I suppose that he, to whom he forgave most. And he said unto him, Thou hast truly judged.

44 Then he turned to the woman, and said unto Simon, Seest thou this woman? I entered into thine house, and thou gavest me no water to my feet: but she hath washed my feet with tears, and wiped them with the hairs of her head.

45 Thou gavest me no kiss: but she since the time I came in, hath not ceased to kiss my feet.

46 Mine head with oil thou didst not anoint: but she hath anointed my feet with ointment.

47 Wherefore I say unto thee, many sins are forgiven her: for she loved much. To whom a little is forgiven, he doth love a little.

48 And he said unto her, Thy sins are forgiven thee.

49 And they that sat at table with him, began to say within themselves, Who is this that even forgiveth sins?

50 And he said to the woman, Thy faith hath saved thee: go in peace.

Luke Chapter 8

1 And it came to pass afterward, that he himself went through every city and town, preaching, and publishing the kingdom of God, and the twelve were with him,

2 And certain women, which were healed of evil spirits, and infirmities, as Mary which was called Magdalene, out of whom went seven devils,

3 And Joanna the wife of Chuza Herod's steward, and Susanna, and many other which ministered unto him of their substance.

4 Now when much people were gathered together, and were come to him out of all cities, he spake by a parable,

5 A sower went out to sow his seed, and as he sowed, some fell by the way side, and it was trodden under feet, and the fowls of heaven devoured it up.

6 And some fell on the stones, and when it was sprung up, it withered away, because it lacked moistness.

7 And some fell among thorns, and the thorns sprang up with it, and choked it.

8 And some fell on good ground, and sprang up, and bare fruit, an hundred fold. And as he said these things, he cried, He that hath ears to hear, let him hear.

9 Then his disciples asked him, demanding what parable that was?

10 And he said, Unto you it is given to know the secrets of the kingdom of God, but to other in parables, that when they see, they should not see, and when they hear, they should not understand.

11 The parable is this, The seed is the word of God.

12 And they that are beside the way, are they that hear: afterward cometh the devil, and taketh away the word out of their hearts, least they should believe, and be saved?

13 But they that are on the stones, are they which when they have heard, receive the word with joy: but they have no roots, which for a while believe, but in the time of temptation go away.

14 And that which fell among thorns, are they which have heard, and after their departure are choked with cares and with riches, and voluptuous living, and bring forth no fruit.

15 But that which fell in good ground, are they which with an honest and good heart hear the word, and keep it, and bring forth fruit with patience.

16 No man when he lighteth a candle, coverth it under a vessel, neither putteth it under the table, but setteth it on a candlestick, that they that enter in, may see the light.

17 For nothing is secret, that shall not be evident: neither anything hid, that shall not be known, and come to light.

18 Take heed therefore how ye hear: for whosoever hath, to him shall be given: and whosoever hath not, from him shall be taken even that, which it seemeth that he hath.

19 Then came to him his mother and his brethren, and could not come near to him for the press.

20 And it was told him by certain which said, Thy mother and thy brethren stand without, and would see thee.

21 But he answered, and said unto them, My mother,and my brethren are these which hear the word of God, and do it.

22 And it came to pass on a certain day, that he went into a ship with his disciples, and he said unto them, Let us go over unto the other side of the lake. And they launched forth.

23 And as they sailed, he fell asleep, and there came down a storm of wind on the lake, and they were filled with water, and were in jeopardy.

24 Then they went to him, and awoke him, saying, Master, Master, we perish. And he arose, and rebuked the wind, and the waves of water: and they ceased, and it was calm.

25 Then he said unto them, Where is your faith? And they feared, and wondered among themselves, saying, Who is this that commandeth both the winds and water, and they obey him!

26 So they sailed unto the region of the Gadarenes, which is over against Galilee.

27 And as he went out to land, there met him a certain man out of the city, which had a devil long time, and he wore no clothes, neither abode in house, but in the graves.

28 And when he saw Jesus, he cried out, and fell down before him, and with a loud voice said, What have I to do with thee, Jesus the Son of God, the most High? I beseech thee torment me not.

29 For he commanded the foul spirit to come out of the man: (for oft times he had caught him: therefore he was bound with chains, and kept in fetters: but he break the bands, and was carried of the devil into wildernesses.)

30 Then Jesus asked him, saying, What is thy name? And he said, Legion, because many devils were entered into him.

31 And they besought him, that he would not command them to go out into the deep.

32 And there was there by, an herd of many swine, feeding on an hill, and the devils besought him, that he would suffer them to enter into them. So he suffered them.

33 Then went the devils out of the man, and entered into the swine: and the herd was carried with violence from a steep down place into the lake, and was choked.

34 When the herdsmen saw what was done, they fled: and when they were departed, they told it in the city and in the country.

35 Then they came out to see what was done, and came to Jesus, and found the man, out of whom the devils were departed, sitting at the feet of Jesus, clothed, and in his right mind: and they were afraid.

36 They also which saw it, told them by what means he that was possessed with the devil, was healed.

37 Then the whole multitude of the country about the Gadarenes, besought him, that he would depart from them: for they were taken with a great fear: and he went into the ship, and returned.

38 Then the man, out of whom the devils were departed, besought him that he might be with him: but Jesus sent him away, saying,

39 Return into thine own house, and show what great things God hath done to thee. So he went his way, and preached throughout all the city, what great things Jesus had done unto him.

40 And it came to pass when Jesus was come again, that the people received him: for they all waited for him.

41 And behold, there came a man named Jairus, and he was the ruler of the Synagogue, who fell down at Jesus feet, and besought him that he would come into his house.

42 For he had but a daughter only, about twelve years of age, and she lay a dying (and as he went, the people thronged him.

43 And a woman having an issue of blood, twelve years long, which had spent all her substance upon physicians, and could not be healed of any:

44 When she came behind him, she touched the hem of his garment, and immediately her issue of blood stanched.

45 Then Jesus said, Who is it that hath touched me? When every man denied, Peter said and they that were with him, Master, the multitude thrust thee, and tread on thee, and sayest you, Who hath touched me?

46 And Jesus said, Someone hath touched me: for I perceive that virtue is gone out of me.

47 When the woman saw that she was not hid, she came trembling, and fell down before him, and told him before all the people, for what cause she had touched him, and how she was healed immediately.

48 And he said unto her, Daughter, be of good comfort: thy faith hath made thee whole: go in peace).

49 While he yet spake there came one from the ruler of the Synagogues house, which said to him, Thy daughter is dead: disease not the Master.

50 When Jesus heard it, he answered him, saying, Fear not: believe only, and she shall be made whole.

51 And when he went into the house, he suffered no man to go in with him, save Peter, and James, and John, and the father and mother of the maid.

52 And all wept, and sorrowed for her: but he said, Weep not: for she is not dead, but sleepeth.

53 And they laughed him to scorn, knowing that she was dead.

54 So he thrust them all out, and took her by the hand, and cried, saying, Maid, arise.

55 And her spirit came again, and she rose straightway: and he commanded to give her meat.

56 Then her parents were astonished: but he commanded them that they should tell no man what was done.

Luke Chapter 9

1 Then called he the twelve disciples together, and gave them power and authority over all devils, and to heal diseases.

2 And he sent them to preach the kingdom of God, and to cure the sick.

3 And he said to them, Take nothing to your journey, neither staves, nor script, neither bread, nor silver, neither have two coats.

4 And whatsoever house ye enter into, there abide, and thence depart.

5 And whosoever will not receive you, when ye go out of that city, shake off the very dust from your feet for a testimony against them.

6 And they went out, and went through every town preaching the Gospel, and healing everywhere.

7 Now Herod the Tetrarch heard of all that was done by him: and he doubted, because that it was said of some, that John was risen again from the dead:

8 And of some, that Elias had appeared: and of some, that one of the old Prophets was risen again.

9 Then Herod said, John have I beheaded: who then is this of whom I hear such things? And he desired to see him.

10 And when the Apostles returned, they told him what great things they had done. Then he took them, and went aside into a solitary place, near to the city called Bethsaida.

11 But when the people knew it, they followed him: and he received them, and spake unto them of the kingdom of God, and healed them that had need to be healed.

12 And when the day began to wear away, the twelve came, and said unto him, Send the people away, that they may go into the towns and villages round about, and lodge, and get meat: for we are here in a desert place.

13 But he said unto them, Give ye them to eat. And they said, We have no more but five loaves and two fishes, except we should go and buy meat for all this people.

14 For they were about five thousand men. Then he said to his disciples, Cause them to sit down by fifties in a company.

15 And they did so, and caused all to sit down.

16 Then he took the five loaves, and the two fishes, and looked up to heaven, and blessed them, and break, and gave to the disciples, to set before the people.

17 So they did all eat, and were satisfied: and there was taken up of that remained to them, twelve baskets full of broken meat.

18 And it came to pass as he was alone praying, his disciples were with him, and he asked them, saying, Whom say the people that I am?

19 They answered, and said, John Baptist: and others say, Elias: and some say, that one of the old Prophets is risen again.

20 And he said unto them, But whom say ye that I am? Peter answered, and said, The Christ of God.

21 And he warned, and commanded them, that they should tell that to no man,

22 Saying, The Son of man must suffer many things, and be reproved of the Elders, and of the high Priests and Scribes, and be slain, and the third day rise again.

23 And he said to them all, If any man will come after me, let him deny himself, and take up his cross daily, and follow me.

24 For whosoever will save his life, shall lose it: and whosoever shall lose his life for my sake, the same shall save it.

25 For what advantageth it a man, if he win the whole world, and destroy himself, or lose himself?

26 For whosoever shall be ashamed of me, and of my words, of him shall the Son of man be ashamed, when he shall come in his glory, and in the glory of the Father, and of the Holy Angels.

27 And I tell you of a surety, there be some standing here, which shall not taste of death, till they have seen the kingdom of God.

28 And it came to pass about an eight days after those words, that he took Peter, and John, and James, and went up into a mountain to pray.

29 And as he prayed, the fashion of his countenance was changed, and his garment was white and glistered.

30 And behold, two men talked with him, which were Moses and Elias,

31 Which appeared in glory, and told of his departing, which he should accomplish at Jerusalem.

32 But Peter and they that were with him, were heavy with sleep, and when they awoke, they saw his glory, and the two men standing with him.

33 And it came to pass, as they departed from him, Peter said unto Jesus, Master, it is good for us to be here: let us therefore make three tabernacles, one for thee, and one for Moses, and one for Elias, and wist not what he said.

34 While he thus spake, there came a cloud and overshadowed them, and they feared when these were entering into the cloud.

35 And there came a voice out of the cloud, saying, This is my beloved Son, hear him.

36 And when the voice was past, Jesus was found alone: and they kept it close, and told no man in those days any of those things which they had seen.

37 And it came to pass on the next day, as they came down from the mountain, much people met him.

38 And behold, a man of the company cried out, saying, Master, I beseech thee, behold my son: for he is all that I have.

39 And lo, a spirit taketh him, and suddenly he cryeth, and he teareth him, that he foameth, and with much pain departeth from him, when he hath bruised him.

40 Now I have besought thy disciples to cast him out, but they could not.

41 Then Jesus answered, and said, O generation faithless, and crooked, how long now shall I be with you, and suffer you? Bring thy son hither.

42 And whiles he was yet coming, the devil rent him, and tare him: and Jesus rebuked the unclean spirit, and healed the child, and delivered him to his father.

43 And they were all amazed at the mighty power of God: and while they all wondered at all things, which Jesus did, he said unto his disciples,

44 Mark these words diligently: for it shall come to pass, that the Son of man shall be delivered into the hands of men.

45 But they understood not that word: for it was hid from them, so that they could not perceive it: and they feared to ask him of that word.

46 Then there arose a disputation among them, which of them should be the greatest.

47 When Jesus saw the thoughts of their hearts, he took a little child, and set him by him,

48 And said unto them, Whosoever receiveth this little child in my Name, receiveth me: and whosoever shall receive me, receiveth him that sent me: for he that is least among you all, he shall be great.

49 And John answered and said, Master, we saw one casting out devils in thy Name, and we forbad him, because he followeth thee not with us.

50 Then Jesus said unto him, Forbid ye him not: for he that is not against us, is with us.

51 And it came to pass, when the days were accomplished, that he should be received up, he settled himself fully to go to Jerusalem,

52 And sent messengers before him: and they went and entered into a town of the Samaritans, to prepare him lodging.

53 But they would not receive him, because his behavior was, as though he would go to Jerusalem.

54 And when his disciples, James and John saw it, they said, Lord, wilt thou that we command, that fire come down from heaven, and consume them, even as Elias did?

55 But Jesus turned about, and rebuked them, and said, Ye know not of what spirit ye are.

56 For the Son of man is not come to destroy men's lives, but to save them. Then they went to another town.

57 And it came to pass that as they went in the way, a certain man said unto him, I will follow thee, Lord, whithersoever thou goest.

58 And Jesus said unto him, The foxes have holes, and the birds of the heaven have nests, but the Son of man hath not whereon to lay his head.

59 But he said unto another, Follow me. And the same said, Lord, suffer me first to go and bury my father.

60 And Jesus said unto him, Let the dead bury their dead: but go thou and preach the kingdom of God.

61 Then another said, I will follow thee, Lord: but let me first go bid them farewell, which are at mine house.

62 And Jesus said unto him, No man that putteth his hand to the plough, and looketh back, is apt to the kingdom of God.

Luke Chapter 10

1 After these things, the Lord appointed other seventy also, and sent them, two and two before him into every city and place, whether he himself should come.

2 And he said unto them, The harvest is great, but the laborers are few: pray therefore the Lord of the harvest to send forth laborers into his harvest.

3 Go your ways: behold, I send you forth as lambs among wolves.

4 Bear no bag, neither script, nor shoes, and salute no man by the way.

5 And into whatsoever house ye enter, first say, Peace be to this house.

6 And if the son of peace be there, your peace shall rest upon him: if not, it shall turn to you again.

7 And in that house tarry still eating, and drinking such things as by them shall be set before you: for the laborer is worthy of his wages. Go not from house to house.

8 But into whatsoever city ye shall enter, if they receive you, eat such things as are set before you,

9 And heal the sick that are there, and say unto them, The kingdom of God is come near unto you.

10 But into whatsoever city ye shall enter, if they will not receive you, go your ways out into the streets of the same, and say,

11 Even the very dust, which cleaveth on us of your city, we wipe off against you: notwithstanding know this, that the kingdom of God was come near unto you.

12 For I say to you, that it shall be easier in that day for them of Sodom, than for that city.

13 Woe be to thee, Chorazin: woe be to thee, Bethsaida: for if the miracles had been done in Tyre and Sidon, which have been done in you, they had a great while ago repented, sitting in sackcloth and ashes.

14 Therefore it shall be easier for Tyre, and Sidon, at the judgment, than for you.

15 And thou, Capernaum, which art exalted to heaven, shalt be thrust down to hell.

16 He that heareth you, heareth me: and he that despiseth you, despiseth me: and he that despiseth me, despiseth him that sent me.

17 And the seventy turned again with joy, saying, Lord, even the devils are subdued to us through thy Name.

18 And he said unto them, I saw Satan, like lightening, fall down from heaven.

19 Behold, I give unto you power to tread on serpents, and scorpions, and over all the power of the enemy, and nothing shall hurt you.

20 Nevertheless, in this rejoice not, that the spirits are subdued unto you: but rather rejoice, because your names are written in heaven.

21 That same hour rejoiced Jesus in the spirit, and said, I confess unto thee, Father, Lord of heaven and earth, that thou hast hid these things from the wise and learned, and hast revealed them to babes: even so, Father, because it so pleased thee.

22 Then he turned to his disciples, and said, All things are given me of my Father: and no man knoweth who the Son is, but the Father: neither who the Father is, save the Son, and he to whom the Son will reveal him.

23 And he returned to his disciples, and said secretly, Blessed are the eyes, which see that ye see.

24 For I tell you that many Prophets and Kings have desired to see those things, which ye see, and have not seen them: and to hear those things, which ye hear, and have not heard them.

25 Then behold, a certain expounder of the Law stood up, and tempted him, saying, Master, what shall I do, to inherit eternal life?

26 And he said unto him, What is written in the Law? How readest thou?

27 And he answered, and said, Thou shalt love thy Lord God with all thine heart, and with all thy soul, and with all thy strength, and with all thy thought, and thy neighbor as thyself.

28 Then he said unto him, Thou hast answered right: this do, and thou shalt live.

29 But he willing to justify himself, said unto Jesus, Who is then my neighbor?

30 And Jesus answered, and said, A certain man went down from Jerusalem to Jericho, and fell among thieves, and they robbed him of his raiment, and wounded him, and departed, leaving him half dead.

31 And by chance there came down a certain Priest that same way, and when he saw him, he passed by on the other side.

32 And likewise also a Levite, when he was come near to the place, went and looked on him, and passed by on the other side.

33 Then a certain Samaritan, as he journeyed, came near unto him, and when he saw him, he had compassion on him,

34 And went to him, and bound up his wounds, and poured in oil and wine, and put him on his own beast, and brought him to an Inn, and made provision for him.

35 And on the morrow when he departed, he took out two pence, and gave them to the host, and said unto him, Take care of him, and whatsoever thou spendest more, when I come again, I will recompense thee.

36 Which now of these three, thinkest thou, was neighbor unto him that fell among the thieves?

37 And he said, He that showed mercy on him. Then said Jesus unto him, Go, and do thou likewise.

38 Now it came to pass as they went, that he entered into a certain town, and a certain woman named Martha, received him into her house.

39 And she had a sister called Mary, which also sat at Jesus' feet, and heard his preaching.

40 But Martha was cumbered about much serving, and came to him, and said, Master, dost thou not care that my sister hath left me to serve alone? bid her therefore, that she help me.

41 And Jesus answered, and said unto her, Martha, Martha, Thou carest, and art troubled about many things:

42 But one thing is needful, Mary hath chosen the good part, which shall not be taken away from her.

Luke Chapter 11

1 And so it was, that as he was praying in a certain place, when he ceased, one of his disciples said unto him, Master, teach us to pray, as John also taught his disciples.

2 And he said unto them, When ye pray, say, Our Father, which art in heaven, hallowed be thy Name: Thy kingdom come: Let thy will be done even in earth, as it is in heaven:

3 Our daily bread give us for the day:

4 And forgive us our sins: for even we forgive every man that is indebted to us: And lead us not into temptation: but deliver us from evil.

5 Moreover he said unto them, Which of you shall have a friend, and shall go to him at midnight, and say unto him, Friend, lend me three loaves?

6 For a friend of mine is come out of the way to me, and I have nothing to set before him:

7 And he within should answer, and say, Trouble me not: the door is now shut, and my children are with me in bed: I cannot rise and give them to thee.

8 I say unto you, though he would not arise and give him, because he is his friend, yet doubtless because of his importunity, he would rise, and give him as many as he needed.

9 And I say unto you, Ask, and it shall be given you: seek, and ye shall find: knock, and it shall be opened unto you.

10 For every one that asketh, receiveth: and he that seeketh, findeth: and to him that knocketh, it shall be opened.

11 If a son shall ask bread of any of you that is a father, will he give him a stone? or if he ask a fish, will he for a fish give him a serpent?

12 Or if he ask an egg, will he give him a scorpion?

13 If ye then which are evil, can give good gifts unto your children, how much more shall your heavenly Father give the Holy Ghost to them, that desire him?

14 Then he cast out a devil which was dumb: and when the devil was gone out, the dumb spake, and the people wondered.
15 But some of them said, He casteth out devils through Beelzebub the chief of the devils.
16 And others tempted him, seeking of him a sign from heaven.
17 But he knew their thoughts, and said unto them, Every kingdom divided against itself, shall be desolate, and an house divided against an house, falleth.
18 So if Satan also be divided against himself, how shall his kingdom stand, because ye say that I cast out devils through Beelzebub?
19 If I through Beelzebub cast out devils, by whom do your children cast them out? Therefore shall they be your judges.
20 But if I by the finger of God cast out devils, doubtless the kingdom of God is come unto you.
21 When a strong man armed, keepeth his palace, the things that he possesseth, are in peace.
22 But when a stronger then he, cometh upon him, and overcometh him: he taketh from him all his armor wherein he trusted, and divideth his spoils.
23 He that is not with me, is against me: and he that gathereth not with me, scattereth.
24 When the unclean spirit is gone out of a man, he walketh through dry places, seeking rest: and when he findeth none, he saith, I will return unto mine house whence I came out.
25 And when he cometh, he findeth it swept and garnished.
26 Then goeth he, and taketh to him seven other spirits worse than himself: and they enter in, and dwell there, so the last state of that man is worse than the first.
27 And it came to pass as he said these things, a certain woman of the company lifted up her voice, and said unto him, Blessed is the womb that bare thee, and the paps which thou hast sucked.
28 But he said, Yea, rather blessed are they that hear the word of God, and keep it.
29 And when the people were gathered thick together, he began to say, This is a wicked generation: they seek a sign, and there shall no sign be given them, but the sign of Jonah the Prophet.
30 For as Jonah was a sign to the Ninivites, so shall also the Son of man be to this generation.
31 The Queen of the South shall rise in judgment, with the men of this generation, and shall condemn them: for she came from the utmost parts of the earth to hear the wisdom of Solomon, and behold, a greater than Solomon is here.
32 The men of Nineveh shall rise in judgment with this generation, and shall condemn it: for they repented at the preaching of Jonah: and behold, a greater than Jonah is here.
33 No man lighteth a candle, and putteth it in a private place, neither under a bushel: but on a candlestick, that they which come in, may see the light.
34 The light of the body is the eye: therefore when thine eye is single, then is thy whole body light: but if thy eye be evil, then thy body is dark.
35 Take heed therefore, that the light which is in thee, be not darkness.
36 If therefore thy whole body shall be light, having no part dark, then shall all be light, even as when a candle doth light thee with the brightness.
37 And as he spake, a certain Pharisee besought him to dine with him: and he went in, and sat down at table.
38 And when the Pharisee saw it, he marveled that he had not first washed before dinner.
39 And the Lord said to him, In deed ye Pharisees make clean the outside of the cup, and of the platter: but the inward part is full of ravening and wickedness.
40 Ye fools, did not he that made that which is without, make that which is within also?

41 Therefore, give alms of those things which are within, and behold, all things shall be clean to you.

42 But woe be to you, Pharisees: for ye tithe the mint and the rue, and all manner herbs, and pass over judgment and the love of God: these ought ye to have done, and not to have left the other undone.

43 Woe be to you, Pharisees: for ye love the uppermost seats in the Synagogues, and greetings in the markets.

44 Woe be to you, Scribes and Pharisees, hypocrites: for ye are as graves which appear not, and the men that walk over them, perceive not.

45 Then answered one of the expounders of the Law, and said unto him, Master, thus saying thou puttest us to rebuke also.

46 And he said, Woe be to you also, ye interpreters of the Law: for ye lade men with burdens grievous to be born, and ye yourselves touch not the burdens with one of your fingers.

47 Woe be to you: for ye build the sepulchers of the Prophets, and your fathers killed them.

48 Truly ye bear witness, and allow the deeds of your fathers: for they killed them, and ye build their sepulchers.

49 Therefore said the wisdom of God, I will send them Prophets and Apostles, and of them they shall slay and persecute,

50 That the blood of all the Prophets, shed from the foundation of the world, may be required of this generation,

51 From the blood of Abel unto the blood of Zechariah, which was slain between the altar and the Temple: Verily I say unto you, it shall be required of this generation.

52 Woe be to you, interpreters of the Law: for ye have taken away the key of knowledge: ye entered not in yourselves, and them that came in, ye forbade.

53 And as he said these things unto them, the Scribes and Pharisees began to urge him sore, and to provoke him to speak of many things,

54 Laying wait for him, and seeking to catch something of his mouth, whereby they might accuse him.

Luke Chapter 12

1 In the mean time, there gathered together an innumerable multitude of people, so that they trod one another: and he began to say unto his disciples first, Take heed to yourselves of the leaven of the Pharisees, which is hypocrisy.

2 For there is nothing covered, that shall not be revealed: neither hid, that shall not be known.

3 Wherefore whatsoever ye have spoken in darkness, it shall be heard in the light: and that which ye have spoken in the ear, in secret places, shall be preached on the houses.

4 And I say unto you, my friends, be not afraid of them that kill the body, and after that are not able to do any more.

5 But I will forewarn you, whom ye shall fear: fear him which after he hath killed, hath power to cast into hell: yea, I say unto you, him fear.

6 Are not five sparrows bought for two farthings, and yet not one of them is forgotten before God?

7 Yea, and all the hairs of your head are numbered: fear not therefore: ye are more of value than many sparrows.

8 Also I say unto you, Whosoever shall confess me before men, him shall the Son of man confess also before the Angels of God.

9 But he that shall deny me before men shall be denied before the Angels of God.

10 And whosoever shall speak a word against the Son of man, it shall be forgiven him: but unto him: that shall blaspheme the Holy Ghost, it shall not be forgiven.

11 And when they shall bring you unto the Synagogues, and unto the rulers and Princes, take no thought how, or what thing ye shall answer, or what ye shall speak.

12 For the Holy Ghost shall teach you in the same hour, what ye ought to say.

13 And one of the company said unto him, Master, bid my brother divide the inheritance with me.

14 And he said unto him, Man, who made me a judge, or a divider over you?

15 Wherefore he said unto them, Take heed, and beware of covetousness: for though a man have abundance, yet his life standeth not in his riches.

16 And he put forth a parable unto them, saying, The ground of a certain rich man brought forth fruits plenteously.

17 Therefore he thought with himself, saying, What shall I do, because I have no room, where I may lay up my fruits?

18 And he said, This will I do, I will pull down my barns, and build greater, and therein will I gather all my fruits, and my goods.

19 And I will say to my soul, Soul, thou hast much goods laid up for many years: live at ease, eat, drink, and take thy pastime.

20 But God said unto him, O fool, this night will they fetch away thy soul from thee: then whose shall those things be which thou hast provided?

21 So is he that gathereth riches to himself, and is not rich in God.

22 And he spake unto his disciples, Therefore I say unto you, Take no thought for your life, what ye shall eat: neither for your body, what ye shall put on.

23 The life is more than meat: and the body more then the raiment.

24 Consider the ravens: for they neither sow nor reap: which neither have storehouse nor barn, and yet God feedeth them: how much more are ye better than fowls?

25 And which of you with taking thought, can add to his stature one cubit?

26 If ye then be not able to do the least thing, why take ye thought for the remnant?

27 Consider the lilies how they grow: they labor not, neither spin they: yet I say unto you, that Solomon himself in all his royalty was not clothed like one of these.

28 If then God so clothes the grass which is today in the field, and tomorrow is cast into the oven, how much more will he clothe you, O ye of little faith?

29 Therefore ask not what ye shall eat, or what ye shall drink, neither stand in doubt.

30 For all such things the people of the world seek for: and your Father knoweth that ye have need of these things.

31 But rather seek ye after the kingdom of God, and all these things shall be ministered unto you.

32 Fear not, little flock: for it is your Father's pleasure, to give you the kingdom.

33 Sell that ye have, and give alms: make you bags, which wax not old, a treasure that can never fail in heaven, where no thief cometh, neither moth corrupteth.

34 For where your treasure is, there will your hearts be also.

35 Let your loins be gird about and your lights burning,

36 And ye yourselves like unto men that wait for their master, when he will return from the wedding, that when he cometh and knocketh, they may open unto him immediately.

37 Blessed are those servants, whom the Lord when he cometh shall find waking: Verily I say unto you, he will gird himself about, and make them to sit down at table, and will come forth, and serve them.

38 And if he come in the second watch, or come in the third watch, and shall find them so, blessed are those servants.

39 Now understand this, that if the good man of the house had known at what hour the thief would have come, he would have watched, and would not have suffered his house to be digged through.

40 Be ye also prepared therefore: for the Son of man will come at an hour when ye think not.

41 Then Peter said unto him, Master, tellest thou this parable unto us, or even to all?

42 And the Lord said, Who is a faithful steward and wise, whom the master shall make ruler over his household, to give them their portion of meat in season?

43 Blessed is that servant, whom his master when he cometh, shall find so doing.

44 Of a truth I say unto you, that he will make him ruler over all that he hath.

45 But if that servant say in his heart, My master doth defer his coming, and shall begin to smite the servants, and maidens, and to eat, and drink, and to be drunken,

46 The master of that servant will come in a day when he thinketh not, and at an hour when he is not aware of, and will cut him off, and give him his portion with the unbelievers.

47 And that servant that knew his master's will, and prepared not himself, neither did according to his will, shall be beaten with many stripes.

48 But he that knew it not, and yet did commit things worthy of stripes, shall be beaten with few stripes: for unto whomsoever much is given, of him shall be much required, and to whom men much commit, the more of him will they ask.

49 I am come to put fire on the earth, and what is my desire, if it be already kindled?

50 Notwithstanding I must be baptized with a baptism, and how am I grieved, till it be ended?

51 Think ye that I am come to give peace on earth? I tell you, nay, but rather debate.

52 For from henceforth there shall be five in one house divided, three against two, and two against three.

53 The father shall be divided against the son, and the son against the father: the mother against the daughter, and the daughter against the mother: the mother in law against her daughter in law, and the daughter in law, against her mother in law.

54 Then said he to the people, When ye see a cloud rise out of the West, straightway ye say, A shower cometh: and so it is.

55 And when ye see the South wind blow, ye say, that it will be hot: and it cometh to pass.

56 Hypocrites, ye can discern the face of the earth, and of the sky: but why discern ye not this time?

57 Yea, and why judge ye not of yourselves what is right?

58 While thou goest with thine adversary to the ruler, as thou art in the way, give diligence in the way, that thou mayest be delivered from him, lest he bring thee to the judge, and the judge deliver thee to the jailer, and the jailer cast thee into prison.

59 I tell thee, thou shalt not depart thence, till thou hast paid the utmost mite.

Luke Chapter 13

1 There were certain men present at the same season, that showed him of the Galileans, whose blood Pilate had mingled with their own sacrifices.

2 And Jesus answered, and said unto them, Suppose ye, that these Galileans were greater sinners than all the other Galileans, because they have suffered such things?

3 I tell you, nay: but except ye amend your lives, ye shall all likewise perish.

4 Or think you that those eighteen, upon whom the tower in Siloam fell, and slew them, were sinners above all men that dwell in Jerusalem?

5 I tell you, nay: but except ye amend your lives, ye shall all likewise perish.

6 He spake also this parable, A certain man had a fig tree planted in his vineyard: and he came and sought fruit thereon, and found none.

7 Then said he to the dresser of his vineyard, Behold, this three years have I come and sought fruit of this fig tree, and find none: cut it down: why keepeth it also the ground barren?

8 And he answered, and said unto him, Lord, let it alone this year also, till I dig round about it, and dung it.

9 And if it bear fruit, well: if not, then after thou shalt cut it down.

10 And he taught in one of the Synagogues on the Sabbath day.

11 And behold, there was a woman which had a spirit of infirmity eighteen years, and was bowed together, and could not lift up herself in any wise.

12 When Jesus saw her, he called her to him, and said to her, Woman, thou art loosed from thy disease.

13 And he laid his hands on her, and immediately she was made straight again, and glorified God.

14 And the ruler of the Synagogue answered with indignation because that Jesus had healed on the Sabbath day, and said unto the people, There are six days in which men ought to work: in them therefore come and be healed, and not on the Sabbath day.

15 Then answered him the Lord, and said, Hypocrite, doth not either one of you on the Sabbath day loose his ox or his ass from the stall, and lead him away to the water?

16 And ought not this daughter of Abraham, whom Satan had bound, lo, eighteen years, be loosed from this bond on the Sabbath day?

17 And when he said these things, all his adversaries were ashamed: but all the people rejoiced at all the excellent things, that were done by him.

18 Then said he, What is the kingdom of God like? Or whereto shall I compare it?

19 It is like a grain of mustard seed, which a man took and sowed in his garden, and it grew, and waxed a great tree, and the fowls of the heaven made nests in the branches thereof.

20 And again he said, Whereunto shall I liken the kingdom of God?

21 It is like leaven, which a woman took, and hid in three pecks of flour, till all was leavened.

22 And he went through all cities and towns, teaching, and journeying towards Jerusalem.

23 Then said one unto him, Lord, are there few that shall be saved? And he said unto them,

24 Strive to enter in at the straight gate: for many, I say unto you, will seek to enter in, and shall not be able.

25 When the good man of the house is risen up, and hath shut to the door, and ye begin to stand without, and to knock at the door, saying, Lord, Lord, open to us, and he shall answer and say unto you, I know you not whence ye are,

26 Then shall ye begin to say, We have eaten and drunk in thy presence, and thou hast taught in our streets.

27 But he shall say, I tell you, I know you not whence ye are: depart from me, all ye workers of iniquity.

28 There shall be weeping and gnashing of teeth when ye shall see Abraham and Isaac, and Jacob, and all the Prophets in the kingdom of God, and yourselves thrust out at doors.

29 Then shall come many from the East, and from the West, and from the North, and from the South, and shall sit at table in the kingdom of God.

30 And behold, there are last, which shall be first, and there are first, which shall be last.

31 The same day there came certain Pharisees, and said unto him, Depart, and go hence: for Herod will kill thee.

32 Then said he unto them, Go ye and tell that fox, Behold, I cast out devils, and will heal still today, and tomorrow, and the third day I shall be perfected.

33 Nevertheless I must walk today, and tomorrow, and the day following: for it cannot be that a Prophet should perish out of Jerusalem.

34 O Jerusalem, Jerusalem, which killest the Prophets, and stonest them that are sent to thee, how often would I have gathered thy children together, as the hen gathered her brood under her wings, and ye would not!

35 Behold, your house is left unto you desolate: and Verily I tell you, ye shall not see me until the time come that ye shall say, Blessed is he that cometh in the Name of the Lord.

Luke Chapter 14

1 And it came to pass that when he was entered into the house of one of the chief Pharisees on the Sabbath day, to eat bread, they watched him.

2 And behold, there was a certain man before him, which had the dropsy.

3 Then Jesus answering, spake unto the expounders of the Law, and Pharisees, saying, Is it lawful to heal on the Sabbath day?

4 And they held their peace. Then he took him, and healed him, and let him go,

5 And answered them, saying, Which of you shall have an ass, or an ox fallen into a pit, and will not straightway pull him out on the Sabbath day?

6 And they could not answer him again to those things.

7 He spake also a parable to the guests, when he marked how they chose out the chief rooms, and said unto them,

8 When thou shalt be bidden of any man to a wedding, set not thyself down in the chiefest place, lest a more honorable man than thou, be bidden of him,

9 And he that bade both him and thee, come, and say to thee, Give this man room, and thou then begin with shame to take the lowest room.

10 But when thou art bidden, go and sit down in the lowest room, that when he that bade thee, cometh, he may say unto thee, Friend, sit up here: then shalt thou have worship in the presence of them that sit at table with thee.

11 For whosoever exalteth himself, shall be brought low, and he that humbleth himself, shall be exalted.

12 Then said he also to him that had bidden him, When thou makest a dinner or a supper, call not thy friends, nor thy brethren, neither thy kinsmen, nor the rich neighbors, lest they also bid thee again, and a recompense be made thee.

13 But when thou makest a feast, call the poor, the maimed, the lame, and the blind,

14 And thou shalt be blessed, because they cannot recompense thee: for thou shalt be recompensed at the resurrection of the just.

15 Now when one of them that sat at table, heard these things, he said unto him, Blessed is he that eateth bread in the kingdom of God.

16 Then said he to him, A certain man made a great supper, and bade many,

17 And sent his servant at supper time to say to them that were bidden, Come: for all things are now ready.

18 But they all with one mind began to make excuse: The first said unto him, I have bought a farm, and I must needs go out and see it: I pray thee, have me excused.

19 And another said, I have bought five yoke of oxen, and I go to prove them: I pray thee, have me excused.

20 And another said, I have married a wife, and therefore I cannot come.

21 So that servant returned, and showed his master these things. Then was the good man of the house angry, and said to his servant, Go out quickly into the places and streets of the city, and bring in hither the poor, and the maimed, and the halt, and the blind.

22 And the servant said, Lord, it is done as thou hast commanded, and yet there is room.

23 Then the master said to the servant, Go out into the highways, and hedges, and compel them to come in, that mine house may be filled.

24 For I say unto you, that none of those men which were bidden, shall taste of my supper.

25 Now there went great multitudes with him, and he turned and said unto them,
26 If any man come to me, and hate not his father, and mother, and wife, and children, and brethren, and sisters: yea, and his own life also, he cannot be my disciple.
27 And whosoever beareth not his cross, and cometh after me, cannot be my disciple.
28 For which of you minding to build a tower, sitteth not down before, and counteth the cost, whether he have sufficient to perform it,
29 Lest that after he hath laid the foundation, and is not able to perform it, all that behold it, begin to mock him,
30 Saying, This man began to build, and was not able to make an end?
31 Or what King going to make war against another King, sitteth not down first, and taketh counsel, whether he be able with ten thousand, to meet him that cometh against him with twenty thousand?
32 Or else while he is yet a great way off, he sendeth an ambassador, and desireth conditions of peace.
33 So likewise, whosoever he be of you, that forsaketh not all that he hath, he cannot be my disciple.
34 Salt is good: but if salt have lost his savor, wherewith shall it be salted?
35 It is neither meet for the land, nor yet for the dunghill, but men cast it out. He that hath ears to hear let him hear.

Luke Chapter 15

1 Then resorted unto him all the Publicans, and sinners, to hear him.
2 Therefore the Pharisees and Scribes murmured, saying, He receiveth sinners, and eateth with them.
3 Then spake he this parable to them, saying,
4 What man of you having an hundred sheep, if he lose one of them, doth not leave ninety and nine in the wilderness, and go after that which is lost, until he find it?
5 And when he hath found it, he layeth it on his shoulders with joy.
6 And when he cometh home, he calleth together his friends and neighbors, saying unto them, Rejoice with me: for I have found my sheep, which was lost.
7 I say unto you, that likewise joy shall be in heaven for one sinner that converteth, more than for ninety and nine just men, which need none amendment of life.
8 Either what woman having ten pieces of silver, if she lose one piece, doth not light a candle, and sweep the house, and seek diligently till she find it?
9 And when she hath found it, she calleth her friends, and neighbors, saying, Rejoice with me: for I have found the piece which I had lost.
10 Likewise I say unto you, there is joy in the presence of the Angels of God, for one sinner that converteth.
11 He said moreover, A certain man had two sons.
12 And the younger of them said to his father, Father, give me the portion of the goods that falleth to me. So he divided unto them his substance.
13 So not long after, when the younger son had gathered all together, he took his journey into a far country, and there he wasted his goods with riotous living.
14 Now when he had spent all, there arose a great dearth throughout that land, and he began to be in necessity.
15 Then he went and clave to a citizen of that country, and he sent him to his farm, to feed swine.
16 And he would feign have filled his belly with the husks that the swine ate: but no man gave them him.

17 Then he came to himself, and said, How many hired servants at my father's have bread enough, and I die for hunger?

18 I will rise and go to my father, and say unto him, Father, I have sinned against heaven, and before thee,

19 And am no more worthy to be called thy son: make me as one of thy hired servants.

20 So he arose and came to his father, and when he was yet a great way off, his father saw him, and had compassion, and ran and fell on his neck, and kissed him.

21 And the son said unto him, Father, I have sinned against heaven, and before thee, and am no more worthy to be called thy son.

22 Then the father said to his servants, Bring forth the best robe, and put it on him, and put a ring on his hand, and shoes on his feet,

23 And bring the fat calf, and kill him, and let us eat, and be merry.

24 For this my son was dead, and is alive again: and he was lost, but he is found. And they began to be merry.

25 Now the Elder brother was in the field, and when he came and drew near to the house, he heard melody, and dancing,

26 And called one of his servants, and asked what those things meant.

27 And he said unto him, Thy brother is come, and thy father hath killed the fatted calf, because he hath received him safe and sound.

28 Then he was angry, and would not go in: therefore came his father out and entreated him.

29 But he answered and said to his father, Lo these many years have I done thee service, neither break I at any time thy commandment, and yet thou never gavest me a kid that I might make merry with my friends.

30 But when this thy son was come, which hath devoured thy goods with harlots, thou hast for his sake killed the fat calf.

31 And he said unto him, Son, thou art ever with me, and all that I have, is thine. It was meet that we should make merry, and be glad: for this thy brother was dead, and is alive again: and he was lost, but he is found.

Luke Chapter 16

1 And he said also unto his disciples, There was a certain rich man, which had a steward, and he was accused unto him, that he wasted his goods.

2 And he called him, and said unto him, How is it that I hear this of thee? Give an accounts of thy stewardship: for thou mayest be no longer steward.

3 Then the steward said within himself, What shall I do: for my master will take away from me the stewardship? I cannot dig, and to beg I am ashamed.

4 I know what I will do, that when I am put out of the stewardship they may receive me into their houses.

5 Then called he every one of his master's debtors, and said unto the first, How much owest thou unto my master?

6 And he said, An hundred measures of oil. And he said to him, Take thy writing, and sit down quickly, and write fifty.

7 Then said he to another, How much owest thou? And he said, An hundred measures of wheat. Then he said to him, Take thy writing, and write four score.

8 And the Lord commended the unjust steward, because he had done wisely. Wherefore the children of this world are in their generation wiser than the children of light.

9 And I say unto you, Make you friends with the riches of iniquity, that when ye shall want, they may receive you into everlasting habitations.

10 He that is faithful in the least, he is also faithful in much: and he that is unjust in the least is unjust also in much.

11 If then ye have not been faithful in the wicked riches, who will trust you in the true treasure?

12 And if ye have not been faithful in another man's goods, who shall give you that which is yours?

13 No servant can serve two masters: for either he shall hate the one, and love the other: or else he shall lean to the one, and despise the other. Ye cannot serve God and riches.

14 All these things heard the Pharisees also which were covetous, and they mocked him.

15 Then he said unto them, Ye are they, which justify yourselves before men: but God knoweth your hearts: for that which is highly esteemed among men, is abomination in the sight of God.

16 The Law and the Prophets endured until John: and since that time the kingdom of God is preached, and every man presseth into it.

17 Now it is more easy that heaven and earth should pass away, than that one tittle of the Law should fall.

18 Whosoever putteth away his wife, and marrieth another, committeth adultery: and whosoever marrieth her that is put away from her husband, committeth adultery.

19 There was a certain rich man, which was clothed in purple and fine linen, and fared well and delicately everyday.

20 Also there was a certain beggar named Lazarus, which was laid at his gate full of sores,

21 And desired to be refreshed with the crumbs that fell from the rich man's table: yea, and the dogs came and licked his sores.

22 And it was so that the beggar died, and was carried by the Angels into Abraham's bosom. The rich man also died and was buried.

23 And being in hell in torments, he lift up his eyes, and saw Abraham afar off, and Lazarus in his bosom.

24 Then he cried, and said, Father Abraham, have mercy on me, and send Lazarus that he may dip the tip of his finger in water, and cool my tongue: for I am tormented in this flame.

25 But Abraham said, Son, remember that thou in thy lifetime receivest thy pleasures, and likewise Lazarus pains: now therefore is he comforted, and thou art tormented.

26 Besides all this, between you and us there is a great gulf set, so that they which would go from hence to you, cannot, neither can they come from hence to us.

27 Then he said, I pray thee therefore father, that thou wouldest send him to my father's house,

28 (For I have five brethren) that he may testify unto them, lest they also come into this place of torment.

29 Abraham said unto him, They have Moses and the Prophets: let them hear them.

30 And he said, Nay, father Abraham: but if one came unto them from the dead, they will amend their lives.

31 Then he said unto him, If they hear not Moses and the Prophets, neither will they be persuaded, though one rise from the dead again.

Luke Chapter 17

1 Then said he to the disciples, It cannot be avoided, but that offences will come, but woe be to him by whom they come.

2 It were better for him that a great millstone were hanged about his neck, and that he were cast into the sea, than that he should offend one of these little ones.

3 Take heed to yourselves: if thy brother trespass against thee, rebuke him: and if he repent, forgive him.

4 And though he sin against thee seven times in a day, and seven times in a day turn again to thee, saying, It repenteth me, thou shalt forgive him.

5 And the Apostles said unto the Lord, Increase our faith.

6 And the Lord said, If ye had faith, as much as is a grain of mustard seed, and should say unto this mulberry tree, pluck thyself up by the roots, and plant thyself in the sea, it should even obey you.

7 Who is it also of you, that having a servant plowing or feeding cattle, would say unto him by and by, when he were come from the field, Go, and sit down at table?

8 And would not rather say to him, Dress wherewith I may sup, and gird thyself, and serve me, till I have eaten and drunken, and afterward eat thou, and drink thou?

9 Doth he thank that servant, because he did that which was commanded unto him? I trow not.

10 So likewise ye, when ye have done all those things, which are commanded you, say, We are unprofitable servants: we have done that which was our duty to do.

11 And so it was when he went to Jerusalem, that he passed through the midst of Samaria and Galilee.

12 And as he entered into a certain town, there met him ten men that were lepers, which stood afar off.

13 And they lift up their voices and said, Jesus, Master, have mercy on us.

14 And when he saw them, he said unto them, Go, show yourselves unto the Priests. And it came to pass, that as they went, they were cleansed.

15 Then one of them, when he saw that he was healed, turned back, and with a loud voice praised God,

16 And fell down on his face at his feet, and gave him thanks: and he was a Samaritan.

17 And Jesus answered, and said, Are there not ten cleansed? but where are the nine?

18 There are none found that returned to give God praise, save this stranger.

19 And he said unto him, Arise, go thy way, thy faith hath made thee whole.

20 And when he was demanded of the Pharisees, when the kingdom of God should come, he answered them, and said, The kingdom of God cometh not with observation.

21 Neither shall men say, Lo here, or lo there: for behold the kingdom of God is within you.

22 And he said unto the disciples, The days will come, when ye shall desire to see one of the days of the Son of man, and ye shall not see it.

23 Then they shall say to you, Behold here, or behold there: but go not thither, neither follow them.

24 For as the lightening that lighteneth out of the one part under heaven, shineth unto the other part under heaven, so shall the Son of man be in his day.

25 But first must he suffer many things, and be reproved of this generation.

26 And as it was in the days of Noah, so shall it be in the days of the Son of man.

27 They ate, they drank, they married wives, and gave in marriage unto the day that Noah went into the Ark: and the flood came, and destroyed them all.

28 Likewise also, as it was in the days of Lot: they ate, they drank, they bought, they sold, they planted, they built.

29 But in the day that Lot went out of Sodom, it rained fire and brimstone from heaven, and destroyed them all.

30 After these ensamples shall it be in the day when the Son of man shall be revealed.

31 At that day he that is upon the house, and his stuff in the house, let him not come down to take it out: and he that is in the field likewise, let him not turn back to that he left behind.

32 Remember Lot's wife.

33 Whosoever will seek to save his soul, shall lose it: and whosoever shall lose it, shall get it life.

34 I tell you, in that night there shall be two in one bed: the one shall be received, and the other shall be left.

35 Two women shall be grinding together: the one shall be taken, and the other shall be left.

36 Two men shall be in the field: one shall be taken, and another shall be left.

37 And they answered, and said to him, Where, Lord? And he said unto them, Wheresoever the body is, thither will also the eagles resort.

Luke Chapter 18

1 And he spake also a parable unto them, to this end, that they ought always to pray, and not to wax faint,

2 Saying, There was a judge in a certain city, which feared not God, neither reverenced man.

3 And there was a widow in that city, which came unto him, saying, Do me justice against mine adversary.

4 And he would not for a time: but afterward he said with himself, Though I fear not God, nor reverence man,

5 Yet because this widow troubleth me, I will do her right, lest at the last she come and make me weary.

6 And the Lord said, Hear what the unrighteous judge saith.

7 Now shall not God avenge his elect, which cry day and night unto him, yea, though he suffer long for them?

8 I tell you he will avenge them quickly: but when the Son of man cometh, shall he find faith on the earth?

9 He spake also this parable unto certain which trusted in themselves that they were just, and despised other,

10 Two men went up into the Temple to pray: the one a Pharisee, and the other a Publican.

11 The Pharisee stood and prayed thus with himself, O God, I thank thee that I am not as other men, extortioners, unjust, adulterers, or even as this Publican.

12 I fast twice in the week: I give tithe of all that ever I possess.

13 But the Publican standing afar off, would not lift up so much as his eyes to heaven, but smote his breast, saying, O God, be merciful to me a sinner.

14 I tell you, this man departed to his house justified, rather than the other: for every man that exalteth himself, shall be brought low, and he that humbleth himself, shall be exalted.

15 They brought unto him also babes, that he should touch them. And when his disciples saw it, they rebuked them.

16 But Jesus called them unto him and said, Suffer the babes to come unto me, and forbid them not: for of such is the kingdom of God.

17 Verily I say unto you, whosoever receiveth not the kingdom of God as a babe, he shall not enter therein.

18 Then a certain ruler asked him, saying, Good master, what ought I to do, to inherit eternal life?

19 And Jesus said unto him, Why callest thou me good? None is good, save one, even God.

20 Thou knowest the commandments, Thou shalt not commit adultery: Thou shalt not kill: Thou shalt not steal: Thou shalt not bear false witness: Honor thy father and thy mother.

21 And he said, All these have I kept from my youth.

22 Now when Jesus heard that, he said unto him, Yet lackest thou one thing. Sell all that ever thou hast, and distribute unto the poor, and thou shalt have treasure in heaven, and come follow me.

23 But when he heard those things, he was very heavy: for he was marvelous rich.

24 And when Jesus saw him sorrowful, he said, With what difficulty shall they that have riches, enter into the kingdom of God?

25 Surely it is easier for a camel to go through a needle's eye, than for a rich man to enter into the kingdom of God.

26 Then said they that heard it, And who then can be saved?

27 And he said, The things which are impossible with men, are possible with God.

28 Then Peter said, Lo, we have left all, and have followed thee.

29 And he said unto them, Verily I say unto you, there is no man that hath left house, or parents, or brethren, or wife, or children for the kingdom of God's sake,

30 Which shall not receive much more in this world, and in the world to come life everlasting.

31 Then Jesus took unto him the twelve, and said unto them, Behold, we go up to Jerusalem, and all things shall be fulfilled to the Son of man, that are written by the Prophets.

32 For he shall be delivered unto the Gentiles, and shall be mocked, and shall be spitefully entreated, and shall be spitted on.

33 And when they have scourged him, they will put him to death: but the third day he shall rise again.

34 But they understood none of these things, and this saying was hid from them, neither perceived they the things, which were spoken.

35 And it came to pass, that as he was come near unto Jericho, a certain blind man sat by the way side, begging.

36 And when he heard the people pass by, he asked what it meant.

37 And they said unto him, that Jesus of Nazareth passed by.

38 Then he cried, saying, Jesus the Son of David, have mercy on me.

39 And they which went before, rebuked him, that he should hold his peace, but he cried much more, O Son of David, have mercy on me.

40 And Jesus stood still, and commanded him to be brought unto him. And when he was come near, he asked him,

41 Saying, What wilt thou that I do unto thee? And he said, Lord, that I may receive my sight.

42 And Jesus said unto him, Receive thy sight: thy faith hath saved thee.

43 Then immediately he received his sight, and followed him, praising God: and all the people, when they saw this, gave praise to God.

Luke Chapter 19

1 Now when Jesus entered and passed through Jericho,

2 Behold, there was a man named Zaccheus, which was the chief receiver of the tribute, and he was rich.

3 And he sought to see Jesus, who he should be, and could not for the press, because he was of a low stature.

4 Wherefore he ran before, and climbed up into a wild fig tree, that he might see him: for he should come that way.

5 And when Jesus came to the place, he looked up, and saw him, and said unto him, Zaccheus, come down at once: for today I must abide at thine house.

6 Then he came down hastily, and received him joyfully.

7 And when all they saw it, they murmured, saying, that he was gone in to lodge with a sinful man.

8 And Zaccheus stood forth, and said unto the Lord, Behold, Lord, the half of my goods I give to the poor: and if I have taken from any man by forged accusation, I restore him four fold.

9 Then Jesus said to him, This day is salvation come unto this house, forasmuch as he is also become the son of Abraham.

10 For the Son of man is come to seek, and to save that which was lost.

11 And whiles they heard these things, he continued and spake a parable, because he was near to Jerusalem, and because also they thought that the kingdom of God should shortly appear.

12 He said therefore, A certain noble man went into a far country, to receive for himself a kingdom, and so to come again.

13 And he called his ten servants, and delivered them ten pieces of money, and said unto them, Occupy till I come.

14 Now his citizens hated him, and sent an ambassador after him, saying, We will not have this man to reign over us.

15 And it came to pass, when he was come again, and had received his kingdom, that he commanded the servants to be called to him, to whom he gave his money, that he might know what every man had gained.

16 Then came the first, saying, Lord, thy piece hath increased ten pieces.

17 And he said unto him, Well, good servant: because thou hast been faithful in a very little thing, take thou authority over ten cities.

18 And the second came, saying, Lord, thy piece hath increased five pieces.

19 And to the same he said, Be thou also ruler over five cities.

20 So the other came and said, Lord, behold thy piece, which I have laid up in a napkin.

21 For I feared thee, because thou art a straight man: thou takest up, that thou laidst not down, and reapest that thou didst not sow.

22 Then he said unto him, Of thine own mouth will I judge thee, O evil servant. Thou knewest that I am a straight man, taking up that I laid not down, and reaping that I did not sow.

23 Wherefore then gavest not thou my money into the bank, that at my coming I might have required it with vantage?

24 And he said to them that stood by, Take from him that piece, and give it him that hath ten pieces.

25 (And they said unto him, Lord, he hath ten pieces.)

26 For I say unto you, that unto all them that have, it shall be given: and from him that hath not, even that he hath shall be taken from him.

27 Moreover those mine enemies, which would not that I should reign over them, bring hither, and slay them before me.

28 And when he had thus spoken, he went forth before, ascending up to Jerusalem.

29 And it came to pass, when he was come near to Bethphage, and Bethany, besides the mount which is called the mount of Olives, he sent two of his disciples,

30 Saying, Go ye to the town which is before you, wherein, as soon as ye are come, ye shall find a colt tied, whereon never man sat: loose him, and bring him hither.

31 And if any man ask you, why ye loose him, thus shall ye say unto him, Because the Lord hath need of him.

32 So they that were sent, went their way, and found it as he had said unto them.

33 And as they were loosing the colt, the owners thereof said unto them, Why loose ye the colt?

34 And they said, The Lord hath need of him.

35 So they brought him to Jesus, and they cast their garments on the colt, and set Jesus thereon.

36 And as he went, they spread their clothes in the way.

37 And when he was now come near to the going down of the Mount of Olives, the whole multitude of the disciples began to rejoice, and to praise God with a loud voice, for all the great works that they had seen,

38 Saying, Blessed be the King that cometh in the Name of the Lord: peace in heaven, and glory in the highest places.

39 Then some of the Pharisees of the company said unto him, Master, rebuke thy disciples.

40 But he answered, and said unto them, I tell you, that if these should hold their peace, the stones would cry.

41 And when he was come near, he beheld the City, and wept for it,

42 Saying, O if thou haddest even known at the least in this thy day those things, which belong unto thy peace: but now are they hid from thine eyes.

43 For the days shall come upon thee, that thine enemies shall cast a trench about thee, and compass thee round, and keep thee in on every side,

44 And shall make thee even with the ground, and thy children which are in thee, and they shall not leave in thee a stone upon a stone, because thou knewest not the time of thy visitation.

45 He went also into the Temple, and began to cast out them that sold therein, and them that bought,

46 Saying unto them, It is written, Mine house is the house of prayer, but ye have made it a den of thieves.

47 And he taught daily in the Temple. And the high Priests and the Scribes, and the chief of the people sought to destroy him.

48 But they could not find what they might do to him: for all the people hanged upon him when they heard him.

Luke Chapter 20

1 And it came to pass that on one of those days, as he taught the people in the Temple, and preached the Gospel, the high Priests and the Scribes came upon him with the Elders,

2 And spake unto him, saying, Tell us by what authority thou doest these things, or who is he that hath given thee this authority?

3 And he answered, and said unto them, I also will ask you one thing: tell me therefore:

4 The baptism of John was it from heaven, or of men?

5 And they reasoned within themselves, saying, If we shall say from heaven, he will say, Why then believed ye him not?

6 But if we shall say, Of men, all the people will stone us: for they be persuaded that John was a Prophet.

7 Therefore they answered, that they could not tell whence it was.

8 Then Jesus said unto them, Neither tell I you, by what authority I do these things.

9 Then began he to speak to the people this parable, A certain man planted a vineyard, and let it forth to husbandmen: and went into a strange country, for a great season.

10 And at a time he sent a servant to the husbandmen, that they should give him of the fruit of the vineyard, but the husbandmen did beat him, and sent him away empty.

11 Again he sent yet another servant: and they did beat him, and foul entreated him, and sent him away empty.

12 Moreover, he sent the third, and him they wounded, and cast out.

13 Then said the Lord of the vineyard, What shall I do? I will send my beloved son: it may be that they will do reverence, when they see him.

14 But when the husbandmen saw him, they reasoned with themselves, saying, This is the heir: come, let us kill him, that the inheritance may be ours.

15 So they cast him out of the vineyard, and killed him. What shall the Lord of the vineyard therefore do unto them?

16 He will come and destroy these husbandmen, and will give out his vineyard to others. But when they heard it, they said, God forbid.

17 And he beheld them, and said, What meaneth this then that is written, The stone that the builders refused, that is made the head of the corner?

18 Whosoever shall fall upon that stone, shall be broken: and on whomsoever it shall fall, it will grind him to powder.

19 Then the high Priests and the Scribes the same hour went about to lay hands on him: (but they feared the people) for they perceived that he had spoken this parable against them.

20 And they watched him, and sent forth spies, which should feign themselves just men, to take him in his talk, and to deliver him unto the power and authority of the governor.

21 And they asked him, saying, Master, we know that thou sayest, and teachest right, neither dost thou accept man's person, but teachest the way of God truly .

22 Is it lawful for us to give Caesar tribute or no?

23 But he perceived their craftiness, and said unto them, Why tempt ye me?

24 Show me a penny. Whose image and superscription hath it? They answered and said, Caesar's.

25 Then he said unto them, Give then unto Caesar the things which are Caesar's, and to God those which are God's.

26 And they could not reprove his saying before the people: but they marveled at his answer, and held their peace.

27 Then came to him certain of the Sadducees (which deny that there is any resurrection) and they asked him,

28 Saying, Master, Moses wrote unto us, If any man's brother die having a wife, and he die without children, that his brother should take his wife, and raise up seed unto his brother.

29 Now there were seven brethren, and the first took a wife, and he died without children.

30 And the second took the wife, and he died childless.

31 Then the third took her: and so likewise the seven died, and left no children.

32 And last of all, the woman died also.

33 Therefore at the resurrection, whose wife of them shall she be? For seven had her to wife.

34 Then Jesus answered, and said unto them, The children of this world marry wives and are married.

35 But they which shall be counted worthy to enjoy that world, and the resurrection from the dead, neither marry wives, neither are married.

36 For they can die no more, forasmuch as they are equal unto the Angels, and are the sons of God, since they are the children of the resurrection.

37 And that the dead shall rise again, even Moses showed it besides the bush, when he said, The Lord is the God of Abraham, and the God of Isaac, and the God of Jacob.

38 For he is not the God of the dead, but of them which live: for all live unto him.

39 Then certain of the Pharisees answered and said, Master, thou hast well said.

40 And after that, durst they not ask him any thing at all.

41 Then said he unto them, How say they that Christ is David's son?

42 And David himself saith in the book of the Psalms, The Lord said unto my Lord, sit at my right hand,

43 Till I shall make thine enemies thy footstool.

44 Seeing David calleth him Lord, how is he then his son?

45 Then in the audience of all the people he said unto his disciples,
46 Beware of the Scribes, which desire to go in long robes, and love salutations in the markets, and the highest seats in the Synagogues, and the chief rooms at feasts:
47 Which devour widow's houses, even under a color of long praying: these shall receive greater damnation.

Luke Chapter 21

1 And as he beheld, he saw the rich men, which cast their gifts into the treasury,
2 And he saw also a certain poor widow, which cast in thither two mites,
3 And he said, Of a truth I say unto you, that this poor widow hath cast in more than they all.
4 For they all have of their superfluity cast into the offerings of God: but she of her penury hath cast in all the living that she had.
5 Now as some spake of the Temple, how it was garnished with goodly stones and with consecrate things, he said,
6 Are these the things that ye look upon? the days will come wherein a stone shall not be left upon a stone, that shall not be thrown down.
7 Then they asked him, saying, Master, but when shall these things be? And what sign shall there be when these things shall come to pass?
8 And he said, Take heed, that ye be not deceived: for many will come in my Name, saying, I am Christ, and the time draweth near: follow ye not them therefore.
9 And when ye hear of wars and seditions, be not afraid: for these things must first come, but the end followeth not by and by.
10 Then said he unto them, Nation shall rise against nation, and kingdom against kingdom,
11 And great earthquakes shall be in diverse places, and hunger, and pestilence, and fearful things, and great signs shall there be from heaven.
12 But before all these, they shall lay their hands on you, and persecute you, delivering you up to the Synagogues, and into prisons, and bring you before Kings and rulers for my Name's sake.
13 And this shall turn to you, for a testimonial.
14 Lay it up therefore in your hearts, that ye premeditate not, what ye shall answer.
15 For I will give you a mouth and wisdom, where against all your adversaries shall not be able to speak, nor resist.
16 Yea, ye shall be betrayed also of your parents, and of your brethren, and kinsmen, and friends, and some of you shall they put to death.
17 And ye shall be hated of all men for my Name's sake.
18 Yet there shall not one hair of your heads perish.
19 By your patience possess your souls.
20 And when ye see Jerusalem besieged with soldiers, then understand that the desolation thereof is near.
21 Then let them which are in Judea, flee to the mountains: and let them which are in the midst thereof, depart out: and let not them that are in the country, enter therein.
22 For these be the days of vengeance, to fulfill all things that are written.
23 But woe be to them that be with child, and to them that give suck in those days: for there shall be great distress in this land, and wrath over this people.
24 And they shall fall on the edge of the sword, and shall be led captive into all nations, and Jerusalem shall be trodden under foot of the Gentiles, until the time of the Gentiles be fulfilled.
25 Then there shall be signs in the sun, and in the moon, and in the stars, and upon the earth trouble among the nations with perplexity: the sea and the waters shall roar.

26 And men's hearts shall fail them for fear, and for looking after those things which shall come on the world: for the powers of heaven shall be shaken,

27 And then shall they see the Son of man come in a cloud, with power and great glory.

28 And when these things begin to come to pass, then look up, and lift up your heads: for your redemption draweth near.

29 And he spake to them a parable, Behold, the fig tree, and all trees,

30 When they now shoot forth, ye seeing them, know of your own selves, that summer is then near.

31 So likewise ye when ye see these things come to pass, know ye that the kingdom of God is near.

32 Verily I say unto you, This age shall not pass, till all these things be done.

33 Heaven and earth shall pass away, but my words shall not pass away.

34 Take heed to yourselves, lest at any time your hearts be oppressed with surfeiting and drunkenness, and cares of this life, and lest that day come on you at unawares.

35 For as a snare shall it come on all them that dwell on the face of the whole earth.

36 Watch therefore, and pray continually, that ye may be counted worthy to escape all these things that shall come to pass, and that ye may stand before the Son of man.

37 Now in the day time he taught in the Temple, and at night he went out, and abode in the mount that is called the Mount of Olives.

38 And all the people came in the morning to him, to hear him in the Temple.

Luke Chapter 22

1 Now the feast of unleavened bread drew near, which is called the Passover.

2 And the high Priests and Scribes sought how they might kill him: for they feared the people.

3 Then entered Satan into Judas, who was called Iscariot, and was of the number of the twelve.

4 And he went his way, and communed with the high Priests and captains, how he might betray him to them.

5 So they were glad, and agreed to give him money.

6 And he consented, and sought opportunity to betray him unto them, when the people were away.

7 Then came the day of unleavened bread when the Passover must be sacrificed.

8 And he sent Peter and John, saying, Go, and prepare us the Passover, that we may eat it.

9 And they said to him, Where wilt thou, that we prepare it?

10 Then he said unto them, Behold, when ye be entered into the city, there shall a man meet you, bearing a pitcher of water: follow him into the house that he entereth in,

11 And say unto the good man of the house, The Master saith unto thee, Where is the lodging where I shall eat my Passover with my disciples?

12 Then he shall show you a great high chamber trimmed: there make it ready.

13 So they went and found as he had said unto them, and made ready the Passover.

14 And when the hour was come, he sat down, and the twelve Apostles with him.

15 Then he said unto them, I have earnestly desired to eat this Passover with you before I suffer.

16 For I say unto you, Henceforth I will not eat of it any more, until it be fulfilled in the kingdom of God.

17 And he took the cup, and gave thanks, and said, Take this, and divide it among you.

18 For I say unto you, I will not drink of the fruit of the vine, until the kingdom of God be come.

19 And he took bread, and when he had given thanks, he break it, and gave to them, saying, This is my body, which is given for you: do this in the remembrance of me.

20 Likewise also after supper he took the cup, saying, This cup is the New Testament in my blood, which is shed for you.

21 Yet behold, the hand of him that betrayeth me, is with me at the table.

22 And truly the Son of man goeth as it is appointed: but woe be to that man, by whom he is betrayed.

23 Then they began to enquire among themselves which of them it should be, that should do that.

24 And there arose also a strife among them, which of them should seem to be the greatest.

25 But he said unto them, The Kings of the Gentiles reign over them, and they that bear rule over them, are called Gracious lords.

26 But ye shall not be so: but let the greatest among you be as the least: and the chiefest as he that serveth.

27 For who is greater, he that sitteth at table, or he that serveth? Is not he that sitteth at table? And I am among you as he that serveth.

28 And ye are they which have continued with me in my temptations.

29 Therefore I appoint unto you a kingdom, as my Father hath appointed to me,

30 That ye may eat, and drink at my table in my kingdom, and sit on seats, and judge the twelve tribes of Israel.

31 And the Lord said, Simon, Simon, behold, Satan hath desired you, to winnow you as wheat.

32 But I have prayed for thee, that thy faith fail not: therefore when thou art converted, strengthen thy brethren.

33 And he said unto him, Lord, I am ready to go with thee into prison, and to death.

34 But he said, I tell thee, Peter, the cock shall not crow this day, before thou hast thrice denied that thou knewest me.

35 And he said unto them, When I sent you without bag, and scrip, and shoes, lacked ye any thing? And they said, Nothing.

36 Then he said to them, But now he that hath a bag, let him take it, and likewise a scrip: and he that hath none, let him sell his coat, and buy a sword.

37 For I say unto you, That yet the same which is written, must be performed in me, Even with the wicked was he numbered: for doubtless those things which are written of me, have an end.

38 And they said, Lord, behold, here are two swords. And he said unto them, It is enough.

39 And he came out, and went (as he was wont) to the Mount of Olives: and his disciples also followed him.

40 And when he came to the place, he said to them, Pray, lest ye enter into temptation.

41 And he gate himself from them, about a stone's cast, and kneeled down, and prayed,

42 Saying, Father, if thou wilt, take away this cup from me: nevertheless, not my will, but thine be done.

43 And there appeared an Angel unto him from heaven, comforting him.

44 But being in an agony, he prayed more earnestly: and his sweat was like drops of blood, trickling down to the ground.

45 And he rose up from prayer, and came to his disciples, and found them sleeping for heaviness.

46 And he said unto them, Why sleep ye? Rise and pray, least ye enter into temptation.

47 And while he yet spake, behold a company, and he that was called Judas one of the twelve, went before them, and came near unto Jesus to kiss him.

48 And Jesus said unto him, Judas, betrayest thou the Son of man with a kiss?

49 Now when they which were about him, saw what would follow, they said unto him, Lord, shall we smite with sword?

50 And one of them smote a servant of the high Priest, and struck off his right ear.

51 Then Jesus answered, and said, Suffer them thus far: and he touched his ear, and healed him.

52 Then Jesus said unto the high Priests, and captains of the Temple, and the Elders which were come to him, Be ye come out as unto a thief with swords and staves?

53 When I was daily with you in the Temple, ye stretched not forth the hands against me: but this is your very hour, and the power of darkness.

54 Then took they him, and led him, and brought him to the high Priest's house. And Peter followed afar off.

55 And when they had kindled a fire in the midst of the hall, and were set down together, Peter also sat down among them.

56 And a certain maid beheld him as he sat by the fire, and having well looked on him, said, This man was also with him.

57 But he denied him, saying, Woman, I know him not.

58 And after a little while, another man saw him, and said, Thou art also of them. But Peter said, Man, I am not.

59 And about the space of an hour after a certain other affirmed, saying, Verily even this man was with him: for he is also a Galilean.

60 And Peter said, Man, I know not what thou sayest. And immediately while he yet spake, the cock crew.

61 Then the Lord turned back, and looked upon Peter: and Peter remembered the word of the Lord, how he had said unto him, Before the cock crow, thou shalt deny me thrice.

62 And Peter went out, and wept bitterly.

63 And the men that held Jesus, mocked him, and struck him.

64 And when they had blindfolded him, they smote him on the face, and asked him, saying, Prophesy who it is that smote thee.

65 And many other things blasphemously spake they against him.

66 And as soon as it was day, the Elders of the people, and the high Priests and the Scribes came together, and led him into their Council,

67 Saying, Art thou the Christ? tell us. And he said unto them, If I tell you, ye will not believe it.

68 And if also I ask you, ye will not answer me, nor let me go.

69 Hereafter shall the Son of man sit at the right hand of the power of God.

70 Then said they all, art thou then the Son of God? And he said to them, ye say that I am.

71 Then said they, What need we any further witness? for we ourselves have heard it of his own mouth.

Luke Chapter 23

1 Then the whole multitude of them arose, and led him unto Pilate.

2 And they began to accuse him, saying, We have found this man perverting the people, and forbidding to pay tribute to Caesar, saying, That he is Christ a King.

3 And Pilate asked him, saying, Art thou the King of the Jews? And he answered him, and said, Thou sayest it.

4 Then said Pilate to the high Priests, and to the people, I find no fault in this man.

5 But they were the more fierce, saying, He moveth the people, teaching throughout all Judea, beginning at Galilee, even to this place.

6 Now when Pilate heard of Galilee, he asked whether the man were a Galilean.

7 And when he knew that he was of Herod's jurisdiction, he sent him to Herod, which was also at Jerusalem in those days.

8 And when Herod saw Jesus, he was exceedingly glad: for he was desirous to see him of a long season, because he had heard many things of him, and trusted to have seen some sign done by him.

9 Then questioned he with him of many things: but he answered him nothing.

10 The high Priests also and Scribes stood forth and accused him vehemently.

11 And Herod with his men of war, despised him, and mocked him, and arrayed him in white, and sent him again to Pilate.

12 And the same day Pilate and Herod were made friends together: for before they were enemies one to another.

13 Then Pilate called together the high Priests, and the rulers, and the people,

14 And said unto them, Ye have brought this man unto me, as one that perverted the people: and behold, I have examined him before you, and have found no fault in this man, of those things whereof ye accuse him:

15 No, nor yet Herod: for I sent you to him: and lo, nothing worthy of death is done to him.

16 I will therefore chastise him, and let him loose.

17 (For of necessity he must have let one loose unto them at the feast.)

18 Then all the multitude cried at once, saying, Away with him, and deliver to us Barabbas:

19 Which for a certain insurrection made in the city, and murder was cast in prison.

20 Then Pilate spake again to them, willing to let Jesus loose.

21 But they cried, saying, Crucify, crucify him.

22 And he said unto them the third time, But what evil hath he done? I find no cause of death in him: I will therefore chastise him, and let him loose.

23 But they were instant with loud voices, and required that he might be crucified: and the voices of them and of the high Priests prevailed.

24 So Pilate gave sentence, that it should be as they required.

25 And he let loose unto them him that for insurrection and murder was cast into prison, whom they desired, and delivered Jesus to do with him what they would.

26 And as they led him away, they caught one Simon of Cyrene, coming out of the field, and on him they laid the cross, to bear it after Jesus.

27 And there followed him a great multitude of people, and of women, which women bewailed and lamented him.

28 But Jesus turned back unto them, and said, Daughters of Jerusalem, weep not for me, but weep for yourselves, and for your children.

29 For behold, the days will come, when men shall say, Blessed are the barren, and the wombs that never bare, and the paps which never gave suck.

30 Then shall they begin to say to the mountains, Fall on us: and to the hills, Cover us.

31 For if they do these things to a green tree, what shall be done to the dry?

32 And there were two others, which were evildoers, led with him to be slain.

33 And when they were come to the place, which is called Calvary, there they crucified him, and the evildoers: one at the right hand, and the other at the left.

34 Then said Jesus, Father, forgive them: for they know not what they do. And they parted his raiment, and cast lots.

35 And the people stood, and beheld: and the rulers mocked him with them, saying, He saved others: let him save himself, if he be the Christ, the Chosen of God.

36 The soldiers also mocked him, and came and offered him vinegar,

37 And said, If thou be the King of the Jews, save thyself.

38 And a superscription was also written over him, in Greek letters, and in Latin, and in Hebrew, THIS IS THE KING OF THE JEWS.

39 And one of the evil doers, which were hanged, railed on him, saying, If thou be the Christ, save thyself and us.

40 But the other answered, and rebuked him, saying, Fearest thou not God, seeing thou art in the same condemnation?

41 We are indeed righteously here: for we receive things worthy of that we have done: but this man hath done nothing amiss.

42 And he said unto Jesus, Lord, remember me, when thou comest into thy kingdom.

43 Then Jesus said unto him, Verily I say unto thee, today shalt thou be with me in Paradise.

44 And it was about the sixth hour: and there was a darkness over all the land, until the ninth hour.

45 And the sun was darkened, and the veil of the Temple rent through the midst.

46 And Jesus cried with a loud voice, and said, Father, into thine hands I commend my spirit. And when he thus had said, He gave up the ghost.

47 Now when the Centurion saw what was done, he glorified God, saying, Of a surety this man was just.

48 And all the people that came together to that sight, beholding the things, which were done , smote their breasts, and returned.

49 And all his acquaintance stood a far off, and the women that followed him from Galilee, beholding these things.

50 And behold, there was a man named Joseph, which was a counselor, a good man and a just.

51 He did not consent to the counsel and deed of them, which was of Arimathea, a city of the Jews: who also himself waited for the kingdom of God.

52 He went unto Pilate, and asked the body of Jesus,

53 And took it down, and wrapped it in a linen cloth, and laid it in a tomb hewn out of a rock, wherein was never man yet laid.

54 And that day was the preparation, and the Sabbath drew on.

55 And the women also that followed after, which came with him from Galilee, beheld the sepulcher, and how his body was laid.

56 And they returned and prepared odors, and ointments, and rested the Sabbath day according to the commandment.

Luke Chapter 24

1 Now the first day of the week early in the morning, they came unto the sepulcher, and brought the odors, which they had prepared, and certain women with them.

2 And they found the stone rolled away from the sepulcher,

3 And went in, but found not the body of the Lord Jesus.

4 And it came to pass, that as they were amazed thereat, behold, two men suddenly stood by them in shining vestures.

5 And as they were afraid, and bowed down their faces to the earth, they said to them, Why seek ye him that liveth, among the dead?

6 He is not here, but is risen: remember how he spake unto you, when he was yet in Galilee,

7 Saying, that the son of man must be delivered into the hands of sinful men, and be crucified, and the third day rise again.

8 And they remembered his words,

9 And returned from the sepulcher, and told all these things unto the eleven, and to all the remnant.

10 Now it was Mary Magdalene and Joanna, and Mary the mother of James, and other women with them, which told these things unto the Apostles.

11 But their words seemed unto them, as a feigned thing, neither believed they them.

12 Then arose Peter, and ran unto the sepulcher, and looked in, and saw the linen clothes laid by themselves, and departed wondering in himself at that which was come to pass.

13 And behold, two of them went that same day to a town which was from Jerusalem about threescore furlongs, called Emmaus.

14 And they talked together of all these things that were done.

15 And it came to pass, as they communed together, and reasoned, that Jesus himself drew near, and went with them.

16 But their eyes were holden, that they could not know him.

17 And he said unto them, What manner of communications are these that ye have one to another as ye walk and are sad?

18 And the one (named Cleophas) answered and said unto him, Art thou only a stranger in Jerusalem, and hath not known the things which are come to pass therein in these days?

19 And he said unto them, What things? And they said unto him, Of Jesus of Nazareth, which was a Prophet, mighty in deed and in word before God, and all the people,

20 And how the high Priests, and our rulers delivered him to be condemned to death, and have crucified him.

21 But we trusted that it had been he that should have delivered Israel, and as touching all these things, today is the third day, that they were done.

22 Yea, and certain women among us made us astonished, which came early unto the sepulcher.

23 And when they found not his body, they came, saying, that they had also seen a vision of Angels, which said that he was alive.

24 Therefore certain of them which were with us, went to the sepulcher, and found it even so as the women had said, but him they saw not.

25 Then he said unto them, O fools and slow of heart to believe all that the Prophets have spoken,

26 Ought not Christ to have suffered these things, and to enter into his glory?

27 And he began at Moses, and at all the Prophets, and interpreted unto them in all the Scriptures the things which were written of him.

28 And they drew near unto the town, which they went to, but he made as though he would have gone further.

29 But they constrained him, saying, Abide with us: for it is towards night, and the day is far spent. So he went in to tarry with them.

30 And it came to pass, as he sat at table with them, he took the bread, and gave thanks, and break it, and gave it to them.

31 Then their eyes were opened, and they knew him: but he was taken out of their sight.

32 And they said between themselves, Did not our hearts burn within us, while he talked with us by the way, and when he opened to us the Scriptures?

33 And they rose up the same hour, and returned to Jerusalem, and found the Eleven gathered together, and them that were with them,

34 Which said, The Lord is risen in deed, and hath appeared to Simon.

35 Then they told what things were done in the way, and how he was known of them in breaking of bread.

36 And as they spake these things, Jesus himself stood in the midst of them, and said unto them, Peace be to you.

37 But they were abashed and afraid, supposing that they had seen a spirit. 38 Then he said unto them, Why are ye troubled? and wherefore do doubts arise in your hearts?

39 Behold mine hands and my feet: for it is I myself: handle me, and see: for a spirit hath not flesh and bones, as ye see me have.

40 And when he had thus spoken, he showed them his hands and feet.

41 And while they yet believed not for joy, and wondered, he said unto them, Have ye here any meat?

42 And they gave him a piece of a broiled fish, and of an honeycomb,

43 And he took it, and did eat before them.

44 And he said unto them, These are the words, which I spake unto you while I was yet with you, that all must be fulfilled which are written of me in the Law of Moses, and in the Prophets, and in the Psalms.

45 Then opened he their understanding, that they might understand the Scriptures,

46 And said unto them, Thus is it written, and thus it behooved Christ to suffer, and to rise again from the dead the third day,

47 And that repentance, and remission of sins should be preached in his Name among all nations, beginning at Jerusalem.

48 Now ye are witnesses of these things.

49 And behold, I will send the promise of my Father upon you: but tarry ye in the city of Jerusalem, until ye be endued with power from an high.

50 Afterward he led them out into Bethany, and lift up his hands, and blessed them.

51 And it came to pass, that as he blessed them, he departed from them, and was carried up into heaven.

52 And they worshipped him, and returned to Jerusalem with great joy,

53 And were continually in the Temple, praising, and lauding God, Amen.

THE HOLY GOSPEL OF JESUS CHRIST, ACCORDING TO JOHN

John Chapter 1

1 In the beginning was the Word, and the Word was with God and that Word was God.

2 The same was in the beginning with God.

3 All things were made by it, and without it was made nothing that was made.

4 In it was life, and the life was the light of men.

5 And the light shineth in the darkness, and the darkness comprehended it not.

6 There was a man sent from God, whose name was John.

7 The same came for a witness, to bear witness of the light, that all men through him might believe.

8 He was not that light, but was sent to bear witness of the light.

9 That was the true light, which lighteth every man that cometh into the world.

10 He was in the world, and the world was made by him: and the world knew him not.

11 He came unto his own, and his own received him not.

12 But as many as received him, to them he gave power to be the sons of God, even to them that believe in his Name,

13 Which are born not of blood, nor of the will of the flesh, nor of the will of man, but of God.

14 And the Word was made flesh, and dwelt among us, (and we saw the glory thereof, as the glory of the only begotten Son of the Father) full of grace and truth.

15 John bare witness of him, and cried, saying, This was he of whom I said, He that cometh after me, is preferred before me: for he was before me.

16 And of his fullness have all we received, and grace for grace.

17 For the Law was given by Moses, but grace and truth came by Jesus Christ.

18 No man hath seen God at any time: the only begotten Son, which is in the bosom of the Father, he hath declared him.

19 Then this is the record of John, when the Jews sent Priests and Levites from Jerusalem, to ask him, Who art thou?

20 And he confessed and denied not, and said plainly, I am not the Christ.

21 And they asked him, What then? Art thou Elias? And he said, I am not. Art thou the Prophet? And he answered, No.

22 Then said they unto him, Who art thou that we may give an answer to them that sent us? What sayest thou of thyself?

23 He said, I am the voice of him that cryeth in the wilderness, Make straight the way of the Lord, as said the Prophet Isaiah.

24 Now they which were sent, were of the Pharisees.

25 And they asked him, and said unto him, Why baptizest thou then, if thou be not the Christ, neither Elias, nor the Prophet?

26 John answered them, saying, I baptize with water: but there is one among you, whom ye know not.

27 He it is that cometh after me, which is preferred before me, whose shoe latchet I am not worthy to unloose.

28 These things were done in Bethabara beyond Jordan, where John did baptize.

29 The next day John seeth Jesus coming unto him, and saith, Behold the Lamb of God, which taketh away the sin of the world.

30 This is he of whom I said, After me cometh a man, which is preferred before me: for he was before me.

31 And I knew him not: but because he should be declared to Israel, therefore am I come, baptizing with water.

32 So John bare record, saying, I saw the Spirit come down from heaven, like a dove, and it abode upon him.

33 And I knew him not: but he that sent me to baptize with water, he said unto me, Upon whom thou shalt see the Spirit come down, and tarry still on him, that is he which baptizeth with the Holy Ghost.

34 And I saw, and bare record that this is the Son of God.

35 The next day, John stood again, and two of his disciples.

36 And he beheld Jesus walking by, and said, Behold the Lamb of God.

37 And the two disciples heard him speak, and followed Jesus.

38 Then Jesus turned about, and saw them follow, and said unto them, What seek ye? And they said unto him, Rabbi (which is to say by interpretation, Master) where dwellest thou?

39 He said unto them, Come, and see. They came and saw where he dwelt, and abode with him that day: for it was about the tenth hour.

40 Andrew, Simon Peters brother, was one of the two which had heard it of John, and that followed him.

41 The same found his brother Simon first, and said unto him, We have found the Messiah, which is by interpretation, the Christ.

42 And he brought him to Jesus. And Jesus beheld him, and said, Thou art Simon the son of Jonah: thou shalt be called Cephas, which is by interpretation, a stone.

43 The day following, Jesus would go into Galilee, and found Philip, and said unto him, Follow me.

44 Now Philip was of Bethsaida, the city of Andrew and Peter.

45 Philip found Nathanael, and said unto him, We have found him of whom Moses did write in the Law, and the Prophets, Jesus of Nazareth the Son of Joseph.

46 Then Nathanael said unto him, Can there any good thing come out of Nazareth? Philip said to him, Come, and see.

47 Jesus saw Nathanael coming to him, and said of him, Behold indeed an Israelite, in whom is no guile.

48 Nathanael said unto him, Whence knewest thou me? Jesus answered, and said unto him, Before that Philip called thee, when thou wast under the fig tree, I saw thee.

49 Nathanael answered, and said unto him, Rabbi, thou art the Son of God: thou art the King of Israel.

50 Jesus answered, and said unto him, Because I said unto thee, I saw thee under the fig tree, believest thou? thou shalt see greater things then these.

51 And he said unto him, Verily, verily, I say unto you, hereafter shall ye see heaven open, and the Angels of God ascending, and descending upon the Son of man.

John Chapter 2

1 And the third day, was there a marriage in Cana a town of Galilee, and the mother of Jesus was there.

2 And Jesus was called also, and his disciples unto the marriage.

3 Now when the wine failed, the mother of Jesus said unto him, They have no wine.

4 Jesus said unto her, Woman, what have I to do with thee? mine hour is not yet come.

5 His mother said unto the servants, Whatsoever he saith unto you, do it.

6 And there were set there, six water pots of stone, after the manner of the purifying of the Jews, containing two or three firkins apiece.

7 And Jesus said unto them, Fill the water pots with water. Then they filled them up to the brim.

8 Then he said unto them, Draw out now and bear unto the governor of the feast. So they bare it.

9 Now when the governor of the feast had tasted the water that was made wine, (for he knew not whence it was: but the servants, which drew the water, knew) the governor of the feast called the bridegroom,

10 And said unto him, All men at the beginning set forth good wine, and when men have well drunk, then that which is worse: but thou hast kept back the good wine until now.

11 This beginning of miracles did Jesus in Cana a town of Galilee, and showed forth his glory: and his disciples believed on him.

12 After that he went down into Capernaum, he and his mother, and his brethren, and his disciples: but they continued not many days there.

13 For the Jews Passover was at hand. Therefore Jesus went up to Jerusalem.

14 And he found in the Temple those that sold oxen, and sheep, and doves, and changers of money, sitting there.

15 Then he made a scourge of small cords, and drove them all out of the Temple with the sheep, and oxen and poured out the changers money, and overthrew the tables,

16 And said unto them that sold doves, Take these things hence: make not my Fathers house, an house of merchandise.

17 And his disciples remembered, that it was written, The zeal of thine house hath eaten me up.

18 Then answered the Jews, and said unto him, What sign showest thou unto us, that thou doest these things?

19 Jesus answered and said unto them, Destroy this Temple, and in three days I will raise it up again.

20 Then said the Jews, Forty and six years was this Temple a building, and wilt thou rear it up in three days?

21 But he spake of the temple of his body.

22 As soon therefore as he was risen from the dead, his disciples remembered that he thus said unto them: and they believed the Scripture, and the word which Jesus had said.

23 Now when he was at Jerusalem at the Passover in the feast, many believed in his Name, when they saw his miracles which he did.

24 But Jesus did not commit himself unto them, because he knew them all,

25 And had no need that any should testify of man: for he knew what was in man.

John Chapter 3

1 There was now a man of the Pharisees, named Nicodemus, a ruler of the Jews.

2 He came to Jesus by night, and said unto him, Rabbi, we know that thou art a teacher come from God: for no man could do these miracles that thou doest, except God were with him.

3 Jesus answered, and said unto him, Verily, verily I say unto thee, except a man be born again, he cannot see the Kingdom of God.

4 Nicodemus said unto him, How can a man be born which is old? can he enter into his mothers womb again, and be born?

5 Jesus answered, Verily, verily I say unto thee, except that a man be born of water and of the Spirit, he cannot enter into the kingdom of God.

6 That which is born of the flesh, is flesh: and that that is born of the Spirit, is spirit.

7 Marvel not that I said to thee, Ye must be born again.

8 The wind bloweth where it listeth, and thou hearest the sound thereof, but canst not tell whence it cometh, and whether it goeth: so is every man that is born of the Spirit.

9 Nicodemus answered, and said unto him, How can these things be?

10 Jesus answered, and said unto him, Art thou a teacher of Israel, and knowest not these things?

11 Verily, verily I say unto thee, we speak that we know, and testify that we have seen: but ye receive not our witness.

12 If when I tell you earthly things, ye believe not, how should ye believe, if I shall tell you of heavenly things?

13 For no man ascendeth up to heaven, but he that hath descended from heaven, the Son of man which is in heaven.

14 And as Moses lift up the serpent in the wilderness, so must the Son of man be lift up,

15 That whosoever believeth in him, should not perish, but have eternal life.

16 For God so loved the world, that he hath given his only begotten Son, that whosoever believeth in him, should not perish, but have everlasting life.

17 For God sent not his Son into the world, that he should condemn the world, but that the world through him might be saved.

18 He that believeth in him, shall not be condemned: but he that believeth not, is condemned already, because he believeth not in the Name of the only begotten Son of God.

19 And this is the condemnation, that light is come into the world, and men loved darkness rather than light, because their deeds were evil.

20 For every man that evil doeth, hateth the light, neither cometh to light, lest his deeds should be reproved.

21 But he that doeth truth, cometh to the light, that his deeds might be made manifest, that they are wrought according to God.

22 After these things, came Jesus and his disciples into the land of Judea, and there tarried with them, and baptized.

23 And John also baptized in Enon besides Salem, because there was much water there: and they came, and were baptized.

24 For John was not yet cast into prison.

25 Then there arose a question between Johns disciples and the Jews, about purifying.

26 And they came unto John, and said unto him, Rabbi, he that was with thee beyond Jordan, to whom thou barest witness, behold, he baptizeth, and all men come to him.

27 John answered, and said, A man can receive nothing, except it be given him from heaven.

28 Ye yourselves are my witnesses, that I said, I am not the Christ, but that I am sent before him.

29 He that hath the bride, is the bridegroom: but the friend of the bridegroom which standeth and heareth him, rejoiceth greatly, because of the bridegrooms voice. This my joy therefore is fulfilled.

30 He must increase, but I must decrease.

31 He that is come from on high, is above all: he that is of the earth, is of the earth, and speaketh of the earth: he that is come from heaven, is above all.

32 And what he hath seen and heard, that he testifieth: but no man receiveth his testimony.

33 He that hath received his testimony, hath sealed that God is true.

34 For he whom God hath sent, speaketh the words of God: for God giveth him not the Spirit by measure.

35 The Father loveth the Son, and hath given all things into his hand.

36 He that believeth in the Son, hath everlasting life, and he that obeyeth not the Son, shall not see life, but the wrath of God abideth on him.

John Chapter 4

1 Now when the Lord knew, how the Pharisees had heard, that Jesus made and baptized more disciples than John,

2 (Though Jesus himself baptized not: but his disciples)

3 He left Judea, and departed again into Galilee.

4 And he must needs go through Samaria.

5 Then came he to a city of Samaria called Sychar, near unto the possession that Jacob gave to his son Joseph.

6 And there was Jacobs well. Jesus then wearied in the journey, sat thus on the well: it was about the sixth hour.

7 There came a woman of Samaria to draw water. Jesus said unto her, Give me drink.

8 For his disciples were gone away into the city, to buy meat.

9 Then said the woman of Samaria unto him, How is it, that thou being a Jew, askest drink of me, which am a woman of Samaria? For the Jews meddle not with the Samaritans.

10 Jesus answered and said unto her, If thou knewest the gift of God, and who it is that saith to thee, Give me drink, thou wouldest have asked of him, and he would have given thee water of life.

11 The woman said unto him, Sir, thou hast nothing to draw with, and the well is deep: from whence then hast thou that water of life?

12 Art thou greater than our father Jacob, which gave us the well, and he himself drank thereof, and his children, and his cattle?

13 Jesus answered, and said unto her, Whosoever drinketh of this water, shall thirst again:

14 But whosoever drinketh of the water that I shall give him, shall never be more a thirst: but the water that I shall give him, shall be in him a well of water, springing up into everlasting life.

15 The woman said unto him, Sir, give me of that water, that I may not thirst, neither come hither to draw.

16 Jesus said unto her, Go, call thine husband, and come hither.

17 The woman answered, and said I have no husband. Jesus said to her, Thou hast well said, I have no husband.

18 For thou hast had five husbands, and he whom thou now hast, is not thine husband: that saidest thou truly .

19 The woman said unto him, Sir, I see that thou art a Prophet.

20 Our fathers worshipped in this mountain, and ye say, that in Jerusalem is the place where men ought to worship.

21 Jesus said unto her, Woman, believe me, the hour cometh, when ye shall neither in this mountain, nor at Jerusalem worship the Father.

22 Ye worship that which ye know not: we worship that which we know: for salvation is of the Jews.

23 But the hour cometh, and now is, when the true worshippers shall worship the Father in spirit, and truth: for the Father requireth even such to worship him.

24 God is a Spirit, and they that worship him, must worship him in spirit and truth.

25 The woman said unto him, I know well that Messiah shall come, which is called Christ: when he is come, he will tell us all things.

26 Jesus said unto her, I am he, that speak unto thee.

27 And upon that, came his disciples, and marveled that he talked with a woman: yet no man said unto him, What askest thou? or why talkest thou with her?

28 The woman then left her water pot, and went her way into the city, and said to the men,

29 Come, see a man which hath told me all things that ever I did: is not he the Christ?

30 Then they went out of the city, and came unto him.

31 In the mean while, the disciples prayed him, saying, Master, eat.

32 But he said unto them, I have meat to eat that ye know not of.

33 Then said the disciples between themselves, Hath any man brought him meat?

34 Jesus said unto them, My meat is that I may do the will of him that sent me, and finish his work.

35 Say not ye, There are yet four months, and then cometh harvest? Behold, I say unto you, Lift up your eyes, and look on the regions: for they are white already unto harvest.

36 And he that reapeth, receiveth wages, and gathereth fruit unto life eternal, that both he that soweth, and he that reapeth, might rejoice together.

37 For herein is the saying true, that one soweth and another reapeth.

38 I sent you to reap that, whereon ye bestowed no labor: other men labored, and ye are entered into their labors.

39 Now many of the Samaritans of that city believed in him, for the saying of the woman which testified, He hath told me all things that ever I did.

40 Then when the Samaritans were come unto him, they besought him, that he would tarry with them: and he abode there two days.

41 And many more believed because of his own word.

42 And they said unto the woman, Now we believe, not because of thy saying: for we have heard him ourselves, and know that this is in deed the Christ the Savior of the world.

43 So two days after he departed thence, and went into Galilee.

44 For Jesus himself had testified that a Prophet hath none honor in his own country.

45 Then when he was come into Galilee, the Galileans received him, which had seen all the things that he did at Jerusalem at the feast: for they went also unto the feast.

46 And Jesus came again into Cana a town of Galilee, where he had made of water wine. And there was a certain ruler, whose son was sick at Capernaum.

47 When he heard that Jesus was come out of Judea into Galilee, he went unto him, and besought him that he would go down, and heal his son: for he was even ready to die.

48 Then said Jesus unto him, Except ye see signs and wonders, ye will not believe.

49 The ruler said unto him, Sir, go down before my son die.

50 Jesus said unto him, Go thy way, thy son liveth: and the man believed the word that Jesus had spoken unto him, and went his way.

51 And as he was now going down, his servants met him, saying, Thy son liveth.

52 Then enquired he of them the hour when he began to amend. And they said unto him, Yesterday the seventh hour the fever left him.

53 Then the father knew, that it was the same hour in the which Jesus had said unto him, Thy son liveth. And he believed, and all his household.

54 This second miracle did Jesus again, after he was come out of Judea into Galilee.

John Chapter 5

1 After that, there was a feast of the Jews, and Jesus went up to Jerusalem.

2 And there is at Jerusalem by the place of the sheep, a pool called in Hebrew Bethesda, having five porches:

3 In the which lay a great multitude of sick folk, of blind, halt, and withered, waiting for the moving of the water.

4 For an Angel went down at a certain season into the pool, and troubled the water: whosoever then first, after the stirring of the water, stepped in, was made whole of whatsoever disease he had.

5 And a certain man was there, which had been diseased eight and thirty years.

6 When Jesus saw him lie, and knew that he now long time had been diseased, he said unto him, Wilt thou be made whole?

7 The sick man answered him, Sir, I have no man, when the water is troubled, to put me into the pool: but while I am coming, another stepeth down before me.

8 Jesus said unto him, Rise: take up thy bed, and walk.

9 And immediately the man was made whole, and took up his bed, and walked: and the same day was the Sabbath.

10 The Jews therefore said to him that was made whole, It is the Sabbath day: it is not lawful for thee to carry thy bed.

11 He answered them, He that made me whole, he said unto me, Take up thy bed, and walk.

12 Then asked they him, What man is that which said unto thee, Take up thy bed, and walk?

13 And he that was healed, knew not who it was: for Jesus had conveyed himself away from the multitude that was in that place.

14 And after that, Jesus found him in the Temple, and said unto him, Behold, thou art made whole: sin no more, lest a worse thing come unto thee.

15 The man departed and told the Jews that it was Jesus, which had made him whole.

16 And therefore the Jews did persecute Jesus, and sought to slay him, because he had done these things on the Sabbath day.

17 But Jesus answered them, My Father worketh hitherto, and I work.

18 Therefore the Jews sought the more to kill him: not only because he had broken the Sabbath: but said also that God was his Father, and made himself equal with God.

19 Then answered Jesus, and said unto them, Verily, verily I say unto you, The Son can do nothing of himself, save that he seeth the Father do: for whatsoever things he doeth, the same things doeth the Son also.

20 For the Father loveth the Son, and showeth him all things, whatsoever he himself doeth, and he will show him greater works than these, that ye should marvel.

21 For likewise as the Father raiseth up the dead, and quickeneth them, so the Son quickeneth whom he will.

22 For the Father judgeth no man, but hath committed all judgment unto the Son,

23 Because that all men should honor the Son, as they honor the Father: he that honoreth not the Son, the same honoreth not the Father, which hath sent him.

24 Verily, verily, I say unto you, he that heareth my word, and believeth in him that sent me, hath everlasting life, and shall not come into condemnation, but hath passed from death unto life.

25 Verily, verily, I say unto you, the hour shall come, and now is, when the dead shall hear the voice of the Son of God: and they that hear it, shall live.

26 For as the Father hath life in himself, so likewise hath he given to the Son to have life in himself,

27 And hath given him power also to execute judgment, in that he is the Son of man.

28 Marvel not at this: for the hour shall come in the which all that are in the graves, shall hear his voice.

29 And they shall come forth, that have done good, unto the resurrection of life: but they that have done evil, unto the resurrection of condemnation.

30 I can do nothing of mine own self: as I hear, I judge: and my judgment is just, because I seek not mine own will, but the will of the Father who hath sent me.

31 If I should bear witness of myself, my witness were not true.

32 There is another that beareth witness of me, and I know that the witness, which he beareth of me, is true.

33 Ye sent unto John, and he bare witness unto the truth.

34 But I receive not the record of man: nevertheless these things I say, that ye might be saved.

35 He was a burning, and a shining candle: and ye would for a season have rejoiced in his light.

36 But I have greater witness then the witness of John: for the works which the Father hath given me to finish, the same works that I do, bear witness of me, that the Father sent me.

37 And the Father himself, which hath sent me, beareth witness of me. Ye have not heard his voice at any time, neither have ye seen his shape.

38 And his word have ye not abiding in you: for whom he hath sent, him ye believed not.

39 Search the Scriptures: for in them ye think to have eternal life, and they are they which testify of me.

40 But ye will not come to me, that ye might have life.

41 I receive not praise of men.

42 But I know you, that ye have not the love of God in you.

43 I am come in my Fathers Name, and ye receive me not: if another shall come in his own name, him will ye receive.

44 How can ye believe, which receive honor one of another, and seek not the honor that cometh of God alone?

45 Do not think that I will accuse you to my Father: there is one that accuseth you, even Moses, in whom ye trust.

46 For had ye believed Moses, ye would have believed me: for he wrote of me.

47 But if ye believe not his writings, how shall ye believe my words?

John Chapter 6

1 After these things, Jesus went his way over the Sea of Galilee, or of Tiberius.

2 And a great multitude followed him, because they saw his miracles, which he did on them that were diseased.

3 Then Jesus went up into a mountain, and there he sat with his disciples.

4 Now the Passover, a feast of the Jews, was near.

5 Then JESUS lift up his eyes, and seeing that a great multitude came unto him, he said unto Philip, Whence shall we buy bread, that these might eat?

6 (And this he said to prove him: for he himself knew what he would do.)

7 Philip answered him, Two hundred penny worth of bread is not sufficient for them, that every one of them may take a little.

8 Then said unto him one of his disciples, Andrew, Simon Peters brother,

9 There is a little boy here, which hath five barley loaves, and two fishes: but what are they among so many?

10 And Jesus said, Make the people sit down. (Now there was much grass in that place.) Then the men sat down in number, about five thousand.

11 And Jesus took the bread, and gave thanks, and gave to the disciples and the disciples, to them that were set down: and likewise of the fishes as much as they would.

12 And when they were satisfied, he said unto his disciples, Gather up the broken meat which remaineth, that nothing be lost.

13 Then they gathered it together, and filled twelve baskets with the broken meat of the five barley loaves, which remained unto them that had eaten.

14 Then the men when they had seen the miracle that Jesus did, said, This is of a truth the Prophet that should come into the world.

15 When Jesus therefore perceived that they would come, and take him to make him a King, he departed again into a mountain himself alone.

16 When even was now come, his disciples went down unto the sea,

17 And entered into a ship, and went over the sea, towards Capernaum: and now it was dark, and Jesus was not come to them.

18 And the Sea arose with a great wind that blew.

19 And when they had rowed about five and twenty, or thirty furlongs, they saw Jesus walking on the sea, and drawing near unto the ship: so they were afraid.

20 But he said unto them, It is I: be not afraid.

21 Then willingly they received him into the ship, and the ship was by and by at the land, whether they went.

22 The day following, the people which stood on the other side of the sea, saw that there was none other ship there, save that one, whereunto his disciples were entered, and that Jesus went not with his disciples in the ship, but that his disciples were gone alone,

23 And that there came other ships from Tiberius near unto the place where they ate the bread, after the Lord had given thanks.

24 Now when the people saw that Jesus was not there, neither his disciples, they also took shipping, and came to Capernaum, seeking for Jesus.

25 And when they had found him on the other side of the sea, they said unto him, Rabbi, when camest thou hither?

26 Jesus answered them; and said, Verily, verily I say unto you, ye seek me not because ye saw the miracles, but because ye ate of the loaves, and were filled.

27 Labor not for the meat which perisheth, but for the meat that endureth unto everlasting life, which the Son of man shall give unto you: for him hath God the Father sealed.

28 Then said they unto him, What shall we do, that we might work the works of God?

29 Jesus answered, and said unto them, This is the work of God, that ye believe in him, whom he hath sent.

30 They said therefore unto him, What sign showest thou then, that we may see it, and believe thee? what doest thou work?

31 Our fathers did eat Manna in the desert, as it is written, He gave them bread from heaven to eat.

32 Then Jesus said unto them, Verily, verily I say unto you, Moses gave you not bread from heaven, but my Father giveth you the true bread from heaven.

33 For the bread of God is he which cometh down from heaven, and giveth life unto the world.

34 Then they said unto him, Lord, evermore give us this bread.

35 And Jesus said unto them, I am the bread of life: he that cometh to me, shall not hunger, and he that believeth in me, shall never thirst.

36 But I said unto you, that ye also have seen me, and believe not.

37 All that the Father giveth me, shall come to me: and him that cometh to me, I cast not away.

38 For I came down from heaven, not to do mine own will, but his will which hath sent me.

39 And this is the Fathers will which hath sent me, that of all which he hath given me, I should lose nothing, but should raise it up again at the last day.

40 And this is the will of him that sent me, that every man which seeth the Son, and believeth in him, should have everlasting life: and I will raise him up at the last day.

41 The Jews then murmured at him because he said, I am the bread, which is come down from heaven.

42 And they said, Is not this Jesus the son of Joseph, whose father and mother we know? How then saith he, I came down from heaven?

43 Jesus then answered, and said unto them, Murmur not among your selves.

44 No man can come to me, except the Father, which hath sent me, draw him: and I will raise him up at the last day.

45 It is written in the Prophets, And they shall be all taught of God. Every man therefore that hath heard, and hath learned of the Father, cometh unto me,

46 Not that any man hath seen the Father, save he which is of God, he hath seen the Father.

47 Verily, verily I say unto you, He that believeth in me, hath everlasting life.

48 I am the bread of life.

49 Your fathers did eat Manna in the wilderness, and are dead.

50 This is the bread, which cometh down from heaven, that he which eateth of it, should not die.

51 I am the living bread, which came down from heaven: if any man eat of this bread, he shall live forever: and the bread that I will give, is my flesh, which I will give for the life of the world.

52 Then the Jews strove among themselves, saying, How can this man give us his flesh to eat?

53 Then Jesus said unto them, Verily, verily I say unto you, Except ye eat the flesh of the Son of man, and drink his blood, ye have no life in you.

54 Whosoever eateth my flesh, and drinketh my blood, hath eternal life, and I will raise him up at the last day.

55 For my flesh is meat indeed, and my blood is drink indeed.

56 He that eateth my flesh, and drinketh my blood, dwelleth in me, and I in him.

57 As the living Father hath sent me, so live I by the Father, and he that eateth me, even he shall live by me.

58 This is the bread which came down from heaven: not as your fathers have eaten Manna, and are dead. He that eateth of this bread, shall live for ever.

59 These things spake he in the Synagogue, as he taught in Capernaum.

60 Many therefore of his disciples (when they heard this) said, This is an hard saying: who can hear it?

61 But Jesus knowing in himself, that his disciples murmured at this, said unto them, Doth this offend you?

62 What then if ye should see the Son of man ascend up where he was before?

63 It is the spirit that quickeneth: the flesh profiteth nothing: the words that I speak unto you, are spirit and life.

64 But there are some of you that believe not: for Jesus knew from the beginning, which they were that believed not, and who should betray him.

65 And he said, Therefore said I unto you, that no man can come unto me, except it be given unto him of my Father.

66 From that time, many of his disciples went back, and walked no more with him.

67 Then said Jesus to the twelve, Will ye also go away?

68 Then Simon Peter answered him, Master to whom shall we go? Thou hast the words of eternal life:

69 And we believe and know that thou art the Christ the Son of the living God.

70 Jesus answered them, Have not I chosen you twelve and one of you is a devil?

71 Now he spake it of Judas Iscariot the son of Simon: for he it was that should betray him, though he was one of the twelve.

John Chapter 7

1 After these things, Jesus walked in Galilee, and would not walk in Judea: for the Jews sought to kill him.

2 Now the Jews feast of the Tabernacles was at hand.

3 His brethren therefore said unto him, Depart hence, and go into Judea, that thy disciples may see thy works that thou doest.

4 For there is no man that doeth any thing secretly, and he himself seeketh to be famous. If thou doest these things, show thyself to the world.

5 For as yet his brethren believed not in him.

6 Then Jesus said unto them, My time is not yet come: but your time is alway ready.

7 The world cannot hate you: but me it hateth, because I testify of it, that the works thereof are evil.

8 Go ye up unto this feast: I will not go up yet unto this feast: for my time is not yet fulfilled.

9 These things he said unto them, and abode still in Galilee.

10 But as soon as his brethren were gone up, then went he also up unto the feast, not openly, but as it were privately.

11 Then the Jews sought him at the feast, and said, Where is he?

12 And much murmuring was there of him among the people. Some said, He is a good man: other said, Nay: but he deceiveth the people.

13 Howbeit no man spake openly of him for fear of the Jews.

14 Now when half the feast was done, Jesus went up into the Temple and taught.

15 And the Jews marveled, saying, How knoweth this man the Scriptures, seeing that he never learned.

16 Jesus answered them, and said, My doctrine is not mine, but his that sent me.

17 If any man will do his will, he shall know of the doctrine, whether it be of God, or whether I speak of myself.

18 He that speaketh of himself, seeketh his own glory: but he that seeketh his glory that sent him, the same is true, and no unrighteousness is in him.

19 Did not Moses give you a Law, and yet none of you keepeth the Law? Why go ye about to kill me?

20 The people answered, and said, Thou hast a devil: who goeth about to kill thee?

21 Jesus answered, and said to them, I have done one work, and ye all marvel.

22 Moses therefore gave unto you circumcision, (not because it is of Moses, but of the fathers) and ye on the Sabbath day circumcise a man.

23 If a man on the Sabbath receive circumcision, that the Law of Moses should not be broken, be ye angry with me, because I have made a man every whit whole on the Sabbath day?

24 Judge not according to the appearance, but judge righteous judgment.

25 Then said some of them of Jerusalem, Is not this he, whom they go about to kill?

26 And behold, he speaketh openly, and they say nothing to him: do the rulers know indeed that this is the very Christ?

27 Howbeit we know this man whence he is: but when the Christ cometh, no man shall know whence he is.

28 Then cried Jesus in the Temple as he taught, saying, Ye both know me, and know whence I am: yet am I not come of myself, but he that sent me, is true, whom ye know not.

29 But I know him: for I am of him, and he hath sent me.

30 Then they sought to take him, but no man laid hands on him, because his hour was not yet come.

31 Now many of the people believed in him, and said, When the Christ cometh, will he do more miracles than this man hath done?

32 The Pharisees heard that the people murmured these things of him, and the Pharisees, and high Priests sent officers to take him.

33 Then said Jesus unto them, Yet am I a little while with you, and then go I unto him that sent me.

34 Ye shall seek me, and shall not find me, and where I am, can ye not come.

35 Then said the Jews among themselves, Whither will he go, that we shall not find him? Will he go unto them that are dispersed among the Grecians, and teach the Grecians?

36 What saying is this that he said, Ye shall seek me, and shall not find me? and where I am, can ye not come?

37 Now in the last and great day of the feast, Jesus stood and cried, saying, If any man thirst, let him come unto me, and drink.

38 He that believeth in me, as saith the Scripture, out of his belly shall flow rivers of water of life.

39 (This spake he of the Spirit which they that believed in him, should receive: for the Holy Ghost was not yet given because that Jesus was not yet glorified.)

40 So many of the people, when they heard this saying, said, Of a truth this is the Prophet.

41 Other said, This is the Christ: and some said, But shall Christ come out of Galilee?

42 Saith not the Scripture that the Christ shall come of the seed of David, and out of the town of Bethlehem, where David was?

43 So was there dissension among the people for him.

44 And some of them would have taken him, but no man laid hands on him.

45 Then came the officers to the high Priests and Pharisees, and they said unto them, Why have ye not brought him?

46 The officers answered, Never man spake like this man.

47 Then answered them the Pharisees, Are ye also deceived?

48 Doth any of the rulers, or of the Pharisees believe in him?

49 But this people, which know not the Law, are cursed.

50 Nicodemus said unto them, (he that came to Jesus by night, and was one of them.)

51 Doth our Law judge a man before it hear him, and know what he hath done?

52 They answered and said unto him, Art thou also of Galilee? Search and look: for out of Galilee ariseth no Prophet.

53 And every man went unto his own house.

John Chapter 8

1 And Jesus went unto the Mount of Olives,

2 And early in the morning came again into the Temple, and all the people came unto him, and he sat down, and taught them.

3 Then the Scribes, and the Pharisees brought unto him a woman, taken in adultery, and set her in the midst,

4 And said unto him, Master, this woman was taken in adultery, in the very act.

5 Now Moses in the Law commanded us, that such should be stoned: what sayest thou therefore?

6 And this they said to tempt him, that they might have, whereof to accuse him. But Jesus stooped down, and with his finger wrote on the ground.

7 And while they continued asking him, he lift himself up, and said unto them, Let him that is among you without sin, cast the first stone at her.

8 And again he stooped down, and wrote on the ground.

9 And when they heard it, being accused by their own conscience, they went out one by one, beginning at the eldest even to the last: so Jesus was left alone, and the woman standing in the midst.

10 When Jesus had lift up himself again, and saw no man, but the woman, he said unto her, Woman, where are those thine accusers? hath no man condemned thee?

11 She said, No man, Lord. And Jesus said, Neither do I condemn thee: go and sin no more.

12 Then spake Jesus again unto them, saying, I am the light of the world: he that followeth me, shall not walk in darkness, but shall have the light of life.

13 The Pharisees therefore said unto him, Thou bearest record of thyself: thy record is not true.

14 Jesus answered, and said unto them, Though I bear record of myself, yet my record is true: for I know whence I came and whether I go: but ye cannot tell whence I come, and whether I go.

15 Ye judge after the flesh: I judge no man.

16 And if I also judge, my judgment is true: for I am not alone, but I and the Father, that sent me.

17 And it is also written in your Law, that the testimony of two men is true.

18 I am one that bear witness of myself, and the Father that sent me, beareth witness of me.

19 Then said they unto him, Where is thy Father? Jesus answered, Ye neither know me, nor my Father. If ye had known me, ye should have known my Father also.

20 These words spake Jesus in the treasury, as he taught in the Temple, and no man laid hands on him: for his hour was not yet come.

21 Then said Jesus again unto them, I go my way, and ye shall seek me, and shall die in your sins, Whether I go, can ye not come.

22 Then said the Jews, Will he kill himself because he saith, Whether I go, can ye not come?

23 And he said unto them, Ye are from beneath: I am from above: ye are of this world: I am not of this world.

24 I said therefore unto you, That ye shall die in your sins: for except ye believe, that I am he, ye shall die in your sins.

25 Then said they unto him, Who art thou? And Jesus said unto them, Even the same thing that I said unto you from the beginning.

26 I have many things to say, and to judge of you: but he that sent me, is true, and the things that I have heard of him, those speak I to the world.

27 They understood not that he spake to them of the Father.

28 Then said Jesus unto them, When ye have lift up the Son of man, then shall ye know that I am he, and that I do nothing of myself, but as my Father hath taught me, so I speak these things.

29 For he that sent me, is with me: the Father hath not left me alone, because I do always those things that please him.

30 As he spake these things, many believed in him.

31 Then said Jesus to the Jews which believed in him, If ye continue in my word, ye are verily my disciples,

32 And shall know the truth, and the truth shall make you free.

33 They answered him, We be Abrahams seed, and were never bound to any man: why sayest thou then, Ye shall be made free?

34 Jesus answered them, Verily, verily I say unto you, that whosoever committeth sin, is the servant of sin.

35 And the servant abideth not in the house forever: but the Son abideth for ever.

36 If the Son therefore shall make you free, you shall be free indeed.

37 I know that ye are Abrahams seed, but ye seek to kill me, because my word hath no place in you.

38 I speak that which I have seen with my Father: and ye do that which ye have seen with your father.

39 They answered, and said unto him, Abraham is our father. Jesus said unto them, If ye were Abrahams children, ye would do the works of Abraham.

40 But now ye go about to kill me, a man that have told you the truth, which I have heard of God: this did not Abraham.

41 Ye do the works of your father. Then said they to him, We are not born of fornication: we have one Father, which is God.

42 Therefore Jesus said unto them, If God were your Father, then would ye love me: for I proceeded forth, and came from God, neither came I of myself, but he sent me.

43 Why do ye not understand my talk? Because ye cannot hear my word.

44 Ye are of your father the devil, and the lusts of your father ye will do: he hath been a murderer from the beginning, and abode not in the truth, because there is no truth in him. When he speaketh a lie, then speaketh he of his own: for he is a liar, and the father thereof.

45 And because I tell you the truth, ye believe me not.

46 Which of you can rebuke me of sin? And if I say the truth, why do ye not believe me?

47 He that is of God, heareth Gods words: ye therefore hear them not, because ye are not of God.

48 Then answered the Jews, and said unto him, Say we not well that thou art a Samaritan, and hast a devil?

49 Jesus answered, I have not a devil, but I honor my Father, and ye have dishonored me.

50 And I seek not mine own praise: but there is one that seeketh it, and judgeth.

51 Verily, verily I say unto you, If a man keep my word, he shall never see death.

52 Then said the Jews to him, Now know we that thou hast a devil. Abraham is dead, and the Prophets, and thou sayest, If a man keep my word, he shall never taste of death.

53 Art thou greater than our father Abraham, which is dead? And the Prophets are dead: whom makest thou thyself?

54 Jesus answered, If I honor myself, mine honor is nothing worth: it is my Father that honoreth me, whom ye say, that he is your God.

55 Yet ye have not known him: but I know him, and if I should say I know him not, I should be a liar like unto you: but I know him, and keep his word.

56 Your father Abraham rejoiced to see my day, and he saw it, and was glad.

57 Then said the Jews unto him, Thou art not yet fifty year old, and hast thou seen Abraham?

58 Jesus said unto them, Verily, verily I say unto you, before Abraham was, I am.

59 Then took they up stones, to cast at him, but Jesus hid himself, and went out of the Temple.

John Chapter 9

1 And as Jesus passed by, he saw a man which was blind from his birth.

2 And his disciples asked him, saying, Master, who did sin, this man, or his parents, that he was born blind?

3 Jesus answered, Neither hath this man sinned, nor his parents, but that the works of God should be showed on him.

4 I must work the works of him that sent me, while it is day: the night cometh when no man can work.

5 As long as I am in the world, I am the light of the world.

6 As soon as he had thus spoken, he spat on the ground, and made clay of the spittle, and anointed the eyes of the blind with the clay,

7 And said unto him, Go wash in the pool of Siloam (which is by interpretation, sent.) He went his way therefore, and washed, and came again seeing.

8 Now the neighbors and they that had seen him before, when he was blind, said, Is not this he that sat and begged?

9 Some said, This is he: and others said, He is like him: but he himself said, I am he.

10 Therefore they said unto him, How were thine eyes opened?

11 He answered, and said, The man that is called Jesus, made clay, and anointed mine eyes, and said unto me, Go to the pool of Siloam and wash. So I went and washed and received sight.

12 Then they said unto him, Where is he? He said, I cannot tell.

13 They brought to the Pharisees him that was once blind.

14 And it was the Sabbath day, when Jesus made the clay, and opened his eyes.

15 Then again the Pharisees also asked him, how he had received sight. And he said unto them, He laid clay upon mine eyes, and I washed, and do see.

16 Then said some of the Pharisees, This man is not of God, because he keepeth not the Sabbath day. Others said, How can a man that is a sinner, do such miracles? and there was a dissension among them.

17 Then spake they unto the blind again, What sayest thou of him, because he hath opened thine eyes? And he said, He is a Prophet.

18 Then the Jews did not believe him (that he had been blind, and received his sight) until they had called the parents of him that had received sight.

19 And they asked them, saying, Is this your son, whom ye say was born blind? How doth he now see then?

20 His parents answered them, and said, We know that this is our son, and that he was born blind:

21 But by what means he now seeth, we know not: or who hath opened his eyes, can we not tell: he is old enough: ask him: he shall answer for himself.

22 These words spake his parents, because they feared the Jews: for the Jews had ordained already, that if any man did confess that he was the Christ, he should be excommunicate out of the Synagogue.

23 Therefore said his parents, He is old enough: ask him.

24 Then again called they the man that had been blind, and said unto him, Give glory unto God: we know that this man is a sinner.

25 Then he answered, and said, Whither he be a sinner or no, I cannot tell: one thing I know, that I was blind, and now I see.

26 Then said they to him again, What did he to thee? How opened he thine eyes?

27 He answered them, I have told you already, and ye have not heard it: wherefore would ye hear it again? Will ye also be his disciples?

28 Then checked they him, and said, Be thou his disciple: we be Moses disciples.

29 We know that God spake with Moses: but this man we know not from whence he is.

30 The man answered, and said unto them, Doubtless, this is a marvelous thing, that ye know not whence he is, and yet he hath opened mine eyes.

31 Now we know that God heareth not sinners: but if any man be a worshipper of God, and doeth his will, him heareth he.

32 Since the world began was it not heard that any man opened the eyes of one that was born blind.

33 If this man were not of God, he could have done nothing.

34 They answered, and said unto him, Thou art altogether born in sins, and doest thou teach us? so they cast him out.

35 Jesus heard that they had cast him out: and when he had found him, he said unto him, Dost thou believe in the Son of God?

36 He answered, and said, Who is he, Lord, that I might believe in him?

37 And Jesus said unto him, Both thou hast seen him, and he it is that talketh with thee.

38 Then he said, Lord, I believe, and worshipped him.

39 And Jesus said, I am come unto judgment into this world, that they which see not, might see: and that they which see, might be made blind.

40 And some of the Pharisees which were with him, heard these things, and said unto him, Are we blind also?

41 Jesus said unto them, If ye were blind, ye should not have sin: but now ye say, We see: therefore your sin remaineth.

John Chapter 10

1 Verily, verily I say unto you, He that entereth not in by the door into the sheepfold, but climbeth up another way, he is a thief and a robber.

2 But he that goeth in by the door, is the shepherd of the sheep.

3 To him the porter openeth, and the sheep hear his voice, and he calleth his own sheep by name, and leadeth them out.

4 And when he hath sent forth his own sheep, he goeth before them, and the sheep follow him: for they know his voice.

5 And they will not follow a stranger, but they flee from him: for they know not the voice of strangers.

6 This parable spake Jesus unto them: but they understood not what things they were which he spake unto them.

7 Then said Jesus unto them again, Verily, verily I say unto you, I am the door of the sheep.

8 All, that ever came before me, are thieves and robbers: but the sheep did not hear them.

9 I am the door: by me if any man enter in, he shall be saved, and shall go in and go out, and find pasture.

10 The thief cometh not, but for to steal, and to kill, and to destroy: I am come that they might have life, and have it in abundance.

11 I am the good shepherd: the good shepherd giveth his life for his sheep.

12 But an hireling, and he which is not the shepherd, neither the sheep are his own, seeth the wolf coming, and he leaveth the sheep, and fleeth, and the wolf catcheth them, and scattereth the sheep.

13 So the hireling fleeth, because he is an hireling, and careth not for the sheep.

14 I am the good shepherd, and know mine, and am known of mine.

15 As the Father knoweth me, so know I the Father: and I lay down my life for my sheep.

16 Other sheep I have also, which are not of this fold: them also must I bring, and they shall hear my voice: and there shall be one sheepfold, and one shepherd.

17 Therefore doth my Father love me, because I lay down my life, that I might take it again.

18 No man taketh it from me, but I lay it down of myself: I have power to lay it down, and have power to take it again: this commandment have I received of my Father.

19 Then there was a dissension again among the Jews for these sayings,

20 And many of them said, He hath a devil, and is mad: why hear ye him?

21 Others said, These are not the words of him that hath a devil: can the devil open the eyes of the blind?

22 And it was at Jerusalem the feast of the Dedication, and it was winter.

23 And Jesus walked in the Temple, in Solomons porch.

24 Then came the Jews round about him, and said unto him, How long dost thou make us doubt? If thou be the Christ, tell us plainly.

25 Jesus answered them, I told you, and ye believe not: the works that I do in my Fathers Name, they bear witness of me.

26 But ye believe not: for ye are not of my sheep, as I said unto you.

27 My sheep hear my voice, and I know them, and they follow me,

28 And I give unto them eternal life, and they shall never perish, neither shall any pluck them out of mine hand.

29 My Father which gave them me, is greater than all, and none is able to take them out of my Fathers hand.

30 I and my Father are one.

31 Then the Jews again took up stones, to stone him.

32 Jesus answered them, Many good works have I showed you from my Father: for which of these works do ye stone me?

33 The Jews answered him, saying, For the good work we stone thee not, but for blasphemy, and that thou being a man, makest thyself God.

34 Jesus answered them, Is it not written in your Law, I said, ye are gods?

35 If he called them gods, unto whom the word of God was given, and the Scripture cannot be broken,

36 Say ye of him, whom the Father hath sanctified, and sent into the world, Thou blasphemest, because I said, I am the Son of God?

37 If I do not the works of my Father, believe me not.

38 But if I do, then though ye believe not me, yet believe the works that ye may know and believe, that the Father is in me, and I in him.

39 Again they went about to take him: but he escaped out of their hands,

40 And went again beyond Jordan, into the place where John first baptized, and there abode.

41 And many resorted unto him, and said, John did no miracle: but all things that John spake of this man, were true.

42 And many believed in him there.

John Chapter 11

1 And a certain man was sick, named Lazarus of Bethany, the town of Mary, and her sister Martha.

2 (And it was that Mary which anointed the Lord with ointment, and wiped his feet with her hair, whose brother Lazarus was sick.)

3 Therefore his sisters sent unto him, saying, Lord, behold, he whom thou lovest, is sick.

4 When Jesus heard it, he said, This sickness is not unto death, but for the glory of God, that the Son of God might be glorified thereby.

5 Now Jesus loved Martha and her sister and Lazarus.

6 And after he had heard that he was sick, yet abode he two days still in the same place where he was.

7 Then after that, said he to his disciples, Let us go into Judea again.

8 The disciples said unto him, Master, the Jews lately sought to stone thee, and dost thou go thither again?

9 Jesus answered, Are there not twelve hours in the day? If a man walk in the day, he stumbleth not, because he seeth the light of this world.

10 But if a man walk in the night, he stumbleth, because there is no light in him.

11 These things spake he, and after he said unto them, Our friend Lazarus sleepeth: but I go to wake him up.

12 Then said his disciples, Lord, if he sleep, he shall be safe.

13 Howbeit, Jesus spake of his death: but they thought that he had spoken of the natural sleep.

14 Then said Jesus unto them plainly, Lazarus is dead.

15 And I am glad for your sakes, that I was not there, that ye may believe: but let us go unto him.

16 Then said Thomas (which is called Didymus) unto his fellow disciples, Let us also go, that we may die with him.

17 Then came Jesus, and found that he had lain in the grave four days already.

18 (Now Bethany was near unto Jerusalem, about fifteen furlongs off.)

19 And many of the Jews were come to Martha and Mary to comfort them for their brother.

20 Then Martha, when she heard that Jesus was coming, went to meet him: but Mary sat still in the house.

21 Then said Martha unto Jesus, Lord, if thou hadst been here, my brother had not been dead.

22 But now I know also, that whatsoever thou askest of God, God will give it thee.

23 Jesus said unto her, Thy brother shall rise again.

24 Martha said unto him, I know that he shall rise again in the resurrection at the last day.

25 Jesus said unto her, I am the resurrection and the life: he that believeth in me, though he were dead, yet shall he live.

26 And whosoever liveth, and believeth in me, shall never die. Believeth thou this?

27 She said unto him, Yea, Lord, I believe that thou art the Christ the Son of God, which should come into the world.

28 And when she had so said, she went her way, and called Mary her sister secretly, saying, The Master is come, and calleth for thee.

29 And when she heard it, she arose quickly, and came unto him.

30 For Jesus was not yet come into the town, but was in the place where Martha met him.

31 The Jews then which were with her in the house, and comforted her, when they saw Mary, that she rose up hastily, and went out, followed her, saying, She goeth unto the grave, to weep there.

32 Then when Mary was come where Jesus was, and saw him, she fell down at his feet, saying unto him, Lord, if thou hadst been here, my brother had not been dead.

33 When Jesus therefore saw her weep, and the Jews also weep which came with her, he groaned in the spirit, and was troubled in himself,

34 And said, Where have ye laid him? They said unto him, Lord, come, and see.

35 And Jesus wept.

36 Then said the Jews, Behold, how he loved him.

37 And some of them said, Could not he, which opened the eyes of the blind, have made also, that this man should not have died?

38 Jesus therefore again groaned in himself, and came to the grave. And it was a cave, and a stone was laid upon it.

39 Jesus said, Take ye away the stone. Martha the sister of him that was dead, said unto him, Lord, he stinketh already: for he hath been dead four days.

40 Jesus said unto her, Said I not unto thee, that if thou didst believe, thou shouldest see the glory of God?

41 Then they took away the stone from the place where the dead was laid. And Jesus lift up his eyes, and said, Father, I thank thee, because thou hast heard me.

42 I know that thou hearest me always, but because of the people that stand by, I said it, that they may believe, that thou hast sent me.

43 As he had spoken these things, he cried with a loud voice, Lazarus, come forth.

44 Then he that was dead, came forth, bound hand and foot with bands, and his face was bound with a napkin. Jesus said unto them, Loose him, and let him go.

45 Then many of the Jews, which came to Mary, and had seen the things, which Jesus did, believed in him.

46 But some of them went their way to the Pharisees, and told them what things Jesus had done.

47 Then gathered the high Priests, and the Pharisees a council, and said, What shall we do? For this man doeth many miracles.

48 If we let him thus alone, all men will believe in him, and the Romans will come and take away both our place, and the nation.

49 Then one of them named Caiaphas, which was the high Priest that same year, said unto them, Ye perceive nothing at all,

50 Nor yet do you consider that it is expedient for us, that one man die for the people, and that the whole nation perish not.

51 This spake he not of himself: but being high Priest that same year, he prophesied that Jesus should die for the nation:

52 And not for the nation only, but that he should gather together in one the children of God, which were scattered.

53 Then from that day forth they consulted together, to put him to death.

54 Jesus therefore walked no more openly among the Jews, but went thence unto a country near to the wilderness, into a city called Ephraim, and there continued with his disciples.

55 And the Jews' Passover was at hand, and many went out of the country up to Jerusalem before the Passover, to purify themselves.

56 Then sought they for Jesus, and spake among themselves, as they stood in the Temple, What think ye, that he cometh not to the feast?

57 Now both the high Priests and the Pharisees had given a commandment, that if any man knew where he were, he should show it, that they might take him.

John Chapter 12

1 Then Jesus six days before the Passover came to Bethany, where Lazarus was, which was dead, whom he had raised from the dead.

2 There they made him a supper, and Martha served: but Lazarus was one of them that sat at the table with him.

3 Then took Mary a pound of ointment of Spikenard very costly, and anointed Jesus feet, and wiped his feet with her hair, and the house was filled with the savor of the ointment.

4 Then said one of his disciples, even Judas Iscariot Simons son, which should betray him,

5 Why was not this ointment sold for three hundred pence, and given to the poor?

6 Now he said this, not that he cared for the poor, but because he was a thief, and had the bag, and bare that which was given.

7 Then said Jesus, Let her alone: against the day of my burying she kept it.

8 For the poor always ye have with you, but me ye shall not have always.

9 Then much people of the Jews knew that he was there: and they came, not for Jesus sake only, but that they might see Lazarus also, whom he had raised from the dead.

10 The high Priests therefore consulted, that they might put Lazarus to death also,

11 Because that for his sake many of the Jews went away, and believed in Jesus.

12 On the morrow a great multitude that were come to the feast, when they heard that Jesus should come to Jerusalem,

13 Took branches of palm trees, and went forth to meet him, and cried, Hosanna, Blessed is the King of Israel that cometh in the Name of the Lord.

14 And Jesus found a young ass, and sat thereon, as it is written,

15 Fear not, daughter of Zion: behold, thy King cometh sitting on an asses colt.

16 But his disciples understood not these things at the first: but when Jesus was glorified, then remembered they, that these things were written of him, and that they had done these things unto him.

17 The people therefore that was with him, bare witness that he called Lazarus out of the grave, and raised him from the dead.

18 Therefore met him the people also, because they heard that he had done this miracle.

19 And the Pharisees said among themselves, Perceive ye how ye prevail nothing? Behold, the world goeth after him.

20 Now there were certain Greeks among them that came up to worship at the feast.

21 And they came to Philip, which was of Bethsaida in Galilee, and desired him, saying, Sir, we would see Jesus.

22 Philip came and told Andrew: and again Andrew and Philip told Jesus.

23 And Jesus answered them, saying, The hour is come, that the Son of man must be glorified.

24 Verily, verily I say unto you, Except the wheat corn fall into the ground and die, it abideth alone: but if it die, it bringeth forth much fruit.

25 He that loveth his life, shall lose it, and he that hateth his life in this world, shall keep it unto life eternal.

26 If any man serve me, let him follow me: for where I am, there shall also my servant be: and if any man serve me, him will my Father honor.

27 Now is my soul troubled: and what shall I say? Father, save me from this hour: but therefore came I unto this hour.

28 Father, glorify thy Name. Then came there a voice from heaven, saying, I have both glorified it, and will glorify it again.

29 Then said the people that stood by and heard, that it was a thunder: others said, An Angel spake to him.

30 Jesus answered, and said, This voice came not because of me, but for your sakes.

31 Now is the judgment of this world: now shall the prince of this world be cast out.

32 And I, if I were lift up from the earth, will draw all men unto me.

33 Now this said he, signifying what death he should die.

34 The people answered him, We have heard out of the Law, that the Christ abideth for ever: and how sayest thou, that the Son of man must be lift up? Who is that Son of man?

35 Then Jesus said unto them, Yet a little while is the light with you: walk while ye have light, lest the darkness come upon you: for he that walketh in the dark, knoweth not whether he goeth.

36 While ye have light, believe in the light, that ye may be the children of the light. These things spake Jesus, and departed, and hid himself from them.

37 And though he had done so many miracles before them, yet believed they not on him,

38 That the saying of Isaiah the Prophet might be fulfilled, that he said, Lord, who believed our report? and to whom is the arm of the Lord revealed?

39 Therefore could they not believe, because that Isaiah saith again,

40 He hath blinded their eyes, and hardened their hearts, that they should not see with their eyes, nor understand with their heart, and should be converted, and I should heal them.

41 These things said Isaiah when he saw his glory, and spake of him.

42 Nevertheless, even among the chief rulers many believed in him: but because of the Pharisees, they did not confess him, lest they should be cast out of the Synagogue.

43 For they loved the praise of men, more then the praise of God.

44 And Jesus cried, and said, He that believeth in me, believeth not in me, but in him that sent me.

45 And he that seeth me, seeth him that sent me.

46 I am come a light into the world, that whosoever believeth in me, should not abide in darkness.

47 And if any man hear my words, and believe not, I judge him not: for I came not to judge the world, but to save the world.

48 He that refuseth me, and receiveth not my words, hath one that judgeth him: the word that I have spoken, it shall judge him in the last day.

49 For I have not spoken of myself: but the Father, which sent me, he gave me a commandment what I should say, and what I should speak.

50 And I know that his commandment is life everlasting: the things therefore that I speak, I speak them so as the Father said unto me.

John Chapter 13

1 Now before the feast of the Passover, when Jesus knew that his hour was come, that he should depart out of this world unto the Father, forasmuch as he loved his own which were in the world, unto the end he loved them.

2 And when supper was done (and that the devil had now put in the heart of Judas Iscariot, Simons son, to betray him)

3 Jesus knowing that the Father had given all things into his hands, and that he was come from God, and went to God,

4 He riseth from supper, and layeth aside his upper garments, and took a towel, and girded himself.

5 After that, he poured water into a basin, and began to wash the disciples' feet, and to wipe them with the towel, wherewith he was girded.

6 Then came he to Simon Peter, who said to him, Lord, dost thou wash my feet?

7 Jesus answered and said unto him, What I do, thou knowest not now: but thou shalt know it hereafter.

8 Peter said unto him, Thou shalt never wash my feet. Jesus answered him, If I wash thee not, thou shalt have no part with me.

9 Simon Peter said unto him, Lord, not my feet only, but also the hands and the head.

10 Jesus said to him, He that is washed, needeth not, save to wash his feet, but is clean every whit: and ye are clean, but not all.

11 For he knew who should betray him: therefore said he, Ye are not all clean.

12 So after he had washed their feet, and had taken his garments, and was set down again, he said unto them, Know ye what I have done to you?

13 Ye call me Master, and Lord, and ye say well: for so am I.

14 If I then your Lord, and Master, have washed your feet, ye also ought to wash one anothers feet.

15 For I have given you an example, that ye should do, even as I have done to you.

16 Verily, verily I say unto you, The servant is not greater than his master, neither the ambassador greater than he that sent him.

17 If ye know these things, blessed are ye, if ye do them.

18 I speak not of you all: I know whom I have chosen: but it is that the Scripture might be fulfilled, He that eateth bread with me, hath lift up his heel against me.

19 From henceforth tell I you before it come, that when it is come to pass, ye might believe that I am he.

20 Verily, verily I say unto you, If I send any, he that receiveth him, receiveth me, and he that receiveth me, receiveth him that sent me.

21 When Jesus had said these things, he was troubled in the Spirit, and testified, and said, Verily, Verily I say unto you, that one of you shall betray me.

22 Then the disciples looked one on another, doubting of whom he spake.

23 Now there was one of his disciples, which leaned on Jesus bosom, whom Jesus loved.

24 To him beckoned therefore Simon Peter, that he should ask who it was of whom he spake.

25 He then, as he leaned on Jesus breast, said unto him, Lord, who is it?

26 Jesus answered, He it is, to whom I shall give a sop, when I have dipped it: and he wet a sop, and gave it to Judas Iscariot, Simons son.

27 And after the sop, Satan entered into him. Then said Jesus unto him, That thou doest, do quickly.

28 But none of them that were at table, knew, for what cause he spake it unto him.

29 For some of them thought because Judas had the bag, that Jesus had said unto him, Buy those things that we have need of against the feast: or that he should give something to the poor.

30 As soon then as he had received the sop, he went immediately out, and it was night.

31 When he was gone out, Jesus said, Now is the Son of man glorified, and God is glorified in him.

32 If God be glorified in him, God shall also glorify him in himself, and shall straightway glorify him.

33 Little children, yet a little while am I with you: ye shall seek me, but as I said unto the Jews, Whither I go, can ye not come: also to you say I now, 34 A new commandment give I unto you, that ye love one another: as I have loved you, that ye also love one another.

35 By this shall all men know that ye are my disciples, if ye have love one to another.

36 Simon Peter said unto him, Lord, whither goest thou? Jesus answered him, Whither I go, thou canst not follow me now: but thou shalt follow me afterwards.

37 Peter said unto him, Lord, why can I not follow thee now? I will lay down my life for thy sake.

38 Jesus answered him, Wilt thou lay down thy life for my sake? Verily, verily I say unto thee, The cock shall not crow, till thou have denied me thrice.

John Chapter 14

1 And He said to his disciples, Let not your heart be troubled: ye believe in God, believe also in me.

2 In my Fathers house are many dwelling places: if it were not so, I would have told you: I go to prepare a place for you.

3 And though I go to prepare a place for you, I will come again, and receive you unto my self, that where I am, there may ye be also.

4 And whither I go, ye know, and the way ye know.

5 Thomas said unto him, Lord, we know not whither thou goest: how can we then know the way?

6 Jesus said unto him, I am the Way, and the Truth, and the Life. No man cometh unto the Father, but by me.

7 If ye had known me, ye should have known my Father also: and from henceforth ye know him, and have seen him.

8 Philip said unto him, Lord, show us thy Father, and it sufficeth us.

9 Jesus said unto him, I have been so long time with you, and hast thou not known me, Philip? he that hath seen me, hath seen my Father: how then sayest thou, Show us thy Father?

10 Believest thou not, that I am in the Father, and the Father is in me? The words that I speak unto you, I speak not of my self: but the Father that dwelleth in me, he doeth the works.

11 Believe me, that I am in the Father, and the Father in me: at the least, believe me for the very works sake.

12 Verily, verily I say unto you, he that believeth in me, the works that I do, he shall do also, and greater than these shall he do: for I go unto my Father.

13 And whatsoever ye ask in my Name, that will I do, that the Father may be glorified in the Son.

14 If ye shall ask any thing in my Name, I will do it.

15 If ye love me, keep my commandments,

16 And I will pray the Father, and he shall give you another Comforter, that he may abide with you for ever,

17 Even the Spirit of truth, whom the world cannot receive, because it seeth him not, neither knoweth him: but ye know him: for he dwelleth with you, and shall be in you.

18 I will not leave you comfortless: but I will come to you. 19 Yet a little while, and the world shall see me no more, but ye shall see me: because I live, ye shall live also.

20 At that day shall ye know that I am in my Father, and you in me, and I in you.

21 He that hath my commandments, and keepeth them, is he that loveth me: and he that loveth me, shall be loved of my Father: and I will love him, and will show mine own self to him.

22 Judas said unto him (not Iscariot) Lord, what is the cause that thou wilt show thyself unto us, and not unto the world?

23 Jesus answered, and said unto him, If any man love me, he will keep my word, and my Father will love him, and we will come unto him, and will dwell with him.

24 He that loveth me not, keepeth not my words, and the word which ye hear, is not mine, but the Father's which sent me.

25 These things have I spoken unto you, being present with you.

26 But the Comforter, which is the Holy Ghost, whom the Father will send in my Name, he shall teach you all things, and bring all things to your remembrance, which I have told you.

27 Peace I leave with you: my peace I give unto you: not as the world giveth, give I unto you. Let not your heart be troubled, nor fear.

28 Ye have heard how I said unto you, I go away, and will come unto you. If ye loved me, ye would verily rejoice, because I said, I go unto the Father: for my Father is greater than I.

29 And now have I spoken unto you, before it come, that when it is come to pass, ye might believe.

30 Hereafter will I not speak many things unto you: for the prince of this world cometh, and hath nought in me.

31 But it is that the world may know that I love my Father: and as the Father hath commanded me, so I do. Arise, let us go hence.

John Chapter 15

1 I am the true vine, and my Father is an husband man.

2 Every branch that beareth not fruit in me, he taketh away: and every one that beareth fruit, he purgeth it, that it may bring forth more fruit.

3 Now are ye clean through the word, which I have spoken unto you.

4 Abide in me, and I in you: as the branch cannot bear fruit of it self, except it abide in the vine, no more can ye, except ye abide in me.

5 I am the vine: ye are the branches: he that abideth in me, and I in him, the same bringeth forth much fruit: for without me can ye do nothing.

6 If a man abide not in me, he is cast forth as a branch, and withereth: and men gather them, and cast them into the fire, and they burn.

7 If ye abide in me and my words abide in you, ask what ye will, and it shall be done to you.

8 Herein is my Father glorified, that ye bear much fruit, and be made my disciples.

9 As the father hath loved me, so have I loved you: continue in my love.

10 If ye shall keep my commandments, ye shall abide in my love, as I have kept my Fathers commandments, and abide in his love.

11 These things have I spoken unto you, that my joy might remain in you, and that your joy might be full.

12 This is my commandment, that ye love one another, as I have loved you.

13 Greater love than this hath no man, when any man bestoweth his life for his friends.

14 Ye are my friends, if ye do whatsoever I command you.

15 Hereforth, call I you not servants: for the servant knoweth not what his master doeth: but I have called you friends: for all things that I have heard of my Father, have I made known to you.

16 Ye have not chosen me, but I have chosen you, and ordained you, that ye go and bring forth fruit, and that your fruit remain, that whatsoever ye shall ask of the Father in my Name, he may give it you.

17 These things command I you, that ye love one another.

18 If the world hate you, ye know that it hated me before you.

19 If ye were of the world, the world would love his own: but because ye are not of the world, but I have chosen you out of the world, therefore the world hateth you.

20 Remember the word that I said unto you, The servant is not greater than his master. If they have persecuted me, they will persecute you also: if they have kept my word, they will also keep yours.

21 But all these things will they do unto you for my Names sake, because they have not known him that sent me.

22 If I had not come and spoken unto them, they should not have had sin: but now have they no cloke for their sin.

23 He that hateth me, hateth my Father also.

24 If I had not done works among them which none other man did, they had not had sin: but now have they both seen, and have hated both me, and my Father.

25 But it is that the word might be fulfilled, that is written in their Law, They hated me without a cause.

26 But when the Comforter shall come, whom I will send unto you from the Father, even the Spirit of truth, which proceedeth of the Father, he shall testify of me.

27 And ye shall witness also, because ye have been with me from the beginning.

John Chapter 16

1 These things have I said unto you, that ye should not be offended.

2 They shall excommunicate you: yea, the time shall come, that whosoever killeth you, will think that he doeth God service.

3 And these things will they do unto you, because they have not known the Father, nor me.

4 But these things have I told you, that when the hour shall come, ye might remember, that I told you them. And these things said I not unto you from the beginning, because I was with you.

5 But now I go my way to him that sent me and none of you asketh me, Whither goest thou?

6 But because I have said these things unto you, your hearts are full of sorrow.

7 Yet I tell you the truth, It is expedient for you that I go away: for if I go not away, the Comforter will not come unto you: but if I depart, I will send him unto you.

8 And when he is come, he will reprove the world of sin, and of righteousness, and of judgment.

9 Of sin, because they believe not in me:

10 Of righteousness, because I go to my Father, and ye shall see me no more:

11 Of judgment, because the prince of this world is judged.

12 I have yet many things to say unto you, but ye cannot bear them now.

13 Howbeit, when he is come which is the Spirit of truth, he will lead you into all truth: for he shall not speak of himself, but whatsoever he shall hear, shall he speak, and he will show you the things to come.

14 He shall glorify me: for he shall receive of mine, and shall show it unto you.

15 All things that the Father hath, are mine: therefore said I, that he shall take of mine, and show it unto you.

16 A little while, and ye shall not see me: and again a little while, and ye shall see me: for I go to my Father.

17 Then said some of his disciples among themselves, What is this that he saith unto us, A little while, and ye shall not see me, and again, a little while, and ye shall see me, and, For I go to my Father?

18 They said therefore, What is this that he saith, A little while? We know not what he saith.

19 Now Jesus knew that they would ask him, and said unto them, Do ye enquire among yourselves, of that I said, A little while, and ye shall not see me: and again, a little while, and ye shall see me?

20 Verily, Verily I say unto you, that ye shall weep and lament, and the world shall rejoice: and ye shall sorrow, but your sorrow shall be turned to joy.

21 A woman when she travaileth, hath sorrow, because her hour is come: but as soon as she is delivered of the child, she remembereth no more the anguish, for joy that a man is born into the world.

22 And ye now therefore are in sorrow: but I will see you again, and your hearts shall rejoice, and your joy shall no man take from you.

23 And in that day shall ye ask me nothing. Verily, verily I say unto you, whatsoever ye shall ask the Father in my Name, he will give it you.

24 Hitherto have ye asked nothing in my Name: ask, and ye shall receive, that your joy may be full.

25 These things have I spoken unto you in parables: but the time will come, when I shall no more speak to you in parables: but I shall show you plainly of the Father.

26 At that day shall ye ask in my Name, and I say not unto you, that I will pray unto the Father for you.

27 For the Father himself loveth you, because ye have loved me, and have believed that I came out from God.

28 I am come out from the Father, and came into the world: again I leave the world, and go to the Father.

29 His disciples said unto him, Lo, now speaketh thou plainly, and thou speaketh no parable.

30 Now know we that thou knowest all things, and needest not that any man should ask thee. By this we believe, that thou art come out from God.

31 Jesus answered them, Do you believe now?

32 Behold, the hour cometh, and is already come, that ye shall be scattered every man into his own, and shall leave me alone: but I am not alone: for the Father is with me.

33 These things have I spoken unto you, that in me ye might have peace: in the world ye shall have affliction, but be of good comfort: I have overcome the world.

John Chapter 17

1 These things spake Jesus, and lift up his eyes to heaven, and said, Father the hour is come: glorify thy Son, that thy Son also may glorify thee.

2 As thou hast given him power over all flesh, that he should give eternal life to all them that thou hast given him.

3 And this is life eternal, that they know thee to be the only very God, and whom thou hast sent, Jesus Christ.

4 I have glorified thee on the earth: I have finished the work which thou gavest me to do.

5 And now glorify me, thou Father, with thine own self, with the glory which I had with thee before the world was.

6 I have declared thy Name unto the men which thou gavest me out of the world: thine they were, and thou gavest them me, and they have kept thy word.

7 Now they know that all things whatsoever thou hast given me, are of thee.

8 For I have given unto them the words, which thou gavest me, and they have received them, and have known surely that I came out from thee, and have believed that thou hast sent me.

9 I pray for them: I pray not for the world, but for them which thou hast given me: for they are thine.

10 And all mine are thine, and thine are mine, and I am glorified in them.

11 And now am I no more in the world, but these are in the world, and I come to thee. Holy Father, keep them in thy Name, even them whom thou hast given me, that they may be one, as we are.

12 While I was with them in the world, I kept them in thy Name: those that thou gavest me, have I kept, and none of them is lost, but the child of perdition, that the Scripture might be fulfilled.

13 And now come I to thee, and these things speak I in the world, that they might have my joy fulfilled in themselves.

14 I have given them thy word, and the world hath hated them, because they are not of the world, as I am not of the world.

15 I pray not that thou shouldest take them out of the world, but that thou keep them from evil.

16 They are not of the world, as I am not of the world.

17 Sanctify them with thy truth: thy word is truth.

18 As thou didst send me into the world, so have I sent them into the world.

19 And for their sakes sanctify I myself, that they also may be sanctified through the truth.

20 I pray not for these alone, but for them also which shall believe in me, through their word,

21 That they all may be one, as thou, O Father, art in me, and I in thee: even that they may be also one in us, that the world may believe that thou hast sent me.

22 And the glory that thou gavest me, I have given them, that they may be one, as we are one,

23 I in them, and thou in me, that they may be made perfect in one, and that the world may know, that thou hast sent me, and hast loved them, as thou hast loved me.

24 Father, I will that they which thou hast given me, be with me even where I am, that they may behold my glory, which thou hast given me: for thou lovest me before the foundation of the world.

25 O righteous Father, the world also hath not known thee, but I have known thee, and these have known, that thou hast sent me.

26 And I have declared unto them thy Name, and will declare it, that the love wherewith thou hast loved me, may be in them, and I in them.

John Chapter 18

1 When Jesus had spoken these things, he went forth with his disciples over the brook Cedron, where was a garden, into the which he entered, and his disciples.

2 And Judas which betrayed him, knew also the place: for Jesus oft times resorted thither with his disciples.

3 Judas then after he had received a band of men and officers of the high Priests, and of the Pharisees, came thither with lanterns and torches, and weapons.

4 Then Jesus, knowing all things that should come unto him, went forth and said unto them, Whom seek ye?

5 They answered him, Jesus of Nazareth. Jesus said unto them, I am he. Now Judas also which betrayed him, stood with them.

6 As soon then as he had said unto them, I am he, they went backwards, and fell to the ground.

7 Then he asked them again, Whom seek ye? And they said, Jesus of Nazareth.

8 Jesus answered, I said unto you, that I am he: therefore if ye seek me, let these go their way,

9 This was that the word might be fulfilled which he spake, Of them which thou gavest me, have I lost none.

10 Then Simon Peter having a sword, drew it, and smote the high Priest's servant, and cut off his right ear. Now the servants name was Malchus.

11 Then said Jesus unto Peter, Put up thy sword into the sheath: shall I not drink of the cup which my Father hath given me?

12 Then the band and the captain, and the officers of the Jews took Jesus, and bound him,

13 And led him away to Annas first (for he was father-in-law to Caiaphas, which was the high Priest that same year)

14 And Caiaphas was he, that gave counsel to the Jews, that it was expedient that one man should die for the people.

15 Now Simon Peter followed Jesus, and another disciple, and that disciple was known of the high Priest: therefore he went in with Jesus into the hall of the high Priest.

16 But Peter stood at the door without. Then went out the other disciple which was known unto the high Priest, and spake to her that kept the door, and brought in Peter.

17 Then said the maid that kept the door, unto Peter, Art not thou also one of this mans disciples? He said, I am not.

18 And the servants and officers stood there, which had made a fire of coals: for it was cold, and they warmed themselves. And Peter also stood among them and warmed himself.

19 (The high Priest then asked Jesus of his disciples, and of his doctrine.

20 Jesus answered him, I spake openly to the world: I ever taught in the Synagogue and in the Temple, whither the Jews resort continually, and in secret have I said nothing.

21 Why askest thou me? ask them which heard me what I said unto them: behold, they know what I said.

22 When he had spoken these things, one of the officers which stood by, smote Jesus with his rod, saying, Answerest thou the high Priest so?

23 Jesus answered him, If I have evil spoken, bear witness of the evil: but if I have well spoken, why smitest thou me?

24 Now Annas had sent him bound unto Caiaphas the high Priest)

25 And Simon Peter stood and warmed himself, and they said unto him, Art not thou also of his disciples? He denied it, and said, I am not.

26 One of the servants of the high Priest, his cousin whose ear Peter smote off, said, Did not I see thee in the garden with him?

27 Peter then denied again, and immediately the cock crew.

28 Then led they Jesus from Caiaphas into the common hall. Now it was morning and they themselves went not into the common hall, lest they should be defiled, but that they might eat the Passover.

29 Pilate then went out unto them, and said, What accusation bring ye against this man?

30 They answered and said unto him, If he were not an evil doer, we would not have delivered him unto thee.

31 Then said Pilate unto them, Take ye him, and judge him after your own Law. Then the Jews said unto him, It is not lawful for us to put any man to death.

32 It was that the word of Jesus might be fulfilled which he spake, signifying what death he should die.

33 So Pilate entered into the common hall again, and called Jesus, and said unto him, Art thou the King of the Jews?

34 Jesus answered him, Sayest thou that of thyself, or did other tell it thee of me?

35 Pilate answered, Am I a Jew? Thine own nation, and the high Priests have delivered thee unto me. What hast thou done?

36 Jesus answered, My kingdom is not of this world: if my kingdom were of this world, my servants would surely fight, that I should not be delivered to the Jews: but now is my kingdom not from hence.

37 Pilate then said unto him, Art thou a King then? Jesus answered, Thou sayest that I am a King: for this cause am I born, and for this cause came I into the world, that I should bear witness unto the truth: every one that is of the truth, heareth my voice.

38 Pilate said unto him, What is truth? And when he had said that, he went out again unto the Jews, and said unto them, I find in him no cause at all.

39 But you have a custom, that I should deliver you one loose at the Passover: will ye then that I loose unto you the King of the Jews?

40 Then cried they all again, saying, Not him, but Barabbas: now this Barabbas was a murderer.

John Chapter 19

1 Then Pilate took Jesus and scourged him.

2 And the soldiers platted a crown of thorns, and put it on his head, and they put on him a purple garment,

3 And said, Hail, King of the Jews. And they smote him with their rods.

4 Then Pilate went forth again, and said unto them, Behold, I bring him forth to you, that ye may know, that I find no fault in him at all.

5 Then came Jesus forth wearing a crown of thorns, and a purple garment. And Pilate said unto them, Behold the man.

6 Then when the high Priests and officers saw him, they cried, saying, Crucify, crucify him. Pilate said unto them, Take ye him and crucify him: for I find no fault in him.

7 The Jews answered him, We have a Law, and by our Law he ought to die, because he made himself the Son of God.

8 When Pilate then heard that word, he was the more afraid,

9 And went again into the common hall and said unto Jesus, Whence art thou? But Jesus gave him none answer.

10 Then said Pilate unto him, Speakest thou not unto me? Knowest thou not that I have power to crucify thee, and have power to loose thee?

11 Jesus answered, Thou couldest have no power at all against me, except it were given thee from above: therefore he that delivered me unto thee, hath the greater sin.

12 From thence forth Pilate sought to loose him, but the Jews cried, saying, If thou deliver him, thou art not Caesars friend: for whosoever maketh himself a King, speaketh against Caesar.

13 When Pilate heard that word, he brought Jesus forth, and sat down in the judgment seat in a place called the Pavement, and in Hebrew, Gabbatha.

14 And it was the Preparation of the Passover, and about the sixth hour: and he said unto the Jews, Behold your King.

15 But they cried, Away with him, away with him, crucify him. Pilate said unto them, Shall I crucify your King? The high Priests answered, We have no King but Caesar.

16 Then delivered he him unto them, to be crucified. And they took Jesus, and led him away.

17 And he bare his cross, and came into a place named of dead mens Skulls, which is called in Hebrew, Golgotha:

18 Where they crucified him, and two other with him, on either side one, and Jesus in the midst.

19 And Pilate wrote also a title and put it on the cross, and it was written, JESUS OF NAZARETH THE KING OF THE JEWS.

20 This title then read many of the Jews: for the place where Jesus was crucified, was near to the city: and it was written in Hebrew, Greek and Latin.

21 Then said the high Priests of the Jews to Pilate, Write not, The King of the Jews, but that he said, I am King of the Jews.

22 Pilate answered, What I have written, I have written.

23 Then the soldiers, when they had crucified Jesus, took his garments and made four parts, to every soldier a part and his coat: and the coat was without seam woven from the top throughout.

24 Therefore they said one to another, Let us not divide it, but cast lots for it, whose it shall be. This was that the Scripture might be fulfilled, which saith, They departed my garments among them, and on my coat did cast lots. So the soldiers did these things indeed.

25 Then stood by the cross of Jesus his mother, and his mothers sister, Mary the wife of Cleopas, and Mary Magdalene.

26 And when Jesus saw his mother, and the disciple standing by whom he loved, he said unto his mother, Woman, behold thy son.

27 Then said he to the disciple, Behold thy mother: and from that hour, the disciple took her home unto him.

28 After, when Jesus knew that all things were performed, that the Scripture might be fulfilled, he said, I thirst.

29 And there was set a vessel full of vinegar: and they filled a sponge with vinegar, and put it about an Hyssop stalk, and put it to his mouth.

30 Now when Jesus had received of the vinegar, he said, It is finished, and bowed his head, and gave up the ghost.

31 The Jews then (because it was the Preparation, that the bodies should not remain upon the cross on the Sabbath day: for that Sabbath was an high day) besought Pilate that their legs might be broken, and that they might be taken down.

32 Then came the soldiers and break the legs of the first, and of the other, which was crucified with Jesus.

33 But when they came to Jesus, and saw that he was dead already, they break not his legs.

34 But one of the soldiers with a spear pierced his side, and forthwith came there out blood and water.

35 And he that saw it, bare record, and his record is true: and he knoweth that he saith true , that ye might believe it.

36 For these things were done, that the Scripture should be fulfilled, Not a bone of him shall be broken.

37 And again another Scripture saith, They shall see him whom they have thrust through.

38 And after these things, Joseph of Arimathea (who was a disciple of Jesus, but secretly for fear of the Jews) besought Pilate that he might take down the body of Jesus. And Pilate gave him license. He came then and took Jesus body.

39 And there came also Nicodemus (which first came to Jesus by night) and brought of myrrh and aloes mingled together about an hundreth pound.

40 Then took they the body of Jesus, and wrapped it in linen clothes with the odors, as the manner of the Jews is to bury.

41 And in that place where Jesus was crucified, was a garden, and in the garden a new sepulcher, wherein was never man yet laid.

42 There then laid they Jesus, because of the Jews Preparation day, for the sepulcher was near.

John Chapter 20

1 Now the first day of the week came Mary Magdalene, early when it was yet dark, unto the sepulcher, and saw the stone taken away from the tomb.

2 Then she ran, and came to Simon Peter, and to the other disciple whom Jesus loved, and said unto them, They have taken away the Lord out of the sepulcher, and we know not where they have laid him.

3 Peter therefore went forth, and the other disciple, and they came unto the sepulcher.

4 So they ran both together, but the other disciple did outrun Peter, and came first to the sepulcher.

5 And he stooped down, and saw the linen clothes lying: yet went he not in.

6 Then came Simon Peter following him, and went into the sepulcher, and saw the linen clothes lie,

7 And the kerchief that was upon his head, not lying with the linen clothes, but wrapped together in a place by itself.

8 Then went in also the other disciple, which came first to the sepulcher, and he saw it, and believed.

9 For as yet they knew not the Scripture, That he must rise again from the dead.

10 And the disciples went away again unto their own home.

11 But Mary stood without at the sepulcher weeping: and as she wept, she bowed herself into the s epulcher,

12 And saw two Angels in white, sitting, the one at the head, and the other at the feet, where the body of Jesus had lain.

13 And they said unto her, Woman, why weepest thou? She said unto them, They have taken away my Lord, and I know not where they have laid him.

14 When she had thus said, she turned herself back and saw Jesus standing, and knew not that it was Jesus.

15 Jesus saith unto her, Woman, why weepest thou? whom seekest thou? She supposing that he had been the gardener, said unto him, Sir, if thou hast borne him hence, tell me where thou hast laid him, and I will take him away.

16 Jesus saith unto her, Mary. She turned herself, and said unto him, Rabboni, which is to say, Master.

17 Jesus saith unto her, Touch me not: for I am not yet ascended to my Father, but go to my brethren, and say unto them, I ascend unto my Father, and to your Father, and to my God, and your God.

18 Mary Magdalene came and told the disciples that she had seen the Lord, and that he had spoken these things unto her.

19 The same day then at night, which was the first day of the week, and when the doors were shut where the disciples were assembled for fear of the Jews, came Jesus and stood in the midst, and said to them, Peace be unto you.

20 And when he had so said, he showed unto them his hands, and his side. Then were the disciples glad when they had seen the Lord.

21 Then said Jesus to them again, Peace be unto you: as my Father sent me, so send I you.

22 And when he had said that, he breathed on them, and said unto them, Receive the Holy Ghost.

23 Whosoevers sins ye remit, they are remitted unto them: and whosoevers sins ye retain, they are retained.

24 But Thomas one of the twelve, called Didymus, was not with them when Jesus came.

25 The other disciples therefore said unto him, We have seen the Lord: but he said unto them, Except I see in his hands the print of the nails, and put my finger into the print of the nails, and put mine hand into his side, I will not believe it.

26 And eight days after, again his disciples were within, and Thomas with them. Then came Jesus, when the doors were shut, and stood in the midst, and said, Peace be unto you.

27 After said he to Thomas, Put thy finger here, and see mine hands, and put forth thine hand, and put it into my side, and be not faithless, but faithful.

28 Then Thomas answered, and said unto him, Thou art my Lord, and my God.

29 Jesus said unto him, Thomas, because thou hast seen me, thou believest: blessed are they that have not seen, and have believed.

30 And many other signs also did Jesus in the presence of his disciples, which are not written in this book.

31 But these things are written, that ye might believe, that Jesus is the Christ the Son of God, and that in believing ye might have life through his Name.

John Chapter 21

1 After these things, Jesus showed himself again to his disciples at the sea of Tiberias: and thus showed he himself.

2 There were together Simon Peter, and Thomas, which is called Didymus, and Nathanael of Cana in Galilee, and the sons of Zebedee, and two other of his disciples.

3 Simon Peter said unto them, I go a fishing. They said unto him, We also will go with thee. They went their way and entered into a ship straightway, and that night caught they nothing.

4 But when the morning was now come, Jesus stood on the shore: nevertheless the disciples knew not that it was Jesus.

5 Jesus then said unto them, Sirs, have ye any meat? They answered him, No.

6 Then he said unto them, Cast out the net on the right side of the ship, and ye shall find. So they cast out, and they were not able at all to draw it, for the multitude of fishes.

7 Therefore said the disciple whom Jesus loved, unto Peter, It is the Lord. When Simon Peter heard that it was the Lord, he girded his coat to him (for he was naked) and cast himself into the sea.

8 But the other disciples came by ship (for they were not far from land, but about two hundreth cubits) and they drew the net with fishes.

9 As soon then as they were come to land, they saw hot coals, and fish laid thereon, and bread.

10 Jesus said unto them, Bring of the fishes, which ye have now caught.

11 Simon Peter stepped forth and drew the net to land, full of great fishes, an hundreth, fifty and three: and albeit there were so many, yet was not the net broken.

12 Jesus said unto them, Come, and dine. And none of the disciples durst ask him, Who art thou? seeing they knew that he was the Lord.

13 Jesus then came and took bread, and gave them, and fish likewise.

14 This is now the third time that Jesus showed himself to his disciples, after that he was risen again from the dead.

15 So when they had dined, Jesus said to Simon Peter, Simon son of Jonas, lovest thou me more than these? He said unto him, Yea Lord, thou knowest that I love thee. He said unto him, Feed my lambs.

16 He said to him again the second time, Simon the son of Jonas, lovest thou me? He said unto him, Yea Lord, thou knowest that I love thee. He said unto him, Feed my sheep.

17 He said unto him the third time, Simon the son of Jonas, lovest thou me? Peter was sorry because he said to him the third time, Lovest thou me: and said unto him, Lord, thou knowest all things: thou knowest that I love thee. Jesus said unto him, Feed my sheep.

18 Verily, verily I say unto thee, When thou wast young, thou girded thyself, and walkest whither thou wouldest: but when thou shalt be old, thou shalt stretch forth thine hands, and another shall gird thee, and lead thee whither thou wouldest not.

19 And this spake he, signifying by what death he should glorify God. And when he had said this, he said to him, Follow me.

20 Then Peter turned about, and saw the disciple whom JESUS loved, following, which had also leaned on his breast at supper, and had said, Lord, which is he that betrayeth thee?

21 When Peter therefore saw him, he said to Jesus, Lord, what shall this man do?

22 Jesus said unto him, If I will that he tarry till I come, what is it to thee? Follow thou me.

23 Then went this word abroad among the brethren, that this disciple should not die. Yet Jesus said not to him, He shall not die: but if I will that he tarry till I come, what is it to thee?

24 This is that disciple, which testifieth of these things, and wrote these things, and we know that his testimony is true.

25 Now there are also many other things which Jesus did, the which if they should be written every one, I suppose the world could not contain the books that should be written, Amen.

THE ACTS OF THE HOLY APOSTLES WRITTEN BY LUKE THE EVANGELIST

Acts Chapter 1

1 I have made the former treatise, O Theophilus, of all that JESUS began to do, and teach,

2 Until the day, that he was taken up, after that he through the Holy Ghost, had given commandments unto the Apostles, whom he had chosen:

3 To whom also he presented himself alive after that he had suffered, by many infallible tokens, being seen of them by the space of forty days, and speaking of those things which appertain to the kingdom of God.

4 And when he had gathered them together, he commanded them, that they should not depart from Jerusalem, but to wait for the promise of the Father, which said he, ye have heard of me.

5 For John indeed baptized with water, but ye shall be baptized with the Holy Ghost within these few days.

6 When they therefore were come together, they asked of him, saying, Lord, wilt thou at this time restore the kingdom to Israel?

7 And he said unto them, It is not for you to know the times, or the seasons, which the Father hath put in his own power,

8 But ye shall receive power of the Holy Ghost, when he shall come on you: and ye shall be witnesses unto me both in Jerusalem, and in all Judea, and in Samaria, and unto the uttermost part of the earth.

9 And when he had spoken these things, while they beheld, he was taken up: for a cloud took him up out of their sight.

10 And while they looked steadfastly toward heaven, as he went, behold, two men stood by them in white apparel,

11 Which also said, Ye men of Galilee, why stand ye gazing into heaven? This Jesus which is taken up from you into heaven, shall so come, as ye have seen him go into heaven.

12 Then returned they unto Jerusalem from the mount that is called the Mount of Olives, which is near to Jerusalem, containing a Sabbath day's journey.

13 And when they were come in, they went up into an upper chamber, where abode both Peter, and James, and John, and Andrew, Philip, and Thomas, Bartholemew, and Matthew, James the son of Alpheus, and Simon Zelotes, and Judas, James' brother.

14 These all continued with one accord in prayer and supplication with the women, and Mary the mother of Jesus, and with his brethren.

15 And in those days Peter stood up in the midst of the disciples and said (now the number of names that were in one place, were about an hundred and twenty.)

16 Ye men and brethren, this Scripture must needs have been fulfilled, which the Holy Ghost by the mouth of David spake before of Judas, which was guide to them that took Jesus.

17 For he was numbered with us, and had obtained fellowship in this ministration.

18 He therefore hath purchased a field with the reward of iniquity: and when he had thrown down himself headlong, he burst asunder in the midst, and all his bowels gushed out.

19 And it is known unto all the inhabitants of Jerusalem, in so much, that that field is called in their own language, Aceldama, that is, The field of blood.

20 For it is written in the book of Psalms, Let his habitation be void, and let no man dwell therein: also, Let another take his charge.

21 Wherefore, of these men which have companied with us, all the time that the Lord Jesus was conversant among us,

22 Beginning from the baptism of John, unto the day that he was taken up from us, must one of them be made a witness with us of his resurrection.

23 And they presented two, Joseph called Barsabas, whose surname was Justus, and Matthias.

24 And they prayed, saying, Thou Lord, which knowest the hearts of all men, show whether of these two thou hast chosen,

25 That he may take the room of this ministration and Apostleship, from which Judas hath gone astray, to go to his own place.

26 Then they gave forth their lots: and the lot fell on Matthias, and he was by a common consent counted with the Eleven Apostles

Acts Chapter 2

1 And when the day of Pentecost was come, they were all with one accord in one place.

2 And suddenly there came a sound from heaven, as of a rushing and mighty wind, and it filled all the house where they sat.

3 And there appeared unto them cloven tongues, like fire, and it sat upon each of them.

4 And they were all filled with the Holy Ghost, and began to speak with other tongues, as the Spirit gave them utterance.

5 And there were dwelling at Jerusalem Jews, men that feared God, of every nation under heaven.

6 Now when this was noised, the multitude came together and were astonished, because that every man heard them speak his own language.

7 And they wondered all, and marveled, saying among themselves, Behold, are not all these which speak, of Galilee?

8 How then hear we every man our own language, wherein we were born?

9 Parthians, and Medes, and Elamites, and the inhabitants of Mesopotamia, and of Judea, and of Cappadocia, of Pontus, and Asia,

10 And of Phrygia, and Pamphylia, of Egypt, and of the parts of Libya, which is beside Cyrene, and strangers of Rome, and Jews, and proselytes,

11 Cretes, and Arabians: we heard them speak in our own tongues the wonderful works of God.

12 They were all then amazed, and doubted, saying one to another, What may this be?

13 And others mocked, and said, They are full of new wine.

14 But Peter standing with the Eleven, lift up his voice, and said unto them, Ye men of Judea, and ye all that inhabit Jerusalem, be this known unto you, and hearken unto my words.

15 For these are not drunken, as ye suppose, since it is but the third hour of the day.

16 But this is that, which was spoken by the Prophet Joel,

17 And it shall be in the last days, saith God, I will pour out of my Spirit upon all flesh, and your sons, and your daughters shall prophesy, and your young men shall see visions, and your old men shall dream dreams.

18 And on my servants, and on mine handmaids I will pour out of my Spirit in those days, and they shall prophesy.

19 And I will show wonders in heaven above, and tokens in the earth beneath, blood, and fire, and the vapor of smoke.

20 The Sun shall be turned into darkness, and the moon into blood, before that great and notable day of the Lord come.

21 And it shall be, that whosoever shall call on the Name of the Lord, shall be saved.

22 Ye men of Israel, hear these words, JESUS of Nazareth, a man approved of God among you with great works, and wonders, and signs, which God did by him in the midst of you, as ye yourselves also know:

23 Him, I say, have ye taken by the hands of the wicked, being delivered by the determinate counsel, and foreknowledge of God, and have crucified and slain:

24 Whom God hath raised up, and loosed the sorrows of death, because it was unpossible that he should be holden of it.

25 For David saith concerning him, I beheld the Lord always before me: for he is at my right hand, that I should not be shaken.

26 Therefore did mine heart rejoice, and my tongue was glad, and moreover also my flesh shall rest in hope,

27 Because thou wilt not leave my soul in grave, neither wilt suffer thine holy one to see corruption.

28 Thou hast showed me the ways of life, and shalt make me full of joy with thy countenance.

29 Men and brethren, I may boldly speak unto you of the Patriarch David, that he is both dead and buried, and his sepulcher remaineth with us unto this day.

30 Therefore, seeing he was a Prophet, and knew that God had sworn with an oath to him, that of the fruit of his loins he would raise up Christ concerning the flesh to set him upon his throne,

31 He knowing this before, spake of the resurrection of Christ, that his soul should not be left in grave, neither his flesh should see corruption.

32 This Jesus hath God raised up, whereof we all are witnesses.

33 Since then that he by the right hand of God hath been exalted, and hath received of his Father the promise of the Holy Ghost, he hath shed forth this which ye now see and hear.

34 For David is not ascended into heaven, but he saith, The Lord said to my Lord, Sit at my right hand,

35 Until I make thine enemies thy footstool.

36 Therefore, let all the house of Israel know for a surety, that God hath made him both Lord, and Christ, this Jesus, I say, whom ye have crucified.

37 Now when they heard it, they were pricked in their hearts,and said unto Peter and the other Apostles, Men and brethren, what shall we do?

38 Then Peter said unto them, Amend your lives, and be baptized every one of you in the Name of Jesus Christ for the remission of sins: and ye shall receive the gift of the Holy Ghost.

39 For the promise is made unto you, and to your children, and to all that are afar off, even as many as the Lord our God shall call.

40 And with many other words he besought, and exhorted them, saying, Save yourselves from this froward generation.

41 Then they that gladly received his word, were baptized: and the same day, there were added to the Church about three thousand souls.

42 And they continued in the Apostles' doctrine, and fellowship, and breaking of bread, and prayers.

43 And fear came upon every soul: and many wonders and signs were done by the Apostles.

44 And all that believed, were in one place, and had all things common.

45 And they sold their possessions and goods and parted them to all men, as every one had need.

46 And they continued daily with one accord in the Temple, and breaking bread at home, did eat their meat together with gladness and singleness of heart,

47 Praising God, and had favor with all the people: and the Lord added to the Church from day to day, such as should be saved.

Acts Chapter 3

1 Now Peter and John went up together into the Temple, at the ninth hour of prayer.

2 And a certain man which was a cripple from his mother's womb, was carried, whom they laid daily at the gate of the Temple called Beautiful, to ask alms of them that entered into the Temple.

3 Who seeing Peter and John, that they would enter into the Temple, desired to receive an alms.

4 And Peter earnestly beholding him with John, said, Look on us.

5 And he gave heed unto them, trusting to receive some thing of them.

6 Then said Peter, Silver and gold have I none, but such as I have, that give I thee: In the Name of Jesus Christ of Nazareth rise up and walk.

7 And he took him by the right hand, and lift him up, and immediately his feet and ankle bones received strength.

8 And he leaped up, stood, and walked, and entered with them into the Temple, walking and leaping, and praising God.

9 And all the people saw him walk, and praising God,

10 And they knew him, that it was he which sat for the alms at the Beautiful gate of the Temple: and they were amazed, and sore astonished at that, which was come unto him.

11 And as the cripple which was healed, held Peter and John, all the people ran amazed unto them in the porch which is called Solomon's.

12 So when Peter saw it, he answered unto the people, Ye men of Israel, why marvel ye at this? or why look ye so steadfastly on us, as though by our own power or godliness, we had made this man go?

13 The GOD of Abraham, and Isaac, and Jacob, the GOD of our fathers hath glorified his Son Jesus, whom ye betrayed, and denied in the presence of Pilate, when he had judged him to be delivered.

14 But ye denied the holy one and the just, and desired a murderer to be given you,

15 And killed the Lord of life, whom God hath raised from the dead, whereof we are witnesses.

16 And his Name hath made this man sound, whom ye see, and know, through faith in his Name: and the faith which is by him, hath given to him this disposition of his whole body in the presence of you all.

17 And now brethren, I know that through ignorance ye did it, as did also your governors.

18 But those things which God before had showed by the mouth of all his Prophets, that Christ should suffer, he hath thus fulfilled.

19 Amend your lives therefore, and turn, that your sins may be put away, when the time of refreshing shall come from the presence of the Lord.

20 And he shall send Jesus Christ, which before was preached unto you,

21 Whom the heaven must contain until the time that all things be restored, which God had spoken by the mouth of all his holy Prophets since the world began.

22 For Moses said unto the Fathers, The Lord your God shall raise up unto you a Prophet, even of your brethren like unto me: ye shall hear him in all things, whatsoever he shall say unto you.

23 For it shall be that every person which shall not hear that Prophet, shall be destroyed out of the people.

24 Also all the Prophets from Samuel, and thenceforth as many as have spoken, have likewise foretold of these days.

25 Ye are the children of the Prophets, and of the covenant, which God hath made unto our fathers, saying to Abraham, Even in thy seed shall all the kindreds of the earth be blessed.

26 First unto you hath God raised up his Son Jesus, and him he hath sent to bless you, in turning every one of you from your iniquities.

Acts Chapter 4

1 And as they spake unto the people, the Priests and the Captain of the Temple, and the Sadducees came upon them,

2 Taking it grievously that they taught the people, and preached in Jesus' Name the resurrection from the dead.

3 And they laid hands on them, and put them in hold, until the next day: for it was now eventide.

4 Howbeit, many of them which heard the word, believed, and the number of the men was about five thousand.

5 And it came to pass on the morrow, that their rulers, and Elders, and Scribes, were gathered together at Jerusalem,

6 And Annas the chief Priest, and Caiaphas, and John, and Alexander, and as many as were of the kindred of the high Priests.

7 And when they had set them before them, they asked, By what power, or in what Name have ye done this?

8 Then Peter full of the Holy Ghost, said unto them, Ye rulers of the people, and Elders of Israel,

9 Forasmuch as we this day are examined of the good deed done to the impotent man, to wit, by what means he is made whole,

10 Be it known unto you all, and to all the people of Israel, that by the Name of Jesus Christ of Nazareth, whom ye have crucified, whom God raised again from the dead, even by him doth this man stand here before you, whole.

11 This is the stone cast aside of you builders, which is become the head of the corner.

12 Neither is there salvation in any other: for among men there is given none other name under heaven, whereby we must be saved.

13 Now when they saw the boldness of Peter and John, and understood that they were unlearned men and without knowledge, they marveled, and knew them, that they had been with Jesus:

14 And beholding also the man which was healed standing with them, they had nothing to say against it.

15 Then they commanded them to go aside out of the Council, and conferred among themselves,

16 Saying, What shall we do to these men? for surely a manifest sign is done by them, and it is openly known to all them that dwell in Jerusalem: and we cannot deny it.

17 But that it be noised no farther among the people, let us threaten and charge them, that they speak henceforth to no man in this Name.

18 So they called them, and commanded them, that in no wise they should speak or teach in the Name of Jesus.

19 But Peter and John answered unto them, and said, Whether it be right in the sight of God, to obey you rather then God, judge ye.

20 For we cannot but speak the things which we have seen and heard.

21 So they threatened them, and let them go, and found nothing how to punish them, because of the people: for all men praised God for that which was done.

22 For the man was above forty years old, on whom this miracle of healing was showed.

23 Then as soon as they were let go, they came to their fellows, and showed all that the high Priests and Elders had said unto them.

24 And when they heard it, they lift up their voices to God with one accord, and said, O Lord, thou art the God which hast made the heaven and the earth, the sea, and all things that are in them.

25 Which by the mouth of thy servant David hast said, Why did the Gentiles rage, and the people imagine vain things?

26 The Kings of the earth assembled, and the rulers came together against the Lord, and against his Christ.

27 For doubtless, against thine holy Son Jesus, whom thou hadst anointed, both Herod and Pontius Pilate, with the Gentiles and the people of Israel gathered themselves together,

28 To do whatsoever thine hand, and thy counsel had determined before to be done.

29 And now, O Lord, behold their threatenings, and grant unto thy servants with all boldness to speak thy word,

30 So that thou stretch forth thine hand, that healing, and signs, and wonders may be done by the Name of thine holy Son Jesus.

31 And when as they had prayed, the place was shaken where they were assembled together, and they were all filled with the Holy Ghost, and they spake the word of God boldly.

32 And the multitude of them that believed, were of one heart, and of one soul: neither any of them said, that anything of that which he possessed, was his own, but they had all things common.

33 And with great power gave the Apostles witness of the resurrection of the Lord Jesus: and great grace was upon them all.

34 Neither was there any among them, that lacked: for as many as were possessors of lands or houses, sold them, and brought the price of the things that were sold,

35 And laid it down at the Apostles' feet, and it was distributed unto every man, according as he had need.

36 Also Joses which was called of the Apostles, Barnabas (that is by interpretation the son of consolation) being a Levite, and of the country of Cyprus,

37 Where as he had land, sold it, and brought the money, and laid it down at the Apostles' feet.

Acts Chapter 5

1 But a certain man named Ananias, with Sapphira his wife, sold a possession,

2 And kept away part of the price, his wife also being of counsel, and brought a certain part, and laid it down at the Apostles' feet.

3 Then said Peter, Ananias, why hath Satan filled thine heart, that thou shouldest lie unto the Holy Ghost, and keep away part of the price of the possession?

4 Whilst it remained, appertained it not unto thee? and after it was sold, was it not in thine own power? how is it that thou hast conceived this thing in thine heart? thou hast not lied unto men, but unto God.

5 Now when Ananias heard these words, he fell down, and gave up the ghost. Then great fear came on all them that heard these things.

6 And the young men rose up, and took him up, and carried him out, and buried him.

7 And it came to pass about the space of three hours after, that his wife came in, ignorant of that which was done.

8 And Peter said unto her, Tell me, sold ye the land for so much? And she said, Yea, for so much.

9 Then Peter said unto her, Why have ye agreed together, to tempt the Spirit of the Lord? behold, the feet of them which have buried thine husband, are at the door, and shall carry thee out.

10 Then she fell down straightway at his feet, and yielded up the ghost: and the young men came in, and found her dead, and carried her out, and buried her by her husband.

11 And great fear came on all the Church, and on as many as heard these things.

12 Thus by the hands of the Apostles were many signs and wonders showed among the people (and they were all with one accord in Solomon's porch.

13 And of the other durst no man join himself to them: nevertheless the people magnified them,

14 Also the number of them that believed in the Lord, both of men and women, grew more and more)

15 Insomuch that they brought the sick into the streets, and laid them on beds and couches, that at the least way the shadow of Peter, when he came by, might shadow some of them.

16 There came also a multitude out of the cities round about unto Jerusalem, bringing sick folks, and them which were vexed with unclean spirits, who were all healed.

17 Then the chief Priest rose up, and all they that were with him (which was the sect of the Sadducees) and were full of indignation,

18 And laid hands on the Apostles, and put them in the common prison.

19 But the Angel of the Lord, by night opened the prison doors, and brought them forth, and said,

20 Go your way, and stand in the Temple, and speak to the people all the words of this life.

21 So when they heard it, they entered into the Temple early in the morning and taught. And the chief Priest came, and they that were with him, and called the Council together, and all the Elders of the children of Israel, and sent to the prison, to cause them to be brought.

22 But when the officers came, and found them not in the prison, they returned and told it,

23 Saying, Certainly we found the prison shut as sure as was possible, and the keepers standing without, before the doors: but when we had opened, we found no man within.

24 Then when the chief Priest, and the captain of the Temple, and the high Priests heard these things, they doubted of them, whereunto this would grow.

25 Then came one and showed them, saying, Behold, the men that ye put in prison, are standing in the Temple, and teach the people.

26 Then went the captain with the officers, and brought them without violence (for they feared the people, lest they should have been stoned)

27 And when they had brought them, they set them before the Council, and the chief Priest asked them,

28 Saying, Did not we straightly command you, that ye should not teach in this Name? and behold, ye have filled Jerusalem with your doctrine, and ye would bring this man's blood upon us.

29 Then Peter and the Apostles answered, and said, We ought rather to obey God than men.

30 The God of our fathers hath raised up Jesus, whom ye slew, and hanged on a tree.

31 Him hath God lift up with his right hand, to be a Prince and a Savior, to give repentance to Israel, and forgiveness of sins.

32 And we are his witnesses concerning these things which we say: yea, and the Holy Ghost, whom God hath given to them that obey him.

33 Now when they heard it, they burst for anger, and consulted to slay them.

34 Then stood there up in the Council a certain Pharisee named Gamaliel, a doctor of the Law, honored of all the people, and commanded to put the Apostles forth a little space,

35 And said unto them, Men of Israel, take heed to yourselves, what ye intend to do touching these men.

36 For before these times, rose up Theudas boasting himself, to whom resorted a number of men, about a four hundred, who was slain: and they all which obeyed him, were scattered, and brought to nought.

37 After this man, arose up Judas of Galilee, in the days of the tribute, and drew away much people after him: he also perished, and all that obeyed him, were scattered abroad.

38 And now I say unto you, Refrain yourselves from these men, and let them alone: for if this counsel, or this work be of men, it will come to nought:

39 But if it be of God, ye cannot destroy it, lest ye be found even fighters against God.

40 And to him they agreed, and called the Apostles: and when they had beaten them, they commanded that they should not speak in the Name of Jesus, and let them go.

41 So they departed from the Council, rejoicing, that they were counted worthy to suffer rebuke for his Name.

42 And daily in the Temple, and from house to house they ceased not to teach, and preach Jesus Christ.

Acts Chapter 6

1 And in those days, as the number of the disciples grew, there arose a murmuring of the Grecians towards the Hebrews, because their widows were neglected in the daily ministering.

2 Then the twelve called the multitude of the disciples together, and said, It is not meet that we should leave the word of God to serve the tables.

3 Wherefore brethren, look ye out among you seven men of honest report, and full of the Holy Ghost, and of wisdom, which we may appoint to this business.

4 And we will give ourselves continually to prayer, and to the ministration of the word.

5 And the saying pleased the whole multitude: and they chose Steven a man full of faith and of the Holy Ghost, and Philip, and Prochorus, and Nicanor, and Timon, and Parmenas, and Nicolas a Proselyte of Antiochia,

6 Which they set before the Apostles: and they prayed, and laid their hands on them.

7 And the word of God increased, and the number of the disciples was multiplied in Jerusalem greatly, and a great company of the Priests were obedient to the faith.

8 Now Steven full of faith and power, did great wonders and miracles among the people.

9 Then there arose certain of the Synagogue, which are called Libertines, and Cyrenians, and of Alexandria, and of them of Cilicia, and of Asia, and disputed with Steven.

10 But they were not able to resist the wisdom, and the Spirit by the which he spake.

11 Then they suborned men, which said, We have heard him speak blasphemous words against Moses, and God.

12 Thus they moved the people and the Elders, and the Scribes: and running upon him, caught him, and brought him to the Council,

13 And set forth false witnesses, which said, This man ceaseth not to speak blasphemous words against this holy place, and the Law.

14 For we have heard him say, that this Jesus of Nazareth shall destroy this place, and shall change the ordinances, which Moses gave us.

15 And as all that sat in the Council, looked steadfastly on him, they saw his face as it had been the face of an Angel.

Acts Chapter 7

1 Then said the chief Priest, Are these things so?

2 And he said, Ye men, brethren and fathers, hearken. The God of glory appeared unto our father Abraham, while he was in Mesopotamia, before he dwelt in Charran,

3 And said unto him, Come out of thy country, and from thy kindred, and come into the land, which I shall show thee.

4 Then came he out of the land of the Chaldeans, and dwelt in Charran. And after that his father was dead, God brought him from thence into this land, wherein ye now dwell,

5 And he gave him none inheritance in it, no, not the breadth of a foot: yet he promised that he would give it to him for a possession, and to his seed after him, when as yet he had no child.

6 But God spake thus, that his seed should be a sojourner in a strange land, and that they should keep it in bondage, and entreat it evil four hundred years.

7 But the nation to whom they shall be in bondage, will I judge, saith God: and after that, they shall come forth and serve me in this place.

8 He gave him also the covenant of circumcision: and so Abraham begat Isaac, and circumcised him the eight day: and Isaac begat Jacob, and Jacob the twelve Patriarchs.

9 And the Patriarchs moved with envy sold Joseph into Egypt: but God was with him,

10 And delivered him out of all his afflictions, and gave him favor and wisdom in the sight of Pharaoh King of Egypt, who made him governor over Egypt, and over his whole house.

11 Then came there a famine over all the land of Egypt and Canaan, and great affliction, that our fathers found no sustenance.

12 But when Jacob heard that there was corn in Egypt, he sent our fathers first.

13 And at the second time, Joseph was known of his brethren, and Joseph's kindred was made known unto Pharaoh.

14 Then sent Joseph and caused his father to be brought, and all his kindred, even threescore and fifteen souls.

15 So Jacob went down into Egypt, and he died, and our fathers,

16 And were removed into Sychem, and were put in the sepulcher, that Abraham had bought for money of the sons of Emor, son of Sychem.

17 But when the time of the promise drew near, which God had sworn to Abraham, the people grew and multiplied in Egypt,

18 Till another King arose, which knew not Joseph.

19 The same dealt subtly with our kindred, and evil entreated our fathers, and made them to cast out their young children, that they should not remain alive.

20 The same time was Moses born, and was acceptable unto God, which was nourished up in his father's house three months.

21 And when he was cast out, Pharaoh's daughter took him up, and nourished him for her own son.

22 And Moses was learned in all the wisdom of the Egyptians, and was mighty in words and in deeds.

23 Now when he was full forty year old, it came into his heart to visit his brethren, the children of Israel.

24 And when he saw one of them suffer wrong, he defended him, and avenged his quarrel that had the harm done to him, and smote the Egyptian.

25 For he supposed his brethren would have understand, that God by his hand should give them deliverance: but they understood it not.

26 And the next day, he showed himself unto them as they strove, and would have set them at one again, saying, Sirs, ye are brethren: why do ye wrong one to another?

27 But he that did his neighbor wrong, thrust him away, saying, Who made thee a prince, and a judge over us?

28 Wilt thou kill me, as thou didst the Egyptian yesterday?

29 Then fled Moses at that saying, and was a stranger in the land of Median, where he begat two sons.

30 And when forty years were expired, there appeared to him in the wilderness of Mount Sinai, an Angel of the Lord in a flame of fire, in a bush.

31 And when Moses saw it, he wondered at the sight: and as he drew near to consider it, the voice of the Lord came unto him, saying,

32 I am the God of thy fathers, the God of Abraham, and the God of Isaac, and the God of Jacob. Then Moses trembled, and durst not behold it.

33 Then the Lord said to him, Put off thy shoes from thy feet: for the place where thou standest, is holy ground.

34 I have seen, I have seen the affliction of my people, which is in Egypt, and I have heard their groaning, and am come down to deliver them: and now come, and I will send thee into Egypt.

35 This Moses whom they forsook, saying, Who made thee a prince and a judge? the same God sent for a prince, and a deliverer by the hands of the Angel, which appeared to him in the bush.

36 He brought them out, doing wonders, and miracles in the land of Egypt, and in the Red Sea, and in the wilderness forty years.

37 This is that Moses, which said unto the children of Israel, A Prophet shall the Lord your God raise up unto you, even of your brethren, like unto me: him shall ye hear.

38 This is he that was in the Congregation, in the wilderness with the Angel, which spake to him in mount Sinai, and with our fathers, who received the lively oracles to give unto us.

39 To whom our fathers would not obey, but refused, and in their hearts turned back again into Egypt,

40 Saying unto Aaron, Make us gods that may go before us: for we know not what is become of this Moses that brought us out of the land of Egypt.

41 And they made a calf in those days, and offered sacrifice unto the idol, and rejoiced in the works of their own hands.

42 Then God turned himself away, and gave them up to serve the host of heaven, as it is written in the book of the Prophets, O house of Israel, have ye offered to me slain beasts and sacrifices by the space of forty years in the wilderness?

43 And ye took up the tabernacle of Moloch, and the star of your god Remphan, figures, which ye made to worship them: therefore I will carry you away beyond Babylon.

44 Our fathers had the tabernacle of witness in the wilderness, as he had appointed, speaking unto Moses, that he should make it according to the fashion that he had seen.

45 Which tabernacle also our fathers received, and brought in with Jesus into the possession of the Gentiles, which God drove out before our fathers, unto the days of David:

46 Who found favor before God, and desired that he might find a tabernacle for the God of Jacob.

47 But Solomon built him an house.

48 Howbeit the most High dwelleth not in temples made with hands, as saith the Prophet,

49 Heaven is my throne, and earth is my footstool: what house will ye build for me, saith the Lord? or what place is it that I should rest in?

50 Hath not mine hand made all these things?

51 Ye stiffnecked and of uncircumcised hearts and ears, ye have always resisted the Holy Ghost: as your fathers did, so do you.

52 Which of the Prophets have not your fathers persecuted? And they have slain them, which showed before of the coming of that Just, of whom ye are now the betrayers and murderers,

53 Which have received the Law by the ordinance of Angels, and have not kept it.

54 But when they heard these things, their hearts burst for anger, and they gnashed at him with their teeth.

55 But he being full of the Holy Ghost, looked steadfastly into heaven, and saw the glory of God, and Jesus standing at the right hand of God,

56 And said, Behold, I see the heavens open, and the Son of man standing at the right hand of God.

57 Then they gave a shout with a loud voice, and stopped their ears, and ran upon him all at once,

58 And cast him out of the city, and stoned him: and the witnesses laid down their clothes at a young man's feet, named Saul.

59 And they stoned Steven, who called on God, and said, Lord Jesus, receive my spirit.

60 And he kneeled down, and cried with a loud voice, Lord, lay not this sin to their charge. And when he had thus spoken, he slept.

Acts Chapter 8

1 And Saul consented to his death, and at that time, there was a great persecution against the Church which was at Jerusalem, and they were all scattered abroad through the regions of Judea and of Samaria, except the Apostles.

2 Then certain men fearing God, carried Steven among them, to be buried, and made great lamentation for him.

3 But Saul made havoc of the Church, and entered into every house, and drew out both men and women, and put them into prison.

4 Therefore they that were scattered abroad, went to and fro preaching the word.

5 Then came Philip into the city of Samaria, and preached Christ unto them.

6 And the people gave heed unto those things which Philip spake, with one accord, hearing and seeing the miracles which he did.

7 For unclean spirits crying with a loud voice, came out of many that were possessed of them: and many taken with palsies, and that halted, were healed.

8 And there was great joy in that city.

9 And there was before in the city a certain man called Simon, which used witchcraft, and bewitched the people of Samaria, saying, that he himself was some great man.

10 To whom they gave heed from the least to the greatest, saying, This man is the great power of God.

11 And they gave heed unto him, because that of long time he had bewitched them with sorceries.

12 But as soon as they believed Philip, which preached the things that concerned the kingdom of God, and in the Name of Jesus Christ, they were baptized both men and women.

13 Then Simon himself believed also and was baptized, and continued with Philip, and wondered, when he saw the signs and great miracles which were done.

14 Now when the Apostles, which were at Jerusalem, heard say, that Samaria had received the word of God, they sent unto them Peter and John.

15 Which when they were come down, prayed for them, that they might receive the Holy Ghost.

16 (For as yet, he was come down on none of them, but they were baptized only in the Name of the Lord Jesus.)

17 Then laid they their hands on them, and they received the Holy Ghost.

18 And when Simon saw, that through laying on of the Apostles hands the Holy Ghost was given, he offered them money,

19 Saying, Give me also this power, that on whomsoever I lay the hands, he may receive the Holy Ghost.

20 Then said Peter unto him, Thy money perish with thee, because thou thinkest that the gift of God may be obtained with money.

21 Thou hast neither part nor fellowship in this business: for thine heart is not right in the sight of God.

22 Repent therefore of this thy wickedness, and pray God, that if it be possible, the thought of thine heart may be forgiven thee.

23 For I see that thou art in the gall of bitterness, and in the bond of iniquity.

24 Then answered Simon, and said, Pray ye to the Lord for me, that none of these things which ye have spoken, come upon me.

25 So they, when they had testified and preached the word of the Lord, returned to Jerusalem, and preached the Gospel in many towns of the Samaritans.

26 Then the Angel of the Lord spake unto Philip, saying, Arise, and go toward the South unto the way that goeth down from Jerusalem unto Gaza, which is waste.

27 And he arose and went on: and behold, a certain Eunuch of Ethiopia Candaces' the Queen of the Ethiopian's chief Governor, who had the rule of all her treasure, and came to Jerusalem to worship:

28 And as he returned sitting in his chariot, he read Isaiah the Prophet.

29 Then the Spirit said unto Philip, Go near and join thyself to yonder chariot.

30 And Philip ran thither, and heard him read the Prophet Isaiah, and said, But understandest thou what thou readest?

31 And he said, How can I, except I had a guide? And he desired Philip, that he would come up and sit with him.

32 Now the place of the Scripture which he read, was this, He was led as a sheep to the slaughter: and like a lamb dumb before his shearer, so opened he not his mouth.

33 In his humility his judgment hath been exalted: but who shall declare his generation? for his life is taken from the earth.

34 Then the Eunuch answered Philip, and said, I pray thee of whom speaketh the Prophet this? of himself, or of some other man?

35 Then Philip opened his mouth, and began at the same Scripture, and preached unto him Jesus.

36 And as they went on their way, they came unto a certain water, and the Eunuch said, See, here is water: what doth let me to be baptized?

37 And Philip said unto him, If thou believest with all thine heart, thou mayest. Then he answered, and said, I believe that that Jesus Christ is the Son of God.

38 Then he commanded the chariot to stand still: and they went down both into the water, both Philip and the Eunuch, and he baptized him.

39 And as soon as they were come up out of the water, the Spirit of the Lord caught away Philip, that the Eunuch saw him no more: so he went on his way rejoicing.

40 But Philip was found at Azotus, and he walked to and fro preaching in all the cities, till he came to Cesarea.

Acts Chapter 9

1 And Saul yet breathing out threatenings and slaughter against the disciples of the Lord, went unto the high Priest,

2 And desired of him letters to Damascus to the Synagogues, that if he found any that were of that way (either men or women) he might bring them bound unto Jerusalem.

3 Now as he journeyed, it came to pass that as he was come near to Damascus, suddenly there shined round about him a light from heaven.

4 And he fell to the earth, and heard a voice, saying to him, Saul, Saul, why persecutest thou me?

5 And he said, Who art thou, Lord? And the Lord said, I am Jesus whom thou persecutest: it is hard for thee to kick against pricks.

6 He then both trembling and astonished, said, Lord, what wilt thou that I do? And the Lord said unto him, Arise and go into the city, and it shall be told thee what thou shalt do.

7 The men also which journeyed with him, stood amazed, hearing his voice, but seeing no man.

8 And Saul arose from the ground, and opened his eyes, but saw no man. Then led they him by the hand, and brought him into Damascus,

9 Where he was three days without sight, and neither ate nor drank.

10 And there was a certain disciple at Damascus named Ananias, and to him said the Lord in a vision, Ananias. And he said, Behold, I am here, Lord.

11 Then the Lord said unto him, Arise, and go into the street which is called Straight, and seek in the house of Judas after one called Saul of Tarsus: for behold, he prayeth.

12 (And he saw in a vision a man named Ananias coming in to him, and putting his hands on him, that he might receive his sight.)

13 Then Ananias answered, Lord, I have heard by many of this man, how much evil he hath done to thy saints at Jerusalem.

14 Moreover here he hath authority of the high Priests, to bind all that call on thy Name.

15 Then the Lord said unto him, Go thy way: for he is a chosen vessel unto me, to bear my Name before the Gentiles, and Kings, and the children of Israel.

16 For I will show him, how many things he must suffer for my Name's sake.

17 Then Ananias went his way, and entered into the house, and put his hands on him, and said, Brother Saul, the Lord hath sent me (even Jesus that appeared unto thee in the way as thou camest) that thou mightest receive thy sight, and be filled with the Holy Ghost.

18 And immediately there fell from his eyes as it had been scales, and suddenly he received sight, and arose, and was baptized,

19 And received meat, and was strengthened. So was Saul certain days with the disciples which were at Damascus.

20 And straightway he preached Christ in the Synagogues, that he was the Son of God,

21 So that all that heard him, were amazed, and said, Is not this he, that destroyed them which called on this Name in Jerusalem, and came hither for that intent, that he should bring them bound unto the high Priests?

22 But Saul increased the more in strength, and confounded the Jews which dwelt at Damascus, confirming, that this was the Christ.

23 And after that many days were fulfilled, the Jews took counsel together, to kill him.

24 But their laying await was known of Saul: now they watched the gates day and night, that they might kill him.

25 Then the disciples took him by night, and put him through the wall, and let him down in a basket.

26 And when Saul was come to Jerusalem, he assayed to join himself with the disciples: but they were all afraid of him, and believed not that he was a disciple.

27 But Barnabas took him, and brought him to the Apostles, and declared to them, how he had seen the Lord in the way, and that he had spoken unto him, and how he had spoken boldly at Damascus in the Name of Jesus.

28 And he was conversant with them at Jerusalem,

29 And spake boldly in the Name of the Lord Jesus, and spake and disputed with the Grecians: but they went about to slay him.

30 But when the brethren knew it, they brought him to Cesarea, and sent him forth to Tarsus.

31 Then had the Churches rest through all Judea, and Galilee, and Samaria, and were edified, and walked in the fear of the Lord, and were multiplied by the comfort of the Holy Ghost.

32 And it came to pass, as Peter walked throughout all quarters, he came also to the saints which dwelt at Lydda.

33 And there he found a certain man named AEneas, which had kept his bed eight years, and was sick of the palsy.

34 Then said Peter unto him, AEneas, Jesus Christ maketh thee whole: arise and make up thy bed. And he arose immediately.

35 And all that dwelt at Lydda and Saron, saw him, and turned to the Lord.

36 There was also at Joppa a certain woman, a disciple named Tabitha (which by interpretation is called Dorcas) she was full of good works and alms which she did.

37 And it came to pass in those days, that she was sick and died: and when they had washed her, they laid her in an upper chamber.

38 Now forasmuch as Lydda was near to Joppa, and the disciples had heard that Peter was there, they sent unto him two men, desiring that he would not delay to come unto them.

39 Then Peter arose and came with them: and when he was come, they brought him into the upper chamber, where all the widows stood by him weeping, and showing the coats and garments, which Dorcas made, while she was with them.

40 But Peter put them all forth, and kneeled down, and prayed, and turned him to the body, and said, Tabitha, arise. And she opened her eyes, and when she saw Peter, sat up.

41 Then he gave her the hand and lift her up, and called the saints and widows, and restored her alive.

42 And it was known throughout all Joppa, and many believed in the Lord.

43 And it came to pass that he tarried many days in Joppa with one Simon a tanner.

Acts Chapter 10

1 Furthermore there was a certain man in Cesarea called Cornelius, a captain of the band called the Italian band,

2 A devout man, and one that feared God with all his household, which gave much alms to the people, and prayed God continually.

3 He saw in a vision evidently (about the ninth hour of the day) an Angel of God coming in to him, and saying unto him, Cornelius.

4 But when he looked on him, he was afraid, and said, What is it, Lord? And he said unto him, Thy prayers and thine alms are come up into remembrance before God.

5 Now therefore send men to Joppa, and call for Simon, whose surname is Peter.

6 He lodgeth with one Simon a tanner, whose house is by the sea side: he shall tell thee what thou oughtest to do.

7 And when the Angel which spake unto Cornelius, was departed, he called two of his servants, and a soldier that feared God, one of them that waited on him,

8 And told them all things, and sent them to Joppa.

9 On the morrow as they went on their journey, and drew near unto the city, Peter went up upon the house to pray, about the sixth hour.

10 Then waxed he an hungered, and would have eaten: but while they made something ready, he fell into a trance.

11 And he saw heaven opened, and a certain vessel come down unto him, as it had been a great sheet, knit at the four corners, and was let down to the earth.

12 Wherein were all manner of four footed beasts of the earth, and wild beasts and creeping things, and fowls of the heaven.

13 And there came a voice to him, Arise, Peter: kill, and eat.

14 But Peter said, Not so, Lord: for I have never eaten any thing that is polluted, or unclean.

15 And the voice spake unto him again the second time, The things that God hath purified, pollute thou not.

16 This was so done thrice: and the vessel was drawn up again into heaven.

17 Now while Peter doubted in himself what this vision which he had seen, meant, behold, the men which were sent from Cornelius, had inquired for Simon's house, and stood at the gate,

18 And called, and asked, whether Simon, which was surnamed Peter, were lodged there.

19 And while Peter thought on the vision, the Spirit said unto him, Behold, three men seek thee.

20 Arise therefore, and get thee down, and go with them, and doubt nothing: for I have sent them.

21 Then Peter went down to the men, which were sent unto him from Cornelius, and said, Behold, I am he whom ye seek: what is the cause wherefore ye are come?

22 And they said, Cornelius the captain, a just man, and one that feareth God, and of good report among all the nation of the Jews, was warned from heaven by an holy Angel, to send for thee into his house, and to hear thy words.

23 Then called he them in, and lodged them, and the next day, Peter went forth with them, and certain brethren from Joppa accompanied him.

24 And the day after, they entered into Cesarea. Now Cornelius waited for them, and had called together his kinsmen, and special friends.

25 And it came to pass as Peter came in, that Cornelius met him, and fell down at his feet and worshipped him.

26 But Peter took him up, saying, Stand up: for even I myself am a man.

27 And as he talked with him, he came in, and found many that were come together.

28 And he said unto them, Ye know that it is an unlawful thing for a man that is a Jew, to company, or come unto one of another nation: but God hath showed me, that I should not call any man polluted, or unclean.

29 Therefore came I unto you without saying nay, when I was sent for. I ask therefore, for what intent have ye sent for me?

30 Then Cornelius said, Four days ago, about this hour, I fasted, and at the ninth hour I prayed in mine house, and behold, a man stood before me in bright clothing,

31 And said, Cornelius, thy prayer is heard, and thine alms are had in remembrance in the sight of God.

32 Send therefore to Joppa, and call for Simon, whose surname is Peter (he is lodged in the house of Simon a tanner by the sea side) who when he cometh, shall speak unto thee.

33 Then sent I for thee immediately, and thou hast well done to come. Now therefore are we all here present before God, to hear all things that are commanded thee of God.

34 Then Peter opened his mouth, and said, Of a truth I perceive, that God is no accepter of persons.

35 But in every nation he that feareth him, and worketh righteousness, is accepted with him.

36 Ye know the word which God hath sent to the children of Israel, preaching peace by Jesus Christ, which is Lord of all.

37 Even the word which came through all Judea beginning in Galilee, after the baptism which John preached,

38 To wit, how God anointed Jesus of Nazareth with the Holy Ghost, and with power: who went about doing good, and healing all that were oppressed of the devil: for God was with him.

39 And we are witnesses of all things which he did both in the land of the Jews, and in Jerusalem: whom they slew, hanging him on a tree.

40 Him God raised up the third day, and caused that he was showed openly:

41 Not to all the people, but unto the witnesses chosen before of God, even to us which did eat and drink with him, after he arose from the dead.

42 And he commanded us to preach unto the people, and to testify, that it is he that is ordained of God a judge of quick and dead.

43 To him also give all the Prophets witness, that through his Name all that believe in him, shall receive remission of sins.

44 While Peter yet spake these words, the Holy Ghost fell on all them which heard the word.

45 So they of the circumcision which believed, were astonished, as many as came with Peter, because that on the Gentiles also was poured out the gift of the Holy Ghost.

46 For they heard them speak with tongues, and magnify God. Then answered Peter,

47 Can any man forbid water, that these should not be baptized, which have received the Holy Ghost, as well as we?

48 So he commanded them to be baptized in the Name of the Lord. Then prayed they him to tarry certain days.

Acts Chapter 11

1 Now the Apostles and the brethren that were in Judea, heard, that the Gentiles had also received the word of God.

2 And when Peter was come up to Jerusalem, they of the circumcision contended against him,

3 Saying, Thou wentest in to men uncircumcised, and hast eaten with them.

4 Then Peter began, and expounded the thing in order to them, saying,

5 I was in the city of Joppa, praying, and in a trance I saw this vision, A certain vessel coming down as it had been a great sheet, let down from heaven by the four corners, and it came to me.

6 Toward the which when I had fastened mine eyes, I considered, and saw four-footed beasts of the earth, and wild beasts, and creeping things, and fowls of the heaven.

7 Also I heard a voice, saying unto me, Arise, Peter: slay and eat.

8 And I said, God forbid, Lord: for nothing polluted or unclean hath at any time entered into my mouth.

9 But the voice answered me the second time from heaven, The things that God hath purified, pollute thou not.

10 And this was done three times, and all were taken up again into heaven.

11 Then behold, immediately there were three men already come unto the house where I was, sent from Cesarea unto me.

12 And the Spirit said unto me, that I should go with them, without doubting: moreover these six brethren came with me, and we entered into the man's house.

13 And he showed us, how he had seen an Angel in his house, which stood and said to him, Send men to Joppa, and call for Simon whose surname is Peter.

14 He shall speak words unto thee, whereby both thou and all thine house shall be saved.

15 And as I began to speak, the Holy Ghost fell on them, even as upon us at the beginning.

16 Then I remembered the word of the Lord, how he said, John baptized with water, but ye shall be baptized with the Holy Ghost.

17 Forasmuch then as God gave them a like gift, as he did unto us, when we believed in the Lord Jesus Christ, who was I, that I could let God?

18 When they heard these things, they held their peace, and glorified God, saying, Then hath God also to the Gentiles granted repentance unto life.

19 And they which were scattered abroad because of the affliction that arose about Steven, walked throughout till they came unto Phenice and Cyprus, and Antiochia, preaching the word to no man, but unto the Jews only.

20 Now some of them were men of Cyprus and of Cyrene, which when they were come into Antiochia, spake unto the Grecians, and preached the Lord Jesus.

21 And the hand of the Lord was with them so that a great number believed and turned unto the Lord.

22 Then tidings of those things came unto the ears of the Church, which was in Jerusalem, and they sent forth Barnabas that he should go unto Antiochia.

23 Who when he was come and had seen the grace of God, was glad, and exhorted all, that with purpose of heart they would cleave unto the Lord.

24 For he was a good man, and full of the Holy Ghost, and faith, and much people joined themselves unto the Lord.

25 Then departed Barnabas to Tarsus to seek Saul:

26 And when he had found him, he brought him unto Antiochia, and it came to pass that a whole year they were conversant with the Church, and taught much people, insomuch, that the disciples were first called Christians in Antiochia.

27 In those days also came Prophets from Jerusalem unto Antiochia.

28 And there stood up one of them named Agabus, and signified by the Spirit, that there should be great famine throughout all the world, which also came to pass under Claudius Cesar.

29 Then the disciples, every man according to his ability, purposed to send succor unto the brethren which dwelt in Judea.

30 Which thing they also did, and sent it to the Elders, by the hands of Barnabas and Saul.

Acts Chapter 12

1 Now about that time, Herod the King stretched forth his hands to vex certain of the Church.

2 And he killed James the brother of John with the sword.

3 And when he saw that it pleased the Jews, he proceeded further, to take Peter also (then were the days of unleavened bread.)

4 And when he had caught him, he put him in prison, and delivered him to four quaternions of soldiers to be kept, intending after the Passover to bring him forth to the people.

5 So Peter was kept in prison, but earnest prayer was made of the Church unto God for him.

6 And when Herod would have brought him out unto the people, the same night slept Peter between two soldiers, bound with two chains, and the keepers before the door kept the prison.

7 And behold, the Angel of the Lord came upon them, and a light shined in the house, and he smote Peter on the side, and raised him up, saying, Arise quickly. And his chains fell off from his hands.

8 And the Angel said unto him, Gird thyself, and bind on thy sandals. And so he did. Then he said unto him, Cast thy garment about thee, and follow me.

9 So Peter came out and followed him, and knew not that it was true, which was done by the Angel, but thought he had seen a vision.

10 Now when they were past the first and the second watch, they came unto the iron gate, that leadeth unto the city, which opened to them by it own accord, and they went out, and passed through one street, and by and by the Angel departed from him.

11 And when Peter was come to himself, he said, Now I know for a truth, that the Lord hath sent his Angel, and hath delivered me out of the hand of Herod, and from all the waiting for of the people of the Jews.

12 And as he considered the thing, he came to the house of Mary, the mother of John, whose surname was Mark, where many were gathered together and prayed.

13 And when Peter knocked at the entry door, a maid came forth to hearken, named Rhoda,

14 But when she knew Peter's voice, she opened not the entry door for gladness, but ran in, and told how Peter stood before the entry.

15 But they said unto her, Thou art mad. Yet she affirmed it constantly, that it was so. Then said they, It is his Angel.

16 But Peter continued knocking, and when they had opened it, and saw him, they were astonished.

17 And he beckoned unto them with the hand, to hold their peace, and told them how the Lord had brought him out of the prison. And he said, Go show these things unto James and to the brethren: and he departed and went into another place.

18 Now as soon as it was day, there was no small trouble among the soldiers, what was become of Peter.

19 And when Herod had sought for him, and found him not, he examined the keepers, and commanded them to be led to be punished. And he went down from Judea to Cesarea, and there abode.

20 Then Herod intended to make war against them of Tyrus and Sidon, but they came all with one accord unto him, and persuaded Blastus the King's Chamberlain, and they desired peace, because their country was nourished by the King's land.

21 And upon a day appointed, Herod arrayed himself in royal apparel, and sat on the judgment seat, and made an oration unto them.

22 And the people gave a shout, saying, The voice of God, and not of man.

23 But immediately the Angel of the Lord smote him, because he gave not glory unto God, so that he was eaten of worms, and gave up the ghost.

24 And the word of God grew, and multiplied.

25 So Barnabas and Saul returned from Jerusalem, when they had fulfilled their office, and took with them John, whose surname was Mark.

Acts Chapter 13

1 There were also in the Church that was at Antiochia, certain Prophets and teachers, as Barnabas, and Simeon called Niger, and Lucius of Cyrene, and Manahen (which had been brought up with Herod the Tetrarch) and Saul.

2 Now as they ministered to the Lord, and fasted, the Holy Ghost said, Separate me Barnabas and Saul, for the work whereunto I have called them.

3 Then fasted they and prayed, and laid their hands on them, and let them go.

4 And they, after they were sent forth of the Holy Ghost, came down unto Seleucia, and from thence they sailed to Cyprus.

5 And when they were at Salamis, they preached the word of God in the Synagogues of the Jews: and they had also John to their minister.

6 So when they had gone throughout the Isle unto Paphus, they found a certain sorcerer, a false prophet, being a Jew, named Barjesus,

7 Which was with the Deputy Sergius Paulus, a prudent man. He called unto him Barnabas and Saul, and desired to hear the word of God.

8 But Elymas, the sorcerer (for so is his name by interpretation) withstood them, and sought to turn away the Deputy from the faith.

9 Then Saul (which also is called Paul) being full of the Holy Ghost, set his eyes on him,

10 And said, O full of all subtlety and all mischief, the child of the devil, and enemy of all righteousness, will thou not cease to pervert the straight ways of the Lord?

11 Now therefore behold, the hand of the Lord is upon thee, and thou shalt be blind, and not see the sun for a season. And immediately there fell on him a mist and a darkness, and he went about, seeking some to lead him by the hand.

12 Then the Deputy when he saw what was done, believed, and was astonished at the doctrine of the Lord.

13 Now when Paul and they that were with him were departed by ship from Paphus, they came to Perga a city of Pamphylia: then John departed from them, and returned to Jerusalem.

14 But when they departed from Perga, they came to Antiochia a city of Pisidia, and went into the Synagogue on the Sabbath day, and sat down.

15 And after the lecture of the Law and Prophets, the rulers of the Synagogue sent unto them, saying, Ye men and brethren, if ye have any word of exhortation for the people, say on.

16 Then Paul stood up and beckoned with the hand, and said, Men of Israel, and ye that fear God, hearken.

17 The God of this people of Israel chose our fathers, and exalted the people when they dwelt in the land of Egypt, and with an high arm brought them out thereof.

18 And about the time of forty years, suffered he their manners in the wilderness.

19 And he destroyed seven nations in the land of Chanaan, and divided their land to them by lot.

20 Then afterward he gave unto them Judges about four hundred and fifty years, unto the time of Samuel the Prophet.

21 So after that they desired a King, and God gave unto them Saul, the son of Cis, a man of the tribe of Benjamin, by the space of forty years.

22 And after he had taken him away, he raised up David to be their King, of whom he witnessed, saying, I have found David the son of Jesse, a man after mine own heart, which will do all things that I will.

23 Of this man's seed hath God according to his promise raised up to Israel, the Savior Jesus:

24 When John had first preached before his coming the baptism of repentance to all the people of Israel.

25 And when John had fulfilled his course, he said, Whom ye think that I am, I am not he: but behold, there cometh one after me, whose shoe of his feet I am not worthy to loose.

26 Ye men and brethren, children of the generation of Abraham, and whosoever among you feareth God, to you is the word of this salvation sent.

27 For the inhabitants of Jerusalem, and their rulers, because they knew him not, nor yet the words of the Prophets, which are read every Sabbath day, they have fulfilled them in condemning him.

28 And though they found no cause of death in him, yet desired they Pilate to kill him.

29 And when they had fulfilled all things that were written of him, they took him down from the tree, and put him in a sepulcher.

30 But God raised him up from the dead.

31 And he was seen many days of them, which came up with him from Galilee to Jerusalem, which are his witnesses unto the people.

32 And we declare unto you, that touching the promise made unto the fathers,

33 God hath fulfilled it unto us their children, in that he raised up Jesus, even as it is written in the second Psalm, Thou art my Son: this day have I begotten thee.

34 Now as concerning that he raised him up from the dead, no more to return to the grave, he hath said thus, I will give you the holy things of David, which are faithful.

35 Wherefore he saith also in another place, Thou wilt not suffer thine Holy one to see corruption.

36 Howbeit, David after he had served his time by the counsel of God, he slept, and was laid with his fathers, and saw corruption.

37 But he whom God raised up, saw no corruption.

38 Be it known unto you therefore, men and brethren, that through this man is preached unto you the forgiveness of sins.

39 And from all things, from which ye could not be justified by the Law of Moses, by him every one that believeth, is justified.

40 Beware therefore, lest that come upon you, which is spoken of in the Prophets,

41 Behold, ye despisers, and wonder, and vanish away: for I work a work in your days, a work which ye shall not believe, if a man would declare it you.

42 And when they were come out of the Synagogue of the Jews, the Gentiles besought, that they would preach these words to them the next Sabbath day.

43 Now when the congregation was dissolved, many of the Jews, and proselytes that feared God, followed Paul and Barnabas, which spake to them, and exhorted them to continue in the grace of God.

44 And the next Sabbath day came almost the whole city together, to hear the word of God.

45 But when the Jews saw the people, they were full of envy, and spake against those things, which were spoken of Paul, contrarying them and railing on them.

46 Then Paul and Barnabas spake boldly, and said, It was necessary that the word of God should first have been spoken unto you: but seeing ye put it from you, and judge yourselves unworthy of everlasting life, lo, we turn to the Gentiles.

47 For so hath the Lord commanded us, saying, I have made thee a light of the Gentiles, that thou shouldest be the salvation unto the end of the world.

48 And when the Gentiles heard it, they were glad, and glorified the word of the Lord: and as many as were ordained unto eternal life, believed.

49 Thus the word of the Lord was published throughout the whole country.

50 But the Jews stirred certain devout and honorable women, and the chief men of the city, and raised persecution against Paul and Barnabas, and expelled them out of their coasts.

51 But they shook off the dust of their feet against them, and came unto Iconium.

52 And the disciples were filled with joy, and with the Holy Ghost.

Acts Chapter 14

1 And it came to pass in Iconium, that they went both together into the Synagogue of the Jews, and so spake, that a great multitude both of the Jews and of the Grecians believed.

2 But the unbelieving Jews stirred up, and corrupted the minds of the Gentiles against the brethren.

3 So therefore they abode there a long time, and spake boldly in the Lord, which gave testimony unto the word of his grace, and caused signs and wonders to be done by their hands.

4 But the people of the city were divided: and some were with the Jews, and some with the Apostles.

5 And when there was an assault made both of the Gentiles, and of the Jews with their rulers, to do them violence, and to stone them,

6 They were ware of it, and fled unto Lystra, and Derbe, cities of Lycaonia, and unto the region round about,

7 And there were preaching the Gospel.

8 Now there sat a certain man at Lystra, impotent in his feet, which was a cripple from his mother's womb, who had never walked.

9 He heard Paul speak: who beholding him, and perceiving that he had faith to be healed,

10 Said with a loud voice, Stand upright on thy feet. And he leaped up, and walked.

11 Then when the people saw what Paul had done, they lift up their voices, saying in the speech of Lycaonia, Gods are come down to us in the likeness of men.

12 And they called Barnabas, Jupiter, and Paul, Mercurius, because he was the chief speaker.

13 Then Jupiter's priest, which was before their city, brought bulls with garlands unto the gates, and would have sacrificed with the people.

14 But when the Apostles, Barnabas and Paul heard it, they rent their clothes, and ran in among the people, crying,

15 And saying, O men, why do ye these things? We are even men subject to the like passions that ye be, and preach unto you, that ye should turn from these vain idols unto the living God, which made heaven and earth, and the sea, and all things that in them are.

16 Who in times past suffered all the Gentiles to walk in their own ways.

17 Nevertheless, he left not himself without witness, in that he did good and gave us rain from heaven, and fruitful seasons, filling our hearts with food, and gladness,

18 And speaking these things, scarce refrained they the people, that they had not sacrificed unto them.

19 Then there came certain Jews from Antiochia and Iconium, which when they had persuaded the people, stoned Paul, and drew him out of the city, supposing he had been dead.

20 Howbeit, as the disciples stood round about him, he arose up, and came into the city, and the next day he departed with Barnabas to Derbe.

21 And after they had preached to that city, and had taught many, they returned to Lystra, and to Iconium, and to Antiochia,

22 Confirming the disciples' hearts, and exhorting them to continue in the faith, affirming that we must through many afflictions enter into the kingdom of God.

23 And when they had ordained them Elders by election in every Church, and prayed, and fasted, they commended them to the Lord in whom they believed.

24 Thus they went throughout Pisidia, and came to Pamphilia.

25 And when they had preached the word in Perga, they came down to Attalia,

26 And thence sailed to Antiochia, from whence they had been commended unto the grace of God, to the work which they had fulfilled.

27 And when they were come and had gathered the Church together, they rehearsed all the things that God had done by them, and how he had opened the door of faith unto the Gentiles.

28 So there they abode a long time with the disciples.

Acts Chapter 15

1 Then came down certain from Judea, and taught the brethren, saying, Except ye be circumcised after the manner of Moses, ye cannot be saved.

2 And when there was great dissension, and disputation by Paul and Barnabas against them, they ordained that Paul and Barnabas, and certain other of them, should go up to Jerusalem unto the Apostles and Elders about this question.

3 Thus being sent forth by the Church, they passed through Phenice, and Samaria, declaring the conversion of the Gentiles: and they brought great joy unto all the brethren.

4 And when they were come to Jerusalem, they were received of the Church, and of the Apostles and Elders, and they declared what things God had done by them.

5 But said they, certain of the sect of the Pharises, which did believe, rose up, saying, that it was needful to circumcise them, and to command them to keep the law of Moses.

6 Then the Apostles and Elders came together to look to this matter.

7 And when there had been great disputation, Peter rose up, and said unto them, Ye men and brethren, ye know that a good while ago, among us God chose out me, that the Gentiles by my mouth should hear the word of the Gospel, and believe.

8 And God which knoweth the hearts, bare them witness, in giving unto them the Holy Ghost, even as he did unto us.

9 And he put no difference between us and them, after that by faith he had purified their hearts.

10 Now therefore, why tempt ye God, to lay a yoke on the disciples' necks, which neither our fathers, nor we were able to bear?

11 But we believe, through the grace of the Lord Jesus Christ to be saved, even as they do.

12 Then all the multitude kept silence, and heard Barnabas and Paul, which told what signs and wonders God had done among the Gentiles by them.

13 And when they held their peace, James answered, saying, Men and brethren, hearken unto me.

14 Simeon hath declared, how God first did visit the Gentiles, to take of them a people unto his Name.

15 And to this agree the words of the Prophets, as it is written,

16 After this I will return, and will build again the tabernacle of David, which is fallen down, and the ruins thereof will I build again, and I will set it up,

17 That the residue of men might seek after the Lord, and all the Gentiles upon whom my Name is called, saith the Lord which doeth all these things.

18 From the beginning of the world God knoweth all his works.

19 Wherefore my sentence is, that we trouble not them of the Gentiles that are turned to God,

20 But that we write unto them, that they abstain themselves from filthiness of idols, and fornication, and that that is strangled, and from blood.

21 For Moses of old time hath in every city them that preach him, seeing he is read in the Synagogues every Sabbath day.

22 Then it seemed good to the Apostles and Elders with the whole Church, to send chosen men of their own company to Antiochia with Paul and Barnabas: to wit, Judas whose surname was Barsabas and Silas, which were chief men among the brethren.

23 And wrote letters by them after this manner, the Elders, and the brethren, unto the brethren which are of the Gentiles in Antiochia, and in Syria, and in Cilicia, send greeting.

24 Forasmuch as we have heard, that certain which departed from us, have troubled you with words, and cumbered your minds, saying, Ye must be circumcised and keep the Law: to whom we gave no such commandment,

25 It seemed therefore good to us, when we were come together with one accord, to send chosen men unto you, with our beloved Barnabas and Paul,

26 Men that have given up their lives for the Name of our Lord Jesus Christ.

27 We have therefore sent Judas and Silas, which shall also tell you the same things by mouth.

28 For it seemed good to the Holy Ghost, and to us, to lay no more burden upon you, than these necessary things,

29 That is, that ye abstain from things offered to idols, and blood, and that that is strangled, and from fornication: from which if ye keep yourselves, ye shall do well. Fare ye well.

30 Now when they were departed, they came to Antiochia, and after that they had assembled the multitude, they delivered the epistle.

31 And when they had read it, they rejoiced for the consolation.

32 And Judas and Silas being Prophets, exhorted the brethren with many words, and strengthened them.

33 And after they had tarried there a space, they were let go in peace of the brethren unto the Apostles.

34 Notwithstanding Silas thought good to abide there still.

35 Paul also and Barnabas continued in Antiochia, teaching and preaching with many other the word of the Lord.

36 But after certain days, Paul said unto Barnabas, Let us return, and visit our brethren in every city, where we have preached the word of the Lord, and see how they do.

37 And Barnabas counseled to take with them John, called Mark.

38 But Paul thought it not meet to take him unto their company, which departed from them from Pamphylia, and went not with them to the work.

39 Then were they so stirred that they departed asunder one from the other, so that Barnabas took Mark, and sailed unto Cyprus.

40 And Paul chose Silas and departed, being commended of the brethren unto the grace of God.

41 And he went through Syria and Cilicia, stablishing the Churches.

Acts Chapter 16

1 Then came he to Derbe and to Lystra: and behold, a certain disciple was there named Timotheus, a woman's son, which was a Jewess and believed, but his father was a Grecian.

2 Of whom the brethren which were at Lystra and Iconium, reported well.

3 Therefore Paul would that he should go forth with him, and took and circumcised him, because of the Jews, which were in those quarters: for they knew all, that his father was a Grecian.

4 And as they went through the cities, they delivered them the decrees to keep, ordained of the Apostles and Elders, which were at Jerusalem.

5 And so were the Churches stablished in the faith, and increased in number daily.

6 Now when they had gone throughout Phrygia, and the region of Galatia, they were forbidden of the Holy Ghost to preach the word in Asia.

7 Then came they to Mysia, and sought to go into Bithynia:but the Spirit suffered them not.

8 Therefore they passed through Mysia, and came down to Troas,

9 Where a vision appeared to Paul in the night. There stood a man of Macedonia, and prayed him, saying, Come into Macedonia, and help us.

10 And after he had seen the vision, immediately we prepared to go into Macedonia, being assured that the Lord had called us to preach the Gospel unto them.

11 Then went we forth from Troas, and with a straight course came to Samothracia, and the next day to Neapolis,

12 And from thence to Philippi, which is the chief city in the parts of Macedonia, and whose inhabitants came from Rome to dwell there, and we were in that city abiding certain days.

13 And on the Sabbath day, we went out of the city, besides a river, where they were wont to pray: and we sat down, and spake unto the women, which were come together.

14 And a certain woman named Lydia, a seller of purple, of the city of the Thyatirians, which worshipped God, heard us: whose heart the Lord opened, that she attended unto the things, which Paul spake.

15 And when she was baptized, and her household, she besought us, saying, If ye have judged me to be faithful to the Lord, come into mine house, and abide there: and she constrained us.

16 And it came to pass that as we went to prayer, a certain maid having a spirit of divination, met us, which gat her masters much vantage with divining.

17 She followed Paul and us, and cried, saying, These men are the servants of the most high God, which show unto us the way of salvation.

18 And this did she many days: but Paul being grieved, turned about, and said to the spirit, I command thee in the Name of Jesus Christ, that thou come out of her. And he came out the same hour.

19 Now when her masters saw that the hope of their gain was gone, they caught Paul and Silas, and drew them into the market place unto the magistrates,

20 And brought them to the governors, saying, These men which are Jews, trouble our city,

21 And preach ordinances, which are not lawful for us to receive, neither to observe, seeing we are Romans.

22 The people also rose up together against them, and the governors rent their clothes, and commanded them to be beaten with rods.

23 And when they had beaten them sore, they cast them into prison, commanding the jailor to keep them surely.

24 Who having received such commandment, cast them into the inner prison, and made their feet fast in the stocks.

25 Now at midnight Paul and Silas prayed, and sang a Psalm unto God: and the prisoners heard them.

26 And suddenly there was a great earthquake, so that the foundation of the prison was shaken: and by and by all the doors opened, and every man's bands were loosed.

27 Then the keeper of the prison waked out of his sleep, and when he saw the prison doors open, he drew out his sword and would have killed himself, supposing the prisoners had been fled.

28 But Paul cried with a loud voice, saying, Do thyself no harm: for we are all here.

29 Then he called for a light and leaped in and came trembling, and fell down before Paul and Silas,

30 And brought them out, and said, Sirs, what must I do to be saved?

31 And they said, Believe in the Lord Jesus Christ, and thou shalt be saved, and thine household.

32 And they preached unto him the word of the Lord, and to all that were in his house.

33 Afterward he took them the same hour of the night, and
washed their stripes, and was baptized with all that belonged unto him, straightway.

34 And when he had brought them into his house, he set meat before them, and rejoiced that he with all his household believed in God.

35 And when it was day, the governors sent the sergeants, saying, Let those men go.

36 Then the keeper of the prison told these words unto Paul, saying, The governors have sent to loose you: now therefore get you hence, and go in peace.

37 Then said Paul unto them, After that they have beaten us openly uncondemned, which are Romans, they have cast us into prison, and now would they put us out privily? nay verily: but let them come and bring us out.

38 And the sergeants told these words unto the governors, who feared when they heard that they were Romans.

39 Then came they and prayed them, and brought them out, and desired them to depart out of the city.

40 And they went out of the prison, and entered into the house of Lydia: and when they had seen the brethren, they comforted them, and departed.

Acts Chapter 17

1 Now as they passed through Amphipolis, and Apollonia, they came to Thessalonica, where was a Synagogue of the Jews.

2 And Paul, as his manner was, went in unto them, and three Sabbath days disputed with them by the Scriptures,

3 Opening, and alleging that Christ must have suffered, and risen again from the dead: and this is Jesus Christ, whom, said he, I preach to you.

4 And some of them believed, and joined in company with Paul and Silas: also of the Grecians that feared God a great multitude, and of the chief women not a few.

5 But the Jews which believed not, moved with envy, took unto them certain vagabonds and wicked fellows, and when they had assembled the multitude, they made a tumult in the city, and made assault against the house of Jason, and sought to bring them out to the people.

6 But when they found them not, they drew Jason and certain brethren unto the heads of the city, crying, These are they which have subverted the state of the world, and here they are,

7 Whom Jason hath received, and these all do against the decrees of Cesar, saying that there is another King, one Jesus.

8 Then they troubled the people, and the heads of the city, when they heard these things.

9 Notwithstanding when they had received sufficient assurance of Jason and of the other, they let them go.

10 And the brethren immediately sent away Paul and Silas by night unto Berea, which when they were come thither, entered into the Synagogue of the Jews.

11 These were also more noble men than they which were at Thessalonica, which received the word with all readiness, and searched the Scriptures daily, whether those things were so.

12 Therefore many of them believed, and of honest women, which were Grecians, and men not a few.

13 But when the Jews of Thessalonica knew, that the word of God was also preached of Paul at Berea, they came thither also, and moved the people.

14 But by and by the brethren sent away Paul to go as it were to the sea: but Silas and Timotheus abode there still.

15 And they that did conduct Paul, brought him unto Athens: and when they had received a commandment unto Silas and Timotheus that they should come to him at once, they departed.

16 Now while Paul waited for them at Athens, his spirit was stirred in him, when he saw the city subject to idolatry.

17 Therefore he disputed in the Synagogue with the Jews, and with them that were religious, and in the market daily with whomsoever he met.

18 Then certain Philosophers of the Epicures, and of the Stoics, disputed with him, and some said, What will this babbler say? Others said, He seemeth to be a setter forth of strange gods (because he preached unto them Jesus, and the resurrection.)

19 And they took him, and brought him into Mars' street, saying, May we not know, what this new doctrine, whereof thou speakest, is?

20 For thou bringest certain strange things unto our ears: we would know therefore, what these things mean.

21 For all the Athenians, and strangers which dwelt there, gave themselves to nothing else, but either to tell, or to hear some news.

22 Then Paul stood in the midst of Mars' street, and said, Ye men of Athens, I perceive that in all things ye are too superstitious.

23 For as I passed by, and beheld your devotions, I found an altar wherein was written, UNTO THE UNKNOWN GOD. Whom ye then ignorantly worship, him show I unto you.

24 God that made the world, and all things that are therein, seeing that he is Lord of heaven and earth, dwelleth not in temples made with hands,

25 Neither is worshipped with men's hands, as though he needed any thing, seeing he giveth to all life and breath and all things,

26 And hath made of one blood all mankind, to dwell on all the face of the earth, and hath assigned the times which were ordained before, and the bounds of their habitation,

27 That they should seek the Lord, if so be they might have groped after him, and found him though doubtless he be not far from every one of us.

28 For in him we live, and move, and have our being, as also certain of your own Poets have said, For we are also his generation.

29 Forasmuch then, as we are the generation of God, we ought not to think that the Godhead is like unto gold, or silver, or stone graven by art and the invention of man.

30 And the time of this ignorance God regarded not: but now he admonisheth all men every where to repent,

31 Because he hath appointed a day in the which he will judge the world in righteousness, by that man whom he hath appointed, whereof he hath given an assurance to all men, in that he hath raised him from the dead.

32 Now when they heard of the resurrection from the dead, some mocked, and other said, We will hear thee again of this thing.

33 And so Paul departed from among them.

34 Howbeit certain men clave unto Paul, and believed: among whom was also Denys Areopagita, and a woman named Damaris, and other with them.

Acts Chapter 18

1 After these things, Paul departed from Athens, and came to Corinthus,

2 And found a certain Jew, named Aquila, born in Pontus, lately come from Italy, and his wife Priscilla (because that Claudius had commanded all Jews to depart from Rome) and he came unto them.

3 And because he was of the same craft, he abode with them and wrought (for their craft was to make tents.)

4 And he disputed in the Synagogue every Sabbath day, and exhorted the Jews, and the Grecians.

5 Now when Silas and Timotheus were come from Macedonia, Paul, burned in spirit, testifying to the Jews that Jesus was the Christ.

6 And when they resisted and blasphemed, he shook his raiment, and said unto them, Your blood be upon your own head: I am clean: from henceforth will I go unto the Gentiles.

7 So he departed thence, and entered into a certain man's house, named Justus, a worshipper of God, whose house joined hard to the Synagogue,

8 And Crispus the chief ruler of the Synagogue, believed in the Lord with all his household: and many of the Corinthians hearing it, believed and were baptized.

9 Then said the Lord to Paul in the night by a vision, Fear not, but speak, and hold not thy peace.

10 For I am with thee, and no man shall lay hands on thee to hurt thee: for I have much people in this city.

11 So he continued there a year and six months, and taught the word of God among them.

12 Now when Gallio was Deputy of Achaia, the Jews arose with one accord against Paul, and brought him to the judgment seat,

13 Saying, This fellow persuadeth men to worship God contrary to the Law.

14 And as Paul was about to open his mouth, Gallio said unto the Jews, If it were a matter of wrong, or an evil deed, O ye Jews, I would according to reason maintain you.

15 But if it be a question of words, and names, and of your Law, look ye to it yourselves: for I will be no judge of those things.

16 And he drove them from the judgment seat.

17 Then took all the Grecians Sosthenes the chief ruler of the Synagogue, and beat him before the judgment seat: but Gallio cared nothing for those things.

18 But when Paul had tarried there yet a good while, he took leave of the brethren, and sailed into Syria (and with him Priscilla and Aquila) after that he had shorn his head in Cenchrea: for he had a vow.

19 Then he came to Ephesus, and left them there: but he entered into the Synagogue and disputed with the Jews.

20 Who desired him to tarry a longer time with them: but he would not consent,

21 But bade them farewell, saying, I must needs keep this feast that cometh, in Jerusalem: but I will return again unto you, if God will. So he sailed from Ephesus.

22 And when he came down to Cesarea, he went up to Jerusalem: and when he had saluted the Church, he went down unto Antiochia.

23 Now when he had tarried there a while, he departed, and went through the country of Galatia and Phrygia by order, strengthening all the disciples. 24 And a certain Jew named Apollos, born at Alexandria, came to Ephesus, an eloquent man, and mighty in the Scriptures.

25 The same was instructed in the way of the Lord, and he spake fervently in the Spirit, and taught diligently the things of the Lord, and knew but the baptism of John only.

26 And he began to speak boldly in the Synagogue. Whom when Aquila and Priscilla had heard, they took him unto them, and expounded unto him the way of God more perfectly.

27 And when he was minded to go into Achaia, the brethren exhorting him, wrote to the disciples to receive him: and after he was come thither, he holp them much which had believed through grace.

28 For mightily he confuted publicly the Jews with great vehemence, showing by the Scriptures, that Jesus was the Christ.

Acts Chapter 19

1 And it came to pass, while Apollos was at Corinthus, that Paul when he passed through the upper coasts, came to Ephesus, and found certain disciples,

2 And said unto them, Have ye received the Holy Ghost since ye believed? And they said unto him, We have not so much as heard whether there be an Holy Ghost.

3 And he said unto them, Unto what were ye then baptized? And they said, Unto John's baptism.

4 Then said Paul, John verily baptized with the baptism of repentance, saying unto the people, that they should believe in him, which should come after him, that is, in Christ Jesus.

5 So when they heard it, they were baptized in the Name of the Lord Jesus.

6 And Paul laid his hands upon them, and the Holy Ghost came on them, and they spake the tongues, and prophesied.

7 And all the men were about twelve.

8 Moreover he went into the Synagogue, and spake boldly for the space of three months, disputing and exhorting to the things that appertain to the kingdom of God.

9 But when certain were hardened, and disobeyed, speaking evil of the way of God before the multitude, he departed from them, and separated the disciples, and disputed daily in the school of one Tyrannus.

10 And this was done by the space of two years, so that all they which dwelt in Asia, heard the word of the Lord Jesus, both Jews and Grecians.

11 And God wrought no small miracles by the hands of Paul,

12 So that from his body were brought unto the sick, kerchiefs or handkerchiefs, and the diseases departed from them, and the evil spirits went out of them.

13 Then certain of the vagabond Jews, exorcists, took in hand to name over them which had evil spirits, the Name of the Lord Jesus, saying, We adjure you by Jesus, whom Paul preacheth.

14 (And there were certain sons of Sceva a Jew, the Priest, about seven which did this)

15 And the evil spirit answered, and said, Jesus I acknowledge, and Paul I know: but who are ye?

16 And the man in whom the evil spirit was, ran on them, and overcame them, and prevailed against them, so that they fled out of that house, naked, and wounded.

17 And this was known to all the Jews and Grecians also, which dwelt at Ephesus, and fear came on them all, and the Name of the Lord Jesus was magnified.

18 And many that believed, came and confessed, and showed their works.

19 Many also of them which used curious arts, brought their books, and burned them before all men: and they counted the price of them, and found it fifty thousand pieces of silver.

20 So the word of God grew mightily, and prevailed.

21 Now when these things were accomplished, Paul purposed by the Spirit to pass through Macedonia and Achaia, and to go to Jerusalem, saying, After I have been there, I must also see Rome.

22 So sent he into Macedonia two of them that ministered unto him, Timotheus and Erastus, but he remained in Asia for a season.

23 And the same time there arose no small trouble about that way.

24 For a certain man named Demetrius a silversmith, which made silver temples of Diana, brought great gains unto the craftsmen:

25 Whom he called together, with the workmen of like things, and said, Sirs, ye know that by this craft we have our goods.

26 Moreover ye see and hear, that not alone at Ephesus, but almost throughout all Asia this Paul hath persuaded, and turned away much people, saying, That they be not gods which are made with hands,

27 So that not only this thing is dangerous unto us, that the state should be reproved, but also that the temple of the great goddess Diana should be nothing esteemed, and that it would come to pass that her magnificence, which all Asia and the world worshippeth, should be destroyed.

28 Now when they heard it, they were full of wrath, and cried out, saying, Great is Diana of the Ephesians.

29 And the whole city was full of confusion, and they rushed into the common place with one assent, and caught Gaius, and Aristarchus, men of Macedonia, and Paul's companions of his journey.

30 And when Paul would have entered in unto the people, the disciples suffered him not.

31 Certain also of the chief of Asia which were his friends, sent unto him, desiring him that he would not present himself in the common place.

32 Some therefore cried one thing, and some another: for the assembly was out of order, and the more part knew not wherefore they were come together.

33 And some of the company drew forth Alexander, the Jews thrusting him forwards. Alexander then beckoned with the hand, and would have excused the matter to the people.

34 But when they knew that he was a Jew, there arose a shout almost for the space of two hours, of all men crying, Great is Diana of the Ephesians.

35 Then the town clerk when he had stayed the people, said, Ye men of Ephesus, what man is it that knoweth not how that the city of the Ephesians is a worshipper of the great goddess Diana, and of the image, which came down from Jupiter?

36 Seeing then that no man can speak against these things, ye ought to be appeased, and to do nothing rashly.

37 For ye have brought hither these men, which have neither commit sacrilege, neither do blaspheme your goddess.

38 Wherefore, if Demetrius and the craftsmen which are with him, have a matter against any man, the law is open, and there are Deputies: let them accuse one another.

39 But if ye inquire any thing concerning other matters it may be determined in a lawful assembly.

40 For we are even in jeopardy to be accused of this day's sedition, forasmuch as there is no cause, whereby we may give a reason of this concourse of people.

41 And when he had thus spoken, he let the assembly depart.

Acts Chapter 20

1 Now after the tumult was ceased, Paul called the disciples unto him, and embraced them, and departed to go into Macedonia.

2 And when he had gone through those parts, and had exhorted them with many words, he came into Grecia.

3 And having tarried there three months, because the Jews laid wait for him, as he was about to sail into Syria, he purposed to return through Macedonia.

4 And there accompanied him into Asia Sopater of Berea, and of them of Thessalonica, Aristarchus, and Secundus, and Gaius of Derbe, and Timotheus, and of them of Asia Tychicus, and Trophimus.

5 These went before, and tarried us at Troas.

6 And we sailed forth from Philippi, after the days of unleavened bread, and came unto them to Troas in five days, where we abode seven days. 7 And the first day of the week, the disciples being come together to break bread, Paul preached unto them, ready to depart on the morrow, and continued the preaching unto midnight.

8 And there were many lights in an upper chamber, where they were gathered together.

9 And there sat in a window a certain young man, named Eutychus, fallen into a deep sleep: and as Paul was long preaching, he overcome with sleep, fell down from the third loft, and was taken up dead.

10 But Paul went down, and laid himself upon him, and embraced him, saying, Trouble not yourselves: for his life is in him.

11 So when Paul was come up again, and had broken bread, and eaten, he commented a long while till the dawning of the day, and so he departed.

12 And they brought the boy alive, and they were not a little comforted.

13 Then we went forth to ship, and sailed unto the city Assos, that we might receive Paul there: for so had he appointed, and would himself go afoot.

14 Now when he was come unto us to Assos, and we had received him, we came to Mitylenes.

15 And we sailed thence, and came the next day over against Chios, and the next day we arrived at Samos, and tarried at Trogyllium: the next day we came to Miletum.

16 For Paul had determined to sail by Ephesus, because he would not spend the time in Asia: for he hasted to be, if he could possible, at Jerusalem, at the day of Pentecost.

17 Wherefore from Miletum he sent to Ephesus, and called the Elders of the Church.

18 Who when they were come to him, he said unto them, Ye know from the first day that I came into Asia, after what manner I have been with you at all seasons,

19 Serving the Lord with all modesty, and with many tears, and temptations, which came unto me by the layings await of the Jews,

20 And how I kept back nothing that was profitable, but have showed you, and taught you openly, and throughout every house,

21 Witnessing both to the Jews, and to the Grecians the repentance toward God, and faith toward our Lord Jesus Christ.

22 And now behold, I go bound in the Spirit unto Jerusalem, and know not what things shall come unto me there,

23 Save that the Holy Ghost witnesseth in every city, saying, that bonds and afflictions abide me.

24 But I pass not at all, neither is my life dear unto myself, so that I may fulfill my course with joy, and the ministration which I have received of the Lord Jesus, to testify the Gospel of the grace of God.

25 And now behold, I know that henceforth ye all, through whom I have gone preaching the kingdom of God, shall see my face no more.

26 Wherefore I take you to record this day, that I am pure from the blood of all men.

27 For I have kept nothing back, but have showed you all the counsel of God.

28 Take heed therefore unto yourselves, and to all the flock, whereof the Holy Ghost hath made you Overseers, to feed the Church of God, which he hath purchased with his own blood.

29 For I know this, that after my departing shall grievous wolves enter in among you, not sparing the flock.

30 Moreover of your own selves shall men arise speaking perverse things, to draw disciples after them.

31 Therefore watch and remember, that by the space of three years I ceased not to warn every one, both night and day with tears.

32 And now brethren, I commend you to God, and to the word of his grace, which is able to build further, and to give you an inheritance, among all them, which are sanctified.

33 I have coveted no man's silver, nor gold, nor apparel.

34 Yea, ye know, that these hands have ministered unto my necessities, and to them that were with me.

35 I have showed you all things, how that so laboring, ye ought to support the weak, and to remember the words of the Lord Jesus, how that he said, It is a blessed thing to give, rather than to receive.

36 And when he had thus spoken, he kneeled down, and prayed with them all.

37 Then they wept all abundantly, and fell on Paul's neck, and kissed him,

38 Being chiefly sorry for the words which he spake, That they should see his face no more. And they accompanied him unto the ship.

Acts Chapter 21

1 And as we launched forth, and were departed from them, we came with a straight course unto Coos, and the day following unto the Rhodes, and from thence unto Patara.

2 And we found a ship that went over unto Phenice, and went aboard, and set forth.

3 And when we had discovered Cyprus, we left it on the left hand, and sailed toward Syria, and arrived at Tyrus: for there the ship unladed the burden.

4 And when we had found disciples, we tarried there seven days. And they told Paul through the Spirit, that he should not go up to Jerusalem.

5 But when the days were ended, we departed, and went our way, and they all accompanied us with their wives and children, even out of the city: and we kneeling down on the shore, prayed.

6 Then when we had embraced one another, we took ship, and they returned home.

7 And when we had ended the course from Tyrus, we arrived at Ptolemais, and saluted the brethren, and abode with them one day.

8 And the next day, Paul and they that were with him, departed, and came unto Cesarea: and we entered into the house of Philip the Evangelist, which was one of the seven Deacons, and abode with him.

9 Now he had four daughters virgins, which did prophesy.

10 And as we tarried there many days, there came a certain Prophet from Judea, named Agabus.

11 And when he was come unto us, he took Paul's girdle, and bound his own hands and feet, and said, Thus saith the Holy Ghost, So shall the Jews at Jerusalem bind the man that owneth this girdle, and shall deliver him into the hands of the Gentiles.

12 And when we had heard these things, both we and other of the same place besought him that he would not go up to Jerusalem.

13 Then Paul answered, and said, What do ye weeping and breaking mine heart? For I am ready not to be bound only, but also to die at Jerusalem for the Name of the Lord Jesus.

14 So when he would not be persuaded, we ceased, saying, The will of the Lord be done.

15 And after those days we trussed up our fardels, and went up to Jerusalem.

16 There went with us also certain of the disciples of Cesarea, and brought with them one Mnason of Cyprus, an old disciple, with whom we should lodge.

17 And when we were come to Jerusalem, the brethren received us gladly. 18 And the next day Paul went in with us unto James: and all the Elders were there assembled.

19 And when he had embraced them, he told by order all things, that God had wrought among the Gentiles by his ministration.

20 So when they heard it, they glorified the Lord, and said unto him, Thou seest, brother, how many thousand Jews there are which believe, and they are all zealous of the Law.

21 Now they are informed of thee, that thou teachest all the Jews, which are among the Gentiles, to forsake Moses, and sayest, that they ought not to circumcise their children, neither to live after the customs.

22 What is then to be done? the multitude must needs come together: for they shall hear that thou art come.

23 Do therefore this that we say to thee. We have four men, which have made a vow.

24 Them take, and purify thyself with them, and contribute with them, that they may shave their heads: and all shall know, that those things, whereof they have been informed concerning thee, are nothing, but that thou thyself also walkest and keepest the Law.

25 For as touching the Gentiles, which believe, we have written, and determined that they observe no such thing, but that they keep themselves from things offered to idols, and from blood, and from that that is strangled, and from fornication.

26 Then Paul took the men, and the next day was purified with them, and entered into the Temple, declaring the accomplishment of the days of the purification, until that an offering should be offered for every one of them.

27 And when the seven days were almost ended, the Jews which were of Asia (when they saw him in the Temple) moved all the people, and laid hands on him,

28 Crying, Men of Israel, help: this is the man that teacheth all men every where against the people, and the Law, and this place: moreover, he hath brought Grecians into the Temple, and hath polluted this holy place.

29 For they had seen before Trophimus an Ephesian with him in the city, whom they supposed that Paul had brought into the Temple.

30 Then all the city was moved, and the people ran together: and they took Paul, and drew him out of the Temple, and forthwith the doors were shut. 31 But as they went about to kill him, tidings came unto the chief Captain of the band, that all Jerusalem was on an uproar.

32 Who immediately took soldiers and Centurions, and ran down unto them: and when they saw the chief Captain and the soldiers, they left beating of Paul.

33 Then the chief Captain came near and took him, and commanded him to be bound with two chains, and demanded who he was, and what he had done.

34 And one cried this, another that, among the people. So when he could not know the certainty for the tumult, he commanded him to be led into the castle.

35 And when he came unto the grieces, it was so that he was born of the soldiers, for the violence of the people.

36 For the multitude of the people followed after, crying, Away with him.

37 And as Paul should have been led into the castle, he said unto the chief Captain, May I speak unto thee? Who said, Canst thou speak Greek?

38 Art not thou the Egyptian, who before these days raised a sedition, and led out into the wilderness four thousand men that were murderers?

39 Then Paul said, Doubtless I am a man which am a Jew, and citizen of Tarsus, a famous city in Cilicia, and I beseech thee, suffer me to speak unto the people.

40 And when he had given him license, Paul stood on the grieces, and beckoned with the hand unto the people: and when there was made great silence, he spake unto them in the Hebrew tongue, saying,

Acts Chapter 22

1 Ye men, brethren and fathers, hear my defense now towards you.

2 (And when they heard that he spake in the Hebrew tongue to them, they kept the more silence, and he said)

3 I am verily a man, which am a Jew, born in Tarsus in Cilicia, but brought up in this city at the feet of Gamaliel, and instructed according to the perfect manner of the Law of the Fathers, and was zealous toward God, as ye all are this day.

4 And I persecuted this way unto the death, binding and delivering into prison both men and women,

5 As also the chief Priest doth bear me witness, and all the state of the Elders: of whom also I received letters unto the brethren, and went to Damascus to bring them which were there, bound unto Jerusalem, that they might be punished.

6 And so it was, as I journeyed and was come near unto Damascus about noon, that suddenly there shone from heaven a great light round about me.

7 So I fell unto the earth, and heard a voice, saying unto me, Saul, Saul, why persecutest thou me?

8 Then I answered, Who art thou, Lord? And he said to me, I am Jesus of Nazareth, whom thou persecutest.

9 Moreover they that were with me, saw indeed a light and were afraid: but they heard not the voice of him that spake unto me.

10 Then I said, What shall I do, Lord? And the Lord said unto me, Arise, and go into Damascus: and there it shall be told thee of all things, which are appointed for thee to do.

11 So when I could not see for the glory of that light, I was led by the hand of them that were with me, and came into Damascus.

12 And one Ananias a godly man, as pertaining to the Law, having good report of all the Jews which dwelt there,

13 Came unto me, and stood, and said unto me, Brother Saul, receive thy sight: and that same hour I looked upon him.

14 And he said, The God of our fathers hath appointed thee, that thou shouldest know his will, and shouldest see that Just one, and shouldest hear the voice of his mouth.

15 For thou shalt be his witness unto all men of the things, which thou hast seen and heard.

16 Now therefore why tarriest thou? Arise, and be baptized, and wash away thy sins, in calling on the Name of the Lord.

17 And it came to pass, that when I was come again to Jerusalem, and prayed in the Temple, I was in a trance,

18 And saw him saying unto me, Make haste, and get thee quickly out of Jerusalem: for they will not receive thy witness concerning me.

19 Then I said, Lord, they know that I prisoned, and beat in every Synagogue them that believed in thee.

20 And when the blood of thy martyr Steven was shed, I also stood by, and consented unto his death, and kept the clothes of them that slew him.

21 Then he said unto me, Depart: for I will send thee far hence unto the Gentiles.

22 And they heard unto this word, but then they lift up their voices, and said, Away with such a fellow from the earth: for it is not meet that he should live.

23 And as they cried and cast off their clothes, and threw dust into the air,

24 The chief captain commanded him to be led into the castle, and bade that he should be scourged, and examined, that he might know wherefore they cried so on him.

25 And as they bound him with thongs, Paul said unto the Centurion that stood by, Is it lawful for you to scourge one that is a Roman, and not condemned?

26 Now when the Centurion heard it, he went, and told the chief captain, saying, Take heed what thou doest: for this man is a Roman.

27 Then the chief captain came, and said to him, Tell me, art thou a Roman? And he said, Yea.

28 And the chief captain answered, With a great sum obtained I this burgeship. Then Paul said, But I was so born.

29 Then straightway they departed from him, which should have examined him: and the chief captain also was afraid, after he knew that he was a Roman, and that he had bound him.

30 On the next day, because he would have known the certainty wherefore he was accused of the Jews, he loosed him from his bonds, and commanded the high Priests and all their Council to come together: and he brought Paul, and set him before them.

Acts Chapter 23

1 And Paul beheld earnestly the Council, and said, Men and brethren, I have in all good conscience served God until this day.

2 Then the high Priest Ananias commanded them that stood by, to smite him on the mouth.

3 Then said Paul to him, God will smite thee, thou whited wall: for thou sittest to judge me according to the Law, and commandest thou me to be smitten contrary to the Law?

4 And they that stood by, said, Revilest thou God's high Priest?

5 Then said Paul, I knew not, brethren, that he was the high Priest: for it is written, Thou shalt not speak evil of the Ruler of thy people.

6 But when Paul perceived that the one part were of the Sadducees, and the other of the Pharisees, he cried in the Council, Men and brethren, I am a Pharisee, the son of a Pharisee: I am accused of the hope and resurrection of the dead.

7 And when he had said this, there was a dissension between the Pharisees and the Sadducees, so that the multitude was divided.

8 For the Sadducees say that there is no resurrection, neither Angel, nor spirit: but the Pharisees confess both.

9 Then there was a great cry: and the Scribes of the Pharisees part rose up, and strove, saying, We find none evil in this man: but if a spirit or an Angel hath spoken to him, let us not fight against God.

10 And when there was a great dissension, the chief captain, fearing lest Paul should have been pulled in pieces of them, commanded the soldiers to go down, and to take him from among them, and to bring him into the castle.

11 Now the night following the Lord stood by him, and said, Be of good courage, Paul: for as thou hast testified of me in Jerusalem, so must thou bear witness also at Rome.

12 And when the day was come, certain of the Jews made an assembly, and bound themselves with an oath, saying, that they would neither eat nor drink, till they had killed Paul.

13 And they were more than forty, which had made this conspiracy.

14 And they came to the chief Priests and Elders, and said, We have bound ourselves with a solemn oath, that we will eat nothing, until we have slain Paul.

15 Now therefore, ye and the Council signify to the chief captain, that he bring him forth unto you tomorrow, as though you would know something more perfectly of him, and we, or ever he come near, will be ready to kill him.

16 But when Paul's sister's son heard of their laying await, he went, and entered into the castle, and told Paul,

17 And Paul called one of the Centurions unto him, and said, Bring this young man unto the chief captain: for he hath a certain thing to show him.

18 So he took him, and brought him to the chief captain, and said, Paul the prisoner called me unto him, and prayed me to bring this young man unto thee, which hath something to say unto thee.

19 Then the chief captain took him by the hand, and went apart with him alone, and asked him, What hast thou to show me?

20 And he said, The Jews have conspired to desire thee, that thou wouldest bring forth Paul tomorrow into the Council, as though they would inquire somewhat of him more perfectly.

21 But let them not persuade thee: for there lie in wait for him of them, more than forty men, which have bound themselves with an oath, that they will neither eat nor drink, till they have killed him: and now are they ready, and wait for thy promise.

22 The chief captain then let the young man depart, and charged him to speak it to no man, that he had showed him these things.

23 And he called unto him two certain Centurions, saying, Make ready two hundred soldiers, that they may go to Caesarea, and horsemen three score and ten, and two hundred, with darts at the third hour of the night.

24 And let them make ready an horse that Paul being set on, may be brought safe unto Felix the Governor.

25 And he wrote an epistle in this manner,

26 Claudius Lysias unto the most noble Governor Felix sendeth greeting.

27 As this man was taken of the Jews, and should have been killed of them, I came upon them with the garrison, and rescued him, perceiving that he was a Roman.

28 And when I would have known the cause, wherefore they accused him, I brought him forth into their Council.

29 There I perceived that he was accused of questions of their Law, but had no crime worthy of death, or of bonds.

30 And when it was showed me, how that the Jews laid wait for the man, I sent him straightway to thee, and commanded his accusers to speak before thee the things that they had against him. Farewell.

31 Then the soldiers as it was commanded them, took Paul, and brought him by night to Antipatris.

32 And the next day, they left the horsemen to go with him, and returned unto the castle.

33 Now when they came to Caesarea, they delivered the epistle to the Governor, and presented Paul also unto him.

34 So when the Governor had read it, he asked of what province he was: and when he understood that he was of Cilicia,

35 I will hear thee, said he, when thine accusers also are come, and commanded him to be kept in Herod's judgment hall.

Acts Chapter 24

1 Now after five days, Ananias the high Priest came down with the Elders, and with Tertullus a certain orator, which appeared before the Governor against Paul.

2 And when he was called forth, Tertullus began to accuse him, saying, Seeing that we have obtained great quietness through thee, and that many worthy things are done unto this nation through thy providence,

3 We acknowledge it wholly, and in all places, most noble Felix, with all thanks.

4 But that I be not tedious unto thee, I pray thee, that thou wouldest hear us of thy courtesy a few words.

5 Certainly we have found this man a pestilent fellow, and a mover of sedition among all the Jews throughout the world and a chief maintainer of the sect of the Nazarites:

6 And hath gone about to pollute the Temple: therefore we took him, and would have judged him according to our Law:

7 But the chief captain Lysias came upon us, and with great violence took him out of our hands,

8 Commanding his accusers to come to thee: of whom thou mayest (if thou wilt inquire) know all these things whereof we accuse him.

9 And the Jews likewise affirmed, saying that it was so.

10 Then Paul, after that the governor had beckoned unto him that he should speak, answered, I do the more gladly answer for myself, forasmuch as I know that thou hast been of many years a judge unto this nation,

11 Seeing that thou mayest know, that there are but twelve days since I came up to worship in Jerusalem.

12 And they neither found me in the Temple disputing with any man, neither making uproar among the people, neither in the Synagogues, nor in the city.

13 Neither can they prove the things, whereof they now accuse me.

14 But this I confess unto thee, that after the way (which they call heresy) so worship I the God of my fathers, believing all things which are written in the Law and the Prophets,

15 And have hope towards God, that the resurrection of the dead which they themselves look for also, shall be both of just and unjust.

16 And herein I endeavor myself to have alway a clear conscience toward God, and toward men.

17 Now after many years, I came and brought alms to my nation and offerings.

18 At what time, certain Jews of Asia found me purified in the Temple,

19 Neither with multitude, nor with tumult.
20 Who ought to have been present before thee, and accuse me, if they had ought against me.
21 Or let these themselves say, if they have found any unjust thing in me, while I stood in the Council,
22 Except it be for this one voice, that I cried standing among them, Of the resurrection of the dead am I accused of you this day.
23 Now when Felix heard these things, he deferred them, and said, When I shall more perfectly know the things which concern this way, by the coming of Lysias the chief Captain, I will decide your matter.
24 Then he commanded a Centurion to keep Paul, and that he should have ease, and that he should forbid none of his acquaintance to minister unto him, or to come unto him.
25 And after certain days, came Felix with his wife Drusilla, which was a Jewess, and he called forth Paul, and heard him of the faith in Christ.
26 And as he disputed of righteousness, and temperance, and of the judgment to come, Felix trembled, and answered, Go thy way for this time, and when I have convenient time, I will call for thee.
27 He hoped also that money should have been given him of Paul, that he might loose him: wherefore he sent for him the oftener, and communed with him.
28 When two years were expired, Porcius Festus came into Felix's room: and Felix willing to get favor of the Jews, left Paul bound.

Acts Chapter 25

1 When Festus was then come into the province, after three days he went up from Caesarea unto Jerusalem.
2 Then the high Priest, and the chief of the Jews appeared before him against Paul: and they besought him,
3 And desired favor against him, that he would send for him to Jerusalem: and they laid wait to kill him by the way.
4 But Festus answered, that Paul should be kept at Caesarea, and that he himself would shortly depart thither.
5 Let them therefore, said he, which among you are able, come down with us: and if there be any wickedness in the man, let them accuse him.
6 Now when he had tarried among them no more than ten days, he went down to Caesarea, and the next day sat in the judgment seat, and commanded Paul to be brought.
7 And when he was come, the Jews which were come from Jerusalem, stood about him and laid many and grievous complaints against Paul, which they could not prove,
8 Forasmuch as he answered, that he had neither offended any thing against the Law of the Jews, neither against the Temple, nor against Caesar.
9 Yet Festus willing to get favor of the Jews, answered Paul, and said, Wilt thou go up to Jerusalem, and there be judged of these things before me?
10 Then said Paul, I stand at Caesar's judgment seat, where I ought to be judged: to the Jews I have done no wrong, as thou very well knowest.
11 For if I have done wrong, or committed any thing worthy of death, I refuse not to die: but if there be none of these things whereof they accuse me, no man can deliver me to them: I appeal unto Caesar.
12 Then when Festus had spoken with the Council, he answered, Hast thou appealed unto Caesar? unto Caesar shalt thou go.
13 And after certain days, King Agrippa and Bernice came down to Caesarea to salute Festus.

14 And when they had remained there many days, Festus proposed Paul's cause unto the King, saying, There is a certain man left in prison by Felix.

15 Of whom when I came to Jerusalem, the high Priests and Elders of the Jews informed me, and desired to have judgment against him.

16 To whom I answered, that it is not the manner of the Romans for favor to deliver any man to the death before that he which is accused, have the accusers before him, and have place to defend himself, concerning the crime.

17 Therefore when they were come hither, without delay the day following I sat on the judgment seat, and commanded the man to be brought forth.

18 Against whom when the accusers stood up, they brought no crime of such things as I supposed:

19 But had certain questions against him of their own superstition, and of one Jesus which was dead, whom Paul affirmed to be alive.

20 And because I doubted of such manner of question, I asked him whether he would go to Jerusalem, and there be judged of these things.

21 But because he appealed to be reserved to the examination of Augustus, I commanded him to be kept, till I might send him to Caesar.

22 Then Agrippa said unto Festus, I would also hear the man myself. Tomorrow, said he, thou shalt hear him.

23 And on the morrow when Agrippa was come and Bernice with great pomp, and were entered into the Common hall with the chief captains and chief men of the city, at Festus' commandment Paul was brought forth.

24 And Festus said, King Agrippa, and all men which are present with us, ye see this man, about whom all the multitude of the Jews have called upon me, both at Jerusalem, and here, crying, that he ought not to live any longer.

25 Yet have I found nothing worthy of death, that he hath committed: nevertheless, seeing that he hath appealed to Augustus, I have determined to send him.

26 Of whom I have no certain thing to write unto my Lord: wherefore I have brought him forth unto you, and specially unto thee, King Agrippa, that after examination had, I might have somewhat to write.

27 For me thinketh it unreasonable to send a prisoner, and not to show the causes which are laid against him.

Acts Chapter 26

1 Then Agrippa said unto Paul, Thou art permitted to speak for thyself. So Paul stretched forth the hand, and answered for himself.

2 I think myself happy, King Agrippa, because I shall answer this day before thee of all the things whereof I am accused of the Jews:

3 Chiefly, because thou hast knowledge of all customs, and questions which are among the Jews: wherefore I beseech thee, to hear me patiently.

4 As touching my life from my childhood and what it was from the beginning among mine own nation at Jerusalem, know all the Jews,

5 Which knew me heretofore (if they would testify) that after the most strait sect of our religion I lived a Pharisee.

6 And now I stand and am accused for the hope of the promise made of God unto our fathers.

7 Whereunto our twelve tribes instantly serving God day and night, hope to come: for the which hope's sake, O King Agrippa, I am accused of the Jews.

8 Why should it be thought a thing incredible unto you, that God should raise again the dead?

9 I also verily thought in myself, that I ought to do many contrary things against the Name of Jesus of Nazareth.

10 Which thing I also did in Jerusalem: for many of the Saints I shut up in prison, having received authority of the high Priests, and when they were put to death, I gave my sentence.

11 And I punished them throughout all the Synagogues, and compelled them to blaspheme, and being more mad against them, I persecuted them, even unto strange cities.

12 At which time, even as I went to Damascus with authority, and commission from the high Priests,

13 At midday, O King, I saw in the way a light from heaven, passing the brightness of the sun, shine round about me, and them which went with me.

14 So when we were all fallen to the earth, I heard a voice speaking unto me, and saying in the Hebrew tongue, Saul, Saul, why persecutest thou me? It is hard for thee to kick against pricks.

15 Then I said, Who art thou, Lord? And he said, I am Jesus whom thou persecutest.

16 But rise and stand up on thy feet: for I have appeared unto thee for this purpose, to appoint thee a minister and a witness, both of the things which thou hast seen, and of the things in the which I will appear unto thee,

17 Delivering thee from the people, and from the Gentiles, unto whom now I send thee,

18 To open their eyes, that they may turn from darkness to light, and from the power of Satan unto God, that they may receive forgiveness of sins, and inheritance among them, which are sanctified by faith in me.

19 Wherefore, King Agrippa, I was not disobedient unto the heavenly vision,

20 But showed first unto them of Damascus, and at Jerusalem, and throughout all the coasts of Judea, and then to the Gentiles, that they should repent, and turn to God, and do works worthy amendment of life.

21 For this cause the Jews caught me in the Temple, and went about to kill me.

22 Nevertheless, I obtained help of God, and continue unto this day, witnessing both to small and to great, saying none other things, than those which the Prophets and Moses did say should come,

23 To wit, that Christ should suffer, and that he should be the first that should rise from the dead, and should show light unto the people, and to the Gentiles.

24 And as he thus answered for himself, Festus said with a loud voice, Paul, thou art besides thyself: much learning doth make thee mad.

25 But he said, I am not mad, O noble Festus, but I speak the words of truth and soberness.

26 For the King knoweth of these things, before whom also I speak boldly: for I am persuaded that none of these things are hid from him: for this thing was not done in a corner.

27 O King Agrippa, believest thou the Prophets? I know that thou believest.

28 Then Agrippa said unto Paul, Almost thou persuadest me to become a Christian.

29 Then Paul said, I would to God that not only thou, but also all that hear me today, were both almost, and altogether such as I am, except these bonds.

30 And when he had thus spoken, the King rose up, and the governor, and Bernice, and they that sat with them.

31 And when they were gone apart, they talked between themselves, saying, This man doeth nothing worthy of death, nor of bonds.

32 Then said Agrippa unto Festus, This man might have been loosed, if he had not appealed unto Caesar.

Acts Chapter 27

1 Now when it was concluded, that we should sail into Italy, they delivered both Paul, and certain other prisoners unto a Centurion named Julius, of the band of Augustus.

2 And we entered into a ship of Adramyttium purposing to sail by the coasts of Asia, and launched forth, and had Aristarchus of Macedonia, a Thessalonian, with us.

3 And the next day we arrived at Sidon: and Julius courteously entreated Paul, and gave him liberty to go unto his friends, that they might refresh him.

4 And from thence we launched, and sailed hard by Cyprus, because the winds were contrary.

5 Then sailed we over the sea by Cilicia, and Pamphilia, and came to Myra, a city in Lycia.

6 And there the Centurion found a ship of Alexandria, sailing into Italy, and put us therein.

7 And when we had sailed slowly many days, and scarce were come against Gnidum, because the wind suffered us not, we sailed hard by Candy, near to Salmone,

8 And with much ado sailed beyond it, and came unto a certain place called the Fair Havens, near unto the which was the city Lasea.

9 So when much time was spent, and sailing was now jeopardous, because also the Fast was now passed, Paul exhorted them,

10 And said unto them, Sirs, I see that this voyage will be with hurt and much damage, not of the lading and ship only, but also of our lives.

11 Nevertheless the Centurion believed rather the governor and the master of the ship, than those things which were spoken of Paul.

12 And because the haven was not commodious to winter in, many took counsel to depart thence, if by any means they might attain to Phenice, there to winter, which is an haven of Candy, and lieth toward the Southwest and by West, and Northwest and by West.

13 And when the Southern wind blew softly, they supposing to obtain their purpose, loosed nearer, and sailed by Candy.

14 But anon after, there arose by it a stormy wind called Euroclydon.

15 And when the ship was caught, and could not resist the wind, we let her go, and were carried away.

16 And we ran under a little Isle named Clauda, and had much a do to get the boat.

17 Which they took up and used all help, undergirding the ship, fearing lest they should have fallen into Syrtes, and they let down the vessel, and so were carried.

18 The next day when we were tossed with an exceeding tempest, they lightened the ship.

19 And the third day we cast out with our own hands the tackling of the ship.

20 And when neither sun nor stars in many days appeared, and no small tempest lay upon us, all hope that we should be saved, was then taken away.

21 But after long abstinence, Paul stood forth in the midst of them, and said, Sirs, ye should have hearkened to me, and not have loosed from Candy: so should ye have gained this hurt and loss.

22 But now I exhort you to be of good courage: for there shall be no loss of any man's life among you, save of the ship only.

23 For there stood by me this night the Angel of God, whose I am, and whom I serve,

24 Saying, Fear not, Paul: for thou must be brought before Caesar: and lo, God hath given unto thee all that sail with thee.

25 Wherefore, sirs, be of good courage: for I believe God, that it shall be so as it hath been told me.

26 Howbeit, we must be cast into a certain Island.

27 And when the fourteenth night was come, as we were carried to and fro in the Adriatical sea about midnight, the shipmen deemed that some country approached unto them,

28 And sounded, and found it twenty fathoms: and when they had gone a little further, they sounded again, and found fifteen fathoms.

29 Then fearing lest they should have fallen into some rough places, they cast four anchors out of the stern, and wished that the day were come.

30 Now as the mariners were about to flee out of the ship, and had let down the boat into the sea under a color as though they would have cast anchors out of the foreship,

31 Paul said unto the Centurion and the soldiers, Except these abide in the ship, ye cannot be safe.

32 Then the soldiers cut off the ropes of the boat, and let it fall away.

33 And when it began to be day, Paul exhorted them all to take meat, saying, This is the fourteenth day that ye have tarried, and continued fasting, receiving nothing.

34 Wherefore I exhort you to take meat: for this is for your safeguard: for there shall not an hair fall from the head of any of you.

35 And when he had thus spoken, he took bread, and gave thanks to God, in presence of them all, and brake it, and began to eat.

36 Then were they all of good courage, and they also took meat.

37 Now we were in the ship in all two hundred, three score and sixteen souls.

38 And when they had eaten enough, they lightened the ship, and cast out the wheat into the sea.

39 And when it was day, they knew not the country, but they spied a certain creek with a bank, into the which they were minded (if it were possible) to thrust in the ship.

40 So when they had taken up the anchors, they committed the ship unto the sea, and loosed the rudder bonds, and hoisted up the main sail to the wind, and drew to the shore.

41 And when they fell into a place, where two seas met, they thrust in the ship: and the forepart stuck fast, and could not be moved, but the hinderpart was broken with the violence of the waves.

42 Then the soldiers counsel was to kill the prisoners, lest any of them, when he had swum out, should flee away.

43 But the Centurion willing to save Paul, stayed them from this counsel, and commanded that they that could swim, should cast themselves first into the sea, and go out to land:

44 And the other, some on boards, and some on certain pieces of the ship: and so it came to pass, that they came all safe to land.

Acts Chapter 28

1 And when they were come safe, then they knew that the Isle was called Melita.

2 And the Barbarians showed us no little kindness: for they kindled a fire, and received us every one, because of the present shower, and because of the cold.

3 And when Paul had gathered a number of sticks, and laid them on the fire, there came a viper out of the heat, and leapt on his hand.

4 Now when the Barbarians saw the worm hang on his hand, they said among themselves, This man surely is a murderer, whom, though he hath escaped the sea, yet Vengeance hath not suffered to live.

5 But he shook off the worm into the fire, and felt no harm.

6 Howbeit they waited when he should have swollen, or fallen down dead suddenly: but after they had looked a great while, and saw no inconvenience come to him, they changed their minds, and said, That he was a God.

7 In the same quarters, the chief man of the Isle (whose name was Publius) had possessions: the same received us, and lodged us three days courteously.

8 And so it was, that the father of Publius lay sick of the fever, and of a bloody flux: to whom Paul entered in, and when he prayed, he laid his hands on him, and healed him.

9 When this then was done, other also in the Isle, which had diseases, came to him and were healed,

10 Which also did us great honor: and when we departed, they laded us with things necessary.

11 Now after three months we departed in a ship of Alexandria, which had wintered in the Isle, whose badge was Castor and Pollux.

12 And when we arrived at Syracuse, we tarried there three days.

13 And from thence we set a compass, and came to Rhegium: and after one day, the South wind blew, and we came the second day to Putioli,

14 Where we found brethren, and were desired to tarry with them seven days, and so we went toward Rome.

15 And from thence, when the brethren heard of us, they came to meet us at the Market of Appius, and at the Three taverns, whom when Paul saw, he thanked God, and waxed bold.

16 So when we came to Rome, the Centurion delivered the prisoners to the general Captain: but Paul was suffered to dwell by himself with a soldier that kept him.

17 And the third day after, Paul called the chief of the Jews together: and when they were come, he said unto them, Men and brethren, though I have committed nothing against the people, or Laws of the fathers, yet was I delivered prisoner from Jerusalem into the hands of the Romans.

18 Who when they had examined me, would have let me go, because there was no cause of death in me.

19 But when the Jews spake contrary, I was constrained to appeal unto Cesar, not because I had aught to accuse my nation of.

20 For this cause therefore have I called for you, to see you, and to speak with you: for the hope of Israel's sake, I am bound with this chain.

21 Then they said unto him, We neither received letters out of Judea concerning thee, neither came any of the brethren that showed or spake any evil of thee.

22 But we will hear of thee what thou thinkest: for as concerning this sect, we know that everywhere it is spoken against.

23 And when they had appointed him a day, there came many unto him into his lodging, to whom he expounded and testified the kingdom of God, and preached unto them concerning Jesus both out of the Law of Moses and out of the Prophets, from morning to night.

24 And some were persuaded with the things, which were spoken, and some believed not.

25 Therefore when they agreed not among themselves, they departed, after that Paul had spoken one word, to wit, Well spake the Holy Ghost by Isaiah the Prophet unto our fathers,

26 Saying, Go unto this people, and say, By hearing ye shall hear, and shall not understand, and seeing ye shall see, and not perceive.

27 For the heart of this people is waxed fat, and their ears are dull of hearing, and with their eyes have they winked, lest they should see with their eyes, and hear with their ears, and understand with their hearts, and should return that I might heal them.

28 Be it known therefore unto you, that this salvation of God is sent to the Gentiles, and they shall hear it.

29 And when he had said these things, the Jews departed, and had great reasoning among themselves.

30 And Paul remained two years full in an house hired for himself, and received all that came in unto him,

31 Preaching the kingdom of God, and teaching those things, which concern the Lord Jesus Christ, with all boldness of speech, without let.

THE EPISTLE OF THE APOSTLE PAUL TO THE ROMANS

Romans Chapter 1

1 Paul a servant of JESUS CHRIST, called to be an Apostle, put apart to preach the Gospel of God,

2 (Which he had promised afore by his Prophets in the Holy Scriptures) 3 Concerning his Son Jesus Christ our Lord (which was made of the seed of David according to the flesh,

4 And declared mightily to be the Son of God, touching the Spirit of sanctification by the resurrection from the dead)

5 By whom we have received grace and Apostleship (that obedience might be given unto the faith) in his Name among all the Gentiles,

6 Among whom ye be also the called of Jesus Christ:

7 To all you that be at Rome beloved of God, called to be Saints: Grace be with you, and peace from God our Father, and from the Lord Jesus Christ.

8 First I thank my God through Jesus Christ for you all, because your faith is published throughout the whole world.

9 For God is my witness (whom I serve in my spirit in the Gospel of his Son) that without ceasing I make mention of you

10 Always in my prayers, beseeching, that by some means one time or other I might have a prosperous journey by the will of God, to come unto you.

11 For I long to see you, that I might bestow among you some spiritual gift, to strengthen you,

12 That is, that I might be comforted together with you, through our mutual faith, both yours and mine.

13 Now my brethren, I would that ye should not be ignorant, how that I have oftentimes purposed to come unto you (but have been let hitherto) that I might have some fruit also among you, as I have among the other Gentiles.

14 I am debtor both to the Grecians, and to the Barbarians, both to the wise men and unto the unwise.

15 Therefore, as much as in me is, I am ready to preach the Gospel to you also that are at Rome.

16 For I am not ashamed of the Gospel of Christ: for it is the power of God unto salvation to every one that believeth, to the Jew first, and also to the Grecian.

17 For by it the righteousness of God is revealed, from faith to faith: as it is written, The just shall live by faith.

18 For the wrath of God is revealed from heaven against all ungodliness, and unrighteousness of men, which withhold the truth in unrighteousness,

19 Forasmuch as that, which may be known of God, is manifest in them: for God hath showed it unto them.

20 For the invisible things of him, that is, his eternal power and Godhead, are seen by the creation of the world, being considered in his works, to the intent that they should be without excuse:

21 Because that when they knew God, they glorified him not as God, neither were thankful, but became vain in their imaginations, and their foolish heart was full of darkness.

22 When they professed themselves to be wise, they became fools.

23 For they turned the glory of the incorruptible God to the similitude of the image of a corruptible man, and of birds, and four footed beasts, and of creeping things.

24 Wherefore also God gave them up to their hearts lusts, unto uncleanness, to defile their own bodies between themselves:

25 Which turned the truth of God unto a lie, and worshipped and served the creature, forsaking the Creator, which is blessed forever, Amen.

26 For this cause God gave them up unto vile affections: for even their women did change the natural use into that which is against nature.

27 And likewise also the men left the natural use of the woman, and burned in their lust one toward another, and man with man wrought filthiness, and received in themselves such recompense of their error, as was meet.

28 For as they regarded not to know God, even so God delivered them up unto a reprobate mind, to do those things which are not convenient,

29 Being full of all unrighteousness, fornication, wickedness, covetousness, maliciousness, full of envy, of murder, of debate, of deceit, taking all things in the evil part, whisperers,

30 Backbiters, haters of God, doers of wrong, proud, boasters, inventors of evil things, disobedient to parents, without understanding, covenant breakers, without natural affection, such as can never be appeased, merciless.

31 Which men, though they knew the Law of God, how that they which commit such things, are worthy of death, yet not only do the same, but also favor them that do them.

Romans Chapter 2

1 Therefore thou art inexcusable, O man, whosoever thou art that judgest: for in that thou judgest another, thou condemnest thy self: for thou that judgest, doest the same things.

2 But we know that the judgment of God is according to truth, against them which commit such things.

3 And thinkest thou this, O thou man, that judgest them which do such things, and doest the same, that thou shalt escape the judgment of God?

4 Or despisest thou the riches of his bountifulness, and patience, and long sufferance, not knowing that the bountifulness of GOD leadeth thee to repentance?

5 But thou, after thine hardness and heart that cannot repent, heapest unto thyself wrath against the day of wrath and of the declaration of the just judgment of God,

6 Who will reward every man according to his works:

7 That is, to them which by continuance in well doing seek glory, and honor, and immortality, eternal life:

8 But unto them that are contentious and disobey the truth, and obey unrighteousness, shall be indignation and wrath.

9 Tribulation and anguish shall be upon the soul of every man that doeth evil: of the Jew first, and also of the Grecian.

10 But to every man that doeth good, shall be glory, and honor, and peace, to the Jew first, and also to the Grecian.

11 For there is no respect of persons with God.

12 For as many as have sinned without the Law, shall perish also without the Law: and as many as have sinned in the Law, shall be judged by the Law

13 (For the hearers of the Law are not righteous before God: but the doers of the Law shall be justified.

14 For when the Gentiles which have not the Law, do by nature the things contained in the Law, they having not the Law, are a Law unto themselves,

15 Which show the effect of the Law written in their hearts, their conscience also bearing witness, and their thoughts accusing one another, or excusing,)

16 At the day when God shall judge the secrets of men by Jesus Christ, according to my Gospel.

17 Behold, thou art called a Jew, and restest in the Law, and gloriest in God,

18 And knowest his will, and allowest the things that are excellent, in that thou art instructed by the Law:

19 And persuadest thy self that thou art a guide of the blind, a light of them which are in darkness.

20 An instructor of them which lack discretion, a teacher of the unlearned, which hast the form of knowledge, and of the truth in the Law.

21 Thou therefore, which teachest another, teachest thou not thy self? thou that preachest, A man should not steal, dost thou steal?

22 Thou that sayest, A man should not commit adultery, dost thou commit adultery? thou that abhorest idols, committest thou sacrilege?

23 Thou that gloriest in the Law, through breaking the Law dishonorest thou God?

24 For the Name of God is blasphemed among the Gentiles through you, as it is written.

25 For circumcision verily is profitable, if thou do the Law: but if thou be a transgressor of the Law, thy circumcision is made uncircumcision.

26 Therefore if the uncircumcision keep the ordinances of the Law, shall not his uncircumcision be counted for circumcision?

27 And shall not uncircumcision which is by nature (if it keep the Law) judge thee, which by the letter and circumcision art a transgressor of the Law?

28 For he is not a Jew, which is one outward: neither is that circumcision, which is outward in the flesh:

29 But he is a Jew which is one within, and the circumcision is of the heart, in the spirit, not in the letter, whose praise is not of men, but of God.

Romans Chapter 3

1 What is then the preferment of the Jew? or what is the profit of circumcision?

2 Much every manner of way: for chiefly, because unto them were committed the oracles of God.

3 For what, though some did not believe? shall their unbelief make the faith of God without effect?

4 God forbid: yea, let God be true, and every man a liar, as it is written, That thou mightest be justified in thy words, and overcome, when thou art judged.

5 Now if our unrighteousness commend the righteousness of God, what shall we say? Is God unrighteous which punisheth? (I speak as a man.)

6 God forbid: else how shall God judge the world?

7 For if the verity of God hath more abounded through my lie unto his glory, why am I yet condemned as a sinner?

8 And (as we are blamed, and as some affirm that we say) why do we not evil, that good may come thereof? whose damnation is just.

9 What then? are we more excellent? No, in no wise: for we have already proved, that all, both Jews and Gentiles are under sin.

10 As it is written, There is none righteous, no not one.

11 There is none that understandeth: there is none that seeketh God.

12 They have all gone out of the way: they have been made altogether unprofitable: there is none that doeth good, no not one.

13 Their throat is an open sepulcher: they have used their tongues to deceit: the poison of asps is under their lips.

14 Whose mouth is full of cursing and bitterness.

15 Their feet are swift to shed blood.

16 Destruction and calamity are in their ways,

17 And the way of peace they have not known.

18 The fear of God is not before their eyes.

NEW TESTAMENT - **ROMANS**

19 Now we know that whatsoever the Law saith, it saith it to them which are under the Law, that every mouth may be stopped, and all the world be culpable before God.

20 Therefore by the works of the Law shall no flesh be justified in his sight: for by the Law cometh the knowledge of sin.

21 But now is the righteousness of God made manifest without the Law, having witness of the Law and of the Prophets,

22 To wit, the righteousness of God by the faith of Jesus Christ, unto all, and upon all that believe.

23 For there is no difference: for all have sinned, and are deprived of the glory of God,

24 And are justified freely by his grace, through the redemption that is in Christ Jesus,

25 Whom God hath set forth to be a reconciliation through faith in his blood to declare his righteousness, by the forgiveness of the sins that are passed through the patience of God,

26 To show at this time his righteousness, that he might be just, and a justifier of him which is of the faith of Jesus.

27 Where is then the rejoicing? It is excluded. By what Law? of works? Nay: but by the Law of faith.

28 Therefore we conclude that a man is justified by faith without the works of the Law.

29 God, is he the God of the Jews only, and not of the Gentiles also? Yes, even of the Gentiles also.

30 For it is one God who shall justify circumcision of faith, and uncircumcision through faith.

31 Do we then make the Law of none effect through faith? God forbid: yea we establish the Law.

Romans Chapter 4

1 What shall we say then, that Abraham our father hath found concerning the flesh?

2 For if Abraham were justified by works, he hath wherein to rejoice, but not with God.

3 For what saith the Scripture? Abraham believed God, and it was counted to him for righteousness.

4 Now to him that worketh, the wages is not counted by favor, but by debt,

5 But to him that worketh not, but believeth in him that justifieth the ungodly, his faith is counted for righteousness.

6 Even as David declareth the blessedness of the man, unto whom God imputeth righteousness without works, saying,

7 Blessed are they, whose iniquities are forgiven, and whose sins are covered.

8 Blessed is the man, to whom the Lord imputeth not sin.

9 Came this blessedness then upon the circumcision only, or upon the uncircumcision also? For we say, that faith was imputed unto Abraham for righteousness.

10 How was it then imputed? when he was circumcised, or uncircumcised? not when he was circumcised, but when he was uncircumcised.

11 After he received the sign of circumcision, as the seal of the righteousness of the faith which he had, when he was uncircumcised, that he should be the father of all them that believe, not being circumcised, that righteousness might be imputed to them also,

12 And the father of circumcision, not unto them only which are of the circumcision, but unto them also that walk in the steps of the faith of our father Abraham, which he had when he was uncircumcised.

13 For the promise that he should be the heir of the world, was not given to Abraham, or to his seed, through the Law, but through the righteousness of faith.

14 For if they which are of the Law, be heirs, faith is made void, and the promise is made of none effect.

15 For the Law causeth wrath: for where no Law is, there is no transgression.
16 Therefore it is by faith, that it might come by grace, and the promise might be sure to all the seed, not to that only which is of the Law: but also to that which is of the faith of Abraham, who is the father of us all,
17 (As it is written, I have made thee a father of many nations) even before God whom he believed, who quickeneth the dead, and calleth those things which be not, as though they were.
18 Which Abraham above hope, believed under hope, that he should be the father of many nations: according to that which was spoken to him, So shall thy seed be.
19 And he not weak in the faith, considered not his own body, which was now dead, being almost an hundredth year old, neither the deadness of Sarah's womb.
20 Neither did he doubt of the promise of God through unbelief, but was strengthened in the faith, and gave glory to God,
21 Being fully assured that he which had promised, was also able to do it.
22 And therefore it was imputed to him for righteousness.
23 Now it is not written for him only, that it was imputed to him for righteousness,
24 But also for us, to whom it shall be imputed for righteousness, which believe in him that raised up Jesus our Lord from the dead.
25 Who was delivered to death for our sins, and is risen again for our justification.

Romans Chapter 5

1 Then being justified by faith, we have peace toward God through our Lord Jesus Christ.
2 By whom also we have access through faith unto this grace, wherein we stand, and rejoice under the hope of the glory of God.
3 Neither do we so only, but also we rejoice in tribulations, knowing that tribulation bringeth forth patience,
4 And patience experience, and experience hope,
5 And hope maketh not ashamed, because the love of God is shed abroad in our hearts by the Holy Ghost, which is given unto us.
6 For Christ, when we were yet of no strength, at his time, died for the ungodly.
7 Doubtless one will scarce die for a righteous man: but yet for a good man it may be that one dare die.
8 But God setteth out his love toward us, seeing that while we were yet sinners, Christ died for us.
9 Much more then, being now justified by his blood, we shall be saved from wrath through him.
10 For if when we were enemies, we were reconciled to God by the death of his Son, much more being reconciled, we shall be saved by his life.
11 And not only so, but we also rejoice in God through our Lord Jesus Christ, by whom we have now received the atonement.
12 Wherefore, as by one man sin entered into the world, and death by sin, and so death went over all men: for as much as all men have sinned.
13 For unto the time of the Law was sin in the world, but sin is not imputed, while there is no Law.
14 But death reigned from Adam to Moses even over them also that sinned not after the like manner of the transgression of Adam, which was the figure of him that was to come.
15 But yet the gift is not so, as is the offence: for if through the offence of one, many be dead, much more the grace of God, and the gift by grace, which is by one man Jesus Christ, hath abounded unto many.
16 Neither is the gift so, as that which entered in by one that sinned: for the fault came of one offence unto condemnation: but the gift is of many offences to justification.

17 For if by the offence of one, death reigned through one, much more shall they which receive the abundance of grace, and of the gift of righteousness, reign in life through one, that is Jesus Christ.

18 Likewise then as by the offence of one the fault came on all men to condemnation, so by the justifying of one the benefit abounded toward all men to the justification of life.

19 For as by one mans disobedience many were made sinners, so by the obedience of one shall many also be made righteous.

20 Moreover the Law entered thereupon that the offence should abound: nevertheless where sin abounded, there grace abounded much more:

21 That as sin had reigned unto death, so might grace also reign by righteousness unto eternal life, through Jesus Christ our Lord.

Romans Chapter 6

1 What shall we say then? Shall we continue still in sin, that grace may abound? God forbid.

2 How shall we, that are dead to sin, live yet therein?

3 Know ye not, that all we which have been baptized into Jesus Christ, have been baptized into his death?

4 We are buried then with him by baptism into his death, that like as Christ was raised up from the dead by the glory of the Father, so we also should walk in newness of life.

5 For if we be grafted with him to the similitude of his death, even so shall we be to the similitude of his resurrection,

6 Knowing this, that our old man is crucified with him, that the body of sin might be destroyed, that henceforth we should not serve sin.

7 For he that is dead, is freed from sin.

8 Wherefore, if we be dead with Christ, we believe that we shall live also with him,

9 Knowing that Christ being raised from the dead, dieth no more: death hath no more dominion over him.

10 For in that he died, he died once to sin: but in that he liveth, he liveth to God.

11 Likewise think ye also, that ye are dead to sin, but are alive to God in Jesus Christ our Lord.

12 Let not sin reign therefore in your mortal body, that ye should obey it in the lusts thereof.

13 Neither give ye your members as weapons of unrighteousness unto sin: but give your selves unto God, as they that are alive from the dead, and give your members as weapons of righteousness unto God.

14 For sin shall not have dominion over you: for ye are not under the Law, but under grace.

15 What then? shall we sin, because we are not under the Law, but under grace? God forbid.

16 Know ye not, that to whomsoever ye give your selves as servants to obey, his servants ye are to whom ye obey, whether it be of sin unto death, or of obedience unto righteousness?

17 But God be thanked, that ye have been the servants of sin, but ye have obeyed from the heart unto the form of the doctrine, whereunto ye were delivered.

18 Being then made free from sin, ye are made the servants of righteousness.

19 I speak after the manner of man, because of the infirmity of your flesh: for as ye have given your members servants to uncleanness and to iniquity, to commit iniquity, so now give your members servants unto righteousness in holiness.

20 For when ye were the servants of sin, ye were freed from righteousness.

21 What fruit had ye then in those things, whereof ye are now ashamed? For the end of those things is death.

22 But now being freed from sin, and made servants unto God, ye have your fruit in holiness, and the end, everlasting life.

23 For the wages of sin is death: but the gift of God is eternal life through Jesus Christ our Lord.

Romans Chapter 7

1 Know ye not, brethren, (for I speak to them that know the Law) that the Law hath dominion over a man as long as he liveth?

2 For the woman which is in subjection to a man, is bound by the law to the man, while he liveth: but if the man be dead, she is delivered from the law of the man.

3 So then, if while the man liveth, she take another man, she shall be called an adulteress: but if the man be dead, she is free from the Law, so that she is not an adulteress, though she take another man.

4 So ye, my brethren, are dead also to the Law by the body of Christ, that ye should be unto another, even unto him that is raised up from the dead, that we should bring forth fruit unto God.

5 For when we were in the flesh, the motions of sins, which were by the Law, had force in our members, to bring forth fruit unto death.

6 But now we are delivered from the Law, being dead unto it, wherein we were holden, that we should serve in newness of Spirit, and not in the oldness of the letter.

7 What shall we say then? Is the Law sin? God forbid. Nay, I knew not sin, but by the Law: for I had not known lust, except the Law had said, Thou shalt not lust.

8 But sin took an occasion by the commandment, and wrought in me all manner of concupiscence: for without the Law sin is dead.

9 For I once was alive, without the Law: but when the commandment came, sin revived,

10 But I died: and the same commandment which was ordained unto life, was found to be unto me unto death.

11 For sin took occasion by the commandment, and deceived me, and thereby slew me.

12 Wherefore the Law is holy, and the commandment is holy, and just, and good.

13 Was that then which is good, made death unto me? God forbid: but sin, that it might appear sin, wrought death in me by that which is good, that sin might be out of measure sinful by the commandment.

14 For we know that the Law is spiritual, but I am carnal, sold under sin.

15 For I allow not that which I do: for what I would, that do I not: but what I hate, that do I.

16 If I do then that which I would not, I consent to the Law, that it is good.

17 Now then, it is no more I, that do it, but the sin that dwelleth in me.

18 For I know, that in me, that is, in my flesh, dwelleth no good thing: for to will is present with me: but I find no means to perform that which is good.

19 For I do not the good thing, which I would, but the evil, which I would not, that do I.

20 Now if I do that I would not, it is no more I that do it, but the sin that dwelleth in me.

21 I find then by the Law, that when I would do good, evil is present with me.

22 For I delight in the Law of God, concerning the inner man:

23 But I see another law in my members, rebelling against the law of my mind, and leading me captive unto the law of sin, which is in my members.

24 O wretched man that I am, who shall deliver me from the body of this death!

25 I thank God through Jesus Christ our Lord. Then I my self in my mind serve the Law of God, but in my flesh the law of sin.

Romans Chapter 8

1 Now then there is no condemnation to them that are in Christ Jesus, which walk not after the flesh, but after the Spirit.

2 For the Law of the Spirit of life, which is in Christ Jesus, hath freed me from the law of sin and of death.

3 For (that that was impossible to the Law, in as much as it was weak, because of the flesh) God sending his own Son, in the similitude of sinful flesh, and for sin, condemned sin in the flesh,

4 That the righteousness of the Law might be fulfilled in us, which walk not after the flesh, but after the Spirit.

5 For they that are after the flesh, savor the things of the flesh: but they that are after the Spirit, the things of the Spirit.

6 For the wisdom of the flesh is death: but the wisdom of the Spirit is life and peace,

7 Because the wisdom of the flesh is enmity against God: for it is not subject to the Law of God, neither in deed can be.

8 So then they that are in the flesh, cannot please God.

9 Now ye are not in the flesh, but in the Spirit, because the Spirit of God dwelleth in you: but if any man hath not the Spirit of Christ, the same is not his.

10 And if Christ be in you, the body is dead, because of sin: but the Spirit is life for righteousness sake.

11 But if the Spirit of him that raised up Jesus from the dead, dwell in you, he that raised up Christ from the dead, shall also quicken your mortal bodies, because that his Spirit dwelleth in you.

12 Therefore brethren, we are debtors not to the flesh, to live after the flesh:

13 For if ye live after the flesh, ye shall die: but if ye mortify the deeds of the body by the Spirit, ye shall live.

14 For as many as are led by the Spirit of God, they are the sons of God.

15 For ye have not received the Spirit of bondage to fear again: but ye have received the Spirit of adoption, whereby we cry Abba, Father.

16 The same Spirit beareth witness with our Spirit, that we are the children of God.

17 If we be children, we are also heirs, even the heirs of God, and heirs annexed with Christ, if so be that we suffer with him, that we may also be glorified with him.

18 For I count that the afflictions of this present time are not worthy of the glory, which shall be showed unto us.

19 For the fervent desire of the creature waiteth when the sons of God shall be revealed,

20 Because the creature is subject to vanity, not of it own will, but by reason of him, which hath subdued it under hope,

21 Because the creature also shall be delivered from the bondage of corruption into the glorious liberty of the sons of God.

22 For we know that every creature groaneth with us also, and travaileth in pain together unto this present.

23 And not only the creature, but we also which have the first fruits of the Spirit, even we do sigh in our selves, waiting for the adoption, even the redemption of our body.

24 For we are saved by hope: but hope that is seen, is not hope: for how can a man hope for that which he seeth?

25 But if we hope for that we see not, we do with patience abide for it.

26 Likewise the Spirit also helpeth our infirmities: for we know not what to pray as we ought: but the Spirit itself maketh request for us with sighs, which cannot be expressed.

27 But he that searcheth the hearts, knoweth what is the meaning of the Spirit: for he maketh request for the Saints, according to the will of God.

28 Also we know that all things work together for the best unto them that love God, even to them that are called of his purpose.

29 For those which he knew before, he also predestinate to be made like to the image of his Son, that he might be the first born among many brethren.

30 Moreover whom he predestinate, them also he called, and whom he called, them also he justified, and whom he justified, them he also glorified.

31 What shall we then say to these things? If God be on our side, who can be against us?

32 Who spared not his own Son, but gave him for us all to death, how shall he not with him give us all things also?

33 Who shall lay any thing to the charge of God's chosen? it is God that justifieth,

34 Who shall condemn? it is Christ, which is dead, yea or rather, which is risen again, who is also at the right hand of God, and maketh request also for us.

35 Who shall separate us from the love of Christ? shall tribulation or anguish, or persecution, or famine, or nakedness, or peril, or sword?

36 As it is written, For thy sake are we killed all day long: we are counted as sheep for the slaughter.

37 Nevertheless, in all these things we are more than conquerors through him that loved us.

38 For I am persuaded that neither death, nor life, nor Angels, nor principalities, nor powers, nor things present, nor things to come,

39 Nor height, nor depth, nor any other creature shall be able to separate us from the love of God, which is in Christ Jesus our Lord.

Romans Chapter 9

1 I say the truth in Christ, I lie not, my conscience bearing me witness in the Holy Ghost,

2 That I have great heaviness and continual sorrow in mine heart.

3 For I would wish myself to be separate from Christ, for my brethren that are my kinsmen according to the flesh,

4 Which are the Israelites, to whom pertaineth the adoption, and the glory, and the Covenants, and the giving of the Law, and the service of God, and the promises.

5 Of whom are the fathers, and of whom concerning the flesh, Christ came, who is God over all blessed forever, Amen.

6 Notwithstanding it cannot be that the word of God should take none effect: for all they are not Israel, which are of Israel:

7 Neither are they all children, because they are the seed of Abraham: but, In Isaac shall thy seed be called:

8 That is, they which are the children of the flesh, are not the children of God: but the children of the promise are counted for the seed.

9 For this is a word of promise, In this same time will I come, and Sara shall have a son.

10 Neither he only felt this, but also Rebecca when she had conceived by one, even by our father Isaac.

11 For ere the children were born, and when they had neither done good, nor evil (that the purpose of God might remain according to election not by works, but by him that calleth)

12 It was said unto her, The elder shall serve the younger.

13 As it is written, I have loved Jacob, and have hated Esau.

14 What shall we say then? Is there unrighteousness with God? God forbid.

15 For he saith to Moses, I will have mercy on him, to whom I will show mercy: and will have compassion on him, on whom I will have compassion.

16 So then it is not in him that willeth, nor in him that runneth, but in God that showeth mercy.

17 For the Scripture saith unto Pharaoh, For this same purpose have I stirred thee up, that I might show my power in thee, and that my Name might be declared throughout all the earth.

18 Therefore he hath mercy on whom he will, and whom he will, he hardeneth.

19 Thou wilt say then unto me, Why doth he yet complain? for who hath resisted his will?

20 But, O man, who art thou which pleadest against God? shall the thing formed say to him that formed it, Why hast thou made me thus?

21 Hath not the potter power of the clay to make of the same lump one vessel to honor, and another unto dishonor?

22 What and if God would, to show his wrath, and to make his power known, suffer with long patience the vessels of wrath, prepared to destruction?

23 And that he might declare the riches of his glory upon the vessels of mercy, which he hath prepared unto glory?

24 Even us, whom he hath called, not of the Jews only, but also of the Gentiles,

25 As he saith also in Osee, I will call them, My people, which were not my people: and her, Beloved, which was not beloved.

26 And it shall be in the place where it was said unto them, Ye are not my people, that there they shall be called, The children of the living God.

27 Also Esaias crieth concerning Israel, Though the number of the children of Israel were as the sand of the sea, yet shall but a remnant be saved.

28 For he will make his account, and gather it into a short sum with righteousness: for the Lord will make a short count in the earth.

29 And as Esaias said before, Except the Lord of hosts had left us a seed, we had been made as Sodom, and had been like to Gomorrah.

30 What shall we say then? That the Gentiles which followed not righteousness, have attained unto righteousness, even the righteousness which is of faith.

31 But Israel which followed the Law of righteousness, could not attain unto the Law of righteousness.

32 Wherefore? Because they sought it not by faith, but as it were by the works of the Law: for they have stumbled at the stumbling stone,

33 As it is written, Behold, I lay in Zion a stumbling stone, and a rock to make men fall: and every one that believeth in him, shall not be ashamed.

Romans Chapter 10

1 Brethren, mine hearts desire and prayer to God for Israel is, that they might be saved.

2 For I bear them record, that they have the zeal of God, but not according to knowledge.

3 For they, being ignorant of the righteousness of God, and going about to stablish their own righteousness, have not submitted themselves to the righteousness of God.

4 For Christ is the end of the Law for righteousness unto every one that believeth.

5 For Moses thus describeth the righteousness which is of the Law, That the man which doeth these things, shall live thereby.

6 But the righteousness which is of faith, speaketh on this wise, Say not in thine heart, Who shall ascend into heaven? (that is to bring Christ from above)

7 Or, Who shall descend into the deep? (that is to bring Christ again from the dead)

8 But what saith it? The word is near thee, even in thy mouth, and in thine heart. This is the word of faith which we preach.

9 For if thou shalt confess with thy mouth the Lord Jesus, and shalt believe in thine heart, that God raised him up from the dead, thou shalt be saved.
10 For with the heart man believeth unto righteousness, and with the mouth man confesseth to salvation.
11 For the Scripture saith, Whosoever believeth in him, shall not be ashamed.
12 For there is no difference between the Jew and the Grecian: for he that is Lord over all, is rich unto all, that call on him.
13 For whosoever shall call upon the Name of the Lord, shall be saved.
14 But how shall they call on him, in whom they have not believed? and how shall they believe in him, of whom they have not heard? and how shall they hear without a preacher?
15 And how shall they preach, except they be sent? as it is written, How beautiful are the feet of them which bring glad tidings of peace, and bring glad tidings of good things!
16 But they have not all obeyed the Gospel: for Esaias saith, Lord, who hath believed our report?
17 Then faith is by hearing, and hearing by the word of God.
18 But I demand, Have they not heard? No doubt their sound went out through all the earth, and their words into the ends of the world.
19 But I demand, Did not Israel know God? First Moses saith, I will provoke you to envy by a nation that is not my nation, and by a foolish nation I will anger you.
20 And Esaias is bold, and saith, I was found of them that sought me not, and have been made manifest to them that asked not after me.
21 And unto Israel he saith, All the day long have I stretched forth mine hand unto a disobedient, and gainsaying people.

Romans Chapter 11

1 I Demand then, Hath God cast away his people? God forbid: for I also am an Israelite, of the seed of Abraham, of the tribe of Benjamin.
2 God hath not cast away his people which he knew before. Know ye not what the Scripture saith of Elias, how he maketh request unto God against Israel, saying,
3 Lord, they have killed thy Prophets, and digged down thine altars: and I am left alone, and they seek my life?
4 But what saith the answer of God to him? I have reserved unto myself seven thousand men, which have not bowed the knee to Baal.
5 Even so then at this present time is there a remnant through the election of grace.
6 And if it be of grace, it is no more of works: or else were grace no more grace: but if it be of works, it is no more grace: or else were work no more work.
7 What then? Israel hath not obtained that he sought: but the election hath obtained it, and the rest have been hardened,
8 According as it is written, God hath given them the spirit of slumber: eyes that they should not see, and ears that they should not hear unto this day.
9 And David saith, Let their table be made a snare, and a net, and a stumbling block, even for a recompense unto them.
10 Let their eyes be darkened that they see not, and bow down their back always.
11 I demand then, Have they stumbled, that they should fall? God forbid: but through their fall salvation cometh unto the Gentiles, to provoke them to follow them.
12 Wherefore if the fall of them be the riches of the world, and the diminishing of them the riches of the Gentiles, how much more shall their abundance be?
13 For in that I speak to you Gentiles, in as much as I am the Apostle of the Gentiles, I magnify mine office,

14 To try if by any means I might provoke them of my flesh to follow them, and might save some of them.
15 For if the casting away of them be the reconciling of the world, what shall the receiving be, but life from the dead?
16 For if the first fruits be holy, so is the whole lump: and if the root be holy, so are the branches.
17 And though some of the branches be broken off, and thou being a wild olive tree, wast graft in for them, and made partaker of the root, and fatness of the olive tree,
18 Boast not thy self against the branches: and if thou boast thy self, thou bearest not the root, but the root thee.
19 Thou wilt say then, The branches are broken off, that I might be graft in.
20 Well: through unbelief they are broken off, and thou standest by faith: be not high minded, but fear.
21 For if God spared not the natural branches, take heed, least he also spare not thee.
22 Behold therefore the bountifulness, and severity of God: toward them which have fallen, severity: but toward thee, bountifulness, if thou continue in his bountifulness: or else thou shalt also be cut off.
23 And they also, if they abide not still in unbelief, shall be grafted in: for God is able to graft them in again.
24 For if thou wast cut out of the olive tree, which was wild by nature, and wast grafted contrary to nature in a right olive tree, how much more shall they that are by nature, be grafted in their own olive tree?
25 For I would not, brethren, that ye should be ignorant of this secret (least ye should be arrogant in your selves) that partly obstinacy is come to Israel, until the fullness of the Gentiles be come in.
26 And so all Israel shall be saved, as it is written, The deliverer shall come out of Zion, and shall turn away the ungodliness from Jacob.
27 And this is my covenant to them, When I shall take away their sins.
28 As concerning the Gospel, they are enemies for your sakes: but as touching the election, they are beloved for the fathers sakes.
29 For the gifts and calling of GOD are without repentance.
30 For even as ye in time past have not believed God, yet have now obtained mercy through their unbelief,
31 Even so now have they not believed by the mercy showed unto you, that they also may obtain mercy.
32 For God hath shut up all in unbelief, that he might have mercy on all.
33 O the deepness of the riches, both of the wisdom, and knowledge of God! how unsearchable are his judgments, and his ways past finding out!
34 For who hath known the mind of the Lord? or who was his counselor?
35 Or who hath given unto him first, and he shall be recompensed?
36 For of him, and through him, and for him are all things: to him be glory for ever. Amen.

Romans Chapter 12

1 I Beseech you therefore, brethren, by the mercies of God, that ye give up your bodies a living sacrifice, holy, acceptable unto God, which is your reasonable serving of God.
2 And fashion not yourselves like unto this world, but be ye changed by the renewing of your mind, that ye may prove what is the good will of God, and acceptable, and perfect.
3 For I say through the grace that is given unto me, to every one that is among you, that no man presume to understand above that which is meet to understand, but that he understand according to sobriety, as God hath dealt to every man the measure of faith.

4 For as we have many members in one body, and all members have not one office,

5 So we being many are one body in Christ, and every one, one anothers members.

6 Seeing then that we have gifts that are divers, according to the grace that is given unto us, whether we have prophecy, let us prophecy according to the portion of faith:

7 Or an office, let us wait on the office: or he that teacheth, on teaching:

8 Or he that exhorteth, on exhortation: he that distributeth, let him do it with simplicity: he that ruleth, with diligence: he that showeth mercy, with cheerfulness.

9 Let love be without dissimulation. Abhor that which is evil, and cleave unto that which is good.

10 Be affectioned to love one another with brotherly love. In giving honor, go one before another,

11 Not slothful to do service: fervent in spirit serving the Lord,

12 Rejoicing in hope, patient in tribulation, continuing in prayer,

13 Distributing unto the necessities of the Saints: giving yourselves to hospitality.

14 Bless them which persecute you: bless, I say, and curse not.

15 Rejoice with them that rejoice, and weep with them that weep.

16 Be of like affection one towards another: be not high minded: but make yourselves equal to them of the lower sort: be not wise in your selves.

17 Recompense to no man evil for evil: procure things honest in the sight of all men.

18 If it be possible, as much as in you is, have peace with all men.

19 Dearly beloved, avenge not yourselves, but give place unto wrath: for it is written, Vengeance is mine: I will repay, saith the Lord.

20 Therefore, if thine enemy hunger, feed him: if he thirst, give him drink: for in so doing, thou shalt heap coals of fire on his head.

21 Be not overcome of evil, but overcome evil with goodness.

Romans Chapter 13

1 Let every soul be subject unto the higher powers: for there is no power but of God: and the powers that be, are ordained of God.

2 Whosoever therefore resisteth the power, resisteth the ordinance of God: and they that resist, shall receive to themselves judgment.

3 For princes are not to be feared for good works, but for evil. Wilt ye then be without fear of the power? do well: so shalt thou have praise of the same.

4 For he is the minister of God for thy wealth: but if thou do evil, fear: for he beareth not the sword for naught: for he is the minister of God to take vengeance on him that doeth evil.

5 Wherefore ye must be subject, not because of wrath only, but also for conscience sake.

6 For, for this cause ye pay also tribute: for they are Gods ministers, applying themselves for the same thing.

7 Give to all men therefore their duty: tribute, to whom ye owe tribute: custom, to whom custom: fear, to whom fear: honor, to whom ye owe honor.

8 Owe nothing to any man, but to love one another: for he that loveth another, hath fulfilled the Law.

9 For this, Thou shalt not commit adultery, Thou shalt not kill, Thou shalt not steal, Thou shalt not bear false witness, Thou shalt not covet: and if there be any other commandment, it is briefly comprehended in this saying, even in this, Thou shalt love thy neighbor as thyself.

10 Love doth not evil to his neighbor: therefore is love the fulfilling of the Law.

11 And that, considering the season, that it is now time that we should arise from sleep: for now is our salvation nearer, then when we believed it.

12 The night is past, and the day is at hand: let us therefore cast away the works of darkness, and let us put on the armor of light,

13 So that we walk honestly, as in the day: not in gluttony, and drunkenness, neither in chambering and wantonness, nor in strife and envying.

14 But put ye on the Lord JESUS CHRIST, and take no thought for the flesh, to fulfill the lusts of it.

Romans Chapter 14

1 Him that is weak in the faith, receive unto you, but not for controversies of disputations.

2 One believeth that he may eat of all things: and another, which is weak, eateth herbs.

3 Let not him that eateth, despise him that eateth not: and let not him which eateth not, judge him that eateth: for God hath received him.

4 Who art thou that condemnest another mans servant? he standeth or falleth to his own master: yea, he shall be established: for God is able to make him stand.

5 This man esteemeth one day above another day, and another man counteth every day alike: let every man be fully persuaded in his mind.

6 He that observeth the day, observeth it to the Lord: and he that observeth not the day, observeth it not to the Lord. He that eateth, eateth to the Lord: for he giveth God thanks: and he that eateth not, eateth not to the Lord, and giveth God thanks.

7 For none of us liveth to himself, neither doth any die to himself.

8 For whether we live, we live unto the Lord: or whether we die, we die unto the Lord: whether we live therefore, or die, we are the Lord's.

9 For Christ therefore died and rose again, and revived, that he might be Lord both of the dead and the quick.

10 But why dost thou judge thy brother? or why dost thou despise thy brother? for we shall all appear before the judgment seat of Christ.

11 For it is written, I live, saith the Lord, and every knee shall bow to me, and all tongues shall confess unto God.

12 So then everyone of us shall give accounts of himself to God.

13 Let us not therefore judge one another any more: but use your judgment rather in this, that no man put an occasion to fall, or a stumbling block before his brother.

14 I know, and am persuaded through the Lord Jesus, that there is nothing unclean of itself: but unto him that judgeth anything to be unclean, to him it is unclean.

15 But if thy brother be grieved for the meat, now walkest thou not charitably: destroy not him with thy meat, for whom Christ died.

16 Cause not your commodity to be evil spoken of.

17 For the kingdom of God is not meat nor drink, but righteousness, and peace, and joy in the Holy Ghost.

18 For whosoever in these things serveth Christ, is acceptable unto God, and is approved of men.

19 Let us then follow those things which concern peace, and wherewith one may edify another.

20 Destroy not the work of God for meats sake: all things indeed are pure: but it is evil for the man which eateth with offence.

21 It is good neither to eat flesh, nor to drink wine, nor anything, whereby thy brother stumbleth, or is offended, or made weak.

22 Hast thou faith? have it with thyself before God: blessed is he that condemneth not himself in that thing which he alloweth.

23 For he that doubteth, is condemned if he eat, because he eateth not of faith: and whatsoever is not of faith, is sin.

Romans Chapter 15

1 We which are strong, ought to bear the infirmities of the weak, and not to please ourselves.

2 Therefore let every man please his neighbor in that that is good to edification.

3 For Christ also would not please himself, but as it is written, The rebukes of them which rebuke thee, fell on me.

4 For whatsoever things are written aforetime, are written for our learning, that we through patience, and comfort of the Scriptures might have hope.

5 Now the God of patience and consolation give you that ye be like minded one towards another, according to Christ Jesus,

6 That ye with one mind, and with one mouth may praise God even the Father of our Lord Jesus Christ.

7 Wherefore receive ye one another, as Christ also received us to the glory of God.

8 Now I say, that Jesus Christ was a minister of the circumcision, for the truth of God, to confirm the promises made unto the fathers.

9 And let the Gentiles praise God for his mercy, as it is written, For this cause I will confess thee among the Gentiles, and sing unto thy Name.

10 And again he saith, Rejoice, ye Gentiles with his people.

11 And again, Praise the Lord, all ye Gentiles, and laud ye him, all people together.

12 And again Esaias saith, There shall be a root of Jesse, and he that shall rise to reign over the Gentiles, in him shall the Gentiles trust.

13 Now the God of hope fill you with all joy, and peace in believing, that ye may abound in hope through the power of the Holy Ghost.

14 And I myself also am persuaded of you, my brethren, that ye also are full of goodness, and filled with all knowledge, and are able to admonish one another.

15 Nevertheless brethren, I have somewhat boldly after a sort written unto you, as one that putteth you in remembrance, through the grace that is given me of God,

16 That I should be the minister of Jesus Christ toward the Gentiles, ministering the Gospel of God, that the offering up of the Gentiles might be acceptable being sanctified by the Holy Ghost.

17 I have therefore whereof I may rejoice in Christ Jesus in those things which pertain to God.

18 For I dare not speak of any thing, which Christ hath not wrought by me, to make the Gentiles obedient in word and deed,

19 With the power of signs and wonders, by the power of the Spirit of God: so that from Jerusalem, and round about unto Illyricum, I have caused to abound the Gospel of Christ.

20 Yea, so I enforced myself to preach the Gospel, not where Christ was named, lest I should have built on another mans foundation.

21 But as it is written, To whom he was not spoken of, they shall see him, and they that heard not, shall understand him.

22 Therefore also I have been oft let to come unto you.

23 But now seeing I have no more place in these quarters, and also have been desirous many years ago to come unto you,

24 When I shall take my journey into Spain, I will come to you: for I trust to see you in my journey, and to be brought on my way thitherward by you, after that I have been somewhat filled with your company.

25 But now go I to Jerusalem, to minister unto the Saints.

26 For it hath pleased them of Macedonia and Achaia, to make a certain distribution unto the poor Saints which are at Jerusalem.

27 For it hath pleased them, and their debtors are they: for if the Gentiles be made partakers of their spiritual things, their duty is also to minister unto them in carnal things.

28 When I have therefore performed this, and have sealed them this fruit, I will pass by you into Spain.

29 And I know when I come, that I shall come to you with abundance of the blessing of the Gospel of Christ.

30 Also brethren I beseech you for our Lord Jesus Christs sake, and for the love of the Spirit, that ye would strive with me by prayers to God for me.

31 That I may be delivered from them which are disobedient in Judea, and that my service which I have to do at Jerusalem, may be accepted of the Saints,

32 That I may come unto you with joy by the will of God, and may with you be refreshed.

33 Thus the God of peace be with you all. Amen.

Romans Chapter 16

1 I commend unto you Phebe our sister which is a servant of the Church of Cenchrea,

2 That ye receive her in the Lord, as it becometh Saints, and that ye assist her in whatsoever business she needeth of your aide: for she hath given hospitality unto many, and to me also.

3 Greet Priscilla and Aquila my fellow helpers in Christ Jesus, 4 (Which have for my life laid down their own neck. Unto whom not I only give thanks, but also all the Churches of the Gentiles.)

5 Likewise greet the Church that is in their house. Salute my beloved Epenetus, which is the first fruits of Achaia in Christ.

6 Greet Mary which bestowed much labor on us.

7 Salute Andronicus and Junia my cousins and fellow prisoners, which are notable among the Apostles, and were in Christ before me.

8 Greet Amplias my beloved in the Lord.

9 Salute Urbane our fellow helper in Christ, and Stachys my beloved. 10 Salute Apelles approved in Christ. Salute them which are of Aristobulus friends.

11 Salute Herodion my kinsman. Greet them which are of the friends of Narcissus which are in the Lord.

12 Salute Tryphena and Tryphosa, which women labor in the Lord. Salute the beloved Persis, which woman hath labored much in the Lord.

13 Salute Rufus chosen in the Lord, and his mother and mine.

14 Greet Asyncritus, Phlegon, Hermas, Patrobas, Mercurius, and the brethren which are with them.

15 Salute Philologus and Julia, Nereus, and his sister, and Olympas, and all the Saints which are with them.

16 Salute one another with an holy kiss. The Churches of Christ salute you.

17 Now I beseech you brethren, mark them diligently which cause division and offences, contrary to the doctrine which ye have learned, and avoid them.

18 For they that are such, serve not the Lord Jesus Christ, but their own bellies, and with fair speech and flattering deceive the hearts of the simple.

19 For your obedience is come abroad among all: I am glad therefore of you: but yet I would have you wise, unto that which is good, and simple concerning evil.

20 The God of peace shall tread Satan under your feet shortly. The grace of our Lord Jesus Christ be with you.

21 Timotheus my companion, and Lucius and Jason, and Sosipater my kinsmen, salute you.

22 I Tertius, which wrote out this epistle, salute you in the Lord.

23 Gaius mine host, and of the whole Church saluteth you. Erastus the chamberlain of the city saluteth you, and Quartus a brother.

24 The grace of our Lord Jesus Christ be with you all. Amen.

25 To him now that is of power to establish you according to my Gospel, and preaching of Jesus Christ, by the revelation of the mystery, which was kept secret since the world began:

26 (But now is opened, and published among all nations by the Scriptures of the Prophets, at the commandment of the everlasting God for the obedience of faith)

27 To God, I say, only wise, be praise through Jesus Christ forever. Amen. Written to the Romans from Corinth, and sent, by Phebe, servant of the Church, which is at Cenchrea.

THE FIRST EPISTLE OF PAUL TO THE CORINTHIANS

1 Corinthians Chapter 1

1 PAUL called to be an Apostle of JESUS CHRIST, through the will of God, and our brother Sosthenes,
2 Unto the Church of God which is at Corinthus, to them that are sanctified in Christ Jesus, Saints by calling, with all that call on the Name of our Lord Jesus Christ in every place, both their Lord, and ours:
3 Grace be with you, and peace from God our Father, and from the Lord Jesus Christ.
4 I thank my God always on your behalf for the grace of God, which is given you in Jesus Christ,
5 That in all things ye are made rich in him, in all kind of speech, and in all knowledge:
6 As the testimony of Jesus Christ hath been confirmed in you.
7 So that ye are not destitute of any gift: waiting for the appearing of our Lord Jesus Christ.
8 Who shall also confirm you unto the end, that ye may be blameless in the day of our Lord Jesus Christ.
9 God is faithful, by whom you are called unto the fellowship of his Son Jesus Christ our Lord.
10 Now I beseech you, brethren, by the Name of our Lord Jesus Christ, that ye all speak one thing, and that there be no dissentions among you: but be ye knit together in one mind, and in one judgment.
11 For it hath been declared unto me, my brethren, of you by them that are of the house of Chloe, that there are contentions among you.
12 Now this I say, that every one of you saith, I am Paul's, and I am Apollos', and I am Cephas', and I am Christ's.
13 Is Christ divided? was Paul crucified for you? either were you baptized into the name of Paul?
14 I thank God, that I baptized none of you, but Crispus, and Gaius,
15 Lest any should say, that I had baptized into mine own name.
16 I baptized also the household of Stephanas: furthermore know I not, whether I baptized any other.
17 For Christ sent me not to baptize, but to preach the Gospel, not with wisdom of words, lest the cross of Christ should be made of none effect.
18 For the preaching of the cross is to them that perish, foolishness: but unto us, which are saved, it is the power of God.
19 For it is written, I will destroy the wisdom of the wise, and will cast away the understanding of the prudent.
20 Where is the wise? where is the Scribe? where is the disputer of this world? hath not God made the wisdom of this world foolishness?
21 For seeing the world by wisdom knew not God in the wisdom of God, it pleased God by the foolishness of preaching to save them that believe:
22 Seeing also that the Jews require a sign, and the Grecians seek after wisdom.
23 But we preach Christ crucified: unto the Jews, even a stumbling block, and unto the Grecians, foolishness:
24 But unto them which are called, both of the Jews and Grecians, we preach Christ, the power of God, and the wisdom of God.
25 For the foolishness of GOD is wiser then men, and the weakness of God is stronger than men.

26 For brethren, you see your calling, how that not many wise men after the flesh, not many mighty, not many noble are called.

27 But God hath chosen the foolish things of the world to confound the wise, and God hath chosen the weak things of the world, to confound the mighty things,

28 And vile things of the world and things which are despised, hath God chosen, and things which are not, to bring to naught things that are,

29 That no flesh should rejoice in his presence.

30 But ye are of him in Christ Jesus, who of God is made unto us wisdom and righteousness, and sanctification, and redemption,

31 That, according as it is written, He that rejoiceth, let him rejoice in the Lord.

1 Corinthians Chapter 2

1 And I, brethren, when I came to you, came not with excellency of words, or of wisdom, showing unto you the testimony of God.

2 For I esteemed not to know any thing among you, save Jesus Christ, and him crucified.

3 And I was among you in weakness, and in fear, and in much trembling.

4 Neither stood my word, and my preaching in the enticing speech of man's wisdom, but in plain evidence of the Spirit and of power,

5 That your faith should not be in the wisdom of men, but in the power of God.

6 And we speak wisdom among them that are perfect: not the wisdom of this world, neither of the princes of this world, which come to naught.

7 But we speak the wisdom of God in a mystery, even the hid wisdom, which God had determined before the world, unto our glory.

8 Which none of the princes of this world hath known: for had they known it, they would not have crucified the Lord of glory.

9 But as it is written, The things which eye hath not seen, neither ear hath heard, neither came into man's heart, are, which God hath prepared for them that love him.

10 But God hath revealed them unto us by his Spirit: for the Spirit searcheth all things, yea, the deep things of God.

11 For what man knoweth the things of a man, save the spirit of a man, which is in him? even so the things of God knoweth no man, but the Spirit of God.

12 Now we have received not the Spirit of the world, but the Spirit, which is of God, that we might know the things that are given to us of God.

13 Which things also we speak, not in the words which man's wisdom teacheth, but which the Holy Ghost teacheth, comparing spiritual things with spiritual things.

14 But the natural man perceiveth not the things of the Spirit of God: for they are foolishness unto him: neither can he know them, because they are spiritually discerned.

15 But he that is spiritual, discerneth all things: yet he himself is judged of no man.

16 For who hath known the mind of the Lord, that he might instruct him? But we have the mind of Christ.

1 Corinthians Chapter 3

1 And I could not speak unto you, brethren, as unto spiritual men, but as unto carnal , even as unto babes in Christ.

2 I gave you milk to drink, and not meat: for you were not yet able to bear it, neither yet now are ye able.

3 For ye are yet carnal: for whereas there is among you envying, and strife, and divisions, are ye not carnal, and walk as men?

4 For when one saith, I am Paul's, and another, I am Apollos', are ye not carnal?

5 Who is Paul then? and who is Apollos, but the ministers by whom ye believed, and as the Lord gave to every man?

6 I have planted, Apollos watered, but God gave the increase.

7 So then, neither is he that planteth, anything, neither he that watereth, but God that giveth the increase.

8 And he that planteth, and he that watereth, are one, and every man shall receive his wages, according to his labor.

9 For we together are God's laborers: ye are God's husbandry, and God's building.

10 According to the grace of God given to me, as a skillful master builder, I have laid the foundation, and another buildeth thereon: but let every man take heed how he buildeth upon it.

11 For other foundation can no man lay, than that which is laid, which is Jesus Christ.

12 And if any man build on this foundation, gold, silver, precious stones, timber, hay, or stubble,

13 Every man's work shall be made manifest: for the day shall declare it, because it shall be revealed by the fire: and the fire shall try every man's work of what sort it is.

14 If any man's work, that he hath built upon, abide, he shall receive wages.

15 If any man's work burn, he shall lose, but he shall be safe himself: nevertheless yet as it were by the fire.

16 Know ye not that ye are the Temple of God, and that the Spirit of God dwelleth in you?

17 If any man destroy the Temple of God, him shall God destroy: for the Temple of God is holy, which ye are.

18 Let no man deceive himself. If any man among you seem to be wise in this world, let him be a fool, that he may be wise.

19 For the wisdom of this world is foolishness with God: for it is written, He catcheth the wise in their own craftiness.

20 And again, The Lord knoweth that the thoughts of the wise be vain.

21 Therefore let no man rejoice in men: for all things are yours.

22 Whether it be Paul, or Apollos, or Cephas, or the world, or life, or death: whether they be things present, or things to come, even all are yours,

23 And ye Christ's, and Christ God's.

1 Corinthians Chapter 4

1 Let a man so think of us, as of the ministers of Christ, and disposers of the secrets of God.

2 And as for the rest, it is required of the disposers, that every man be found faithful.

3 As touching me, I pass very little, to be judged of you, or of man's judgment: no, I judge not mine own self.

4 For I know nothing by myself, yet am I not thereby justified: but he that judgeth me, is the Lord.

5 Therefore judge nothing before the time, until the Lord come, who will lighten things that are hid in darkness, and make the counsels of the hearts manifest: and then shall every man have praise of God.

6 Now these things, brethren, I have figuratively applied unto mine own self and Apollos, for your sakes, that ye might learn by us, that no man presume above that which is written, that one swell not against another for any man's cause.

7 For who separateth thee? and what hast thou, that thou hast not received? if thou hast received it, why rejoicest thou, as though thou hast not received it?

8 Now ye are full: now ye are made rich: ye reign as Kings without us, and would to God ye did reign, that we also might reign with you.

9 For I think that God hath set forth us the last Apostles, as men appointed to death: for we are made a gazing stock unto the world, and to the Angels, and to men.

10 We are fools for Christ's sake, and ye are wise in Christ: we are weak, and ye strong: ye are honorable, and we are despised.

11 Unto this hour we both hunger, and thirst, and are naked, and are buffeted, and have no certain dwelling place,

12 And labor, working with our own hands: we are reviled, and yet we bless: we are persecuted, and suffer it.

13 We are evil spoken of, and we pray: we are made as the filth of the world, the offscouring of all things, unto this time.

14 I write not these things to shame you, but as my beloved children I admonish you.

15 For though ye have ten thousand instructors in Christ, yet have ye not many fathers: for in Christ Jesus I have begotten you through the Gospel.

16 Wherefore, I pray you, be ye followers of me.

17 For this cause have I sent unto you Timotheus, which is my beloved son, and faithful in the Lord, which shall put you in remembrance of my ways in Christ as I teach every where in every Church.

18 Some are puffed up as though I would not come to you.

19 But I will come to you shortly, if the Lord will, and will know, not the speech of them which are puffed up, but the power.

20 For the kingdom of God is not in word, but in power. 21 What will ye? Shall I come unto you with a rod, or in love, and in the spirit of meekness?

1 Corinthians Chapter 5

1 It is heard certainly that there is fornication among you, and such fornication as is not once named among the Gentiles, that one should have his father's wife.

2 And ye are puffed up and have not rather sorrowed, that he which hath done this deed, might be put from among you.

3 For I verily as absent in body, but present in spirit, have determined already as though I were present, that he that hath thus done this thing,

4 When ye are gathered together, and my spirit, in the Name of our Lord Jesus Christ, that such one, I say, by the power of our Lord Jesus Christ,

5 Be delivered unto Satan, for the destruction of the flesh, that the spirit may be saved in the day of the Lord Jesus.

6 Your rejoicing is not good: know ye not that a little leaven, leaveneth the whole lump?

7 Purge out therefore the old leaven, that ye may be a new lump, as ye are unleavened: for Christ our Passover is sacrificed for us.

8 Therefore let us keep the feast, not with old leaven, neither in the leaven of maliciousness and wickedness: but with the unleavened bread of sincerity and truth.

9 I wrote unto you in an epistle, that ye should not company together with fornicators,

10 And not altogether with the fornicators of this world, or with the covetous, or with extortioners, or with idolaters: for then ye must go out of the world.

11 But now I have written unto you, that ye company not together: if any that is called a brother, be a fornicator, or covetous, or an idolater, or a railer, or a drunkard, or an extortioner, with such one eat not.

12 For what have I to do, to judge them also, which are without? do ye not judge them that are within?

13 But God judgeth them that are without. Put away therefore from among yourselves that wicked man.

1 Corinthians Chapter 6

1 Dare any of you, having business against another, be judged under the unjust, and not under the Saints?
2 Do ye not know, that the Saints shall judge the world? If the world then shall be judged by you, are ye unworthy to judge the smallest matters?
3 Know ye not that we shall judge the Angels? how much more things that pertain to this life?
4 If then ye have judgments of things pertaining to this life, set up them which are least esteemed in the Church.
5 I speak it to your shame. Is it so that there is not a wise man among you? no not one, that can judge between his brethren?
6 But a brother goeth to law with a brother, and that under the infidels.
7 Now therefore there is utterly a fault among you, because ye go to law one with another: why rather suffer ye not wrong? why rather sustain ye not harm?
8 Nay, ye yourselves do wrong, and do harm, and that to your brethren.
9 Know ye not that the unrighteous shall not inherit the kingdom of God? Be not deceived: neither fornicators, nor idolaters, nor adulterers, nor wantons, nor buggerers,
10 Nor thieves, nor covetous, nor drunkards, nor railers, nor extortioners shall inherit the kingdom of God.
11 And such were some of you: but ye are washed, but ye are sanctified, but ye are justified in the Name of the Lord Jesus, and by the Spirit of our God.
12 All things are lawful unto me: but all things are not profitable. I may do all things, but I will not be brought under the power of any thing.
13 Meats are ordained for the belly, and the belly for the meats: but God shall destroy both it, and them. Now the body is not for fornication, but for the Lord, and the Lord for the body.
14 And God hath also raised up the Lord, and shall raise us up by his power.
15 Know ye not, that your bodies are the members of Christ? shall I then take the members of Christ, and make them the members of an harlot? God forbid.
16 Do ye not know, that he which coupleth himself with an harlot, is one body? for two, saith he, shall be one flesh.
17 But he that is joined unto the Lord, is one spirit.
18 Flee fornication: every sin that a man doeth, is without the body: but he that committeth fornication, sinneth against his own body.
19 Know ye not, that your body is the temple of the Holy Ghost, which is in you, whom ye have of God? And ye are not your own.
20 For ye are bought for a price: therefore glorify God in your body, and in your spirit: for they are God's.

1 Corinthians Chapter 7

1 Now concerning the things whereof ye wrote unto me, It were good for a man not to touch a woman.
2 Nevertheless, to avoid fornication, let every man have his wife, and let every woman have her own husband.
3 Let the husband give unto the wife due benevolence, and likewise also the wife unto the husband.

4 The wife hath not the power of her own body, but the husband: and likewise also the husband hath not the power of his own body, but the wife.

5 Defraud not one another, except it be with consent for a time, that ye may give yourselves to fasting and prayer, and again come together that Satan tempt you not for your incontinency.

6 But I speak this by permission, not by commandment.

7 For I would that all men were even as I myself am: but every man hath his proper gift of God, one after this manner, and another after that.

8 Therefore I say unto the unmarried, and unto the widows, it is good for them if they abide even as I do.

9 But if they cannot abstain, let them marry: for it is better to marry than to burn.

10 And unto the married I command, not I, but the Lord, Let not the wife depart from her husband.

11 But and if she depart, let her remain unmarried, or be reconciled unto her husband, and let not the husband put away his wife.

12 But to the remnant I speak, and not the Lord, If any brother have a wife, that believeth not, if she be content to dwell with him, let him not forsake her.

13 And the woman which hath an husband that believeth not, if he be content to dwell with her, let her not forsake him.

14 For the unbelieving husband is sanctified by the wife, and the unbelieving wife is sanctified by the husband, else were your children unclean: but now are they holy.

15 But if the unbelieving depart, let him depart: a brother or a sister is not in subjection in such things: but God hath called us in peace.

16 For what knowest thou, O wife, whether thou shalt save thine husband? Or what knowest thou, O man, whether thou shalt save thy wife?

17 But as God hath distribute to every man, as the Lord hath called every one, so let him walk: and so ordain I, in all Churches.

18 Is any man called being circumcised? let him not gather his uncircumcision: is any called uncircumcised? let him not be circumcised.

19 Circumcision is nothing, and uncircumcision is nothing, but the keeping of the commandments of God.

20 Let every man abide in the same vocation wherein he was called.

21 Art thou called being a servant? care not for it: but if yet thou mayest be free, use it rather.

22 For he that is called in the Lord, being a servant, is the Lord's freeman: likewise also he that is called being free, is Christ's servant.

23 Ye are bought with a price: be not the servants of men.

24 Brethren, let every man, wherein he was called, therein abide with God.

25 Now concerning virgins, I have no commandment of the Lord: but I give mine advice, as one that hath obtained mercy of the Lord to be faithful.

26 I suppose then this to be good for the present necessity: I mean that it is good for a man so to be.

27 Art thou bound unto a wife? seek not to be loosed: art thou loosed from a wife? seek not a wife.

28 But if thou takest a wife, thou sinnest not: and if a virgin marry, she sinneth not: nevertheless, such shall have trouble in the flesh: but I spare you.

29 And this I say, brethren, because the time is short, here after that both they which have wives, be as though they had none:

30 And they that weep, as though they wept not: and they that rejoice, as though they rejoiced not: and they that buy, as though they possessed not:

31 And they that use this world, as though they used it not: for the fashion of this world goeth away.

32 And I would have you without care. The unmarried careth for the things of the Lord, how he may please the Lord.

33 But he that is married, careth for the things of the world, how he may please his wife.

34 There is difference also between a virgin and a wife: the unmarried woman careth for the things of the Lord, that she may be holy, both in body and in spirit: but she that is married, careth for the things of the world, how she may please her husband.

35 And this I speak for your own commodity, not to tangle you in a snare, but that ye follow that, which is honest, and that ye may cleave fast unto the Lord without separation.

36 But if any man think that it is uncomely for his virgin, if she pass the flower of her age, and need so require, let him do what he will, he sinneth not: let them be married.

37 Nevertheless he that standeth firm in his heart, that he hath no need, but hath power over his own will, and hath so decreed in his heart, that he will keep his virgin, he doeth well.

38 So then he that giveth her to marriage, doeth well, but he that giveth her not to marriage, doeth better.

39 The wife is bound by the law, as long as her husband liveth: but if her husband be dead, she is at liberty to marry with whom she will, only in the Lord.

40 But she is more blessed, if she so abide, in my judgment: and I think that I have also the Spirit of God.

1 Corinthians Chapter 8

1 And as touching things sacrificed unto idols, we know that we all have knowledge: knowledge puffeth up, but love edifieth.

2 Now, if any man think that he knoweth anything, he knoweth nothing yet as he ought to know.

3 But if any man love God, the same is known of him.

4 Concerning therefore meat sacrificed unto idols, we know that an idol is nothing in the world, and that there is none other God but one.

5 For though there be that are called gods, whether in heaven, or in earth, (as there be many gods, and many lords)

6 Yet unto us there is but one God , which is the Father, of whom are all things, and we in him: and one Lord Jesus Christ, by whom are all things, and we by him.

7 But every man hath not knowledge: for some having conscience of the idol, until this hour, eat as a thing sacrificed unto the idol, and so their conscience being weak, is defiled.

8 But meat maketh not us acceptable to God: for neither if we eat, have we the more: neither if we eat not, have we the less.

9 But take heed lest by any means this power of yours be an occasion of falling to them that are weak.

10 For if any man see thee which hast knowledge, sit at table in the idol's temple, shall not the conscience of him which is weak, be boldened to eat those things which are sacrificed to idols?

11 And through thy knowledge shall the weak brother perish, for whom Christ died.

12 Now when ye sin so against the brethren, and wound their weak conscience, ye sin against Christ.

13 Wherefore if meat offend my brother, I will eat no flesh while the world standeth, that I may not offend my brother.

1 Corinthians Chapter 9

1 Am I not an Apostle? am I not free? have I not seen Jesus Christ our Lord? are ye not my work in the Lord?

2 If I be not an Apostle unto other, yet doubtless I am unto you: for ye are the seal of mine Apostleship in the Lord.

3 My defense to them that examine me, is this,

4 Have we not power to eat and to drink?

5 Or have we not power to lead about a wife being a sister, as well as the rest of the Apostles, and as the brethren of the Lord, and Cephas?

6 Or I only and Barnabas, have not we power not to work?

7 Who goeth a warfare any time at his own cost? Who planteth a vineyard, and eateth not of the fruit thereof? or who feedeth a flock, and eateth not of the milk of the flock?

8 Say I these things according to man? saith not the Law the same also?

9 For it is written in the Law of Moses, Thou shalt not muzzle the mouth of the ox that treadeth out the corn: doth God take care for oxen?

10 Either saith he it not altogether for our sakes? For our sakes no doubt it is written, that he which heareth, should hear in hope: and that he that thresheth in hope, should be partaker of his hope.

11 If we have sown unto you spiritual things, is it a great thing if we reap your carnal things?

12 If others with you be partakers of this power, are not we rather?
nevertheless, we have not used this power: but suffer all things, that we should not hinder the Gospel of Christ.

13 Do ye not know, that they which minister about the holy things, eat of the things of the Temple? and they which wait at the altar, are partakers with the altar?

14 So also hath the Lord ordained, that they which preach the Gospel, should live of the Gospel.

15 But I have used none of these things: neither wrote I these things, that it should be so done unto me: for it were better for me to die, than that any man should make my rejoicing vain.

16 For though I preach the Gospel, I have nothing to rejoice of: for necessity is laid upon me, and woe is unto me, if I preach not the Gospel.

17 For if I do it willingly, I have a reward: but if I do it against my will, notwithstanding the dispensation is committed unto me.

18 What is my reward then? verily that when I preach the Gospel, I make the Gospel of Christ free that I abuse not mine authority in the Gospel.

19 For though I be free from all men, yet have I made myself servant unto all men, that I might win the more.

20 And unto the Jews I become as a Jew, that I may win the Jews: to them that are under the Law, as though I were under the Law, that I may win them that are under the Law:

21 To them that are without Law, as though I were without Law (when I am not without Law as pertaining to God, but am in the Law through Christ) that I may win them that are without Law.

22 To the weak I become as weak, that I may win the weak: I am made all things to all men, that I might by all means save some.

23 And this I do for the Gospel's sake, that I might be partaker thereof with you.

24 Know ye not, that they which run in a race, run all, yet one receiveth the price? so run that ye may obtain.

25 And every man that proveth masteries, abstaineth from all things: and they do it to obtain a corruptible crown: but we for an uncorruptible.

26 I therefore so run, not as uncertainly: so fight I, not as one that beateth the air.

27 But I beat down my body, and bring it into subjection, lest by any means after that I have preached to other, I myself should be reproved.

1 Corinthians Chapter 10

1 Moreover, brethren, I would not that ye should be ignorant, that all our fathers were under the cloud, and all passed through the sea,

2 And were all baptized unto Moses, in the cloud, and in the sea,

3 And did all eat the same spiritual meat,

4 And did all drink the same spiritual drink (for they drank of the spiritual Rock that followed them: and the Rock was Christ)

5 But with many of them God was not pleased: for they were overthrown in the wilderness.

6 Now these are ensamples to us, to the intent that we should not lust after evil things as they also lusted.

7 Neither be ye idolaters as were some of them, as it is written, The people sat down to eat and drink, and rose up to play.

8 Neither let us commit fornication, as some of them committed fornication, and fell in one day three and twenty thousand.

9 Neither let us tempt Christ, as some of them also tempted him, and were destroyed of serpents.

10 Neither murmur ye, as some of them also murmured, and were destroyed of the destroyer.

11 Now all these things came unto them for ensamples, and were written to admonish us, upon whom the ends of the world are come.

12 Wherefore, let him that thinketh he standeth, take heed lest he fall.

13 There hath no temptation taken you, but such as appertaineth to man: and God is faithful, which will not suffer you to be tempted above that you be able, but will even give the issue with the temptation, that ye may be able to bear it.

14 Wherefore my beloved, flee from idolatry.

15 I speak as unto them which have understanding: judge ye what I say.

16 The cup of blessing which we bless, is it not the communion of the blood of Christ? The bread which we break, is it not the communion of the body of Christ?

17 For we that are many, are one bread and one body, because we all are partakers of one bread.

18 Behold Israel, which is after the flesh: are not they which eat of the sacrifices, partakers of the altar?

19 What say I then? that the idol is anything? or that that which is sacrificed to idols, is anything?

20 Nay, but that these things which the Gentiles sacrifice, they sacrifice to devils, and not unto God: and I would not that ye should have fellowship with the devils.

21 Ye cannot drink the cup of the Lord, and the cup of the devils. Ye cannot be partakers of the Lord's table, and of the table of devils.

22 Do we provoke the Lord to anger? are we stronger than he?

23 All things are lawful for me, but all things are not expedient: all things are lawful for me, but all things edify not.

24 Let no man seek his own, but every man another's wealth.

25 Whatsoever is sold in the shambles, eat ye, and ask no question for conscience sake.

26 For the earth is the Lord's, and all that therein is.

27 If any of them which believe not, call you to a feast, and if ye will go, whatsoever is set before you, eat, asking no question for conscience sake.

28 But if any man say unto you, This is sacrificed unto idols, eat it not, because of him that showed it, and for the conscience (for the earth is the Lord's, and all that therein is)

29 And the conscience I say, not thine, but of that other: for why should my liberty be condemned of another man's conscience?

30 For if I through God's benefit be partaker, why am I evil spoken of, for that wherefore I give thanks?

31 Whether therefore ye eat or drink, or whatsoever ye do, do all to the glory of God.

32 Give none offence, neither to the Jews, nor to the Grecians, nor to the Church of God:

33 Even as I please all men in all things, not seeking mine own profit, but the profit of many, that they might be saved.

1 Corinthians Chapter 11

1 Be ye followers of me, even as I am of Christ.

2 Now brethren, I commend you, that ye remember all my things, and keep the ordinances, as I delivered them to you.

3 But I will that ye know, that Christ is the head of every man: and the man is the woman's head: and God is Christ's head.

4 Every man praying or prophesying having any thing on his head, dishonoreth his head.

5 But every woman that prayeth or prophesieth bareheaded, dishonoreth her head: for it is even one very thing, as though she were shaven.

6 Therefore if the woman be not covered, let her also be shorn: and if it be shame for a woman to be shorn or shaven, let her be covered.

7 For a man ought not to cover his head: for as much as he is the image and glory of God: but the woman is the glory of the man.

8 For the man is not of the woman, but the woman of the man.

9 For the man was not created for the woman's sake: but the woman for the man's sake.

10 Therefore ought the woman to have power on her head, because of the Angels.

11 Nevertheless, neither is the man without the woman, neither the woman without the man in the Lord.

12 For as the woman is of the man, so is the man also by the woman: but all things are of God.

13 Judge in yourselves, Is it comely that a woman pray unto God uncovered?

14 Does not nature itself teach you, that if a man have long hair, it is a shame unto him?

15 But if a woman have long hair, it is a praise unto her: for her hair is given her for a covering.

16 But if any man lust to be contentious, we have no such custom, neither the Churches of God.

17 Now in this that I declare, I praise you not, that you come together, not with profit, but with hurt.

18 For first of all, when ye come together in the Church, I hear that there are dissentions among you: and I believe it to be true in some part.

19 For there must be heresies even among you, that they which are approved among you, might be known.

20 When ye come together therefore into one place, this is not to eat the Lord's Supper.

21 For every man when they should eat, taketh his own supper afore, and one is hungry, and another is drunken.

22 Have ye not houses to eat and to drink in? despise ye the Church of God, and shame them that have not? what shall I say to you? shall I praise you in this? I praise you not.

23 For I have received of the Lord that which I also have delivered unto you, to wit, That the Lord Jesus in the night that he was betrayed, took bread.

24 And when he had given thanks, he brake it, and said, Take, eat: this is my body, which is broken for you: this do ye in remembrance of me.

25 After the same manner also he took the cup, when he had supped, saying, This cup is the New Testament in my blood: this do as oft as ye drink it, in remembrance of me.

26 For as often as ye shall eat this bread, and drink this cup, ye show the Lord's death till he come.

27 Wherefore, whosoever shall eat this bread, and drink the cup of the Lord unworthily, shall be guilty of the body and blood of the Lord.

28 Let a man therefore examine himself, and so let him eat of this bread, and drink of this cup.

29 For he that eateth and drinketh unworthily, eateth and drinketh his own damnation, because he discerneth not the Lord's body.

30 For this cause many are weak, and sick among you, and many sleep.

31 For if we would judge ourselves, we should not be judged.

32 But when we are judged, we are chastened of the Lord, because we should not be condemned with the world.

33 Wherefore, my brethren, when ye come together to eat, tarry one for another.

34 And if any man be hungry, let him eat at home, that ye come not together unto condemnation. Other things will I set in order when I come.

1 Corinthians Chapter 12

1 Now concerning spiritual gifts, brethren, I would not have you ignorant.

2 Ye know that ye were Gentiles, and were carried away unto the dumb idols, as ye were led.

3 Wherefore, I declare unto you, that no man speaking by the Spirit of God, calleth Jesus execrable: also no man can say that Jesus is the Lord, but by the Holy Ghost.

4 Now there are diversities of gifts, but the same Spirit.

5 And there are diversities of administrations, but the same Lord,

6 And there are diversities of operations, but God is the same, which worketh all in all.

7 But the manifestation of the Spirit is given to every man, to profit withal.

8 For to one is given by the Spirit the word of wisdom: and to another the word of knowledge, by the same Spirit:

9 And to another is given faith, by the same Spirit: and to another the gifts of healing, by the same Spirit:

10 And to another the operations of great works: and to another prophecy: and to another, the discerning of spirits: and to another, diversities of tongues: and to another the interpretation of tongues.

11 And all these things worketh even the selfsame Spirit, distributing to every man severally as he will.

12 For as the body is one, and hath many members, and all the members of the body, which is one, though they be many, yet are but one body: even so is Christ.

13 For by one Spirit are we all baptized into one body, whether we be Jews, or Grecians, whether we be bond, or free, and have been all made to drink into one Spirit.

14 For the body also is not one member, but many.

15 If the foot would say, Because I am not the hand, I am not of the body, is it therefore not of the body?

16 And if the ear would say, Because I am not the eye, I am not of the body, is it therefore not of the body?

17 If the whole body were an eye, where were the hearing? If the whole were hearing, where were the smelling?

18 But now hath God disposed the members every one of them in the body at his own pleasure.

19 For if they were all one member, where were the body?

20 But now are there many members, yet but one body.

21 And the eye cannot say unto the hand, I have no need of thee: nor the head again to the feet, I have no need of you.

22 Yea, much rather those members of the body, which seem to be more feeble, are necessary.

23 And upon those members of the body, which we think most unhonest, put we more honesty on: and our uncomely parts have more comeliness on.

24 For our comely parts need it not: but God hath tempered the body together, and hath given the more honor to that part which lacked,

25 Lest there should be any division in the body: but that the members should have the same care one for another.

26 Therefore if one member suffer, all suffer with it: if one member be had in honor, all the members rejoice with it.

27 Now ye are the body of Christ, and members for your part.

28 And God hath ordained some in the Church: as first Apostles, secondly Prophets, thirdly teachers, then them that do miracles: after that, the gifts of healing, helpers, governors, diversity of tongues.

29 Are all Apostles? are all Prophets? are all teachers?

30 Are all doers of miracles? have all the gifts of healing? do all speak with tongues? do all interpret?

31 But desire you the best gifts, and I will yet show you a more excellent way.

1 Corinthians Chapter 13

1 Though I speak with the tongues of men and Angels, and have not love, I am as sounding brass, or a tinkling cymbal.

2 And though I had the gift of prophecy, and knew all secrets and all knowledge, yea, if I had all faith, so that I could remove mountains and had not love, I were nothing.

3 And though I feed the poor with all my goods, and though I give my body, that I be burned, and have not love, it profiteth me nothing.

4 Love suffereth long: it is bountiful: love envieth not: love doth not boast itself: it is not puffed up:

5 It distaineth not: it seeketh not her own things: it is not provoked to anger: it thinketh not evil:

6 It rejoiceth not in iniquity, but rejoiceth in the truth:

7 It suffereth all things: it believeth all things: it hopeth all things: it endureth all things.

8 Love doth never fall away, though that prophesyings be abolished, or the tongues cease, or knowledge vanish away.

9 For we know in part, and we prophesy in part.

10 But when that which is perfect, is come, then that which is in part, shall be abolished.

11 When I was a child, I spake as a child, I understood as a child, I thought as a child: but when I became a man, I put away childish things.

12 For now we see through a glass darkly: but then shall we see face to face. Now I know in part: but then shall I know even as I am known.

13 And now abideth faith, hope and love, even these three: but the chiefest of these is love.

1 Corinthians Chapter 14

1 Follow after love, and covet spiritual gifts, and rather that ye may prophecy.

2 For he that speaketh a strange tongue, speaketh not unto men, but unto God: for no man heareth him: howbeit in the spirit he speaketh secret things.

3 But he that prophesieth, speaketh unto men to edifying, and to exhortation, and to comfort.

4 He that speaketh strange language, edifieth himself: but he that prophesieth, edifieth the Church.

5 I would that ye all spake strange languages, but rather that ye prophesied: for greater is he that prophesieth, than he that speaketh diverse tongues, except he expound it, that the Church may receive edification.

6 And now, brethren, if I come unto you speaking diverse tongues, what shall I profit you, except I speak to you, either by revelation, or by knowledge, or by prophesying, or by doctrine?

7 Moreover things without life which give a sound, whether it be a pipe or an harp, except they make a distinction in the sounds, how shall it be known what is piped or harped?

8 And also if the trumpet give an uncertain sound, who shall prepare himself to battle?

9 So likewise you, by the tongue, except ye utter words that have signification, how shall it be understand what is spoken? For ye shall speak in the air.

10 There are so many kinds of voices (as it cometh to pass) in the world, and none of them is dumb.

11 Except I know then the power of the voice, I shall be unto him that speaketh a barbarian, and he that speaketh, shall be a barbarian unto me.

12 Even so, forasmuch as ye covet spiritual gifts, seek that ye may excel unto the edifying of the Church.

13 Wherefore, let him that speaketh a strange tongue, pray, that he may interpret.

14 For if I pray in a strange tongue, my spirit prayeth: but mine understading is without fruit.

15 What is it then? I will pray with the spirit, but I will pray with the understanding also: I will sing with the spirit, but I will sing with the understanding also.

16 Else, when thou blessest with the spirit, how shall he that occupieth the room of the unlearned, say Amen, at the giving of thanks, seeing he knoweth not what thou sayest?

17 For thou verily givest thanks well, but the other is not edified.

18 I thank my God, I speak languages more than ye all.

19 Yet had I rather in the Church to speak five words with mine understanding that I might also instruct others, then ten thousand words in a strange tongue.

20 Brethren, be not children in understanding, but as concerning maliciousness be children, but in understanding be of a ripe age.

21 In the Law it is written, By men of other tongues, and by other languages will I speak unto this people: yet so shall they not hear me, saith the Lord.

22 Wherefore strange tongues are for a sign, not to them that believe, but to them that believe not: but prophesying serveth not for them that believe not, but for them which believe.

23 If therefore, when the whole Church is come together in one, and all speak strange tongues, there come in they that are unlearned, or they which believe not, will they not say, that ye are out of your wits?

24 But if all prophesy, and there come in one that believeth not, or one unlearned, he is rebuked of all men, and is judged of all,

25 And so are the secrets of his heart made manifest, and so he will fall down on his face and worship God, and say plainly that God is in you indeed.

26 What is to be done then, brethren? when ye come together, according as every one of you hath a Psalm, or hath doctrine, or hath a tongue, or hath revelation, or hath interpretation, let all things be done unto edifying.

27 If any man speak a strange tongue, let it be by two, or at the most, by three, and that by course, and let one interpret.

28 But if there be no interpreter, let him keep silence in the Church, which speaketh languages, and let him speak to himself, and to God.
29 Let the Prophets speak two, or three, and let the other judge.
30 And if any thing be revealed to another that sitteth by, let the first hold his peace.
31 For ye may all prophesy one by one, that all may learn, and all may have comfort.
32 And the spirits of the Prophets are subject to the Prophets.
33 For God is not the author of confusion, but of peace, as we see in all the Churches of the Saints.
34 Let your women keep silence in the Churches: for it is not permitted unto them to speak: but they ought to be subject, as also the Law saith.
35 And if they will learn any thing, let them ask their husbands at home: for it is a shame for women to speak in the Church.
36 Came the word of God out from you? either came it unto you only?
37 If any man think himself to be a Prophet, or spiritual, let him acknowledge, that the things, that I write unto you, are the commandments of the Lord.
38 And if any man be ignorant, let him be ignorant.
39 Wherefore, brethren, covet to prophesy, and forbid not to speak languages.
40 Let all things be done honestly and by order.

1 Corinthians Chapter 15

1 Moreover, brethren, I declare unto you the Gospel, which I preached unto you, which ye have also received, and wherein ye continue,
2 And whereby ye are saved, if ye keep in memory, after what manner I preached it unto you, except ye have believed in vain.
3 For first of all, I delivered unto you that which I received, how that Christ died for our sins, according to the Scriptures,
4 And that he was buried, and that he arose the third day according to the Scriptures,
5 And that he was seen of Cephas, then of the twelve.
6 After that, he was seen of more than five hundred brethren at once: whereof many remain unto this present, and some also are asleep.
7 After that, he was seen of James: then of all the Apostles.
8 And last of all he was seen also of me as of one, born out of due time.
9 For I am the least of the Apostles, which am not meet to be called an Apostle, because I persecuted the Church of God.
10 But by the grace of God, I am that I am: and his grace which is in me, was not in vain: but I labored more abundantly than they all: yet not I, but the grace of God which is with me.
11 Wherefore whether it were I, or they, so we preach, and so have ye believed.
12 Now if it be preached, that Christ is risen from the dead, how say some among you, that there is no resurrection of the dead?
13 For if there be no resurrection of the dead, then is Christ not rise.
14 And if Christ be not risen, then is our preaching vain, and your faith is also vain.
15 And we are found also false witnesses of God: for we have testified of God, that he hath raised up Christ: whom he hath not raised up, if so be the dead be not raised.
16 For if the dead be not raised, then is Christ not raised.
17 And if Christ be not raised, your faith is vain: ye are yet in your sins.
18 And so they which are asleep in Christ, are perished.
19 If in this life only we have hope in Christ, we are of all men the most miserable.
20 But now is Christ risen from the dead , and was made the first fruits of them that slept.
21 For since by man came death, by man came also the resurrection of the dead.
22 For as in Adam all die, even so in Christ shall all be made alive,

23 But every man in his own order: the first fruits is Christ, afterward, they that are of Christ, at his coming shall rise again.

24 Then shall be the end, when he hath delivered up the kingdom to God, even the Father, when he hath put down all rule, and all authority and power.

25 For he must reign till he hath put all his enemies under his feet.

26 The last enemy that shall be destroyed , is death.

27 For he hath put down all things under his feet. (And when he saith that all things are subdued to him, it is manifest that he is excepted, which did put down all things under him.)

28 And when all things shall be subdued unto him, then shall the Son also himself be subject unto him, that did subdue all things under him, that God may be all in all.

29 Else what shall they do which are baptized for dead? If the dead rise not at all, why are they then baptized for dead?

30 Why are we also in jeopardy every hour?

31 By our rejoicing which I have in Christ Jesus our Lord, I die daily.

32 If I have fought with beasts at Ephesus after the manner of men, what advantageth it me, if the dead be not raised up? Let us eat and drink: for tomorrow we shall die.

33 Be not deceived: evil speakings corrupt good manners.

34 Awake to live righteously, and sin not: for some have not the knowledge of God, I speak this to your shame.

35 But some man will say, How are the dead raised up? And with what body come they forth?

36 O fool, that which thou sowest, is not quickened, except it die.

37 And that which thou sowest, thou sowest not that body that shall be, but bare corn, as it falleth, of wheat, or of some other.

38 But God giveth it a body at his pleasure, even to every seed his own body,

39 All flesh is not the same flesh, but there is one flesh of men, and another flesh of beasts, and another of fishes, and another of birds.

40 There are also heavenly bodies, and earthly bodies: but the glory of the heavenly is one, and the glory of the earthly is another.

41 There is another glory of the sun, and another glory of the moon, and another glory of the stars: for one star differeth from another star in glory.

42 So also is the resurrection of the dead. The body is sown in corruption, and is raised in incorruption.

43 It is sown in dishonor, and is raised in glory: it is sown in weakness, and is raised in power.

44 It is sown a natural body, and is raised a spiritual body: there is a natural body, and there is a spiritual body.

45 As it is also written, The first man Adam was made a living soul: and the last Adam was made a quickening Spirit.

46 Howbeit that was not first made which is spiritual: but that which is natural, and afterward that which is spiritual.

47 The first man is of the earth, earthly: the second man is the Lord from heaven.

48 As is the earthly, such are they that are earthly: and as is the heavenly, such are they also that are heavenly.

49 And as we have born the image of the earthly, so shall we bear the image of the heavenly.

50 This say I, brethren, that flesh and blood cannot inherit the kingdom of God, neither doth corruption inherit incorruption.

51 Behold, I show you a secret thing, We shall not all sleep, but we shall all be changed,

52 In a moment, in the twinkling of an eye at the last trumpet: for the trumpet shall blow, and the dead shall be raised up incorruptible, and we shall be changed.

53 For this corruptible must put on incorruption: and this mortal must put on immortality.
54 So when this corruptible hath put on incorruption, and this mortal hath put on immortality, then shall be brought to pass the saying that is written, Death is swallowed up into victory.
55 O death, where is thy sting? O grave where is thy victory?
56 The sting of death is sin: and the strength of sin is the Law.
57 But thanks be unto God, which hath given us victory through our Lord Jesus Christ.
58 Therefore my beloved brethren, be ye steadfast, unmoveable, abundant always in the work of the Lord, forasmuch as ye know that your labor is not in vain in the Lord.

1 Corinthians Chapter 16

1 Concerning the gathering for the Saints, as I have ordained in the Churches of Galatia, so do ye also.
2 Every first day of the week, let every one of you put aside by himself, and lay up as God hath prospered him, that then there be no gatherings when I come.
3 And when I am come, whosoever ye shall allow by letters, them will I send to bring your liberality unto Jerusalem.
4 And if it be meet that I go also, they shall go with me.
5 Now I will come unto you, after I have gone through Macedonia (for I will pass through Macedonia.)
6 And it may be that I will abide, yea, or winter with you, that you may bring me on my way whithersoever I go.
7 For I will not see you now in my passage, but I trust to abide a while with you, if the Lord permit.
8 And I will tarry at Ephesus until Pentecost.
9 For a great door and effectual is opened unto me: but there are many adversaries.
10 Now if Timotheus come, see that he be without fear with you: for he worketh the work of the Lord, even as I do.
11 Let no man therefore despise him: but convey him forth in peace, that he may come unto me: for I look for him with the brethren.
12 As touching our brother Apollos, I greatly desired him, to come unto you with the brethren: but his mind was not at all to come at this time: howbeit he will come when he shall have convenient time.
13 Watch ye: stand fast in the faith: quiet you like men, and be strong.
14 Let all your things be done in love.
15 Now, brethren, I beseech you (ye know the house of Stephanas, that it is the first fruits of Achaia, and that they have given themselves to minister unto the Saints)
16 That ye be obedient even unto such, and to all that help with us and labor.
17 I am glad of the coming of Stephanas, and Fortunatus, and Achaicus: for they have supplied the want of you.
18 For they have comforted my spirit and yours: acknowledge therefore such men.
19 The Churches of Asia salute you: Aquila and Priscilla with the Church that is in their house, salute you greatly in the Lord.
20 All the brethren greet you. Greet ye one another with an holy kiss.
21 The salutation of me Paul with mine own hand.
22 If any man love not the Lord Jesus Christ, let him be had in execration , yea excommunicate to death.
23 The grace of our Lord Jesus Christ be with you.
24 My love be with you all in Christ Jesus, Amen.
The first Epistle to the Corinthians, written from Philippi, and sent by Stephanas, and Fortunatus, and Achaicus, and Timotheus.

NEW TESTAMENT - **1 CORINTHIANS**

THE SECOND EPISTLE OF PAUL TO THE CORINTHIANS

2 Corinthians Chapter 1

1 Paul an Apostle of JESUS CHRIST by the will of God, and our brother Timotheus, to the Church of God, which is at Corinthus with all the Saints, which are in all Achaia:

2 Grace be with you, and peace from God our Father, and from the Lord Jesus Christ.

3 Blessed be God even the Father of our Lord Jesus Christ, the Father of mercies, and the God of all comfort,

4 Which comforteth us in all our tribulation, that we may be able to comfort them which are in any affliction by the comfort wherewith we ourselves are comforted of God.

5 For as the sufferings of Christ abound in us, so our consolation aboundeth through Christ.

6 And whether we be afflicted, it is for your consolation and salvation, which is wrought in the enduring of the same sufferings, which we also suffer: or whether we be comforted, it is for your consolation and salvation.

7 And our hope is steadfast concerning you, in as much as we know that as ye are partakers of the sufferings, so shall ye be also of the consolation.

8 For brethren, we would not have you ignorant of our affliction, which came unto us in Asia, how we were pressed out of measure passing strength, so that we altogether doubted, even of life.

9 Yea, we received the sentence of death in ourselves, because we should not trust in ourselves, but in God, which raiseth the dead.

10 Who delivered us from so great a death, and doth deliver us: in whom we trust, that yet hereafter he will deliver us,

11 So that ye labor together in prayer for us, that for the gift bestowed upon us for many, thanks may be given by many persons for us.

12 For our rejoicing is this, the testimony of our conscience, that in simplicity and godly pureness, and not in fleshly wisdom, but by the grace of God we have had our conversation in the world, and most of all to you wards.

13 For we write none other things unto you, than that ye read or else that ye acknowledge, and I trust ye shall acknowledge unto the end.

14 Even as ye have acknowledged us partly, that we are your rejoicing, even as ye are ours, in the day of our Lord Jesus.

15 And in this confidence was I minded first to come unto you, that ye might have had a double grace,

16 And to pass by you into Macedonia, and to come again out of Macedonia unto you, and to be led forth toward Judea of you.

17 When I therefore was thus minded, did I use lightness? or mind I those things which I mind, according to the flesh, that with me should be, Yea, yea, and Nay, nay?

18 Yea, God is faithful, that our word toward you was not Yea, and Nay.

19 For the Son of God Jesus Christ who was preached among you by us, that is by me, and Silvanus, and Timotheus, was not Yea, and Nay: but in him it was Yea.

20 For all the promises of God in him are Yea, and are in him Amen, unto the glory of God through us.

21 And it is God which stablisheth us with you in Christ, and hath anointed us.

22 Who hath also sealed us, and hath given the earnest of the Spirit in our hearts.

23 Now, I call God for a record unto my soul, that to spare you, I came not as yet unto Corinthus.

24 Not that we have dominion over your faith, but we are helpers of your joy: for by faith ye stand.

2 Corinthians Chapter 2

1 But I determined thus in myself, that I would not come again to you in heaviness.
2 For if I make you sorry, who is he then that should make me glad, but the same which is made sorry by me?
3 And I wrote this same thing unto you, lest when I came, I should take heaviness of them, of whom I ought to rejoice: this confidence have I in you all, that my joy is the joy of you all.
4 For in great affliction, and anguish of heart I wrote unto you with many tears: not that ye should be made sorry, but that ye might perceive the love which I have, specially unto you.
5 And if any hath caused sorrow, the same hath not made me sorry, but partly (lest I should more charge him) you all.
6 It is sufficient unto the same man, that he was rebuked of many.
7 So that now contrariwise ye ought rather to forgive him and comfort him, lest the same should be swallowed up with over much heaviness.
8 Wherefore, I pray you, that you would confirm your love towards him.
9 For this cause also did I write, that I might know the proof of you, whether ye would be obedient in all things.
10 To whom ye forgive any thing, I forgive also: for verily if I forgave anything, to whom I forgave it, for your sakes forgave I it in the sight of Christ,
11 Lest Satan should circumvent us: for we are not ignorant of his enterprises.
12 Furthermore, when I came to Troas to preach Christ's Gospel, and a door was opened unto me of the Lord,
13 I had no rest in my spirit, because I found not Titus my brother, but took my leave of them, and went away into Macedonia.
14 Now thanks be unto God which always maketh us to triumph in Christ, and maketh manifest the savour of his knowledge by us in every place.
15 For we are unto God the sweet savor of Christ, in them that are saved, and in them which perish.
16 To the one we are the savor of death, unto death, and to the other the savor of life, unto life, and who is sufficient for these things?
17 For we are not as many, which make merchandise of the word of God: but as of sincerity, but as of God in the sight of God speak we in Christ.

2 Corinthians Chapter 3

1 Do we begin to praise ourselves again? or need we as some other, epistles of recommendation unto you, or letters of recommendation from you?
2 Ye are our epistle, written in our hearts, which is understand and read of all men,
3 In that ye are manifest, to be the Epistle of Christ, ministered by us, and written, not with ink, but with the Spirit of the living God, not in tables of stone, but in fleshly tables of the heart.
4 And such trust have we through Christ to God:
5 Not that we are sufficient of ourselves, to think any thing, as of ourselves: but our sufficiency is of God.
6 Who also hath made us able ministers of the New testament, not of the letter but of the Spirit: for the letter killeth, but the Spirit giveth life.
7 If then the ministration of death written with letters and engraven in stones, was glorious so that the children of Israel could not behold the face of Moses for the glory of his countenance (which glory is done away)

8 How shall not the ministration of the Spirit be more glorious?

9 For if the ministry of condemnation was glorious, much more doth the ministration of righteousness exceed in glory.

10 For even that which was glorified, was not glorified in this point , that is, as touching the exceeding glory.

11 For if that which should be abolished, was glorious, much more shall that which remaineth, be glorious.

12 Seeing then that we have such trust, we use great boldness of speech.

13 And we are not as Moses, which put a vail upon his face, that the children of Israel should not look unto the end of that which should be abolished.

14 Therefore their minds are hardened: for until this day remaineth the same covering untaken away in the reading of the Old Testament, which vail in Christ is put away.

15 But even unto this day, when Moses is read, the veil is laid over their hearts.

16 Nevertheless when their heart shall be turned to the Lord, the vail shall be taken away.

17 Now the Lord is the Spirit, and where the Spirit of the
Lord is, there is liberty.

18 But we all behold as in a mirror the glory of the Lord with open face, and are changed into the same image, from glory to glory, as by the Spirit of the Lord.

2 Corinthians Chapter 4

1 Therefore, seeing that we have this ministry, as we have received mercy, we faint not:

2 But have cast from us the cloaks of shame and walk not in craftiness, neither handle we the word of God deceitfully: but in declaration of the truth we approve ourselves to every man's conscience in the sight of God.

3 If our Gospel be then hid, it is hid to them, that are lost.

4 In whom the God of this world hath blinded the minds, that is, of the infidels, that the light of the glorious Gospel of Christ, which is the image of God, should not shine unto them.

5 For we preach not ourselves, but Christ Jesus the Lord, and ourselves your servants for Jesus' sake.

6 For God that commanded the light to shine out of darkness, is he which hath shined in our hearts, to give the light of the knowledge of the glory of God in the face of Jesus Christ.

7 But we have this treasure in earthen vessels, that the excellency of that power might be of God and not of us.

8 We are afflicted on every side, yet are we not in distress: in poverty,but not overcome of poverty.

9 We are persecuted, but not forsaken: cast down, but we perish not.

10 Every where we bear about in our body the dying of the Lord Jesus, that the life of Jesus might also be made manifest in our bodies.

11 For we which live, are always delivered unto death for Jesus' sake, that the life also of Jesus might be made manifest in our mortal flesh.

12 So then death worketh in us, and life in you.

13 And because we have the same Spirit of faith, according as it is written, I believed, and therefore have I spoken, we also believe, and therefore speak,

14 Knowing that he which hath raised up the Lord Jesus, shall raise us up also by Jesus, and shall set us with you.

15 For all things are for your sakes that most plenteous grace by the thanksgiving of many may redound to the praise of God.

16 Therefore we faint not, but though our outward man perish, yet the inward man is renewed daily.

17 For our light affliction which is but for a moment, causeth unto us a far most excellent and an eternal weight of glory:

18 While we look not on the things which are seen, but on the things, which are not seen: for the things which are seen, are temporal: but the things which are not seen, are eternal.

2 Corinthians Chapter 5

1 For we know that if our earthly house of this tabernacle be destroyed, we have a building given of God, that is, an house not made with hands, but eternal in the heavens.

2 For therefore we sigh, desiring to be clothed with our house, which is from heaven.

3 Because that if we be clothed, we shall not be found naked.

4 For indeed we that are in this tabernacle, sigh and are burdened, because we would not be unclothed, but would be clothed upon, that mortality might be swallowed up of life.

5 And he that hath created us for this thing, is God, who also hath given unto us the earnest of the Spirit.

6 Therefore we are alway bold, though we know that whilst we are at home in the body, we are absent from the Lord.

7 (For we walk by faith, and not by sight.)

8 Nevertheless, we are bold, and love rather to remove out of the body, and to dwell with the Lord.

9 Wherefore also we covet, that both dwelling at home, and removing from home, we may be acceptable to him.

10 For we must all appear before the judgment seat of Christ, that every man may receive the things which are done in his body, according to that he hath done, whether it be good or evil.

11 Knowing therefore the terror of the Lord, we persuade men, and we are made manifest unto God, and I trust also that we are made manifest in your consciences.

12 For we praise not ourselves again unto you, but give you an occasion to rejoice of us, that ye may have to answer against them, which rejoice in the face, and not in the heart.

13 For whether we be out of our wit, we are it to God: or whether we be in our right mind, we are it unto you.

14 For the love of Christ constraineth us: because we thus judge, that if one be dead for all, then were all dead,

15 And he died for all, that they which live, should not henceforth live unto themselves, but unto him which died for them, and rose again.

16 Wherefore, henceforth know we no man after the flesh, yea though we had known Christ after the flesh, yet now henceforth know we him no more.

17 Therefore if any man be in Christ, let him be a new creature. Old things are passed away: behold, all things are become new.

18 And all things are of God, which hath reconciled us unto himself by Jesus Christ, and hath given unto us the ministry of reconciliation.

19 For God was in Christ, and reconciled the world to himself, not imputing their sins unto them, and hath committed to us the word of reconciliation.

20 Now then are we ambassadors for Christ: as though God did beseech you through us, we pray you in Christ's stead, that ye be reconciled to God.

21 For he hath made him to be sin for us, which knew no sin, that we should be made the righteousness of God in him.

2 Corinthians Chapter 6

1 So we therefore as workers together beseech you, that ye receive not the grace of God in vain.

2 For he saith, I have heard thee in a time accepted, and in the day of salvation have I succoured thee: behold now the accepted time, behold now the day of salvation.

3 We give no occasion of offense in any thing, that our ministry should not be reprehended.

4 But in all things we approve ourselves as the ministers of God, in much patience, in afflictions, in necessities, in distresses,

5 In stripes, in prisons, in tumults, in labors,

6 By watchings, by fastings, by purity, by knowledge, by long suffering, by kindness, by the Holy Ghost, by love unfeigned,

7 By the word of truth, by the power of God, by the armor of righteousness on the right hand and on the left,

8 By honor, and dishonor, by evil report and good report, as deceivers, and yet true:

9 As unknown, and yet known: as dying, and behold, we live: as chastened, and yet not killed:

10 As sorrowing, and yet alway rejoicing: as poor, and yet make many rich: as having nothing, and yet possessing all things.

11 O Corinthians, our mouth is open unto you: our heart is made large.

12 Ye are not kept strait in us, but ye are kept strait in your own bowels.

13 Now for the same recompense, I speak as to my children, Be you also enlarged.

14 Be not unequally yoked with the infidels: for what fellowship hath righteousness with unrighteousness? and what communion hath light with darkness?

15 And what concord hath Christ with Belial? or what part hath the believer with the infidel?

16 And what agreement hath the Temple of God with idols? for ye are the Temple of the living God: as God hath said, I will dwell among them, and walk there: and I will be their God, and they shall be my people.

17 Wherefore come out from among them, and separate yourselves, saith the Lord: and touch none unclean thing, and I will receive you.

18 And I will be a Father unto you, and ye shall be my sons and daughters, saith the Lord almighty.

2 Corinthians Chapter 7

1 Seeing then we have these promises, dearly beloved, let us cleanse ourselves from all filthiness of the flesh and spirit, and grow up unto full holiness in the fear of God.

2 Receive us: we have done wrong to no man: we have consumed no man: we have defrauded no man.

3 I speak it not to your condemnation: for I have said before, that ye are in our hearts, to die and live together.

4 I use great boldness of speech toward you: I rejoice greatly in you: I am filled with comfort, and am exceeding joyous in all our tribulation.

5 For when we were come into Macedonia, our flesh had no rest, but we were troubled on every side, fightings without, and terrors within.

6 But God, that comforteth the abject, comforted us at the coming of Titus:

7 And not by his coming only, but also by the consolation wherewith he was comforted of you, when he told us your great desire, your mourning, your fervent mind to meward, so that I rejoiced much more.

8 For though I made you sorry with a letter, I repent not, though I did repent: for I perceive that the same epistle made you sorry, though it were but for a season.

9 I now rejoice, not that ye were sorry, but that ye sorrowed to repentance: for ye sorrowed godly, so that in nothing ye were hurt by us.

10 For godly sorrow causeth repentance unto salvation, not to be repented of: but the worldly sorrow causeth death.

11 For behold, this thing that ye have been godly sorry, what great care it hath wrought in you: yea, what clearing of yourselves: yea, what indignation: yea, what fear: yea, how great desire: yea, what a zeal: yea, what punishment: in all things ye have showed yourselves, that ye are pure in this matter.

12 Wherefore, though I wrote unto you, I did not it for his cause that had done the wrong, neither for his cause that had the injury, but that our care toward you in the sight of God might appear unto you.

13 Therefore we were comforted, because ye were comforted: but rather we rejoiced much more for the joy of Titus, because his spirit was refreshed by you all.

14 For if that I have boasted anything to him of you, I have not been ashamed: but as I have spoken unto you all things in truth, even so our boasting unto Titus was true.

15 And his inward affection is more abundant toward you, when he remembereth the obedience of you all, and how with fear and trembling ye received him.

16 I rejoice therefore that I may put my confidence in you in all things.

2 Corinthians Chapter 8

1 We do you also to wit, brethren, of the grace of God bestowed upon the Churches of Macedonia,

2 Because in great trial of affliction their joy abounded, and their most extreme poverty abounded unto their rich liberality.

3 For to their power (I bear record) yea, and beyond their power, they were willing,

4 And prayed us with great instance that we would receive the grace, and fellowship of the ministring which is toward the Saints.

5 And this they did, not as we looked for: but gave their own selves, first to the Lord, and after unto us by the will of God,

6 That we should exhort Titus, that as he had begun, so he would also accomplish the same grace among you also.

7 Therefore, as ye abound in everything, in faith and word, and knowledge, and in all diligence, and in your love towards us, even so see that ye abound in this grace also.

8 This say I not by commandment, but because of the diligence of others: therefore prove I the naturalness of your love.

9 For ye know the grace of our Lord Jesus Christ, that he being rich, for your sakes became poor, that ye through his poverty might be made rich.

10 And I show my mind herein: for this is expedient for you, which have begun not to do only, but also to will, a year ago.

11 Now therefore perform to do it also, that as there was a readiness to will, even so ye may perform it of that which ye have.

12 For if there be first a willing mind, it is accepted according to that a man hath, and not according to that he hath not.

13 Neither is it that other men should be eased and you grieved.

14 But upon like condition, at this time your abundance supplieth their lack, that also their abundance may be for your lack, that there may be equality:

15 As it is written, He that gathered much, had nothing over, and he that gathered little, had not the less.

16 And thanks be unto God, which hath put in the heart of Titus the same care for you.

17 Because he accepted the exhortation, yea, he was so careful that of his own accord he went unto you.

18 And we have sent also with him the brother, whose praise is in the Gospel throughout all the Churches.

19 (And not so only, but is also chosen of the Churches to be a fellow in our journey concerning this grace that is ministered by us unto the glory of the same Lord, and declaration of your prompt mind)

20 Avoiding this, that no man should blame us in this abundance that is ministered by us,

21 Providing for honest things, not only before the Lord, but also before men.

22 And we have sent with them our brother, whom we have oft times proved to be diligent in many things, but now much more diligent, for the great confidence, which I have in you.

23 Whether any do inquire of Titus, he is my fellow and helper to you ward: or of our brethren, they are messengers of the Churches, and the glory of Christ.

24 Wherefore show toward them, and before the Churches the proof of your love, and of the rejoicing that we have of you.

2 Corinthians Chapter 9

1 For as touching the ministering to the Saints, it is superfluous for me to write unto you.

2 For I know your readiness of mind, whereof I boast myself of you unto them of Macedonia, and say, that Achaia was prepared a year ago, and your zeal hath provoked many.

3 Now have I sent the brethren, lest our rejoicing over you should be in vain in this behalf, that you (as I have said) be ready:

4 Lest if they of Macedonia come with me, and find you unprepared, we (I need not to say, you) should be ashamed in this my constant boasting.

5 Wherefore, I thought it necessary to exhort the brethren to come before unto you, and to finish your benevolence appointed afore, that it might be ready, and come as of benevolence, and not as of sparing.

6 This yet remember, that he which soweth sparingly, shall reap also sparingly, and he that soweth liberally, shall reap also liberally.

7 As every man wisheth in his heart, so let him give not grudgingly, or of necessity: for God loveth a cheerful giver.

8 And God is able to make all grace to abound toward you, that ye always having all sufficiency in all things, may abound in every good work,

9 As it is written, He hath sparsed abroad and hath given to the poor: his benevolence remaineth for ever.

10 Also he that findeth seed to the sower, will minister likewise bread for food, and multiply your seed, and increase the fruits of your benevolence,

11 That on all parts ye may be made rich unto all liberality, which causeth through us thanksgiving unto God.

12 For the ministration of this service not only supplieth the necessities of the Saints, but also is abundant by the thanksgiving of many unto God,

13 (Which by the experiment of this ministration praise God for your voluntary submission to the Gospel of Christ, and for your liberal distribution to them, and to all men)

14 And by their prayer for you, desiring after you greatly, for the abundant grace of God in you.

15 Thanks therefore be unto God for his unspeakable gift.

2 Corinthians Chapter 10

1 Now I Paul myself beseech you by the meekness, and gentleness of Christ, which when I am present among you, am base, but am bold toward you being absent:

2 And this I require you, that I need not to be bold when I am present, with that same confidence, wherewith I think to be bold against some, which esteem us as though we walked according to the flesh.

3 Nevertheless, though we walk in the flesh, yet we do not war after the flesh,

4 (For the weapons of our warfare are not carnal, but mighty through God, to cast down holds)

5 Casting down the imaginations, and every high thing that is exalted against the knowledge of God, and bringing into captivity every thought to the obedience of Christ,

6 And having ready the vengeance against all disobedience, when your obedience is fulfilled.

7 Look ye on things after the appearance? If any man trust in himself that he is Christ's, let him consider this again of himself, that as he is Christ's, even so are we Christ's.

8 For though I should boast somewhat more of our authority, which the Lord hath given us for edification, and not for your destruction, I should have no shame.

9 This I say that I may not seem as it were to fear you with letters.

10 For the letters, saith he, are sore and strong, but his bodily presence is weak, and his speech is of no value.

11 Let such one think this, that such as we are in word by letters when we are absent, such will we be also in deed, when we are present.

12 For we dare not make ourselves of the number, or to compare ourselves to them, which praise themselves: but they understand not that they measure themselves with themselves, and compare themselves with themselves.

13 But we will not rejoice of things, which are not within our measure, but according to the measure of the line, whereof God hath distributed unto us a measure to attain even unto you.

14 For we stretch not ourselves beyond our measure, as though we had not attained unto you: for even to you also have we come in preaching the Gospel of Christ,

15 Not boasting of things which are without our measure: that is, of other men's labors: and we hope, when your faith shall increase, to be magnified by you according to our line abundantly,

16 And to preach the Gospel in those regions which are beyond you: not to rejoice in another man's line, that is in the things that are prepared already.

17 But let him that rejoiceth, rejoice in the Lord.

18 For he that praiseth himself, is not allowed, but he whom the Lord praiseth.

2 Corinthians Chapter 11

1 Would to God, ye could suffer a little my foolishness, and in deed, ye suffer me.

2 For I am jealous over you, with godly jealousy: for I have prepared you for one husband, to present you as a pure virgin to Christ:

3 But I fear lest as the serpent beguiled Eve through his subtlety, so your minds should be corrupt from the simplicity that is in Christ.

4 For if he that cometh, preacheth another Jesus than him whom we have preached: or if ye receive another spirit than that which ye have received: either another Gospel, than that ye have received, ye might well have suffered him.

5 Verily I suppose that I was not inferior to the very chief Apostles.

6 And though I be rude in speaking, yet I am not so in knowledge, but among you we have been made manifest to the utmost, in all things.

7 Have I committed an offence, because I abased myself, that ye might be exalted, and because I preached to you the Gospel of God freely?

8 I robbed other Churches, and took wages of them to do you service.

9 And when I was present with you, and had need, I was not slothful to the hinderance of any man: for that which was lacking unto me, the brethren which came from Macedonia, supplied, and in all things I kept and will keep myself that I should not be grievous to you.

10 The truth of Christ is in me, that this rejoicing shall not be shut up against me in the regions of Achaia.

11 Wherefore? Because I love you not? God knoweth.

12 But what I do, that will I do: that I may cut away occasion from them which desire occasion, that they might be found like unto us in that wherein they rejoice.

13 For such false apostles are deceitful workers, and transform themselves into the Apostles of Christ.

14 And no marvel: for Satan himself is transformed into an Angel of light.

15 Therefore it is no great thing, though his ministers transform themselves, as though they were the ministers of righteousness, whose end shall be according to their works.

16 I say again, let no man think, that I am foolish: or else take me even as a fool, that I also may boast myself a little.

17 That I speak, I speak it not after the Lord: but as it were foolishly, in this my great boasting.

18 Seeing that many rejoice after the flesh, I will rejoice also.

19 For ye suffer fools gladly, because that ye are wise.

20 For ye suffer even if a man bring you into bondage, if a man devour you, if a man take your goods, if a man exalt himself, if a man smite you on the face.

21 I speak as concerning the reproach: as though that we had been weak: but wherein any man is bold (I speak foolishly) I am bold also.

22 They are Hebrews, so am I: they are Israelites, so am I: they are the seed of Abraham, so am I:

23 They are the ministers of Christ (I speak as a fool) I am more: in labors more abundant: in stripes above measure: in prison more plenteously: in death oft.

24 Of the Jews five times received I forty stripes save one. 25 I was thrice beaten with rods: I was once stoned: I suffered thrice shipwreck: night and day have I been in the deep sea.

26 In journeying I was often, in perils of waters, in perils of robbers, in perils of mine own nation, in perils among the Gentiles, in perils in the city, in perils in wilderness, in perils in the sea, in perils among false brethren,

27 In weariness and painfulness, in watching often, in hunger and thirst, in fastings often, in cold and in nakedness.

28 Beside the things which are outward, I am cumbered daily, and have the care of all the Churches.

29 Who is weak, and I am not weak? who is offended, and I burn not?

30 If I must needs rejoice, I will rejoice of mine infirmities.

31 The God, even the Father of our Lord Jesus Christ, which is blessed for evermore, knoweth that I lie not.

32 In Damascus the governor of the people under King Aretas, laid watch in the city of the Damascenes, and would have caught me.

33 But at a window was I let down in a basket through the wall, and escaped his hands.

2 Corinthians Chapter 12

1 It is not expedient for me no doubt to rejoice: for I will come to visions and revelations of the Lord.

2 I know a man in Christ above fourteen years agone, (whether he were in the body, I can not tell, or out of the body, I cannot tell: God knoweth) which was taken up into the third heaven.

3 And I know such a man (whether in the body, or out of the body, I cannot tell: God knoweth,)

4 How that he was taken up into Paradise, and heard words which cannot be spoken, which are not possible for man to utter.

5 Of such a man will I rejoice: of myself will I not rejoice, except it be of mine infirmities.

6 For though I would rejoice, I should not be a fool: for I will say the truth, but I refrain, lest any man should think of me above that he seeth in me, or that he heareth of me.

7 And lest I should be exalted out of measure through the abundance of revelations, there was given unto me a prick in the flesh, the messenger of Satan to buffet me, because I should not be exalted out of measure.

8 For this thing I besought the Lord thrice, that it might depart from me.

9 And he said unto me, My grace is sufficient for thee: for my power is made perfect through weakness. Very gladly therefore will I rejoice rather in mine infirmities, that the power of Christ may dwell in me.

10 Therefore I take pleasure in infirmities, in reproaches, in necessities, in persecutions, in anguish for Christ's sake: for when I am weak, then am I strong.

11 I was a fool to boast myself: ye have compelled me: for I ought to have been commended of you: for in nothing was I inferior unto the very chief Apostles, though I be nothing.

12 The signs of an Apostle were wrought among you with all patience, with signs, and wonders, and great works.

13 For what is it, wherein ye were inferiors unto other Churches, except that I have not been slothful to your hinderance? forgive me this wrong.

14 Behold, the third time I am ready to come unto you, and yet will I not be slothful to your hinderance: for I seek not yours, but you: for the children ought not to lay up for the fathers, but the fathers for the children.

15 And I will most gladly bestow, and will be bestowed for your souls: though the more I love you, the less I am loved.

16 But be it that I charged you not: yet for as much as I was crafty, I took you with guile.

17 Did I pill you by any of them whom I sent unto you?

18 I have desired Titus, and with him I have sent a brother: did Titus pill you of any-thing? walked we not in the selfsame spirit? walked we not in the same steps?

19 Again, think ye that we excuse ourselves unto you? We speak before God in Christ. But we do all things, dearly beloved, for your edifying.

20 For I fear lest when I come, I shall not find you such as I would: and that I shall be found unto you such as ye would not, and lest there be strife, envying, wrath, contentions, backbitings, whisperings, swellings and discord.

21 I fear lest when I come again, my God abase me among you, and I shall bewail many of them which have sinned already, and have not repented of the uncleanness, and fornication, and wantonness which they have committed.

2 Corinthians Chapter 13

1 This is the third time that I come unto you. In the mouth of two or three witnesses shall every word stand

2 I told you before, and tell you before: as though I had been present the second time, so write I now being absent to them which heretofore have sinned, and to all others, that if I come again, I will not spare,

3 Seeing that ye seek experience of Christ, that speaketh in me, which toward you is not weak, but is mighty in you.

4 For though he was crucified concerning his infirmity, yet liveth he through the power of God. And we no doubt are weak in him: but we shall live with him, through the power of God toward you.

5 Prove yourselves whether ye are in the faith: examine yourselves: know ye not your own selves, how that Jesus Christ is in you, except ye be reprobates?

6 But I trust that ye shall know that we are not reprobates.

7 Now I pray unto God that ye do none evil, not that we should seem approved, but that ye should do that which is honest: though we be as reprobates.

8 For we cannot do any thing against the truth, but for the truth.

9 For we are glad when we are weak, and that ye are strong: this also we wish for even your perfection.

10 Therefore write I these things being absent, lest when I am present, I should use sharpness, according to the power which the Lord hath given me, to edification, and not to destruction.

11 Finally brethren, fare ye well: be perfect: be of good comfort: be of one mind: live in peace, and the God of love and peace shall be with you.

12 Greet one another with an holy kiss. All the Saints salute you.

13 The grace of our Lord Jesus Christ, and the love of God, and the communion of the Holy Ghost be with you all, Amen.

The second Epistle to the Corinthians, written from Philippi, a city in Macedonia, and sent by Titus and Lucas.

THE EPISTLE OF THE APOSTLE PAUL TO THE GALATIANS

Galatians Chapter 1

1 Paul an Apostle (not of men, neither by man, but by JESUS CHRIST, and God the Father which hath raised him from the dead)
2 And all the brethren which are with me, unto the Churches of Galatia:
3 Grace be with you and peace from God the Father, and from our Lord Jesus Christ,
4 Which gave himself for our sins, that he might deliver us from this present evil world according to the will of God even our Father,
5 To whom be glory for ever and ever, Amen.
6 I marvel that ye are so soon removed away unto another Gospel, from him that had called you in the grace of Christ,
7 Which is not another Gospel, save that there be some which trouble you, and intend to pervert the Gospel of Christ.
8 But though that we, or an Angel from heaven preach unto you otherwise, then that which we have preached unto you, let him be accursed.
9 As we said before, so say I now again, If any man preach unto you otherwise, than that ye have received, let him be accursed.
10 For now preach I man's doctrine, or God's? or go I about to please men? for if I should yet please men, I were not the servant of Christ.
11 Now I certify you, brethren, that the Gospel which was preached of me, was not after man.
12 For neither received I it of man, neither was I taught it, but by the revelation of Jesus Christ.
13 For ye have heard of my conversation in time past, in the Jewish religion, how that I persecuted the Church of God extremely, and wasted it,
14 And profited in the Jewish religion above many of my companions of mine own nation, and was much more zealous of the traditions of my fathers.
15 But when it pleased God (which had separated me from my mother's womb, and called me by his grace)
16 To reveal his Son in me, that I should preach him among the Gentiles, immediately I communicated not with flesh and blood:
17 Neither came I again to Jerusalem to them which were Apostles before me, but I went into Arabia, and turned again unto Damascus.
18 Then after three years I came again to Jerusalem to visit Peter, and abode with him fifteen days.
19 And none other of the Apostles saw I, save James the Lord's brother.
20 Now the things which I write unto you, behold, I witness before God, that I lie not.
21 After that, I went into the coasts of Syria and Cilicia: for I was unknown by face unto the Churches of Judea, which were in Christ.
22 But they had heard only some say, He which persecuted us in time past, now preacheth the faith which before he destroyed.
23 And they glorified God for me.

Galatians Chapter 2

1 Then fourteen years after, I went up again to Jerusalem with Barnabas, and took with me Titus also.

2 And I went up by revelation, and communicated with them of the Gospel which I preach among the Gentiles, but particularly with them that were the chief, lest by any means I should run, or had run in vain:

3 But neither yet Titus which was with me, though he were a Grecian, was compelled to be circumcised

4 For all the false brethren that crept in: who came in privily to spy out our liberty, which we have in Christ Jesus, that they might bring us into bondage.

5 To whom we gave not place by subjection for an hour, that the truth of the Gospel might continue with you.

6 And of them which seemed to be great, I was not taught (what they were in time passed, it maketh no matter to me: God accepteth no man's person) nevertheless they that are the chief, did communicate nothing with me.

7 But contrariwise, when they saw that the Gospel over the uncircumcision was committed unto me, as the Gospel over the Circumcision was unto Peter:

8 (For he that was mighty by Peter in the Apostleship over the Circumcision, was also mighty by me toward the Gentiles)

9 And when James, and Cephas, and John knew of the grace that was given unto me, which are counted to be pillars, they gave to me and to Barnabas the right hands of fellowship, that we should preach unto the Gentiles, and they unto the Circumcision,

10 Warning only that we should remember the poor: which thing also I was diligent to do.

11 And when Peter was come to Antiochia, I withstood him to his face: for he was to be blammed.

12 For before that certain came from James, he ate with the Gentiles: but when they were come, he withdrew and separated himself, fearing them which were of the Circumcision.

13 And the other Jews played dissembled likewise with him, insomuch that Barnabas was brought into their dissimulation also.

14 But when I saw, that they went not the right way to the truth of the Gospel, I said unto Peter before all men, If thou being a Jew, livest as the Gentiles, and not like the Jews, why constrainest thou the Gentiles to do like the Jews?

15 We which are Jews by nature, and not sinners of the Gentiles,

16 Know that a man is not justified by the works of the Law, but by the faith of Jesus Christ: even we, I say, have believed in Jesus Christ, that we might be justified by the faith of Christ, and not by the works of the Law, because that by the works of the Law no flesh shall be justified.

17 If then while we seek to be made righteous by Christ, we ourselves are found sinners, is Christ therefore the minister of sin? God forbid.

18 For if I build again the things that I have destroyed, I make myself a trespasser.

19 For I through the Law am dead to the Law, and that I might live unto God, I am crucified with Christ.

20 Thus I live, yet not I now, but Christ liveth in me: and in that that I now live in the flesh, I live by the faith in the Son of God, who hath loved me, and given himself for me.

21 I do not abrogate the grace of God: for if righteousness be by the Law, then Christ died without a cause.

Galatians Chapter 3

1 O foolish Galatians, who hath bewitched you that ye should not obey the truth, to whom Jesus Christ before was described in your sight, and among you crucified?

2 This only would I learn of you, Received ye the Spirit by the works of the Law, or by the hearing of faith preached?

3 Are ye so foolish, that after ye have begun in the Spirit, ye would now be made perfect by the flesh?

4 Have ye suffered so many things in vain? if so be it be even in vain.

5 He therefore that ministereth to you the Spirit, and worketh miracles among you, doeth he it through the works of the Law, or by the hearing of faith preached?

6 Yea rather as Abraham believed God, and it was imputed to him for righteousness.

7 Know ye therefore, that they which are of faith, the same are the children of Abraham.

8 For the Scripture foreseeing, that God would justify the Gentiles through faith, preached before the Gospel unto Abraham, saying, In thee shall all the Gentiles be blessed.

9 So then they which be of faith, are blessed with faithful Abraham.

10 For as many as are of the works of the Law, are under the curse: for it is written, Cursed is every man that continueth not in all things, which are written in the book of the Law, to do them.

11 And that no man is justified by the Law in the sight of God, it is evident: for the just shall live by faith.

12 And the Law is not of faith: but the man that shall do those things, shall live in them.

13 Christ hath redeemed us from the curse of the Law, when he was made a curse for us (for it is written, Cursed is every one that hangeth on tree)

14 That the blessing of Abraham might come on the Gentiles through Christ Jesus, that we might receive the promise of the Spirit through faith.

15 Brethren, I speak as men do, Though it be but a man's covenant when it is confirmed, yet no man doth abrogate it, or addeth any thing thereto.

16 Now to Abraham and his seed were the promises made. He saith not, And to the seeds, as speaking of many: but, And to thy seed, as of one, which is Christ.

17 And this I say, that the Law which was four hundred and thirty years after, cannot disannul the covenant that was confirmed afore of God in respect of Christ, that it should make the promise of none effect.

18 For if the inheritance be of the Law, it is no more by the promise, but God gave it unto Abraham by promise.

19 Wherefore then serveth the Law? It was added because of the transgressions, till the seed came unto the which the promise was made: and it was ordained by Angels in the hand of a Mediator.

20 Now a Mediator is not a Mediator of one: but God is one. 21 Is the Law then against the promises of God? God forbid: For if there had been a Law given which could have given life, surely righteousness should have been by the Law.

22 But the Scripture hath concluded all under sin, that the promise by the faith of Jesus Christ should be given to them that believe.

23 But before faith came, we were kept under the Law, and shut up unto the faith, which should afterward be revealed.

24 Wherefore the Law was our schoolmaster to bring us to Christ, that we might be made righteous by faith.

25 But after that faith is come, we are no longer under a schoolmaster.

26 For ye are all the sons of God by faith, in Christ Jesus.

27 For all ye that are baptized into Christ, have put on Christ.

28 There is neither Jew nor Grecian: there is neither bond nor free: there is neither male nor female: for ye are all one in Christ Jesus.

29 And if ye be Christ's, then are ye Abraham's seed, and heirs by promise.

Galatians Chapter 4

1 Then I say, that the heir as long as he is a child, differeth nothing from a servant, though he be Lord of all,

2 But is under tutors and governors, until the time appointed of the Father. 3 Even so, we when we were children, were in bondage under the rudiments of the world.

4 But when the fulness of time was come, God sent forth his Son made of a woman, and made under the Law,

5 That he might redeem them which were under the Law, that we might receive the adoption of the sons.

6 And because ye are sons, God hath sent forth the Spirit of his Son into your hearts, which crieth, Abba, Father.

7 Wherefore, thou art no more a servant, but a son: now if thou be a son, thou art also the heir of God through Christ.

8 But even then, when ye knew not God, ye did service unto them, which by nature are not gods.

9 But now seeing ye know God, yea, rather are known of God, how turn ye again unto impotent and beggarly rudiments, whereunto as from the beginning ye will be in bondage again?

10 Ye observe days, and months, and times, and years.

11 I am in fear of you, lest I have bestowed on you labor in vain.

12 Be ye as I: for I am even as you brethren, I beseech you: ye have not hurt me at all.

13 And ye know, how through infirmity of the flesh I preached the Gospel unto you at the first.

14 And the trial of me which was in my flesh, ye despised not, neither abhorred: but ye received me as an Angel of God, yea, as Christ Jesus.

15 What was then your felicity? for I bear you record, that if it had been possible, ye would have plucked out your own eyes, and have given them to me.

16 Am I therefore become your enemy, because I tell you the truth?

17 They are jealous over you amiss: yea, they would exclude you, that ye should altogether love them.

18 But it is a good thing to love earnestly always in a good thing, and not only when I am present with you,

19 My little children, of whom I travail in birth again, until Christ be formed in you.

20 And I would I were with you now, that I might change my voice: for I am in doubt of you.

21 Tell me, ye that will be under the Law, do ye not hear the Law?

22 For it is written, that Abraham had two sons, one by a servant, and one by a free woman.

23 But he which was of the servant, was born after the flesh: and he which was of the free woman, was born by promise.

24 By the which things another thing is meant: for these mothers are the two testaments, the one which is Agar of mount Sinai, which gendereth unto bondage.

25 (For Agar or Sinai is a mountain in Arabia, and it answereth to Jerusalem which now is) and she is in bondage with her children.

26 But Jerusalem, which is above, is free: which is the mother of us all.

27 For it is written, Rejoice thou barren that bearest no children: break forth, and cry, thou that travailest not: for the desolate hath many more children, than she which hath an husband.

28 Therefore, brethren, we are after the manner of Isaac, children of the promise.

29 But as then he that was born after the flesh, persecuted him that was born after the Spirit, even so it is now.

30 But what saith the Scripture? Put out the servant and her son: for the son of the servant shall not be heir with the son of the free woman.

31 Then brethren, we are not children of the servant, but of the free woman.

Galatians Chapter 5

1 Stand fast therefore in the liberty wherewith Christ hath made us free, and be not entangled again with the yoke of bondage.
2 Behold, I Paul say unto you, that if ye be circumcised, Christ shall profit you nothing.
3 For I testify again to every man, which is circumcised, that he is bound to keep the whole Law.
4 Ye are abolished from Christ: whosoever are justified by the Law, ye are fallen from grace.
5 For we through the Spirit wait for the hope of righteousness through faith.
6 For in Jesus Christ neither Circumcision availeth anything, neither uncircumcision, but faith which worketh by love.
7 Ye did run well: who did let you, that ye did not obey the truth?
8 It is not the persuasion of him that calleth you.
9 A little leaven doth leaven the whole lump.
10 I have trust in you through the Lord, that ye will be none otherwise minded: but he that troubleth you, shall bear his condemnation, whosoever he be.
11 And brethren, if I yet preach circumcision, why do I yet suffer persecution? Then is the slander of the cross abolished.
12 Would to God they were even cut off, which do disquiet you.
13 For brethren, ye have been called unto liberty: only use not your liberty as an occasion unto the flesh, but by love serve one another.
14 For all the Law is fulfilled in one word, which is this, Thou shalt love thy neighbor as thyself.
15 If ye bite and devour one another, take heed lest ye be consumed one of another.
16 Then I say, Walk in the Spirit, and ye shall not fulfill the lusts of the flesh.
17 For the flesh lusteth against the Spirit, and the Spirit against the flesh: and these are contrary one to another, so that ye cannot do the same things that ye would.
18 And if ye be led by the Spirit, ye are not under the law.
19 Moreover the works of the flesh are manifest, which are adultery, fornication, uncleanness, wantonness,
20 Idolatry, witchcraft, hatred, debate, emulations, wrath, contentions, seditions, heresies,
21 Envy, murders, drunkenness, gluttony, and such like, whereof I tell you before, as I also have told you before, that they which do such things, shall not inherit the kingdom of God.
22 But the fruit of the Spirit is love, joy, peace, long suffering, gentleness, goodness, faith,
23 Meekness, temperancy: against such there is no law.
24 For they that are Christ's, have crucified the flesh with the affections and the lusts.
25 If we live in the Spirit, let us also walk in the Spirit.
26 Let us not be desirous of vain glory, provoking one another, envying one another.

Galatians Chapter 6

1 Brethren, if a man be fallen by occasion into any fault, ye which are spiritual, restore such one with the spirit of meekness, considering thyself, lest thou also be tempted.
2 Bear ye one another's burden, and so fulfill the Law of Christ.

3 For if any man seem to himself, that he is somewhat, when he is nothing, he deceiveth himself in his imagination.

4 But let every man prove his own work, and then shall he have rejoicing in himself only and not in another.

5 For every man shall bear his own burden.

6 Let him that is taught in the word, make him that hath taught him, partaker of all his goods.

7 Be not deceived: God is not mocked: for whatsoever a man soweth, that shall he also reap.

8 For he that soweth to his flesh, shall of the flesh reap corruption: but he that soweth to the spirit, shall of the spirit reap life everlasting.

9 Let us not therefore be weary of well doing: for in due season we shall reap, if we faint not.

10 While we have therefore time, let us do good unto all men, but specially unto them, which are of the household of faith.

11 Ye see how large a letter I have written unto you with mine own hand.

12 As many as desire to make a fair show in the flesh, they constrain you to be circumcised, only because they would not suffer persecution for the cross of Christ.

13 For they themselves which are circumcised, keep not the Law, but desire to have you circumcised, that they might rejoice in your flesh.

14 But God forbid that I should rejoice, but in the cross of our Lord Jesus Christ, whereby the world is crucified unto me, and I unto the world.

15 For in Christ Jesus neither circumcision availeth anything, nor uncircumcision, but a new creature.

16 And as many as walk according to this rule, peace shall be upon them, and mercy, and upon the Israel of God.

17 From henceforth let no man put me to business: for I bear in my body the marks of the Lord Jesus.

18 Brethren, the grace of our Lord Jesus Christ be with your spirit, Amen. Unto the Galatians written from Rome.

THE EPISTLE OF PAUL TO THE EPHESIANS

Ephesians Chapter 1

1 Paul an Apostle of Jesus Christ, by the will of God, to the Saints, which are at Ephesus, and to the faithful in Christ Jesus:
2 Grace be with you, and peace from God our Father, and from the Lord Jesus Christ.
3 Blessed be God even the Father of our Lord Jesus Christ, which hath blessed us with all spiritual blessing in heavenly things in Christ,
4 As he hath chosen us in him, before the foundation of the world, that we should be holy, and without blame before him in love:
5 Who hath predestinate us, to be adopted through Jesus Christ unto himself, according to the good pleasure of his will,
6 To the praise of the glory of his grace, wherewith he hath made us accepted in his beloved,
7 By whom we have redemption through his blood, even the forgiveness of sins, according to his rich grace:
8 Whereby he hath been abundant toward us in all wisdom and understanding,
9 And hath opened unto us the mystery of his will according to his good pleasure, which he had purposed in him,
10 That in the dispensation of the fullness of the times he might gather together in one all things, both which are in heaven and which are in earth , even in Christ:
11 In whom also we are chosen when we were predestinate according to the purpose of him, which worketh all things after the counsel of his own will,
12 That we, which first trusted in Christ, should be unto the praise of his glory:
13 In whom also ye have trusted after that ye heard the word of truth, even the Gospel of your salvation, wherein also after that ye believed, ye were sealed with the Holy Spirit of promise,
14 Which is the earnest of our inheritance, until the redemption of the possession purchased unto the praise of his glory.
15 Therefore also after that I heard of the faith, which ye have in the Lord Jesus, and love toward all the Saints,
16 I cease not to give thanks for you, making mention of you in my prayers,
17 That the God of our Lord Jesus Christ the Father of glory, might give unto you the Spirit of wisdom, and revelation through the knowledge of him,
18 That the eyes of your understanding may be lightened that ye may know what the hope is of his calling, and what the riches of his glorious inheritance is in the Saints,
19 And what is the exceeding greatness of his power toward us, which believe, according to the working of his mighty power,
20 Which he wrought in Christ, when he raised him from the dead, and set him at his right hand in the heavenly places,
21 Far above all principality, and power, and might, and domination, and every Name, that is named, not in this world only, but also in that that is to come,
22 And hath made all things subject under his feet, and hath appointed him over all things to be the head to the Church,
23 Which is his body, even the fullness of him that filleth all in all things.

Ephesians Chapter 2

1 And you hath he quickened, that were dead in trespasses and sins,

2 Wherein, in time past ye walked, according to the course of this world, and after the prince that ruleth in the air, even the spirit, that now worketh in the children of disobedience,

3 Among whom we also had our conversation in time past, in the lusts of our flesh, in fulfilling the will of the flesh, and of the mind, and were by nature the children of wrath, as well as others.

4 But God which is rich in mercy, through his great love wherewith he loved us,

5 Even when we were dead by sins, hath quickened us together in Christ, by whose grace ye are saved,

6 And hath raised us up together, and made us sit together in the heavenly places in Christ Jesus,

7 That he might show in the ages to come the exceeding riches of his grace, through his kindness toward us in Christ Jesus.

8 For by grace are ye saved through faith, and that not of yourselves: it is the gift of God,

9 Not of works, lest any man should boast himself.

10 For we are his workmanship created in Christ Jesus unto good works, which God hath ordained, that we should walk in them.

11 Wherefore remember that ye being in time past Gentiles in the flesh, and called uncircumcision of them, which are called circumcision in the flesh, made with hands,

12 That ye were, I say, at that time without Christ, and were aliens from the commonwealth of Israel, and were strangers from the covenants of promise, and had no hope, and were without God in the world.

13 But now in Christ Jesus, ye which once were far off, are made near by the blood of Christ.

14 For he is our peace, which hath made of both one, and hath broken the stop of the partition wall,

15 In abrogating through his flesh the hatred, that is, the Law of commandments which standeth in ordinances, for to make of twain one new man in himself, so making peace,

16 And that he might reconcile both unto God in one body by his cross, and slay hatred thereby,

17 And came, and preached peace to you which were afar off, and to them that were near.

18 For through him we both have an entrance unto the Father by one Spirit.

19 Now therefore ye are no more strangers and foreigners: but citizens with the Saints, and of the household of God,

20 And are built upon the foundation of the Apostles and Prophets, Jesus Christ himself being the chief corner stone,

21 In whom all the building coupled together, groweth unto an holy Temple in the Lord,

22 In whom ye also are built together to be the habitation of God by the Spirit.

Ephesians Chapter 3

1 For this cause, I Paul am the prisoner of Jesus Christ for you Gentiles,

2 If ye have heard of the dispensation of the grace of God, which is given me to you-ward,

3 That is, that God by revelation hath showed this mystery unto me (as I wrote above in few words,

4 Whereby when ye read, ye may know mine understanding in the mystery of Christ)

5 Which in other ages was not opened unto the sons of men, as it is now revealed unto his holy Apostles and Prophets by the Spirit,

6 That the Gentiles should be inheritors also, and of the same body, and partakers of his promise in Christ by the Gospel,

7 Whereof I am made a minister by the gift of the grace of God given unto me through the working of his power.

8 Even unto me the least of all Saints is this grace given, that I should preach among the Gentiles the unsearchable riches of Christ,

9 And to make clear unto all men what the fellowship of the mystery is, which from the beginning of the world hath been hid in God, who hath created all things by Jesus Christ,

10 To the intent, that now unto principalities and powers in heavenly places might be known by the Church the manifold wisdom of God,

11 According to the eternal purpose, which he wrought in Christ Jesus our Lord.

12 By whom we have boldness and entrance with confidence, by faith in him.

13 Wherefore I desire that ye faint not at my tribulations for your sakes, which is your glory.

14 For this cause I bow my knees unto the Father of our Lord Jesus Christ,

15 (Of whom is named the whole family in heaven and in earth)

16 That he might grant you according to the riches of his glory, that ye may be strengthened by his Spirit in the inner man,

17 That Christ may dwell in your hearts by faith, that ye, being rooted and grounded in love,

18 May be able to comprehend with all Saints, what is the breadth, and length, and depth, and height:

19 And to know the love of Christ, which passeth knowledge, that ye may be filled with all fullness of God.

20 Unto him therefore that is able to do exceeding abundantly above all that we ask or think, according to the power that worketh in us,

21 Be praise in the Church by Christ Jesus, throughout all generations forever, Amen.

Ephesians Chapter 4

1 I therefore, being prisoner in the Lord, pray you that ye walk worthy of the vocation whereunto ye are called,

2 With all humbleness of mind, and meekness, with longsuffering, supporting one another through love,

3 Endeavoring to keep the unity of the Spirit in the bond of peace.

4 There is one body, and one Spirit, even as ye are called in one hope of your vocation.

5 There is one Lord, one Faith, one Baptism,

6 One God and Father of all, which is above all, and through all, and in you all.

7 But unto every one of us is given grace, according to the measure of the gift of Christ.

8 Wherefore he saith, When he ascended up on high, he led captivity captive, and gave gifts unto men.

9 (Now, in that he ascended, what is it but that he had also descended first into the lowest parts of the earth?

10 He that descended, is even the same that ascended, far above all heavens, that he might fill all things)

11 He therefore gave some to be Apostles, and some Prophets, and some Evangelists, and some Pastors, and Teachers,

12 For the gathering together of the Saints, for the work of the ministry, and for the edification of the body of Christ, 13 Till we all meet together (in the unity of faith and knowledge of the Son of God) unto a perfect man, and unto the measure of the age of the fullness of Christ,

14 That we henceforth be no more children, wavering and carried about with every wind of doctrine, by the deceit of men, and with craftiness, whereby they lay in wait to deceive.

15 But let us follow the truth in love, and in all things grow up into him, which is the head, that is Christ,

16 By whom all the body being coupled and knit together by every joint, for the furniture thereof (according to the effectual power, which is in the measure of every part) receiveth increase of the body, unto the edifying of itself in love.

17 This I say therefore and testify in the Lord, that ye henceforth walk not as other Gentiles walk, in vanity of their mind,

18 Having their cogitation darkened, and being strangers from the life of God through the ignorance that is in them, because of the hardness of their heart:

19 Which being past feeling, have given themselves unto wantonness, to work all uncleanness, even with greediness.

20 But ye have not so learned Christ.

21 If so be ye have heard him, and have been taught by him, as the truth is in Jesus,

22 That is, that ye cast off, concerning the conversation in time past, the old man, which is corrupt through the deceiveable lusts,

23 And be renewed in the spirit of your mind,

24 And put on the new man, which after God is created in righteousness, and true holiness.

25 Wherefore cast off lying, and speak every man truth unto his neighbor: for we are members one of another.

26 Be angry, but sin not: let not the sun go down upon your wrath,

27 Neither give place to the devil.

28 Let him that stole, steal no more: but let him rather labor and work with his hands the thing which is good, that he may have to give unto him that needeth.

29 Let no corrupt communication proceed out of your mouths: but that which is good, to the use of edifying, that it may minister grace unto the hearers.

30 And grieve not the Holy Spirit of God by whom ye are sealed unto the day of redemption.

31 Let all bitterness, and anger, and wrath, crying, and evil speaking be put away from you, with all maliciousness.

32 Be ye courteous one to another, and tender hearted, forgiving one another, even as God for Christ's sake forgave you.

Ephesians Chapter 5

1 Be ye therefore followers of God, as dear children,

2 And walk in love, even as Christ hath loved us, and hath given himself for us, to be an offering and a sacrifice of a sweet-smelling savor to God.

3 But fornication, and all uncleanness, or covetousness, let it not be once named among you, as it becometh Saints,

4 Neither filthiness, neither foolish talking, neither jesting, which are things not comely, but rather giving of thanks.

5 For this ye know, that no whoremonger, neither unclean person, nor covetous person, which is an idolator, hath any inheritance in the kingdom of Christ, and of God.

6 Let no man deceive you with vain words: for from such things cometh the wrath of God upon the children of disobedience.

7 Be not therefore companions with them.

8 For ye were once darkness, but are now light in the Lord: walk as children of light,

9 (For the fruit of the Spirit is in all goodness, and righteousness, and truth) 10 Approving that which is pleasing to the Lord.

11 And have no fellowship with the unfruitful works of darkness, but even reprove them rather.

12 For it is shame even to speak of the things which are done of them in secret.

13 But all things when they are reproved of the light, are manifest: for it is light that maketh all things manifest.

14 Wherefore he saith, Awake thou that sleepest, and stand up from the dead, and Christ shall give thee light.

15 Take heed therefore that ye walk circumspectly, not as fools, but as wise,

16 Redeeming the time: for the days are evil.

17 Wherefore, be ye not unwise, but understand what the will of the Lord is.

18 And be not drunk with wine, wherein is excess: but be fulfilled with the Spirit,

19 Speaking unto yourselves in psalms, and hymns, and spiritual songs, singing, and making melody to the Lord in your hearts,

20 Giving thanks always for all things unto God even the Father, in the Name of our Lord Jesus Christ,

21 Submitting yourselves one to another in the fear of God.

22 Wife's, submit yourselves unto your husbands, as unto the Lord.

23 For the husband is the wives head, even as Christ is the head of the Church, and the same is the savior of his body.

24 Therefore as the Church is in subjection to Christ, even so let the wives be to their husbands in every thing.

25 Husbands, love your wives, even as Christ loved the Church, and gave himself for it,

26 That he might sanctify it, and cleanse it by the washing of water through the word,

27 That he might make it unto himself a glorious Church, not having spot or wrinkle, or any such thing: but that it should be holy and without blame.

28 So ought men to love their wives, as their own bodies: he that loveth his wife, loveth himself.

29 For no man ever yet hated his own flesh, but nourisheth and cherisheth it, even as the Lord doth the Church.

30 For we are members of his body, of his flesh, and of his bones.

31 For this cause shall a man leave father and mother, and shall cleave to his wife, and they twain shall be one flesh.

32 This is a great secret, but I speak concerning Christ, and concerning the Church.

33 Therefore every one of you, do ye so: let every one love his wife, even as himself, and let the wife see that she fear her husband.

Ephesians Chapter 6

1 Children, obey your parents in the Lord: for this is right.

2 Honor thy father and mother (which is the first commandment with promise)

3 That it may be well with thee, and that thou mayest live long on earth.

4 And ye, fathers, provoke not your children to wrath: but bring them up in instruction and information of the Lord.

5 Servants, be obedient unto them that are your masters, according to the flesh, with fear and trembling in singleness of your hearts as unto Christ,

6 Not with service to the eye, as men pleasers, but as the servants of Christ, doing the will of God from the heart,

7 With good will serving the Lord, and not men.

8 And know ye that whatsoever good thing any man doeth, that same shall he receive of the Lord, whether he be bond or free.

9 And ye masters, do the same things unto them, putting away threatening: and know that even your master also is in heaven, neither is there respect of person with him.

10 Finally, my brethren, be strong in the Lord, and in the power of his might.

11 Put on the whole armor of God, that ye may be able to stand against the assaults of the devil.

12 For we wrestle not against flesh and blood, but against principalities, against powers, and against the worldly governors, the princes of the darkness of this world, against spiritual wickednesses, which are in the high places.

13 For this cause take unto you the whole armor of God, that ye may be able to resist in the evil day, and having finished all things, stand fast.

14 Stand therefore, and your loins gird about with verity, and having on the breastplate of righteousness,

15 And your feet shod with the preparation of the Gospel of peace.

16 Above all, take the shield of faith, wherewith ye may quench all the fiery darts of the wicked,

17 And take the helmet of salvation, and the sword of the Spirit, which is the word of God.

18 And pray always with all manner prayer and supplication in the Spirit: and watch thereunto with all perseverance and supplication for all Saints,

19 And for me, that utterance may be given unto me, that I may open my mouth boldly to publish the secret of the Gospel,

20 Whereof I am the ambassador in bonds, that therein I may speak boldly, as I ought to speak.

21 But that ye may also know mine affairs, and what I do, Tychicus my dear brother and faithful minister in the Lord, shall show you of all things,

22 Whom I have sent unto you for the same purpose, that ye might know mine affairs, and that he might comfort your hearts.

23 Peace be with the brethren, and love with faith from God the Father, and from the Lord Jesus Christ.

24 Grace be with all them which love our Lord Jesus Christ, to their immortality, Amen.

Written from Rome unto the Ephesians, and sent by Tychicus.

THE EPISTLE OF PAUL TO THE PHILIPPIANS

Philippians Chapter 1

1 Paul and Timotheus the servants of JESUS CHRIST, to all the Saints in Christ Jesus which are at Philippi, with the Bishops, and Deacons:
2 Grace be with you, and peace from God our Father, and from the Lord Jesus Christ.
3 I thank my God, having you in perfect memory,
4 (Always in all my prayers for all you, praying with gladness) 5 Because of the fellowship which ye have in the Gospel, from the first day unto now.
6 And I am persuaded of this same thing that he that hath begun this good work in you, will perform it until the day of Jesus Christ,
7 As it becometh me so to judge of you all, because I have you in remembrance that both in my bands, and in my defense, and confirmation of the Gospel you all were partakers of my grace.
8 For God is my record, how I long after you all from the very heart root in Jesus Christ.
9 And this I pray, that your love may abound, yet more and more in knowledge, and in all judgment,
10 That ye may discern things that differ one from another, that ye may be pure, and without offense until the day of Christ,
11 Filled with the fruits of righteousness, which are by Jesus Christ unto the glory and praise of God.
12 I would ye understood, brethren, that the things which have come unto me, are turned rather to the furthering of the Gospel,
13 So that my bands in Christ are famous throughout all the judgment hall, and in all other places,
14 In so much that many of the brethren in the Lord are boldened through my bands, and dare more frankly speak the word.
15 Some preach Christ even through envy and strife, and some also of good will.
16 The one part preacheth Christ of contention and not purely, supposing to add more affliction to my bands.
17 But the others of love, knowing that I am set for the defense of the Gospel.
18 What then? yet Christ is preached all manner ways, whether it be under a pretense, or sincerely: and I therein joy: yea and will joy.
19 For I know that this shall turn to my salvation, through your prayer, and by the help of the Spirit of Jesus Christ,
20 As I heartily look for, and hope, that in nothing I shall be ashamed, but that with all confidence, as always, so now Christ shall be magnified in my body, whether it be by life or by death.
21 For Christ is to me both in life, and in death advantage.
22 And whether to live in the flesh were profitable for me, and what to choose I know not.
23 For I am greatly in doubt on both sides, desiring to be loosed and to be with Christ, which is best of all.
24 Nevertheless, to abide in the flesh, is more needful for you.
25 And this am I sure of, that I shall abide, and with you all continue, for your furtherance and joy of your faith,
26 That ye may more abundantly rejoice in Jesus Christ for me, by my coming to you again.

27 Only let your conversation be, as it becometh the Gospel of Christ, that whether I come and see you, or else be absent, I may hear of your matters that ye continue in one Spirit, and in one mind fighting together through the faith of the Gospel.

28 And in nothing fear your adversaries, which is to them a token of perdition, and to you of salvation, and that of God.

29 For unto you it is given for Christ, that not only ye should believe in him, but also suffer for his sake,

30 Having the same fight, which ye saw in me, and now hear to be in me.

Philippians Chapter 2

1 If there be therefore any consolation in Christ, if any comfort of love, if any fellowship of the Spirit, if any compassion and mercy,

2 Fulfill my joy, that ye be like minded, having the same love, being of one accord, and of one judgment,

3 That nothing be done through contention or vain glory, but that in meekness of mind every man esteem other better than himself.

4 Look not every man on his own things, but every man also on the things of other men.

5 Let the same mind be in you that was even in Christ Jesus,

6 Who being in the form of God, thought it no robbery to be equal with God:

7 But he made himself of no reputation, and took on him the form of a servant, and was made like unto men, and was found in shape as a man.

8 He humbled himself, and became obedient unto the death, even the death of the cross.

9 Wherefore God hath also highly exalted him, and given him a Name above every name,

10 That at the Name of Jesus should every knee bow, both of things in heaven, and things in earth, and things under the earth,

11 And that every tongue should confess that Jesus Christ is the Lord, unto the glory of God the Father.

12 Wherefore my beloved, as ye have always obeyed, not as in my presence only, but now much more in mine absence, so make an end of your own salvation with fear and trembling.

13 For it is God which worketh in you, both the will and the deed, even of his good pleasure.

14 Do all things without murmuring and reasonings,

15 That ye may be blameless, and pure, and the sons of God without rebuke in the midst of a naughty and crooked nation, among whom ye shine as lights in the world,

16 Holding forth the word of life, that I may rejoice in the day of Christ, that I have not run in vain, neither have labored in vain.

17 Yea, and though I be offered up upon the sacrifice, and service of your faith, I am glad, and rejoice with you all.

18 For the same cause also be ye glad, and rejoice with me.

19 And I trust in the Lord Jesus, to send Timotheus shortly unto you, that I also may be of good comfort, when I know your state.

20 For I have no man like minded, who will faithfully care for your matters.

21 For all seek their own, and not that which is Jesus Christ's.

22 But ye know the proof of him, that as a son with the father, he hath served with me in the Gospel.

23 Him therefore I hope to send as soon as I know how it will go with me,

24 And trust in the Lord, that I also myself shall come shortly.

25 But I supposed it necessary to send my brother Epaphroditus unto you, my companion in labor, and fellow soldier, even your messenger, and he that ministered unto me such things as I wanted.

26 For he longed after all you, and was full of heaviness, because ye had heard, that he had been sick.

27 And no doubt he was sick, very near unto death: but God had mercy on him, and not on him only, but on me also, lest I should have sorrow upon sorrow.

28 I sent him therefore the more diligently, that when ye should see him again, ye might rejoice, and I might be the less sorrowful.

29 Receive him therefore in the Lord with all gladness, and make much of such:

30 Because that for the work of Christ he was near unto death, and regarded not his life, to fulfill that service which was lacking on your part toward me.

Philippians Chapter 3

1 Moreover, my brethren, rejoice in the Lord. It grieveth me not to write the same things to you, and for you it is a sure thing.

2 Beware of dogs: beware of evil workers: beware of the concision. 3 For we are the circumcision, which worship God in the spirit, and rejoice in Christ Jesus, and have no confidence in the flesh:

4 Though I might also have confidence in the flesh. If any other man thinketh that he hath whereof he might trust in the flesh, much more I:

5 Circumcised the eight day, of the kindred of Israel, of the tribe of Benjamin, an Hebrew of the Hebrews, by the Law a Pharisee.

6 Concerning zeal, I persecuted the Church: touching the righteousness which is in the Law, I was unrebukeable.

7 But the things that were vantage unto me, the same I counted loss for Christ's sake.

8 Yea, doubtless I think all things but loss for the excellent knowledge sake of Christ Jesus my Lord, for whom I have counted all things loss, and do judge them to be dung, that I might win Christ,

9 And might be found in him, that is, not having mine own righteousness, which is of the Law, but that which is through the faith of Christ, even the righteousness which is of God through faith,

10 That I may know him, and the virtue of his resurrection, and the fellowship of his afflictions, and be made conformable unto his death,

11 If by any means I might attain unto the resurrection of the dead:

12 Not as though I had already attained to it, either were already perfect: but I follow, if that I may comprehend that for whose sake also I am comprehended of Christ Jesus.

13 Brethren, I count not myself, that I have attained to it, but one thing I do: I forget that which is behind, and endeavor myself unto that which is before,

14 And follow hard toward the mark, for the prize of the high calling of God in Christ Jesus.

15 Let us therefore as many as be perfect, be thus minded: and if ye be otherwise minded, God shall reveal even the same unto you.

16 Nevertheless, in that whereunto we are come, let us proceed by one rule, that we may mind one thing.

17 Brethren, be followers of me, and look on them, which walk so, as ye have us for an ensample.

18 For many walk, of whom I have told you often, and now tell you weeping, that they are the enemies of the Cross of Christ:

19 Whose end is damnation, whose God is their belly, and whose glory is to their shame, which mind earthly things.

20 But our conversation is in heaven, from whence also we look for the Savior, even the Lord Jesus Christ,

21 Who shall change our vile body, that it may be fashioned like unto his glorious body, according to the working, whereby he is able even to subdue all things unto himself.

Philippians Chapter 4

1 Therefore, my brethren, beloved and longed for, my joy and my crown, so continue in the Lord, ye beloved.

2 I pray Euodias, and beseech Syntyche, that they be of one accord in the Lord,

3 Yea, and I beseech thee, faithful yokefellow, help those women, which labored with me in the Gospel, with Clement also, and with other my fellow laborers, whose names are in the book of life.

4 Rejoice in the Lord alway, again I say, rejoice.

5 Let your patient mind be known unto all men. The Lord is at hand.

6 Be nothing careful, but in all things let your requests be showed unto God in prayer, and supplication with giving of thanks.

7 And the peace of God which passeth all understanding, shall preserve your hearts and minds in Christ Jesus.

8 Furthermore, brethren, whatsoever things are true, whatsoever things are honest, whatsoever things are just, whatsoever things are pure, whatsoever things pertain to love, whatsoever things are of good report, if there be any virtue, or if there be any praise, think on these things,

9 Which ye have both learned and received, and heard, and seen in me: those things do, and the God of peace shall be with you.

10 Now I rejoice also in the Lord greatly, that now at the last ye are revived again to care for me, wherein notwithstanding ye were careful, but ye lacked opportunity.

11 I speak not because of want: for I have learned in whatsoever state I am, therewith to be content.

12 And I can be abased, and I can abound: everywhere in all things I am instructed both to be full, and to be hungry, and to abound, and to have want.

13 I am able to do all things through the help of Christ, which strengtheneth me.

14 Notwithstanding ye have well done, that ye did communicate to mine affliction.

15 And ye Philippians know also that in the beginning of the Gospel, when I departed from Macedonia, no Church communicated with me concerning the matter of giving and receiving, but ye only.

16 For even when I was in Thessalonica, ye sent once, and afterward again for my necessity,

17 Not that I desire a gift: but I desire the fruit which may further your reckoning.

18 Now I have received all, and have plenty: I was even filled, after that I had received of Epaphroditus that which came from you, an odor that smelleth sweet, a sacrifice acceptable and pleasant to God.

19 And my God shall fulfill all your necessities through his riches with glory in Jesus Christ.

20 Unto God even our Father be praise for evermore, Amen. 21 Salute all the Saints in Christ Jesus. The brethren, which are with me, greet you.

22 All the Saints salute you, and most of all they which are of Cesar's household.

23 The grace of our Lord Jesus Christ be with you all, Amen. Written to the Philippians from Rome, and sent by Epaphroditus.

THE EPISTLE OF PAUL TO THE COLOSSIANS

Colossians Chapter 1

1 Paul an Apostle of Jesus Christ, by the will of God, and Timotheus our brother,

2 To them which are at Colosse, Saints and faithful brethren in Christ: Grace be with you, and peace from God our Father, and from the Lord Jesus Christ.

3 We give thanks to God even the Father of our Lord Jesus Christ, always praying for you:

4 Since we heard of your faith in Christ Jesus, and of your love toward all Saints,

5 For the hope's sake, which is laid up for you in heaven, whereof ye have heard before by the word of truth, which is the Gospel,

6 Which is come unto you, even as it is unto all the world, and is fruitful, as it is also among you, from the day that ye heard and truly knew the grace of God,

7 As ye also learned of Epaphras our dear fellow servant, which is for you a faithful minister of Christ:

8 Who hath also declared unto us your love which ye have by the Spirit.

9 For this cause we also, since the day we heard of it, cease not to pray for you, and to desire that ye might be fulfilled with knowledge of his will, in all wisdom, and spiritual understanding,

10 That ye might walk worthy of the Lord, and please him in all things, being fruitful in all good works, and increasing in the knowledge of God,

11 Strengthened with all might through his glorious power, unto all patience, and long suffering with joyfulness,

12 Giving thanks unto the Father, which hath made us meet to be partakers of the inheritance of the Saints in light,

13 Who hath delivered us from the power of darkness, and hath translated us into the kingdom of his dear Son,

14 In whom we have redemption through his blood, that is, the forgiveness of sins,

15 Who is the image of the invisible God, the first born of every creature.

16 For by him were all things created, which are in heaven, and which are in earth, things visible and invisible: whether they be Thrones or Dominions, or Principalities, or Powers, all things were created by him, and for him,

17 And he is before all things, and in him all things consist.

18 And he is the head of the body of the Church: he is the beginning, and the first-born of the dead, that in all things he might have the preeminence.

19 For it pleased the Father, that in him should all fullness dwell,

20 And by him to reconcile all things unto himself, and to set at peace through the blood of his cross both the things in earth, and the things in heaven.

21 And you which were in times past strangers and enemies, because your minds were set in evil works, hath he now also reconciled,

22 In the body of his flesh through death, to make you holy, and unblameable and without fault in his sight,

23 If you continue, grounded and stablished in the faith, and be not moved away from the hope of the Gospel, whereof ye have heard, and which hath been preached to every creature which is under heaven whereof I Paul am a minister.

24 Now rejoice I in my sufferings for you, and fulfill the rest of the afflictions of Christ in my flesh, for his body's sake, which is the Church,

25 Whereof I am a minister, according to the dispensation of God, which is given me unto you-ward, to fulfill the word of God,

26 Which is the mystery hid since the world began, and from all ages, but now is made manifest to his Saints,
27 To whom God would make known what is the riches of this glorious mystery among the Gentiles, which riches is Christ in you, the hope of glory,
28 Whom we preach, admonishing every man, and teaching every man in all wisdom, that we may present every man perfect in Christ Jesus,
29 Whereunto I also labor and strive, according to his working which worketh in me mightily.

Colossians Chapter 2

1 For I would ye knew what great fighting I have for your sakes, and for them of Laodicea, and for as many as have not seen my person in the flesh,
2 That their hearts might be comforted and they knit together in love, and in all riches of the full assurance of understanding, to know the mystery of God even the Father, and of Christ:
3 In whom are hid all the treasures of wisdom and knowledge.
4 And this I say, lest any man should beguile you with enticing words.
5 For though I be absent in the flesh, yet am I with you in the spirit rejoicing, and beholding your order, and your steadfast faith in Christ.
6 As ye have therefore received Christ Jesus the Lord, so walk in him,
7 Rooted and built in him, and stablished in the faith, as ye have been taught, abounding therein with thanksgiving.
8 Beware lest there be any man that spoil you through philosophy, and vain deceit, through the traditions of men, according to the rudiments of the world, and not after Christ.
9 For in him dwelleth all the fullness of the Godhead bodily.
10 And ye are complete in him, which is the head of all principality and Power.
11 In whom also ye are circumcised with circumcision made without hands, by putting off the sinful body of the flesh, through the circumcision of Christ,
12 In that ye are buried with him through baptism, in whom ye are also raised up together through the faith of the operation of God which raised him from the dead.
13 And ye which were dead in sins, and in the uncircumcision of your flesh, hath he quickened together with him, forgiving you all your trespasses.
14 And putting out the handwriting of ordinances that was against us, which was contrary to us, he even took it out of the way, and fastened it upon the cross,
15 And hath spoiled the Principalities, and Powers, and hath made a show of them openly, and hath triumphed over them in the same cross.
16 Let no man therefore condemn you in meat and drink, or in respect of an holy day, or of the new moon, or of the Sabbath days,
17 Which are but a shadow of things to come: but the body is in Christ.
18 Let no man at his pleasure bear rule over you by humbleness of mind, and worshipping of Angels, advancing himself in those things which he never saw, rashly puft up with his fleshly mind,
19 And holdeth not the head, whereof all the body furnished and knit together by joints and bands, increaseth with the increasing of God.
20 Wherefore if ye be dead with Christ from the ordinances of the world, why, as though ye lived in the world, are ye burdened with traditions?
21 As, Touch not, Taste not, Handle not.
22 Which all perish with the using, and are after the commandments and doctrines of men.

23 Which things have indeed a show of wisdom, in voluntary religion and humbleness of mind, and in not sparing the body, neither have they it any estimation to satisfy the flesh.

Colossians Chapter 3

1 If ye then be risen with Christ, seek those things which are above, where Christ sitteth at the right hand of God.
2 Set your affections on things which are above, and not on things which are on the earth.
3 For ye are dead, and your life is hid with Christ in God.
4 When Christ which is our life, shall appear, then shall ye also appear with him in glory.
5 Mortify therefore your members which are on the earth, fornication, uncleanness, the inordinate affection, evil concupiscence, and covetousness, which is idolatry.
6 For the which things' sake the wrath of God cometh on the children of disobedience.
7 Wherein ye also walked once, when ye lived in them.
8 But now put ye away even all these things, wrath, anger, maliciousness, cursed speaking, filthy speaking, out of your mouth.
9 Lie not one to another, seeing that you have put off the old man with his works,
10 And have put on the new, which is renewed in knowledge after the image of him that created him,
11 Where is neither Grecian nor Jew, circumcision nor uncircumcision, Barbarian, Scythian, bond, free: but Christ is all and in all things.
12 Now therefore as the elect of God holy and beloved, put on the tender mercy, kindness, humbleness of mind, meekness, long suffering:
13 Forbearing one another, and forgiving one another, if any man have a quarrel to another: even as Christ forgave you, even so do ye.
14 And above all these things put on love, which is the bond of perfectness.
15 And let the peace of God rule in your hearts, to the which ye are called in one body, and be ye amiable.
16 Let the word of Christ dwell in you plenteously in all wisdom, teaching and admonishing your own selves, in Psalms, and hymns, and spiritual songs, singing with a grace in your hearts to the Lord.
17 And whatsoever ye shall do, in word or deed, do all in the Name of the Lord Jesus, giving thanks to God even the Father by him.
18 Wives, submit yourselves unto your husbands, as it is comely in the Lord.
19 Husbands, love your wives, and be not bitter unto them.
20 Children, obey your parents in all things: for that is well pleasing unto the Lord.
21 Fathers, provoke not your children to anger, lest they be discouraged.
22 Servants, be obedient unto them that are your masters according to the flesh in all things, not with eye service as men-pleasers, but in singleness of heart, fearing God.
23 And whatsoever ye do, do it heartily, as to the Lord, and not unto men,
24 Knowing that of the Lord ye shall receive the reward of the inheritance: for ye serve the Lord Christ.
25 But he that doeth wrong, shall receive for the wrong that he hath done, and there is no respect of persons.

Colossians Chapter 4

1 Ye masters, do unto your servants, that which is just, and equal, knowing that ye also have a master in heaven.
2 Continue in prayer, and watch in the same with thanksgiving,

3 Praying also for us, that God may open unto us the door of utterance, to speak the mystery of Christ: wherefore I am also in bonds,

4 That I may utter it, as it becometh me to speak.

5 Walk wisely toward them that are without, and redeem the time.

6 Let your speech be gracious always, and powdered with salt, that ye may know how to answer every man.

7 Tychicus our beloved brother, and faithful minister, and fellow servant in the Lord, shall declare unto you my whole state:

8 Whom I have sent unto you for the same purpose that he might know your state, and might comfort your hearts,

9 With Onesimus a faithful and a beloved brother, who is one of you. They shall show you of all things here.

10 Aristarchus my prison fellow saluteth you, and Marcus, Barnabas sister's son (touching whom ye received commandment, If he come unto you, receive him)

11 And Jesus which is called Justus, which are of the circumcision. These only are my workfellows unto the kingdom of God, which have been unto my consolation.

12 Epaphras the servant of Christ, which is one of you, saluteth you, and always striveth for you in prayers, that ye may stand perfect, and full in all the will of God.

13 For I bear him record, that he hath a great zeal for you, and for them of Laodicea, and them of Hierapolis.

14 Luke the beloved physician greeteth you, and Demas.

15 Salute the brethren which are of Laodicea, and Nymphas, and the Church which is in his house.

16 And when this Epistle is read of you, cause that it be read in the Church of the Laodiceans also, and that ye likewise read the Epistle written from Laodicea.

17 And say to Archippus, Take heed to the ministry, that thou hast received in the Lord, that thou fulfill it.

18 The salutation by the hand of me Paul. Remember my bands.

Grace be with you, Amen.

Written from Rome to the Colossians, and sent by Tychicus, and Onesimus.

THE FIRST EPISTLE OF PAUL TO THE THESSALONIANS

1 Thessalonians Chapter 1

1 Paul and Silvanus, and Timotheus, unto the Church of the Thessalonians, which is in God the Father, and in the Lord Jesus Christ: Grace be with you, and peace from God our Father, and from the Lord Jesus Christ.
2 We give God thanks always for you all, making mention of you in our prayers
3 Without ceasing, remembering your effectual faith, and diligent love and the patience of your hope in our Lord Jesus Christ in the sight of God even our Father,
4 Knowing, beloved brethren, that ye are elect of God.
5 For our Gospel was not unto you in word only, but also in power, and in the Holy Ghost, and in much assurance, as ye know after what manner we were among you for your sakes.
6 And ye became followers of us, and of the Lord, and received the word in much affliction, with joy of the Holy Ghost,
7 So that ye were as ensamples to all that believe in Macedonia and Achaia.
8 For from you sounded out the word of the Lord, not in Macedonia and in Achaia only: but your faith also which is toward God, spread abroad in all quarters, that we need not to speak anything.
9 For they themselves show of you what manner of entering in we had unto you, and how ye turned to God from idols, to serve the living and true God,
10 And to look for his Son from heaven, whom he raised from the dead, even Jesus which delivereth us from the wrath to come.

1 Thessalonians Chapter 2

1 For ye yourselves know, brethren, that our entrance in unto you was not in vain,
2 But even after that we had suffered before, and were shamefully entreated at Philippi, (as ye know) we were bold in our God, to speak unto you the Gospel of God with much striving.
3 For our exhortation was not by deceit, nor by uncleanness, nor by guile.
4 But as we were allowed of God, that the Gospel should be committed unto us, so we speak, not as they that please men, but God, which trieth our hearts.
5 Neither yet did we ever use flattering words, as ye know, nor colored covetousness, God is record.
6 Neither sought we praise of men, neither of you, nor of others,
7 When we might have been chargeable, as the Apostles of Christ: but we were gentle among you, even as a nurse cherisheth her children.
8 Thus being affectioned toward you, our good will was to have dealt unto you, not the Gospel of God only, but also our own souls, because ye were dear unto us.
9 For ye remember, brethren, our labor and travail: for we labored day and night, because we would not be chargeable unto any of you, and preached unto you the Gospel of God.
10 You are witnesses, and God also, how holily, and justly, and unblameably we behaved ourselves among you that believe.
11 As ye know how that we exhorted you, and comforted, and besought every one of you (as a father his children)
12 That ye would walk worthy of God, who hath called you unto his kingdom and glory.
13 For this cause also thank we God without ceasing, that when ye received of us the word of the preaching of God, ye received it not as the word of men, but as it is indeed the word of God, which also worketh in you that believe.

NEW TESTAMENT - **1 THESSALONIANS**

14 For brethren, ye are become followers of the Churches of God, which in Judea are in Christ Jesus, because ye have also suffered the same things of your own countrymen, even as they have of the Jews,

15 Who both killed the Lord Jesus and their own Prophets, and have persecuted us, and God they please not, and are contrary to all men,

16 And forbid us to preach unto the Gentiles, that they might be saved, to fulfill their sins always: for the wrath of God is come on them, to the utmost.

17 Forasmuch brethren, as we were kept from you for a season, concerning sight, but not in the heart, we enforced the more to see your face with great desire.

18 Therefore we would have come unto you (I Paul, at least once or twice) but Satan hindered us.

19 For what is our hope or joy, or crown of rejoicing? Are not even you it in the presence of our Lord Jesus Christ at his coming?

20 Yes, ye are our glory and joy.

1 Thessalonians Chapter 3

1 Wherefore since we could no longer forbear, we thought it good to remain at Athens alone,

2 And have sent Timotheus our brother and minister of God, and our labor fellow in the Gospel of Christ, to establish you, and to comfort you touching your faith,

3 That no man should be moved with these afflictions: for ye yourselves know, that we are appointed thereunto.

4 For verily when we were with you, we told you before that we should suffer tribulations, even as it came to pass, and ye know it.

5 Even for this cause, when I could no longer forbear, I sent him that I might know of your faith, lest the tempter had tempted you in any sort, and that our labor had been in vain.

6 But now lately when Timotheus came from you unto us, and brought us good tidings of your faith and love, and that ye have good remembrance of us always, desiring to see us, as we also do you,

7 Therefore, brethren, we had consolation in you, in all our affliction and necessity through your faith.

8 For now are we alive, if ye stand fast in the Lord.

9 For what thanks can we recompense to God again for you for all the joy wherewith we rejoice for your sakes before our God,

10 Night and day praying exceedingly that we might see your face, and might accomplish that which is lacking in your faith?

11 Now God himself, even our Father, and our Lord Jesus Christ, guide our journey unto you.

12 And the Lord increase you and make you abound in love one toward another, and toward all men, even as we do toward you:

13 To make your hearts stable and unblameable in holiness before God even our Father, at the coming of our Lord Jesus Christ with all his Saints.

1 Thessalonians Chapter 4

1 And furthermore we beseech you, brethren, and exhort you in the Lord Jesus that ye increase more and more, as ye have received of us, how ye ought to walk, and to please God.

2 For ye know what commandments we gave you by the Lord Jesus.

3 For this is the will of God even your sanctification, and that ye should abstain from fornication,

4 That every one of you should know, how to possess his vessel in holiness and honor,

5 And not in the lust of concupiscence, even as the Gentiles which know not God:

6 That no man oppress or defraud his brother in any matter: for the Lord is avenger of all such things, as we also have told you before time and testified.

7 For God hath not called us unto uncleanness, but unto holiness.

8 He therefore that despiseth these things, despiseth not man, but God who hath even given you his Holy Spirit.

9 But as touching brotherly love, ye need not that I write unto you: for ye are taught of God to love one another.

10 Yea, and that thing verily ye do unto all the brethren, which are throughout all Macedonia: but we beseech you, brethren, that ye increase more and more,

11 And that ye study to be quiet, and to meddle with your own business, and to work with your own hands, as we commanded you,

12 That ye may behave yourselves honestly toward them that are without, and that nothing be lacking unto you.

13 I would not, brethren, have you ignorant concerning them which are asleep, that ye sorrow not even as other which have no hope.

14 For if we believe that Jesus is dead, and is risen, even so them which sleep in Jesus, will God bring with him.

15 For this say we unto you by the word of the Lord, that we which live, and are remaining in the coming of the Lord, shall not prevent them which sleep.

16 For the Lord himself shall descend from heaven with a shout, and with the voice of the Archangel, and with the trumpet of God: and the dead in Christ shall rise first.

17 Then shall we which live and remain, be caught up with them also in the clouds, to meet the Lord in the air: and so shall we ever be with the Lord.

18 Wherefore, comfort yourselves one another with these words.

1 Thessalonians Chapter 5

1 But of the times and seasons, brethren, ye have no need that I write unto you.

2 For ye yourselves know perfectly, that the day of the Lord shall come, even as a thief in the night.

3 For when they shall say, Peace, and safety, then shall come upon them sudden destruction, as the travail upon a woman with child, and they shall not escape,

4 But ye, brethren, are not in darkness, that that day should come on you, as it were a thief.

5 You are all the children of light, and the children of the day: we are not of the night neither of darkness.

6 Therefore let us not sleep as do other, but let us watch and be sober.

7 For they that sleep, sleep in the night, and they that be drunken, are drunken in the night.

8 But let us which are of the day, be sober, putting on the breastplate of faith and love, and of the hope of salvation for an helmet.

9 For God hath not appointed us unto wrath, but to obtain salvation by the means of our Lord Jesus Christ,

10 Which died for us, that whether we wake or sleep, we should live together with him.

11 Wherefore exhort one another, and edify one another, even as ye do.

12 Now we beseech you, brethren, that ye know them, which labor among you, and are over you in the Lord, and admonish you,

13 That ye have them in singular love for their works' sake. Be at peace among yourselves.

14 We desire you, brethren, admonish them that are unruly: comfort the feeble minded: bear with the weak: be patient toward all men.

15 See that none recompense evil for evil unto any man: but ever follow that which is good, both toward yourselves, and toward all men.

16 Rejoice evermore.

17 Pray continually.

18 In all things give thanks: for this is the will of God in Christ Jesus toward you.

19 Quench not the Spirit.

20 Despise not prophesying.

21 Try all things, and keep that which is good.

22 Abstain from all appearance of evil.

23 Now the very God of peace sanctify you throughout: and I pray God that your whole spirit and soul and body, may be kept blameless unto the coming of our Lord Jesus Christ.

24 Faithful is he which calleth you, which will also do it.

25 Brethren, pray for us.

26 Greet all the brethren with an holy kiss.

27 I charge you in the Lord, that this Epistle be read unto all the brethren the Saints.

28 The grace of our Lord Jesus Christ be with you,
Amen.

SECOND EPISTLE OF PAUL TO THE THESSALONIANS

2 Thessalonians Chapter 1

1 Paul and Silvanus, and Timotheus unto the Church of the Thessalonians, which is in God our Father, and in the Lord Jesus Christ:
2 Grace be with you, and peace from God our Father, and from the Lord Jesus Christ.
3 We ought to thank God always for you, brethren, as it is meet, because that your faith groweth exceedingly, and the love of every one of you toward another aboundeth,
4 So that we ourselves rejoice of you in the Churches of God, because of your patience and faith in all your persecutions and tribulations that ye suffer,
5 Which is a token of the righteous judgment of God, that ye may be counted worthy of the kingdom of God, for the which ye also suffer.
6 For it is a righteous thing with God, to recompense tribulation to them that trouble you,
7 And to you which are troubled, rest with us when the Lord Jesus shall show himself from heaven with his mighty Angels,
8 In flaming fire, rendering vengeance unto them, that do not know God, and which obey not unto the Gospel of our Lord Jesus Christ.
9 Which shall be punished with everlasting perdition, from the presence of the Lord, and from the glory of his power,
10 When he shall come to be glorified in his Saints, and to be made marvelous in all them that believe (because our testimony toward you was believed) in that day.
11 Wherefore, we also pray always for you, that our God may make you worthy of his calling, and fulfill all the good pleasure of his goodness, and the work of faith with power,
12 That the Name of our Lord Jesus Christ may be glorified in you, and ye in him, according to the grace of our God, and of the Lord Jesus Christ.

2 Thessalonians Chapter 2

1 Now we beseech you, brethren, by the coming of our Lord Jesus Christ, and by our assembling unto him,
2 That ye be not suddenly moved from your mind, nor troubled neither by spirit, nor by word, nor by letter, as it were from us, as though the day of Christ were at hand.
3 Let no man deceive you by any means: for that day shall not come, except there come a departing first, and that that man of sin be disclosed, even the son of perdition,
4 Which is an adversary, and exalteth himself against all that is called God, or that is worshipped: so that he doth sit as God in the Temple of God, showing himself that he is God.
5 Remember ye not, that when I was yet with you, I told you these things?
6 And now ye know what withholdeth, that he might be revealed in his time.
7 For the mystery of iniquity doth already work: only he which now withholdeth, shall let till he be taken out of the way.
8 And then shall the wicked man be revealed, whom the Lord shall consume with the Spirit of his mouth, and shall abolish with the brightness of his coming,
9 Even him whose coming is by the working of Satan, with all power and signs, and lying wonders,
10 And in all deceivableness of unrighteousness, among them that perish, because they received not the love of the truth, that they might be saved.
11 And therefore God shall send them strong delusion, that they should believe lies,

12 That all they might be damned which believed not the truth, but had pleasure in unrighteousness.

13 But we ought to give thanks alway to God for you, brethren beloved of the Lord, because that God hath from the beginning chosen you to salvation, through sanctification of the Spirit, and the faith of truth,

14 Whereunto he called you by our Gospel, to obtain the glory of our Lord Jesus Christ.

15 Therefore, brethren, stand fast and keep the instructions, which ye have been taught, either by word, or by our Epistle.

16 Now the same Jesus Christ our Lord and our God even the Father which hath loved us, and hath given us everlasting consolation and good hope through grace,

17 Comfort your hearts, and stablish you in every word and good work.

2 Thessalonains Chapter 3

1 Furthermore, brethren, pray for us, that the word of the Lord may have free passage, and be glorified, even as it is with you,

2 And that we may be delivered from unreasonable and evil men: for all men have not faith.

3 But the Lord is faithful, which will stablish you, and keep you from evil.

4 And we are persuaded of you through the Lord, that ye both do, and will do the things which we command you.

5 And the Lord guide your hearts to the love of God, and the waiting for of Christ.

6 We command you, brethren, in the Name of our Lord Jesus Christ, that ye withdraw yourselves from every brother that walketh inordinately, and not after the instruction, which he received of us.

7 For ye yourselves know how ye ought to follow us: for we behaved not ourselves inordinately among you,

8 Neither took we bread of any man for naught: but we wrought with labor and travail night and day, because we would not be chargeable to any of you.

9 Not but that we had authority, but that we might make ourselves an ensample unto you to follow us.

10 For even when we were with you, this we warned you of, that if there were any, which would not work, that he should not eat.

11 For we heard, that there are some which walk among you inordinately, and work not at all, but are busy bodies.

12 Therefore them that are such, we command and exhort by our Lord Jesus Christ, that they work with quietness, and eat their own bread.

13 And ye, brethren, be not weary in well doing.

14 If any man obey not our sayings, note him by a letter, and have no company with him, that he may be ashamed.

15 Yet count him not as an enemy, but admonish him as a brother.

16 Now the Lord of peace give you peace always by all means. The Lord be with you all.

17 The salutation of me Paul, with mine own hand, which is the token in every Epistle: so I write,

18 The grace of our Lord Jesus Christ be with you all, Amen.

FIRST EPISTLE OF PAUL TO TIMOTHEUS

1 Timothy Chapter 1

1 Paul an Apostle of Jesus Christ, by the commandment of God our Savior, and of our Lord Jesus Christ our hope,
2 Unto Timotheus my natural son in the faith: Grace, mercy, and peace from God our Father, and from Christ Jesus our Lord.
3 As I besought thee to abide still in Ephesus, when I departed into Macedonia, so do, that thou mayest command some, that they teach none other doctrine,
4 Neither that they give heed to fables and genealogies which are endless, which breed questions rather than godly edifying which is by faith.
5 For the end of the commandment is love out of a pure heart, and of a good conscience, and of faith unfeigned.
6 From the which things some have erred, and have turned unto vain jangling.
7 They would be doctors of the Law, and yet understand not what they speak, neither whereof they affirm.
8 And we know, that the Law is good, if a man use it lawfully,
9 Knowing this, that the Law is not given unto a righteous man, but unto the lawless and disobedient, to the ungodly, and to sinners, to the unholy, and to the profane, to murderers of fathers and mothers, to manslayers,
10 To whoremongers, to buggerers, to mensteelers, to liars, to the perjured, and if there be any other thing, that is contrary to wholesome doctrine,
11 Which is according to the glorious Gospel of the blessed God, which is committed unto me.
12 Therefore I thank him, which hath made me strong, that is, Christ Jesus our Lord: for he counted me faithful, and put me in his service:
13 When before I was a blasphemer, and a persecutor, and an oppressor: but I was received to mercy: for I did it ignorantly through unbelief.
14 But the grace of our Lord was exceeding abundant with faith and love, which is in Christ Jesus.
15 This is a true saying, and by all means worthy to be received, that Christ Jesus came into the world to save sinners, of whom I am chief.
16 Notwithstanding, for this cause was I received to mercy, that Jesus Christ should first show on me all long suffering unto the ensample of them, which shall in time to come believe in him unto eternal life.
17 Now unto the King everlasting, immortal, invisible, unto God only wise, be honor and glory forever, and ever, Amen.
18 This commandment commit I unto thee, son Timotheus, according to the prophecies, which went before upon thee, that thou by them shouldest fight a good fight,
19 Having faith and a good conscience, which some have put away, and as concerning faith, have made shipwreck.
20 Of whom is Hymeneus, and Alexander, whom I have delivered unto Satan, that they might learn not to blaspheme.

1 Timothy Chapter 2

1 I Exhort therefore, that first of all supplications, prayers, intercessions and giving of thanks be made for all men,
2 For Kings, and for all that are in authority, that we may lead a quiet and a peaceable life, in all godliness and honesty.

264

3 For this is good and acceptable in the sight of God our Savior,

4 Who will that all men shall be saved, and come unto the knowledge of the truth.

5 For there is one God, and one Mediator between God and man, which is the man Christ Jesus,

6 Who gave himself a ransom for all men, to be a testimony in due time,

7 Whereunto I am ordained a preacher and an Apostle (I speak the truth in Christ, and lie not) even a teacher of the Gentiles in faith and verity.

8 I will therefore that the men pray, everywhere lifting up pure hands without wrath, or doubting.

9 Likewise also the women, that they array themselves in comely apparel, with shamefacedness and modesty, not with braided hair, or gold, or pearls, or costly apparel,

10 But (as becometh women that profess the fear of God) with good works.

11 Let the woman learn in silence with all subjection.

12 I permit not a woman to teach, neither to usurp authority over the man, but to be in silence.

13 For Adam was first formed, then Eve.

14 And Adam was not deceived, but the woman was deceived, and was in the transgression.

15 Notwithstanding, through bearing of children she shall be saved if they continue in faith, and love, and holiness with modesty.

1 Timothy Chapter 3

1 This is a true saying, If any man desire the office of a Bishop, he desireth a worthy work.

2 A Bishop therefore must be unreprovable, the husband of one wife, watching, sober, modest, harborous, apt to teach,

3 Not given to wine, no striker, not given to filthy lucre, but gentle, no fighter, not covetous,

4 One that can rule his own house honestly, having children under obedience with all honesty.

5 For if any cannot rule his own house, how shall he care for the Church of God?

6 He may not be a young scholar, lest he being puffed up fall into the condemnation of the devil.

7 He must also be well reported of, even of them which are without, lest he fall into rebuke, and the snare of the devil.

8 Likewise must Deacons be honest, not double-tongued, not given unto much wine, neither to filthy lucre,

9 Having the mystery of the faith in pure conscience.

10 And let them first be proved: then let them minister, if they be found blameless.

11 Likewise their wives must be honest, not evil speakers, but sober, and faithful in all things.

12 Let the Deacons be the husbands of one wife, and such as can rule their children well, and their own households.

13 For they that have ministered well, get themselves a good degree, and great liberty in the faith, which is in Christ Jesus.

14 These things write I unto thee, trusting to come very shortly unto thee.

15 But if I tarry long, that thou mayest yet know, how thou oughtest to behave thyself in the house of God, which is the Church of the living God, the pillar and ground of truth.

16 And without controversy, great is the mystery of godliness, which is, God is manifested in the flesh, justified in the Spirit, seen of Angels, preached unto the Gentiles, believed on in the world, and received up in glory.

1 Timothy Chapter 4

1 Now the Spirit speaketh evidently, that in the latter times some shall depart from the faith, and shall give heed unto spirits of error, and doctrines of devils,
2 Which speak lies through hypocrisy, and have their consciences burned with an hot iron,
3 Forbidding to marry, and commanding to abstain from meats which God hath created to be received with giving thanks of them which believe and know the truth.
4 For every creature of God is good, and nothing ought to be refused, if it be received with thanksgiving.
5 For it is sanctified by the word of God, and prayer.
6 If thou put the brethren in remembrance of these things, thou shalt be a good minister of Jesus Christ, which hast been nourished up in the words of faith, and of good doctrine, which thou hast continually followed.
7 But cast away profane, and old wives' fables, and exercise thyself unto godliness.
8 For bodily exercise profiteth little: but godliness is profitable unto all things, which hath the promise of the life present, and of that that is to come.
9 This is a true saying, and by all means worthy to be received.
10 For therefore we labor and are rebuked, because we trust in the living God, which is the Savior of all men, especially of those that believe.
11 These things command and teach.
12 Let no man despise thy youth, but be unto them that believe, an ensample, in word, in conversation, in love, in spirit, in faith, and in pureness.
13 Till I come, give attendance to reading, to exhortation, and to doctrine.
14 Despise not the gift that is in thee which was given thee by prophecy with the laying on of the hands of the company of the Eldership.
15 These things exercise, and give thyself unto them, that it may be seen how thou profitest among all men.
16 Take heed unto thyself, and unto learning: continue therein: for in doing this thou shalt both save thyself, and them that hear thee.

1 Timothy Chapter 5

1 Rebuke not an Elder, but exhort him as a father, and the younger men as brethren,
2 The elder women as mothers, the younger as sisters, with all pureness.
3 Honor widows, which are widows indeed.
4 But if any widow have children or nephews, let them learn first to show godliness toward their own house, and to recompense their kindred: for that is an honest thing and acceptable before God.
5 And she that is a widow indeed and left alone, trusteth in God, and continueth in supplications and prayers night and day.
6 But she that liveth in pleasure, is dead, while she liveth.
7 These things therefore command, that they may be blameless.
8 If there be any that provideth not for his own, and namely for them of his household, he denieth the faith, and is worse then an infidel.
9 Let not a widow be taken into the number under three score year old, that hath been the wife of one husband,

10 And well reported of for good works: if she have nourished her children, if she have lodged the strangers, if she have washed the Saints' feet, if she have ministered unto them which were in adversity, if she were continually given unto every good work.

11 But refuse the younger widows: for when they have begun to wax wanton against Christ, they will marry,

12 Having damnation, because they have broken the first faith.

13 And likewise also being idle they learn to go about from house to house: yea, they are not only idle, but also prattlers and busybodies, speaking things which are not comely.

14 I will therefore that the younger women marry, and bear children, and govern the house, and give none occasion to the adversary to speak evil.

15 For certain are already turned back after Satan.

16 If any faithful man, or faithful woman have widows, let them minister unto them, and let not the Church be charged, that there may be sufficient for them that are widows indeed.

17 The Elders that rule well, are worthy of double honor, specially they which labor in the word and doctrine,

18 For the Scripture saith, Thou shalt not muzzle the mouth of the ox that treadeth out the corn: and, The laborer is worthy of his wages.

19 Against an Elder receive none accusation, but under two or three witnesses.

20 Them that sin, rebuke openly, that the rest also may fear.

21 I charge thee before God and the Lord Jesus Christ, and the elect Angels, that thou observe these things without preferring one to another, and do nothing partially.

22 Lay hands suddenly on no man, neither be partaker of other men's sins: keep thyself pure.

23 Drink no longer water, but use a little wine for thy stomach's sake, and thine often infirmities.

24 Some men's sins are open beforehand, and go before unto judgment: but some men's follow after.

25 Likewise also the good works are manifest beforehand, and they that are otherwise, cannot be hid.

1 Timothy Chapter 6

1 Let as many servants as are under the yoke, count their masters worthy of all honor, that the Name of God, and his doctrine be not evil spoken of.

2 And they which have believing masters, let them not despise them, because they are brethren, but rather do service, because they are faithful, and beloved, and partakers of the benefit. These things teach and exhort.

3 If any man teach otherwise, and consenteth not to the wholesome words of our Lord Jesus Christ, and to the doctrine, which is according to godliness,

4 He is puffed up and knoweth nothing, but doteth about questions and strife of words, whereof cometh envy, strife, railings, evil surmisings,

5 Vain disputations of men of corrupt minds, and destitute of the truth, which think that gain is godliness: from such separate thyself.

6 But godliness is great gain, if a man be content with that he hath.

7 For we brought nothing into the world, and it is certain, that we can carry nothing out.

8 Therefore when we have food and raiment, let us therewith be content.

9 For they that will be rich, fall into temptation and snares, and into many foolish and noisome lusts, which drown men in perdition and destruction.

10 For the desire of money is the root of all evil, which while some lusted after, they erred from the faith, and pierced themselves through with many sorrows.

11 But thou, O man of God, flee these things, and follow after righteousness, godliness, faith, love, patience, and meekness.

12 Fight the good fight of faith: lay hold of eternal life, whereunto thou art also called, and hast professed a good profession before many witnesses.

13 I charge thee in the sight of God, who quickeneth all things, and before Jesus Christ, which under Pontius Pilate witnessed a good confession,

14 That thou keep this commandment without spot, and unrebukeable, until the appearing of our Lord Jesus Christ,

15 Which in due time he shall show, that is blessed and Prince only, the King of Kings and Lord of Lords.

16 Who only hath immortality, and dwelleth in the light that none can attain unto, whom never man saw, neither can see, unto whom be honor and power everlasting, Amen.

17 Charge them that are rich in this world, that they be not high minded, and that they trust not in uncertain riches, but in the living God, (which giveth us abundatly all things to enjoy)

18 That they do good, and be rich in good works, and ready to distribute, and communicate,

19 Laying up in store for themselves a good foundation against the time to come, that they may obtain eternal life.

20 O Timotheus, keep that which is committed unto thee, and avoid profane and vain babblings, and oppositions of science falsely so called,

21 Which while some profess, they have erred concerning the faith. Grace be with thee, Amen.

The first Epistle to Timotheus, written from Laodicea, which is the chiefest city of Phrygia Pacaciana.

THE SECOND EPISTLE OF PAUL TO TIMOTHEUS

2 Timotheus Chapter 1

1 Paul an Apostle of Jesus Christ, by the will of God, according to the promise of life, which is in CHRIST JESUS,
2 To Timotheus my beloved son: Grace, mercy, and peace from God the Father, and from Jesus Christ our Lord.
3 I thank God, whom I serve from mine elders with pure conscience, that without ceasing I have remembrance of thee in my prayers night and day,
4 Desiring to see thee, mindful of thy tears, that I may be filled with joy:
5 When I call to remembrance the unfeigned faith that is in thee, which dwelt first in thy grandmother Lois, and in thy mother Eunice, and am assured that it dwelleth in thee also.
6 Wherefore, I put thee in remembrance that thou stir up the gift of God which is in thee, by the putting on of mine hands.
7 For God hath not given to us the Spirit of fear, but of power, and of love, and of a sound mind.
8 Be not therefore ashamed of the testimony of our Lord, neither of me his prisoner: but be partaker of the afflictions of the Gospel, according to the power of God,
9 Who hath saved us, and called us with an holy calling, not according to our works, but according to his own purpose and grace, which was given to us through Christ Jesus before the world was,
10 But is now made manifest by the appearing of our Savior Jesus Christ, who hath abolished death, and hath brought life and immortality unto light through the Gospel.
11 Whereunto I am appointed a preacher, and Apostle, and a teacher of the Gentiles.
12 For the which cause I also suffer these things, but I am not ashamed: for I know whom I have believed, and I am persuaded that he is able to keep that which I have committed to him against that day.
13 Keep the true pattern of the wholesome words, which thou hast heard of me in faith and love which is in Christ Jesus.
14 That worthy thing, which was committed to thee, keep through the Holy Ghost, which dwelleth in us.
15 This thou knowest, that all they which are in Asia, be turned from me: of which sort are Phygellus and Hermogenes.
16 The Lord give mercy unto the house of Onesiphorus: for he oft refreshed me, and was not ashamed of my chain.
17 But when he was at Rome, he sought me out very diligently, and found me.
18 The Lord grant unto him, that he may find mercy with the Lord at that day, and in how many things he hath ministered unto me at Ephesus, thou knowest very well.

2 Timotheus Chapter 2

1 Thou therefore, my son, be strong in the grace that is in Christ Jesus.
2 And what things thou hast heard of me, by many witnesses, the same deliver to faithful men, which shall be able to teach other also.
3 Thou therefore suffer affliction as a good soldier of Jesus Christ.
4 No man that warreth, entangleth himself with the affairs of this life, because he would please him that hath chosen him to be a soldier.
5 And if any man also strive for a Mastery, he is not crowned, except he strive as he ought to do.
6 The husbandman must labor before he receive the fruits.

7 Consider what I say: and the Lord give thee understanding in all things:

8 Remember that Jesus Christ, made of the seed of David, was raised again from the dead according to my Gospel,

9 Wherein I suffer trouble as an evildoer, even unto bonds: but the word of God is not bound.

10 Therefore I suffer all things, for the elect's sake, that they might also obtain the salvation which is in Christ Jesus, with eternal glory.

11 It is a true saying, For if we be dead with him, we also shall live with him.

12 If we suffer, we shall also reign with him: if we deny him, he also will deny us.

13 If we believe not, yet abideth he faithful: he cannot deny himself.

14 Of these things put them in remembrance, and protest before the Lord, that they strive not about words, which is to no profit, but to the perverting of the hearers.

15 Study to show thyself approved unto God, a workman that needeth not to be ashamed, dividing the word of truth aright.

16 Stay profane, and vain babblings: for they shall increase unto more ungodliness.

17 And their word shall fret as a canker: of which sort is Hymeneus and Philetus,

18 Which as concerning the truth have erred, saying that the resurrection is past already, and do destroy the faith of certain.

19 But the foundation of God remaineth sure, and hath this seal, The Lord, knoweth who are his, and, Let every one that calleth on the Name of Christ, depart from iniquity.

20 Notwithstanding in a great house are not only vessels of gold and of silver, but also of wood and of earth, and some for honor, and some unto dishonor.

21 If any man therefore purge himself from these, he shall be a vessel unto honor, sanctified, and meet for the Lord, and prepared unto every good work.

22 Flee also from the lusts of youth, and follow after righteousness, faith, love, and peace, with them that call on the Lord with pure heart.

23 And put away foolish, and unlearned questions, knowing that they engender strife.

24 But the servant of the Lord must not strive, but must be gentle toward all men apt to teach, suffering the evil men patiently.

25 Instructing them with meekness that are contrary minded, proving if God at any time will give them repentance, that they may know the truth,

26 And that they may come to amendment out of the snare of the devil, which are taken of him at his will.

2 Timotheus Chapter 3

1 This know also, that in the last days shall come perilous times.

2 For men shall be lovers of their own selves, covetous, boasters, proud, cursed speakers, disobedient to parents, unthankful, unholy,

3 Without natural affection, truce-breakers, false accusers, intemperate, fierce, despisers of them which are good,

4 Traitors, heady, high-minded, lovers of pleasures more than lovers of God,

5 Having a show of godliness, but have denied the power thereof: turn away therefore from such.

6 For of this sort are they which creep into houses, and lead captive simple women laden with sins, and led with diverse lusts,

7 Which women are ever learning, and are never able to come to the knowledge of the truth.

8 And as Jannes and Jambres withstood Moses, so do these also resist the truth, men of corrupt minds, reprobate concerning the faith.

9 But they shall prevail no longer: for their madness shall be evident unto all men, as theirs also was.

10 But thou hast fully known my doctrine, manner of living, purpose, faith, long suffering, love, patience,

11 Persecutions, and afflictions which came unto me at Antiochia, at Iconium, and at Lystri, which persecutions I suffered: but from them all the Lord delivered me.

12 Yea, and all that will live godly in Christ Jesus, shall suffer persecution.

13 But the evil men and deceivers, shall wax worse and worse, deceiving, and being deceived.

14 But continue thou in the things which thou hast learned, and art persuaded there of, knowing of whom thou hast learned them:

15 And that thou hast known the holy Scriptures of a child, which are able to make thee wise unto salvation, through the faith which is in Christ Jesus.

16 For the whole Scripture is given by inspiration of God, and is profitable to teach, to improve, to correct, and to instruct in righteousness,

17 That the man of God may be absolute, being made perfect unto all good works.

2 Timotheus Chapter 4

1 I charge thee therefore before God, and before the Lord Jesus Christ, which shall judge the quick and dead at that his appearing, and in his kingdom,

2 Preach the word: be instant, in season and out of season: improve, rebuke, exhort with all long suffering and doctrine.

3 For the time will come, when they will not suffer wholesome doctrine: but having their ears itching, shall after their own lusts get them an heap of teachers,

4 And shall turn their ears from the truth, and shall be given unto fables.

5 But watch thou in all things: suffer adversity: do the work of an Evangelist: make thy ministry fully known.

6 For I am now ready to be offered, and the time of my departing is at hand.

7 I have fought a good fight, and have finished my course: I have kept the faith.

8 For henceforth is laid up for me the crown of righteousness, which the Lord the righteous judge shall give me at that day: and not to me only, but unto all them also that love his appearing.

9 Make speed to come unto me at once.

10 For Demas hath forsaken me, and hath embraced this present world, and is departed unto Thessalonica. Crescens is gone to Galatia, Titus unto Dalmatia.

11 Only Luke is with me. Take Mark and bring him with thee: for he is profitable unto me to minister.

12 And Tychicus have I sent to Ephesus.

13 The cloak that I left at Troas with Carpus, when thou comest, bring with thee, and the books, but specially the parchments.

14 Alexander the coppersmith hath done me much evil: the Lord reward him according to his works.

15 Of whom be thou ware also: for he withstood our preaching sore.

16 At my first answering no man assisted me, but all forsook me: I pray God, that it may not be laid to their charge.

17 Notwithstanding the Lord assisted me, and strengthened me, that by me the preaching might be fully known, and that all the Gentiles should hear: and I was delivered out of the mouth of the lion.

18 And the Lord will deliver me from every evil work, and will preserve me unto his heavenly kingdom: to whom be praise forever and ever, Amen.

19 Salute Prisca and Aquila, and the household of Onesiphorus.

20 Erastus abode at Corinth: Trophimus I left at Miletum sick.

21 Make speed to come before winter. Eubulus greeteth thee, and Pudens, and Linus, and Claudia, and all the brethren.
22 The Lord Jesus Christ be with thy spirit. Grace be with you, Amen.

THE EPISTLE OF PAUL TO TITUS

Titus Chapter 1

1 Paul a servant of God, and an Apostle of JESUS CHRIST, according to the faith of God's elect and the knowledge of the truth, which is according to godliness,
2 Under the hope of eternal life, which God that cannot lie, hath promised before the world began:
3 But hath made his word manifest in due time through the preaching, which is committed unto me, according to the commandment of God our Savior:
4 To Titus my natural son according to the common faith, Grace, mercy and peace from God the Father, and from the Lord Jesus Christ our Savior.
5 For this cause left I thee in Creta, that thou shouldest continue to redress the things that remain, and should ordain Elders in every city, as I appointed thee,
6 If any be unreprovable, the husband of one wife, having faithful children, which are not slandered of riot, neither are disobedient.
7 For a Bishop must be unreprovable, as God's steward, not froward, not angry, not given to wine, no striker, not given to filthy lucre,
8 But harborous, one that loveth goodness, wise, righteous, holy, temperate,
9 Holding fast the faithful word according to doctrine, that he also may be able to exhort with wholesome doctrine, and improve them that say against it.
10 For there are many disobedient and vain talkers and deceivers of minds, chiefly they of the Circumcision,
11 Whose mouths must be stopped, which subvert whole houses, teaching things, which they ought not, for filthy lucre's sake.
12 One of themselves, even one of their own prophets said, The Cretians are always liars, evil beasts, slow bellies.
13 This witness is true: wherefore rebuke them sharply, that they may be sound in the faith,
14 And not taking heed to Jewish fables and commandments of men, that turn from the truth.
15 Unto the pure are all things pure, but unto them that are defiled, and unbelieving, is nothing pure, but even their minds and consciences are defiled.
16 They profess that they know God, but by works they deny him, and are abominable and disobedient, and unto every good work reprobate.

Titus Chapter 2

1 But speak thou the things which become wholesome doctrine,
2 That the elder men be sober, honest, discrete, sound in the faith, in love, and in patience:
3 The elder women likewise, that they be in such behavior as becometh holiness, not false accusers, not given to much wine, but teachers of honest things,
4 That they may instruct the young women to be sober minded, that they love their husbands, that they love their children,
5 That they be discrete, chaste, keeping at home, good and subject unto their husbands, that the word of God be not evil spoken of.
6 Exhort young men likewise, that they be sober minded.
7 Above all things show thyself an ensample of good works with uncorrupt doctrine, with gravity, integrity,

8 And with the wholesome word, which cannot be reproved, that he which withstandeth, may be ashamed, having nothing concerning you to speak evil of.

9 Let servants be subject to their masters, and please them in all things, not answering again,

10 Neither pickers, but that they show all good faithfulness, that they may adorn the doctrine of God our Savior in all things.

11 For the grace of God, that bringeth salvation unto all men, hath appeared,

12 And teacheth us that we should deny ungodliness, and worldly lusts, and that we should live soberly and righteously, and godly in this present world,

13 Looking for the blessed hope, and appearing of the glory of the mighty God, and of our Savior Jesus Christ,

14 Who gave himself for us, that he might redeem us from all iniquity, and purge us to be a peculiar people unto himself, zealous of good works.

15 These things speak, and exhort, and rebuke with all authority. See that no man despise thee.

Titus Chapter 3

1 Put them in remembrance that they be subject to the Principalities and powers, and that they be obedient, and ready to every good work,

2 That they speak evil of no man, that they be no fighters, but soft, showing all meekness unto all men.

3 For we ourselves also were in times past unwise, disobedient, deceived, serving the lusts and diverse pleasures, living in maliciousness and envy, hateful, and hating one another.

4 But when that bountifulness and love of God our Savior toward man appeared,

5 Not by the works of righteousness, which we had done, but according to his mercy he saved us, by the washing of the new birth, and the renewing of the Holy Ghost,

6 Which he shed on us abundantly, through Jesus Christ our Savior,

7 That we, being justified by his grace, should be made heirs according to the hope of eternal life.

8 This is a true saying, and these things I will thou shouldest affirm, that they which have believed in God, might be careful to show forth good works. These things are good and profitable unto men.

9 But stay foolish questions, and genealogies, and contentions, and brawlings about the Law: for they are unprofitable and vain.

10 Reject him that is an heretic, after once or twice admonition,

11 Knowing that he that is such, is perverted, and sinneth being damned of his own self.

12 When I shall send Artemas unto thee, or Tychicus, be diligent to come to me unto Nicopolis: for I have determined there to winter.

13 Bring Zenas the expounder of the Law, and Apollos on their journey diligently, that they lack nothing.

14 And let ours also learn to show forth good works for necessary uses, that they be not unfruitful.

15 All that are with me, salute thee. Greet them that love us in the faith. Grace be with you all, Amen.

To Titus, elect the first bishop of the Church of the Cretians, written from Nicopolis in Macedonia.

The Epistle Of Paul To Philemon

1 Paul a prisoner of Jesus Christ, and our brother Timotheus, unto Philemon our dear friend, and fellow helper,

2 And to our dear sister Apphia, and to Archippus our fellow soldier, and to the Church that is in thine house:

3 Grace be with you, and peace from God our Father, and from the Lord Jesus Christ.

4 I give thanks to my God, making mention always of thee in my prayers,

5 (When I hear of thy love and faith, which thou hast toward the Lord Jesus, and toward all Saints)

6 That the fellowship of thy faith may be made effectual, and that whatsoever good thing is in you through Christ Jesus, may be known.

7 For we have great joy and consolation in thy love, because by thee, brother, the Saints' bowels are comforted.

8 Wherefore, though I be very bold in Christ to command thee that which is convenient,

9 Yet for love's sake I rather beseech thee, though I be as I am, even Paul aged, and even now a prisoner for Jesus Christ.

10 I beseech thee for my son Onesimus, whom I have begotten in my bonds,

11 Which in times past was to thee unprofitable, but now profitable both to thee and to me,

12 Whom I have sent again: thou therefore receive him, that is mine own bowels,

13 Whom I would have retained with me, that in thy stead he might have ministered unto me in the bonds of the Gospel.

14 But without thy mind would I do nothing, that thy benefit should not be as it were of necessity, but willingly.

15 It may be that he therefore departed for a season, that thou shouldest receive him for ever,

16 Not now as a servant, but above a servant, even as a brother beloved, specially to me: how much more then unto thee, both in the flesh and in the Lord?

17 If therefore thou count our things common, receive him as myself.

18 If he hath hurt thee, or oweth thee ought, that put on mine accounts.

19 I Paul have written this with mine own hand: I will recompense it, albeit I do not say to thee, that thou owest moreover unto me even thine own self.

20 Yea, brother, let me obtain this pleasure of thee in the Lord: comfort my bowels in the Lord.

21 Trusting in thine obedience, I wrote unto thee, knowing that thou wilt do even more then I say.

22 Moreover also prepare me lodging: for I trust through your prayers I shall be freely given unto you.

23 There salute thee Epaphras my fellow prisoner in Christ Jesus,

24 Marcus, Aristarchus, Demas and Luke, my fellow helpers.

25 The grace of our Lord Jesus Christ be with your spirit, Amen.

THE EPISTLE TO THE HEBREWS

Hebrews Chapter 1

1 At sundry times and in diverse manners God spake in the old time to our fathers by the Prophets:

2 In these last days he has spoken unto us by his Son, whom he hath made heir of all things, by whom also he made the worlds,

3 Who being the brightness of the glory, and the engraved form of his person, and bearing up all things by his mighty word, hath by himself purged our sins, and sitteth at the right hand of the Majesty in the highest places,

4 And is made so much more excellent than the Angels, inasmuch as he hath obtained a more excellent name than they.

5 For unto which of the Angels said he at any time, Thou art my Son, this day begat I thee? and again, I will be his Father, and he shall be my Son?

6 And again when he bringeth in his first begotten Son into the world, he saith, And let all the Angels of God worship him.

7 And of the Angels he saith, He maketh the spirits his messengers, and his ministers a flame of fire.

8 But unto the Son he saith, O God, thy throne is forever and ever: the scepter of thy kingdom is a scepter of righteousness.

9 Thou hast loved righteousness and hated iniquity. Wherefore God, even thy God, hath anointed thee with the oil of gladness above thy fellows.

10 And, Thou, Lord, in the beginning hast established the earth, and the heavens are the works of thine hands.

11 They shall perish, but thou dost remain: and they all shall wax old as doth a garment.

12 And as a vesture shalt thou fold them up, and they shall be changed: but thou art the same and thy years shall not fail.

13 Unto which also of the Angels said he at any time, Sit at my right hand, till I make thine enemies thy footstool?

14 Are they not all ministering spirits, sent forth to minister, for their sakes which shall be heirs of salvation?

Hebrews Chapter 2

1 Wherefore we ought diligently to give heed to the things which we have heard, lest at any time we should let them slip.

2 For if the word spoken by Angels was steadfast, and every transgression, and disobedience received a just recompense of reward,

3 How shall we escape, if we neglect so great salvation, which at the first began to be preached by the Lord, and afterward was confirmed unto us by them that heard him,

4 God bearing witness thereto, both with signs and wonders, and with diverse miracles, and gifts of the Holy Ghost, according to his own will?

5 For he hath not put in subjection unto the Angels the world to come, whereof we speak.

6 But one in a certain place witnessed, saying, What is man, that thou shouldest be mindful of him? or the son of man that thou wouldest consider him?

7 Thou madest him a little inferior to the Angels: thou crowned him with glory and honor, and hast set him above the works of thine hands.

8 Thou hast put all things in subjection under his feet. And in that he hath put all things in subjection under him, he left nothing that should not be subject unto him. But we yet see not all things subdued unto him,

9 But we see Jesus crowned with glory and honor, which was made a little inferior to the Angels, through the suffering of death, that by God's grace he might taste death for all men.
10 For it became him, for whom are all things, and by whom are all things, seeing that he brought many children unto glory, that he should consecrate the Prince of their salvation through afflictions.
11 For he that sanctifieth, and they which are sanctified, are all of one: wherefore he is not ashamed to call them brethren,
12 Saying, I will declare thy Name unto my brethren: in the midst of the Church will I sing praises to thee.
13 And again, I will put my trust in him. And again, Behold, here am I, and the children which God hath given me.
14 Forasmuch then as the children were partakers of flesh and blood, he also himself likewise took part with them, that he might destroy through death, him that had the power of death, that is the devil,
15 And that he might deliver all them, which for fear of death were all their lifetime subject to bondage.
16 For he in no sort took the Angels , but he took the seed of Abraham.
17 Wherefore in all things it became him to be made like unto his brethren, that he might be merciful, and a faithful high Priest in things concerning God, that he might make reconciliation for the sins of the people.
18 For in that he suffered, and was tempted, he is able to sucker them that are tempted.

Hebrews Chapter 3

1 Therefore, holy brethren, partakers of the heavenly vocation, consider the Apostle and high Priest of our profession Christ Jesus:
2 Who was faithful to him that hath appointed him, even as Moses was in all his house.
3 For this man is counted worthy of more glory than Moses, inasmuch as he which hath builded the house, hath more honor than the house.
4 For every house is builded of some man, and he that hath built all things, is God.
5 Now Moses verily was faithful in all his house, as a servant, for a witness of the things which should be spoken after.
6 But Christ is as the Son, over his own house, whose house we are, if we hold fast the confidence and the rejoicing of the hope unto the end.
7 Wherefore, as the holy Ghost saith, Today if ye shall hear his voice,
8 Harden not your hearts, as in the provocation, according to the day of the temptation in the wilderness,
9 Where your fathers tempted me, proved me, and saw my works forty years long.
10 Wherefore I was grieved with that generation, and said, They err ever in their heart, neither have they known my ways.
11 Therefore I swear in my wrath, If they shall enter into my rest.
12 Take heed, brethren, lest at any time there be in any of you an evil heart, and unfaithful, to depart away from the living God.
13 But exhort one another daily, while it is called Today, lest any of you be hardened through the deceitfulness of sin.
14 For we are made partakers of Christ, if we keep sure unto the end the beginning, wherewith we are upholden,

15 So long as it is said, Today if ye hear his voice, harden not your hearts, as in the provocation.

16 For some when they heard, provoked him to anger: howbeit, not all that came out of Egypt by Moses.

17 But with whom was he displeased forty years? Was he not displeased with them that sinned, whose carcasses fell in the wilderness?

18 And to whom sware he that they should not enter into his rest, but unto them, that obeyed not?

19 So we see that they could not enter in because of unbelief.

Hebrews Chapter 4

1 Let us fear therefore, lest at any time by forsaking the promise of entering into his rest any of you should seem to be deprived.

2 For unto us was the Gospel preached as also unto them: but the word that they heard, profited not them, because it was not mixed with faith in those that heard it.

3 For we which have believed, do enter into rest, as he said to the other, As I have sworn in my wrath, If they shall enter into my rest: although the works were finished from the foundation of the world.

4 For he spake in a certain place of the seventh day on this wise, And God did rest the seventh day from all his works.

5 And in this place again, If they shall enter into my rest.

6 Seeing therefore it remaineth that some must enter thereinto, and they to whom it was first preached, entered not therein for unbelief's sake:

7 Again he appointed in David a certain day, by Today, after so long a time, saying, as it is said, This day, if ye hear his voice, harden not your hearts.

8 For if Jesus had given them rest, then would he not after this day have spoken of another.

9 There remaineth therefore a rest to the people of God.

10 For he that is entered into his rest, hath also ceased from his own works, as God did from his.

11 Let us study therefore to enter into that rest, lest any man fall after the same ensample of disobedience.

12 For the word of God is lively, and mighty in operation, and sharper than any two-edged sword, and entereth through, even unto the dividing asunder of the soul and the spirit, and of the joints, and the marrow, and is a discerner of the thoughts, and the intents of the heart.

13 Neither is there any creature, which is not manifest in his sight: but all things are naked and open unto his eyes, with whom we have to do.

14 Seeing then that we have a great high Priest, which is entered into heaven, even Jesus the Son of God, let us hold fast our profession.

15 For we have not an high Priest, which cannot be touched with the feeling of our infirmities, but was in all things tempted in like sort, yet without sin.

16 Let us therefore go boldly unto the throne of grace, that we may receive mercy, and find grace to help in time of need.

Hebrews Chapter 5

1 For every high Priest is taken from among men, and is ordained for men, in things pertaining to God, that he may offer both gifts and sacrifices for sins,

2 Which is able sufficiently to have compassion on them that are ignorant, and that are out of the way, because that he also is compassed with infirmity,

3 And for the same's sake he is bound to offer for sins, as well for his own part, as for the people's.

4 And no man taketh this honor unto himself, but he that is called of God, as was Aaron.

5 So likewise Christ took not to himself this honor, to be made the high Priest, but he that said unto him, Thou art my Son, this day begat I thee, gave it him.

6 As he also in another place speaketh, Thou art a Priest forever after the order of Melchisedec.

7 Which in the days of his flesh did offer up prayers and supplications, with strong crying and tears unto him, that was able to save him from death, and was also heard in that which he feared.

8 And though he were the Son, yet learned he obedience, by the things which he suffered.

9 And being consecrate was made the author of eternal salvation unto all them that obey him:

10 And is called of God an high Priest after the order of Melchisedec.

11 Of whom we have many things to say, which are hard to be uttered, because ye are dull of hearing.

12 For when as concerning the time ye ought to be teachers, yet have ye need again that we teach you the first principles of the word of God: and are become such as have need of milk, and not of strong meat.

13 For every one that useth milk, is inexpert in the word of righteousness: for he is a babe.

14 But strong meat belongeth to them that are of age, which through long custom have their wits exercised, to discern both good and evil.

Hebrews Chapter 6

1 Therefore, leaving the doctrine of the beginning of Christ, let us be led forward unto perfection, not laying again the foundation of repentance from dead works, and of faith toward God,

2 Of the doctrine of baptisms, and laying on of hands, and of the resurrection from the dead, and of eternal judgment.

3 And this will we do if God permit.

4 For it is impossible that they, which were once lightened, and have tasted of the heavenly gift, and were made partakers of the holy Ghost,

5 And have tasted of the good word of God, and of the powers of the world to come,

6 If they fall away, should be renewed again by repentance: seeing they crucify again to themselves the Son of God and make a mock of him.

7 For the earth which drinketh in the rain that cometh oft upon it, and bringeth forth herbs meet for them by whom it is dressed, receiveth blessing of God.

8 But that which beareth thorns and briars, is reproved, and is near unto cursing, whose end is to be burned.

9 But beloved, we have persuaded ourselves better things of you, and such as accompany salvation, though we thus speak.

10 For God is not unrighteous, that he should forget your work, and labor of love, which ye showed toward his Name, in that ye have ministered unto the Saints, and yet minister.

11 And we desire that every one of you show the same diligence, to the full assurance of hope unto the end,

12 That ye be not slothful, but followers of them, which through faith and patience, inherit the promises.

13 For when God made the promise to Abraham, because he had no greater to swear by, he swear by himself,

14 Saying, Surely I will abundantly bless thee and multiply thee marvelously.

15 And so after that he had tarried patiently, he enjoyed the promise.

16 For men verily swear by him that is greater than themselves, and an oath for confirmation is among them an end of all strife.

17 So God willing more abundantly to show unto the heirs of promise the stableness of his counsel, bound himself by an oath,

18 That by two immutable things, wherein it is unpossible that God should lie, we might have strong consolation, which have our refuge to hold fast the hope that is set before us,

19 Which we have, as an anchor of the soul, both sure and steadfast, and it entereth into that which is within the vale,

20 Whether the forerunner is for us entered in, even Jesus that is made an high Priest forever after the order of Melchisedec.

Hebrews Chapter 7

1 For this Melchisedec was King of Salem, the Priest of the most high God, who met Abraham, as he returned from the slaughter of the Kings, and blessed him:

2 To whom also Abraham gave the tithe of all things: who first is by interpretation King of righteousness: after that, he is also King of Salem, that is, King of peace,

3 Without father, without mother, without kindred, and hath neither beginning of his days, neither end of life: but is likened unto the Son of God, and continueth a Priest forever.

4 Now consider how great this man was, unto whom even the Patriarch Abraham gave the tithe of the spoils.

5 For verily they which are the children of Levi, which receive the office of the Priesthood, have a commandment to take, according to the Law, tithes of the people (that is, of their brethren) though they came out of the loins of Abraham.

6 But he whose kindred is not counted among them, received tithes of Abraham, and blessed him that had the promises.

7 And without all contradiction the less is blessed of the greater.

8 And here men that die, receive tithes: but there he receiveth them, of whom it is witnessed, that he liveth.

9 And to say as the thing is, Levi also which receiveth tithes, paid tithes in Abraham.

10 For he was yet in the loins of his father Abraham, when Melchisedec met him.

11 If therefore perfection had been by the Priesthood of the Levites (for under it the Law was established to the people) what needed it furthermore, that another Priest should rise after the order of Melchisedec, and not to be called after the order of Aaron?

12 For if the Priesthood be changed, then of necessity must there be a change of the Law.

13 For he of whom these things are spoken, pertaineth unto another tribe, whereof no man served at the altar.

14 For it is evident, that our Lord sprung out of Juda, concerning the which tribe Moses spake nothing, touching the Priesthood.

15 And it is yet a more evident thing, because that after the similitude of Melchisedec, there is risen up another Priest,

16 Which is not made Priest after the Law of the carnal commandment, but after the power of the endless life.

17 For he testifieth thus, Thou art a Priest forever, after the order of Melchisedec.

18 For the commandment that went afore, is disannuled, because of the weakness thereof, and unprofitableness.

19 For the Law made nothing perfect, but the bringing in of a better hope made perfect, whereby we draw near unto God.

20 And forasmuch as it is not without an oath (for these are made Priests without an oath:

21 But this, he is made with an oath by him that said unto him, The Lord hath sworn, and will not repent, Thou art a Priest forever, after the order of Melchisedec)

22 By so much is Jesus made a surety of a better Testament.

23 And among them many were made Priests, because they were not suffered to endure, by the reason of death.

24 But this man, because he endureth ever, hath an everlasting Priesthood.

25 Wherefore, he is able also perfectly to save them that come unto God by him, seeing he ever liveth, to make intercession for them.

26 For such an high Priest it became us to have, which is holy, harmless, undefiled, separate from sinners, and made higher than the heavens:

27 Which needed not daily as those high Priests to offer up sacrifice, first for his own sins, and then for the peoples: for that did he once, when he offered up himself.

28 For the Law maketh men high Priests, which have infirmity: but the word of the oath that was since the Law, maketh the Son, who is consecrated forevermore.

Hebrews Chapter 8

1 Now of the things which we have spoken, this is the sum, that we have such an high Priest, that sitteth at the right hand of the throne of the Majesty in heavens,

2 And is a minister of the Sanctuary, and of that true Tabernacle which the Lord pight, and not man.

3 For every high Priest is ordained to offer both gifts and sacrifices: wherefore it was of necessity, that this man should have somewhat also to offer.

4 For he were not a Priest, if he were on the earth, seeing there are Priests that according to the Law offer gifts,

5 Who serve unto the pattern and shadow of heavenly things, as Moses was warned by God, when he was about to finish the Tabernacle. See, said he, that thou make all things according to the pattern, showed to thee in the mount.

6 But now our high Priest hath obtained a more excellent office, in as much as he is the Mediator of a better Testament, which is established upon better promises.

7 For if that first Testament had been faultless, no place should have been sought for the second.

8 For in rebuking them he saith, Behold, the days will come, saith the Lord, when I shall make with the house of Israel, and with the house of Juda a new Testament:

9 Not like the Testament that I made with their fathers, in the day that I took them by the hand, to lead them out of the land of Egypt: for they continued not in my Testament, and I regarded them not, saith the Lord.

10 For this is the Testament that I will make with the house of Israel, After those days, saith the Lord, I will put my Laws in their mind, and in their heart I will write them, and I will be their God, and they shall be my people,

11 And they shall not teach every man his neighbor and every man his brother, saying, Know the Lord: for all shall know me, from the least of them to the greatest of them.

12 For I will be merciful to their unrighteousness, and I will remember their sins and their iniquities no more.

13 In that he saith a new Testament, he hath abrogate the old: now that which is disannuled and waxed old, is ready to vanish away.

Hebrews Chapter 9

1 Then the first Testament had also ordinances of religion, and a worldly Sanctuary.

2 For the first Tabernacle was made, wherein was the candlestick, and the table, and the showbread, which Tabernacle is called the Holy places.

3 And after the second veil was the Tabernacle, which is called the Holiest of all,

4 Which had the golden censer, and the Ark of the Testament overlaid round about with gold, wherein the golden pot which had Manna, was, and Aaron's rod that had budded, and the tables of the Testament.

5 And over the Ark were the glorious Cherubims, shadowing the mercy seat: of which things we will not now speak particularly.

6 Now when these things were thus ordained, the Priests went always into the first Tabernacle, and accomplished the service.

7 But into the second went the high Priest alone, once every year, not without blood which he offered for himself, and for the ignorances of the people.

8 Whereby the Holy Ghost this signified, that the way into the Holiest of all was, not yet opened, while as yet the first tabernacle was standing,

9 Which was a figure for the time present, wherein were offered gifts and sacrifices that could not make holy, concerning the conscience, him that did the service,

10 Which only stood in meats and drinks, and diverse washings, and carnal rites, until the time of reformation.

11 But Christ being come an high Priest of good things to come, by a greater and a more perfect Tabernacle, not made with hands, that is, not of this building,

12 Neither by the blood of goats and calves: but by his own blood entered he in once unto the holy place, and obtained eternal redemption for us.

13 For if the blood of bulls and of goats, and the ashes of an heifer, sprinkling them that are unclean, sanctifieth as touching the purifying of the flesh,

14 How much more shall the blood of Christ which through the eternal Spirit offered himself without spot to God, purge your conscience from dead works, to serve the living God?

15 And for this cause is he the Mediator of the new Testament, that through death which was for the redemption of the transgressions that were in the former Testament, they which were called, might receive the promise of eternal inheritance.

16 For where a Testament is, there must be the death of him that made the Testament.

17 For the Testament is confirmed when men are dead: for it is yet of no force as long as he that made it, is alive.

18 Wherefore neither was the first ordained without blood.

19 For when Moses had spoken every precept to the people, according to the Law, he took the blood of calves and of goats, with water and purple wool and hyssop, and sprinkled both the book, and all the people,

20 Saying, This is the blood of the Testament, which God hath appointed unto you.

21 Moreover, he sprinkled likewise the Tabernacle with blood also, and all the ministering vessels.

22 And almost all things are by the Law purged with blood, and without shedding of blood is no remission.

23 It was then necessary, that the similitudes of heavenly things should be purified with such things: but the heavenly things themselves are purified with better sacrifices than are these.

24 For Christ is not entered into the holy places that are made with hands, which are similitudes of the true Sanctuary: but is entered into very heaven, to appear now in the sight of God for us,

25 Not that he should offer himself often, as the high Priest entered into the Holy place every year with other blood,

26 (For then must he have often suffered since the foundation of the world) but now in the end of the world hath he appeared once to put away sin, by the sacrifice of himself.

27 And as it is appointed unto men that they shall once die, and after that cometh the judgment:

28 So Christ was once offered to take away the sins of many, and unto them that look for him, shall he appear the second time without sin unto salvation.

Hebrews Chapter 10

1 For the Law having the shadow of good things to come, and not the very image of the things, can never with those sacrifices, which they offer year by year continually, sanctify the comers thereunto.

2 For would they not then have ceased to have been offered, because that the offerers once purged, should have had no more conscience of sins?

3 But in those sacrifices there is a remembrance again of sins every year.

4 For it is unpossible that the blood of bulls and goats should take away sins.

5 Wherefore when he cometh into the world, he saith, Sacrifice and offering thou wouldest not: but a body hast thou ordained me.

6 In burnt offerings, and sin offerings thou hast had no pleasure.

7 Then I said, Lo, I come (In the beginning of the book it is written of me) that I should do thy will, O God.

8 Above, when he said, Sacrifice and offering, and burnt offerings, and sin offerings thou wouldest not have, neither hadest pleasure therein (which are offered by the Law)

9 Then said he, Lo, I come to do thy will, O God, he taketh away the first, that he may stablish the second.

10 By the which will we are sanctified, even by the offering of the body of Jesus Christ once made.

11 And every Priest appeareth daily ministering, and oft times offereth one manner of offering, which can never take away sins:

12 But this man after he had offered one sacrifice for sins, sitteth forever at the right hand of God,

13 And from henceforth tarrieth, till his enemies be made his footstool.

14 For with one offering hath he consecrated forever them that are sanctified.

15 For the holy Ghost also beareth us record: for after that he had said before,

16 This is the Testament that I will make unto them after those days, saith the Lord, I will put my Laws in their heart, and in their minds I will write them.

17 And their sins and iniquities will I remember no more.

18 Now where remission of these things is, there is no more offering for sin.

19 Seeing therefore, brethren, that by the blood of Jesus we may be bold to enter into the Holy place

20 By the new and living way, which he hath prepared for us, through the veil, that is, his flesh:

21 And seeing we have an high Priest, which is over the house of God,

22 Let us draw near with a true heart in assurance of faith, sprinkled in our hearts from an evil conscience, and washed in our bodies with pure water.

23 Let us keep the profession of our hope, without wavering, (for he is faithful that promised)

24 And let us consider one another, to provoke unto love, and to good works,

25 Not forsaking the fellowship that we have among ourselves, as the manner of some is: but let us exhort one another, and that so much the more, because ye see that the day draweth near.

26 For if we sin willingly after that we have received the knowledge of the truth, there remaineth no more sacrifice for sins,

27 But a fearful looking for of judgment, and violent fire, which shall devour the adversaries.

28 He that despiseth Moses' Law, dieth without mercy under two, or three witnesses:

29 Of how much sorer punishment suppose ye shall he be worthy, which treadeth under foot the Son of God, and counteth the blood of the Testament as an unholy thing, wherewith he was sanctified, and doth despite the Spirit of grace?

30 For we know him that hath said, Vengeance belongeth unto me: I will recompense, saith the Lord. And again, The Lord shall judge his people.

31 It is a fearful thing to fall into the hands of the living God. 32 Now call to remembrance the days that are passed, in the which, after ye had received light, ye endured a great fight in afflictions,

33 Partly while you were made a gazing stock both by reproaches and afflictions, and partly while ye became companions of them which were so tossed to and fro.

34 For both ye sorrowed with me for my bonds, and suffered with joy the spoiling of your goods, knowing in yourselves how that ye have in heaven a better, and an enduring substance.

35 Cast not away therefore your confidence which hath great recompense of reward.

36 For ye have need of patience, that after ye have done the will of God, ye might receive the promise.

37 For yet a very little while, and he that shall come, will come, and will not tarry.

38 Now the just shall live by faith: but if any withdraw himself, my soul shall have no pleasure in him.

39 But we are not they which withdraw ourselves unto perdition, but follow faith unto the conservation of the soul.

Hebrews Chapter 11

1 Now faith is the ground of things, which are hoped for, and the evidence of things which are not seen.

2 For by it our elders were well reported of.

3 Through faith we understand that the world was ordained by the word of God, so that the things which we see, are not made of things which did appear.

4 By faith Abel offered unto God a greater sacrifice than Cain, by the which he obtained witness that he was righteous, God testifying of his gifts: by the which faith also he being dead, yet speaketh.

5 By faith was Enoch taken away, that he should not see death: neither was he found: for God had taken him away: for before he was taken away, he was reported of, that he had pleased God.

6 But without faith it is unpossible to please him: for he that cometh to God, must believe that God is, and that he is a rewarder of them that seek him.

7 By faith Noah being warned of God of the things which were as yet not seen, moved with reverence, prepared the Ark to the saving of his household, through the which Ark he condemned the world, and was made heir of the righteousness, which is by faith.

8 By faith Abraham, when he was called, obeyed God, to go out into a place, which he should afterward receive for inheritance, and he went out, not knowing whether he went.

9 By faith he abode in the land of promise, as in a strange country, as one that dwelt in tents with Isaac and Jacob, heirs with him of the same promise.

10 For he looked for a city having a foundation, whose builder and maker is God.

11 Through faith Sara also received strength to conceive seed, and was delivered of a child when she was past age, because she judged him faithful which had promised.

12 And therefore sprang there of one, even of one which was dead, so many as the stars of the sky in multitude, and as the sand of the sea shore which is innumerable.

13 All these died in faith, and received not the promises, but saw them afar off, and believed them, and received them thankfully, and confessed that they were strangers and pilgrims on the earth.

14 For they that say such things, declare plainly, that they seek a country.

15 And if they had been mindful of that country, from whence they came out, they had leisure to have returned.

16 But now they desire a better, that is an heavenly: wherefore God is not ashamed of them to be called their God: for he hath prepared for them a city.

17 By faith Abraham offered up Isaac, when he was tried, and he that had received the promises, offered his only begotten son.

18 (To whom it was said, In Isaac shall thy seed be called.)

19 For he considered that God was able to raise him up even from the dead: from whence he received him also after a sort.

20 By faith Isaac blessed Jacob and Esau, concerning things to come.

21 By faith Jacob when he was a dying, blessed both the sons of Joseph, and leaning on the end of his staff, worshipped God.

22 By faith Joseph when he died, made mention of the departing of the children of Israel, and gave commandment of his bones.

23 By faith Moses when he was born, was hid three months of his parents, because they saw he was a proper child, neither feared they the King's commandment.

24 By faith Moses when he was come to age, refused to be called the son of Pharaoh's daughter,

25 And chose rather to suffer adversity with the people of God, than to enjoy the pleasures of sins for a season,

26 Esteeming the rebuke of Christ greater riches than the treasures of Egypt: for he had respect unto the recompense of the reward.

27 By faith he forsook Egypt, and feared not the fierceness of the king: for he endured, as he that saw him which is invisible.

28 Through faith he ordained the Passover and the effusion of blood, lest he that destroyed the firstborn, should touch them.

29 By faith they passed through the Red sea as by dry land, which when the Egyptians had assayed to do, they were drowned.

30 By faith the walls of Jericho fell down after they were compassed about seven days.

31 By faith the harlot Rahab perished not with them which obeyed not, when she had received the spies peaceably.

32 And what shall I more say? for the time would be too short for me to tell of Gideon, of Barak, and of Sampson, and of Jephthah, also of David, and Samuel, and of the Prophets:

33 Which through faith subdued kingdoms, wrought righteousness, obtained the promises, stopped the mouths of lions,

34 Quenched the violence of fire, escaped the edge of the sword, of weak were made strong, waxed valiant in battle, turned to flight the armies of the aliens.

35 The women received their dead raised to life: other also were racked, and would not be delivered, that they might receive a better resurrection.

36 And others have been tried by mockings and scourgings, yea, moreover by bonds and prisonment.

37 They were stoned, they were hewn asunder, they were tempted, they were slain with the sword, they wandered up and down in sheepskins, and in goatskins, being destitute, afflicted, and tormented:

38 Whom the world was not worthy of: they wandered in wildernesses and mountains, and dens, and caves of the earth.

39 And these all through faith obtained good report, and received not the promise,

40 God providing a better thing for us, that they without us should not be made perfect.

Hebrews Chapter 12

1 Wherefore, let us also, seeing that we are compassed with so great a cloud of witnesses, cast away every thing that presseth down, and the sin that hangeth so fast on: let us run with patience the race that is set before us,

2 Looking unto Jesus the author and finisher of our faith, who for the joy that was set before him, endured the cross, and despised the shame, and is set at the right hand of the throne of God.

3 Consider therefore him that endured such speaking against of sinners, lest ye should be wearied and faint in your minds.

4 Ye have not yet resisted unto blood, striving against sin.

5 And ye have forgotten the consolation, which speaketh unto you as unto children, My son, despise not the chastening of the Lord, neither faint when thou art rebuked of him.

6 For whom the Lord loveth, he chasteneth: and he scourgeth every son that he receiveth:

7 If you endure chastening, God offereth himself unto you as unto sons: for what son is it whom the father chasteneth not?

8 If therefore ye be without correction, whereof all are partakers, then are ye bastards, and not sons.

9 Moreover we have had the fathers of our bodies which corrected us, and we gave them reverence: should we not much rather be in subjection unto the Father of spirits, that we might live?

10 For they verily for a few days chastened us after their own pleasure: but he chasteneth us for our profit, that we might be partakers of his holiness.

11 Now no chastising for the present seemeth to be joyous, but grievous: but afterward, it bringeth the quiet fruit of righteousness, unto them which are thereby exercised.

12 Wherefore lift up your hands which hang down, and your weak knees,

13 And make straight steps unto your feet, lest that which is halting, be turned out of the way, but let it rather be healed.

14 Follow peace with all men, and holiness, without the which no man shall see the Lord.

15 Take heed, that no man fall away from the grace of God: let no root of bitterness spring up and trouble you, lest thereby many be defiled.

16 Let there be no fornicator, or profane person as Esau, which for a portion of meat sold his birthright.

17 For ye know how that afterward also when he would have inherited the blessing, he was rejected: for he found no place to repentance, though he sought the blessing with tears.

18 For ye are not come unto the mount that might be touched, nor unto burning fire, nor to blackness and darkness, and tempest,

19 Neither unto the sound of a trumpet, and the voice of words, which they that heard it, excused themselves, that the word should not be spoken to them any more,

20 (For they were not able to abide that which was commanded, Yea, though a beast touch the mountain, it shall be stoned, or thrust through with a dart:

21 And so terrible was the sight which appeared, that Moses said, I fear and quake.)

22 But ye are come unto the mount Zion, and to the city of the living God, the celestial Jerusalem, and to the company of innumerable Angels,

23 And to the congregation of the firstborn, which are written in heaven, and to God the judge of all, and to the spirits of just and perfect men,

24 And to Jesus the Mediator of the New Testament, and to the blood of sprinkling that speaketh better things than that of Abel.

25 See that ye despise not him that speaketh: for if they escaped not which refused him, that spake on earth: much more shall we not escape, if we turn away from him, that speaketh from heaven.

26 Whose voice then shook the earth, and now hath declared, saying, Yet once more will I shake, not the earth only, but also heaven.

27 And this word, Yet once more, signifieth the removing of those things, which are shaken, as of things which are made with hands, that the things which are not shaken, may remain.

28 Wherefore seeing we receive a kingdom, which cannot be shaken, let us have grace, whereby we may so serve God, that we may please him with reverence and fear.

29 For even our God is a consuming fire.

Hebrews Chapter 13

1 Let brotherly love continue.

2 Be not forgetful to lodge strangers: for thereby some have received Angels into their houses unawares.

3 Remember them that are in bonds, as though ye were bound with them: and them that are in affliction, as if ye were also afflicted in the body.

4 Marriage is honorable among all, and the bed undefiled: but whoremongers and adulterers God will judge.

5 Let your conversation be without covetousness, and be content with those things that ye have, for he hath said, I will not fail thee, neither forsake thee:

6 So that we may boldly say, The Lord is mine helper, neither will I fear what man can do unto me.

7 Remember them which have the oversight of you, which have declared unto you the word of God: whose faith follow, considering what hath been the end of their conversation.

8 Jesus Christ yesterday, and today, the same also is forever.

9 Be not carried about with diverse and strange doctrines: for it is a good thing that the heart be stablished with grace, and not with meats, which have not profited them that have been occupied therein.

10 We have an altar whereof they have no authority to eat which serve in the tabernacle.

11 For the bodies of those beasts whose blood is brought into the Holy place by the high Priest for sin, are burned without the camp.

12 Therefore even Jesus, that he might sanctify the people with his own blood, suffered without the gate.

13 Let us go forth therefore out of the camp, bearing his reproach.

14 For here have we no continuing city: but we seek one to come.

15 Let us therefore by him offer the sacrifice of praise always to God, that is, the fruit of the lips, which confess his Name.

16 To do good, and to distribute forget not: for with such sacrifices God is pleased.

17 Obey them that have the oversight of you, and submit yourselves: for they watch for your souls, as they that must give accounts, that they may do it with joy, and not with grief: for that is unprofitable for you.

18 Pray for us: for we are assured that we have a good conscience in all things, desiring to live honestly.

19 And I desire you somewhat the more earnestly, that ye so do, that I may be restored to you more quickly.

20 The God of peace that brought again from the dead our Lord Jesus, the great shepherd of the sheep, through the blood of the everlasting Covenant,

21 Make you perfect in all good works, to do his will, working in you that which is pleasant in his sight through JESUS CHRIST, to whom be praise forever and ever, Amen.
22 I beseech you also, brethren, suffer the words of exhortation: for I have written unto you in few words.
23 Know that our brother Timotheus is delivered, with whom (if he come shortly) I will see you.
24 Salute all them that have the oversight of you, and all the Saints. They of Italy salute you.
25 Grace be with you all, Amen.
Written to the Hebrews from Italy, and sent by Timotheus.

THE GENERAL EPISTLE OF JAMES

James Chapter 1

1 James a servant of God, and of the Lord JESUS CHRIST, to the twelve Tribes, which are scattered abroad, salutation.

2 My brethren, count it exceeding joy, when ye fall into diverse temptations,

3 Knowing that the trying of your faith bringeth forth patience,

4 And let patience have her perfect work, that ye may be perfect and entire, lacking nothing.

5 If any of you lack wisdom, let him ask of God, which giveth to all men liberally, and reproacheth no man, and it shall be given him.

6 But let him ask in faith, and waver not: for he that wavereth, is like a wave of the sea, tossed of the wind, and carried away.

7 Neither let that man think that he shall receive any thing of the Lord.

8 A wavering minded man is unstable in all his ways.

9 Let the brother of low degree rejoice in that he is exalted:

10 Again he that is rich, in that he is made low: for as the flower of the grass, shall he vanish away.

11 For as when the sun riseth with heat, then the grass withereth, and his flower falleth away, and the beauty of the fashion of it perisheth: even so shall the rich man fade away in all his ways.

12 Blessed is the man, that endureth temptation: for when he is tried, he shall receive the crown of life, which the Lord hath promised to them that love him.

13 Let no man say when he is tempted, I am tempted of God: for God cannot be tempted with evil, neither tempteth he any man.

14 But every man is tempted, when he is drawn away by his own concupiscence, and is enticed.

15 Then when lust hath conceived, it bringeth forth sin, and sin when it is finished, bringeth forth death.

16 Err not, my dear brethren.

17 Every good giving, and every perfect gift is from above, and cometh down from the Father of lights, with whom is no variableness, neither shadowing by turning.

18 Of his own will begat he us with the word of truth, that we should be as the first fruits of his creatures.

19 Wherefore my dear brethren, let every man be swift to hear, slow to speak, and slow to wrath.

20 For the wrath of man doth not accomplish the righteousness of God.

21 Wherefore lay apart all filthiness, and superfluity of maliciousness, and receive with meekness the word that is grafted in you, which is able to save your souls.

22 And be ye doers of the word, and not hearers only, deceiving your own selves.

23 For if any hear the word, and do it not, he is like unto a man, that beholdeth his natural face in a glass.

24 For when he hath considered himself, he goeth his way, and forgetteth immediately what manner of one he was.

25 But who so looketh in the perfect Law of liberty, and continueth therein, he not being a forgetful hearer, but a doer of the work, shall be blessed in his deed.

26 If any man among you seemeth religious, and restraineth not his tongue, but deceiveth his own heart, this man's religion is vain.

27 Pure religion and undefiled before God, even the Father, is this, to visit the fatherless, and widows in their adversity, and to keep himself unspotted of the world.

James Chapter 2

1 My brethren, have not the faith of our glorious Lord Jesus Christ in respect of persons.
2 For if there come into your company a man with a gold ring, and in goodly apparel, and there come in also a poor man in vile raiment,
3 And ye have a respect to him that weareth the gay clothing; and say unto him, Sit thou here in a good place, and say unto the poor, Stand thou there, or sit here under my footstool,
4 Are ye not partial in yourselves, and are become judges of evil thoughts?
5 Hearken my beloved brethren, hath not God chosen the poor of this world, that they should be rich in faith, and heirs of the kingdom which he promised to them that love him?
6 But ye have despised the poor. Do not the rich oppress you by tyranny, and do not they draw you before the judgment seats?
7 Do not they blaspheme the worthy Name after which ye be named?
8 But if ye fulfill the royal Law according to the Scripture, which saith, Thou shalt love thy neighbor as thyself, ye do well.
9 But if ye regard the persons, ye commit sin, and are rebuked of the Law, as transgressors.
10 For whosoever shall keep the whole Law, and yet faileth in one point, he is guilty of all.
11 For he that said, Thou shalt not commit adultery, said also, Thou shalt not kill. Now though thou doest none adultery, yet if thou killest, thou art a transgressor of the Law.
12 So speak ye, and so do, as they that shall be judged by the Law of liberty.
13 For there shall be judgment merciless to him that showeth no mercy, and mercy rejoiceth against judgment.
14 What availeth it, my brethren, though a man saith he hath faith, when he hath no works? Can the faith save him?
15 For if a brother or a sister be naked and destitute of daily food,
16 And one of you say unto them, Depart in peace: warm yourselves, and fill your bellies, notwithstanding ye give them not those things which are needful to the body, what helpeth it?
17 Even so the faith, if it have no works, is dead in itself.
18 But some man might say, Thou hast the faith, and I have works: show me thy faith out of thy works, and I will show thee my faith by my works.
19 Thou believest that there is one God: thou doest well: the devils also believe it, and tremble.
20 But wilt thou understand, O thou vain man, that the faith which is without works, is dead?
21 Was not Abraham our father justified through works, when he offered Isaac his son upon the altar?
22 Seest thou not that the faith wrought with his works? And through the works was the faith made perfect.
23 And the Scripture was fulfilled which saith, Abraham believed God, and it was imputed unto him for righteousness: and he was called the friend of God.
24 Ye see then how that of works a man is justified, and not of faith only.
25 Likewise also was not Rahab the harlot justified through works, when she had received the messengers, and sent them out another way?
26 For as the body without the spirit is dead, even so the faith without works is dead.

James Chapter 3

1 My brethren, be not many masters, knowing that we shall receive the greater condemnation.

2 For in many things we sin all. If any man sin not in word, he is a perfect man, and able to bridle all the body.

3 Behold, we put bits into the horses' mouths that they should obey us, and we turn about all their body.

4 Behold also the ships, which though they be so great, and are driven of fierce winds, yet are they turned about with a very small rudder, whithersoever the governor listeth.

5 Even so the tongue is a little member, and boasteth of great things: behold, how great a thing a little fire kindleth.

6 And the tongue is fire, yea, a world of wickedness: so is the tongue set among our members, that it defileth the whole body, and setteth on fire the course of nature, and it is set on fire of hell.

7 For the whole nature of beasts, and of birds and of creeping things, and things of the sea is tamed and hath been tamed of the nature of man.

8 But the tongue can no man tame. It is an unruly evil, full of deadly poison.

9 Therewith bless we God even the Father, and therewith curse we men, which are made after the similitude of God.

10 Out of one mouth proceedeth blessing and cursing: my brethren, these things ought not so to be.

11 Doth a fountain send forth at one place sweet water and bitter?

12 Can the fig tree, my brethren, bring forth olives, other a vine figs? So can no fountain make both salt water and sweet.

13 Who is a wise man and endued with knowledge among you? let him show by good conversation his works in meekness of wisdom.

14 But if ye have bitter envying and strife in your hearts, rejoice not, neither be liars against the truth.

15 This wisdom descendeth not from above, but is earthly, sensual, and devilish.

16 For where envying and strife is, there is sedition, and all manner of evil works.

17 But the wisdom that is from above, is first pure, then peaceable, gentle, easy to be entreated, full of mercy and good fruits without judging, and without hypocrisy.

18 And the fruit of righteousness is sown in peace, of them that make peace.

James Chapter 4

1 From whence are wars and contentions among you? are they not hence, even of your lusts, that fight in your members?

2 Ye lust, and have not: ye envy, and have indignation, and cannot obtain: ye fight and war, and get nothing, because ye ask not.

3 Ye ask, and receive not because ye ask amiss, that ye might consume it on your lusts.

4 Ye adulterers and adulteresses, know ye not that the amity of the world is the enmity of God? Whosoever therefore will be a friend of the world, maketh himself the enemy of God.

5 Do ye think that the Scripture saith in vain, The spirit that dwelleth in us, lusteth after envy?

6 But the Scripture offereth more grace, and therefore saith, God resisteth the proud, and giveth grace to the humble.

7 Submit yourselves to God: resist the devil, and he will flee from you.

8 Draw near to God, and he will draw near to you. Cleanse your hands, ye sinners, and purge your hearts, ye wavering minded.

9 Suffer afflictions, and sorrow ye, and weep: let your laughter be turned into mourning, and your joy into heaviness.

10 Cast down yourselves before the Lord, and he will lift you up.

11 Speak not evil one of another, brethren. He that speaketh evil of his brother, or he that condemneth his brother, speaketh evil of the Law, and condemneth the Law: and if thou condemnest the Law, thou art not an observer of the Law, but a judge.

12 There is one Lawgiver, which is able to save, and to destroy. Who art thou that judgest another man?

13 Go to now ye that say, Today or tomorrow we will go into such a city, and continue there a year, and buy and sell, and get gain,

14 (And yet ye cannot tell what shall be tomorrow. For what is your life? It is even a vapor that appeareth for a little time, and afterward vanisheth away)

15 For that ye ought to say, If the Lord will, and, If we live, we will do this or that.

16 But now ye rejoice in your boastings: all such rejoicing is evil.

17 Therefore, to him that knoweth how to do well, and doeth it not, to him it is sin.

James Chapter 5

1 Go to now, ye rich men: weep, and howl for your miseries that shall come upon you.

2 Your riches are corrupt, and your garments are moth eaten.

3 Your gold and silver is cankered, and the rust of them shall be a witness against you, and shall eat your flesh, as it were fire. Ye have heaped up treasure for the last days.

4 Behold, the hire of the laborers, which have reaped your fields (which is of you kept back by fraud) cryeth, and the cries of them which have reaped, are entered into the ears of the Lord of hosts.

5 Ye have lived in pleasure on the earth, and in wantonness. Ye have nourished your hearts, as in a day of slaughter.

6 Ye have condemned and have killed the just, and he hath not resisted you.

7 Be patient therefore, brethren, unto the coming of the Lord. Behold, the husbandman waiteth for the precious fruit of the earth, and hath long patience for it, until he receive the former, and the latter rain.

8 Be ye also patient therefore and settle your hearts: for the coming of the Lord draweth near.

9 Grudge not one against another, brethren, lest ye be condemned: behold, the judge standeth before the door.

10 Take, my brethren, the Prophets for an ensample of suffering adversity, and of long patience, which have spoken in the Name of the Lord.

11 Behold, we count them blessed which endure. Ye have heard of the patience of Job, and have known what end the Lord made. For the Lord is very pitiful and merciful.

12 But before all things, my brethren, swear not, neither by heaven, nor by earth, nor by any other oath: but let your yea, be yea, and your nay, nay, lest ye fall into condemnation.

13 Is any among you afflicted? Let him pray. Is any merry? Let him sing.

14 Is any sick among you? Let him call for the Elders of the Church, and let them pray for him, and anoint him with oil in the Name of the Lord.

15 And the prayer of faith shall save the sick, and the Lord shall raise him up: and if he have committed sin, it shall be forgiven him.

16 Acknowledge your faults one to another, and pray one for another, that ye may be healed: for the prayer of a righteous man availeth much, if it be fervent.

17 Elias was a man subject to like passions as we are, and he prayed earnestly that it might not rain, and it rained not on the earth for three years and six months.
18 And he prayed again, and the heaven gave rain, and the earth brought forth her fruit.
19 Brethren, if any of you hath erred from the truth, and some man hath converted him,
20 Let him know that he which hath converted the sinner from going astray out of his way, shall save a soul from death, and shall hide a multitude of sins.

THE FIRST EPISTLE GENERAL OF PETER

1 Peter Chapter 1

1 Peter an Apostle of JESUS CHRIST, to the strangers that dwell here and there throughout Pontus, Galatia, Cappadocia, Asia and Bithynia,

2 Elect according to the foreknowledge of God the Father unto sanctification of the Spirit, through obedience and sprinkling of the blood of Jesus Christ: Grace and peace be multiplied unto you.

3 Blessed be God even the Father of our Lord Jesus Christ, which according to his abundant mercy hath begotten us again unto a lively hope by the resurrection of Jesus Christ from the dead,

4 To an inheritance immortal and undefiled, and that fadeth not away, reserved in heaven for you,

5 Which are kept by the power of God through faith unto salvation, which is prepared to be showed in the last time:

6 Wherein ye rejoice, though now for a season (if need require) ye are in heaviness, through manifold temptations,

7 That the trial of your faith, being much more precious than gold that perisheth (though it be tried with fire) might be found unto your praise, and honor and glory at the appearing of Jesus Christ:

8 Whom ye have not seen, and yet love him, in whom now, though ye see him not, yet do you believe, and rejoice with joy unspeakable and glorious,

9 Receiving the end of your faith, even the salvation of your souls.

10 Of the which salvation the Prophets have inquired and searched, which prophesied of the grace that should come unto you,

11 Searching when or what time the Spirit which testified before of Christ which was in them, should declare the sufferings that should come unto Christ, and the glory that should follow.

12 Unto whom it was revealed, that not unto themselves, but unto us they should minister the things which are now showed unto you by them which have preached unto you the Gospel by the Holy Ghost sent down from heaven, the which things the Angels desire to behold.

13 Wherefore, gird up the loins of your mind: be sober, and trust perfectly on the grace that is brought unto you, by the revelation of Jesus Christ,

14 As obedient children, not fashioning yourselves unto the former lusts of your ignorance:

15 But as he which hath called you, is holy, so be ye holy in all manner of conversation,

16 Because it is written, Be ye holy, for I am holy.

17 And if ye call him Father, which without respect of person judgeth according to every man's work, pass the time of your dwelling here in fear,

18 Knowing that ye were not redeemed with corruptible things, as silver and gold, from your vain conversation, received by the traditions of the fathers,

19 But with the precious blood of Christ, as of a Lamb undefiled, and without spot.

20 Which was ordained before the foundation of the world, but was declared in the last times for your sakes,

21 Which by his means do believe in God that raised him from the dead, and gave him glory, that your faith and hope might be in God,

22 Seeing your souls are purified in obeying the truth through the spirit, to love brotherly without feigning, love one another with a pure heart fervently,

23 Being born anew, not of mortal seed, but of immortal, by the word of God, who liveth and endureth forever.

24 For all flesh is as grass, and all the glory of man is as the flower of grass. The grass withereth, and the flower falleth away.

25 But the word of the Lord endureth forever: and this is the word which is preached among you.

1 Peter Chapter 2

1 Wherefore, laying aside all maliciousness and all guile, and dissimulation, and envy, and all evil speaking,

2 As newborn babes desire the sincere milk of the word, that ye may grow thereby,

3 If so be that ye have tasted how bountiful the Lord is.

4 To whom ye come as unto a living stone disallowed of men, but chosen of God and precious.

5 And ye as lively stones, be made a spiritual house, an holy Priesthood to offer up spiritual sacrifices acceptable to God by Jesus Christ.

6 Wherefore it is contained in the Scripture, Behold, I put in Zion a chief corner stone, elect and precious: and he that believeth therein, shall not be ashamed.

7 Unto you therefore which believe, it is precious: but unto them which be disobedient, the stone which the builders disallowed, the same is made the head of the corner,

8 And a stone to stumble at, and a rock of offense, even to them which stumble at the word being disobedient, unto the which thing they were even ordained.

9 But ye are a chosen generation, a royal Priesthood, an holy nation, a peculiar people, that ye should show forth the virtues of him that hath called you out of darkness into his marvelous light,

10 Which in time past were not a people, yet are now the people of God: which in time past were not under mercy, but now have obtained mercy.

11 Dearly beloved, I beseech you, as strangers and pilgrims, abstain from fleshly lusts, which fight against the soul,

12 And have your conversation honest among the Gentiles, that they which speak evil of you as of evil doers, may by your good works which they shall see, glorify God in the day of the visitation.

13 Submit yourselves unto all manner ordinance of man for the Lord's sake, whether it be unto the King, as unto the superior,

14 Or unto governors, as unto them that are sent of him, for the punishment of evildoers, and for the praise of them that do well.

15 For so is the will of God, that by well doing ye may put to silence the ignorance of the foolish men,

16 As free, and not as having the liberty for a cloak of maliciousness, but as the servants of God.

17 Honor all men: love brotherly fellowship: fear God: honor the King.

18 Servants, be subject to your masters with all fear, not only to the good and courteous, but also to the froward.

19 For this is thankworthy, if a man for conscience toward God endure grief suffering wrongfully.

20 For what praise is it, if when ye be buffeted for your faults, ye take it patiently? but and if when ye do well, ye suffer wrong and take it patiently, this is acceptable to God.

21 For here unto ye are called: for Christ also suffered for us, leaving us an ensample that ye should follow his steps.

22 Who did no sin, neither was there guile found in his mouth.

23 Who when he was reviled, reviled not again: when he suffered, he threatened not, but committed it to him that judgeth righteously.

24 Who his own self bear our sins in his body on the tree, that we being delivered from sin, should live in righteousness: by whose stripes ye were healed.

25 For ye were as sheep going astray: but are now returned unto the shepherd and bishop of your souls.

1 Peter Chapter 3

1 Likewise let the wives be subject to their husbands that even they which obey not the word, may without the word be won by the conversation of the wives,

2 While they behold your pure conversation, which is with fear.

3 Whose apparelling let it not be outward, with braided hair, and gold put about, or in putting on of apparel.

4 But let the hidden man of the heart be uncorrupt, with a meek and quiet spirit, which is before God a thing much set by.

5 For even after this manner in time past did the holy women, which trusted in God, tire themselves, and were subject to their husbands.

6 As Sara obeyed Abraham, and called him Sir: whose daughters ye are, while ye do well, not being afraid of any terror.

7 Likewise ye husbands, dwell with them as men of knowledge, giving honor unto the woman, as unto the weaker vessel, even as they which are heirs together of the grace of life, that your prayers be not interrupted.

8 Finally, be ye all of one mind: one suffer with another: love as brethren: be pitiful: be courteous,

9 Not rendering evil for evil, neither rebuke for rebuke: but contrarywise bless, knowing that ye are thereunto called, that ye should be heirs of blessing.

10 For if any man long after life, and to see good days, let him refrain his tongue from evil, and his lips that they speak not guile.

11 Let him eschew evil and do good: let him seek peace, and follow after it.

12 For the eyes of the Lord are over the righteous, and his ears are open unto their prayers: and the face of the Lord is upon them that do evil.

13 And who is it that will harm you, if ye follow that which is good?

14 Notwithstanding blessed are ye, if ye suffer for righteousness' sake. Yea, fear not their fear, neither be troubled.

15 But sanctify the Lord God in your hearts: and be ready always to give an answer to every man that asketh you a reason of the hope that is in you,

16 And that with meekness and reverence, having a good conscience, that when they speak evil of you as of evildoers, they may be ashamed, which blame your good conversation in Christ.

17 For it is better (if the will of God be so) that ye suffer for well doing, than for evil doing.

18 For Christ also hath once suffered for sins, the just for the unjust, that he might bring us to God, and was put to death concerning the flesh, but was quickened in the spirit.

19 By the which he also went, and preached unto the spirits that were in prison.

20 Which were in time past disobedient, when once the long suffering of God abode in the days of Noah, while the Ark was preparing, wherein few, that is, eight souls were saved in the water.

21 To the which also the figure that now saveth us, even Baptism agreeth (not the putting away of the filth of the flesh, but in that a good conscience maketh request to God) by the resurrection of Jesus Christ,

22 Which is at the right hand of God, gone into heaven, to whom the Angels, and Powers, and might are subject.

1 Peter Chapter 4

1 Forasmuch then as Christ hath suffered for us in the flesh, arm yourselves likewise with the same mind, which is that he which hath suffered in the flesh, hath ceased from sin,
2 That he hence forward should live (as much time as remaineth in the flesh) not after the lusts of men, but after the will of God.
3 For it is sufficient for us that we have spent the time past of the life, after the lust of the Gentiles, walking in wantonness, lusts, drunkenness, in gluttony, drinkings, and in abominable idolatries.
4 Wherein it seemeth to them strange that ye run not with them unto the same excess of riot: therefore speak they evil of you.
5 Which shall give accounts to him, that is ready to judge quick and dead.
6 For unto this purpose was the Gospel preached also unto the dead, that they might be condemned, according to men, in the flesh, but might live according to God in the spirit.
7 Now the end of all things is at hand. Be ye therefore sober, and watching in prayer.
8 But above all things have fervent love among you: for love covereth the multitude of sins.
9 Be ye harborous one to another, without grudging.
10 Let every man as he hath received the gift, minister the same one to another, as good disposers of the manifold grace of God.
11 If any man speak, let him talk as the words of God. If any man minister, let him do it as of the ability which God ministereth, that God in all things may be glorified through Jesus Christ, to whom is praise and dominion for ever, and ever, Amen.
12 Dearly beloved, think it not strange concerning the fiery trial, which is among you to prove you, as though some strange thing were come unto you:
13 But rejoice, inasmuch as ye are partakers of Christ's sufferings, that when his glory shall appear, ye may be glad and rejoice.
14 If ye be railed upon for the Name of Christ, blessed are ye: for the spirit of glory, and of God resteth upon you: which on their part is evil spoken of: but on your part is glorified.
15 But let none of you suffer as a murderer, or as a thief, or an evildoer, or as a busybody in other men's matters.
16 But if any man suffer as a Christian, let him not be ashamed: but let him glorify God in this behalf.
17 For the time is come, that judgment must begin at the house of God. If it first begin at us, what shall the end be of them which obey not the Gospel of God?
18 And if the righteous scarcely be saved, where shall the ungodly and the sinner appear?
19 Wherefore let them that suffer according to the will of God, commit their souls to him in well doing, as unto a faithful Creator.

1 Peter Chapter 5

1 The elders which are among you, I beseech which am also an elder, and a witness of the sufferings of Christ, and also a partaker of the glory that shall be revealed,
2 Feed the flock of God, which dependeth upon you, caring for it not by constraint, but willingly: not for filthy lucre, but of a ready mind:
3 Not as though ye were lords over God's heritage, but that ye may be ensamples to the flock.

4 And when the chief shepherd shall appear, ye shall receive an incorruptible crown of glory.

5 Likewise ye younger, submit yourselves unto the elders, and submit yourselves every man, one to another: deck yourselves inwardly in lowliness of mind: for God resisteth the proud and giveth grace to the humble.

6 Humble yourselves therefore under the mighty hand of God, that he may exalt you in due time.

7 Cast all your care on him: for he careth for you.

8 Be sober and watch: for your adversary the devil as a roaring lion walketh about, seeking whom he may devour:

9 Whom resist steadfast in the faith, knowing that the same afflictions are accomplished in your brethren which are in the world.

10 And the God of all grace, which hath called us unto his eternal glory by Christ Jesus, after that ye have suffered a little, make you perfect, confirm, strengthen and establish you.

11 To him be glory and dominion forever and ever. Amen.

12 By Silvanus a faithful brother unto you, as I suppose, have I written briefly, exhorting and testifying how that this is the true grace of God, wherein ye stand.

13 The Church that is at Babylon elected together with you, saluteth you, and Marcus my son.

14 Greet ye one another with the kiss of love. Peace be with you all which are in Christ Jesus. Amen.

THE SECOND EPISTLE GENERAL OF PETER

2 Peter Chapter 1

1 Simon Peter a servant and an Apostle of JESUS CHRIST, to you which have obtained like precious faith with us by the righteousness of our God and Savior Jesus Christ:
2 Grace and peace be multiplied to you, by the knowledge of God and of Jesus our Lord,
3 According as his godly power hath given unto us all things that pertain unto life and godliness, through the knowledge of him that hath called us unto glory and virtue.
4 Whereby most great, and precious promises are given unto us, that by them ye should be partakers of the godly nature, in that ye flee the corruption, which is in the world through lust.
5 Therefore give even all diligence thereunto: join moreover virtue with your faith: and with virtue, knowledge:
6 And with knowledge, temperance: and with temperance, patience: and with patience, godliness:
7 And with godliness, brotherly kindness: and with brotherly kindness, love.
8 For if these things be among you, and abound, they will make you that ye neither shall be idle, nor unfruitful in the knowledge of our Lord Jesus Christ:
9 For he that hath not these things, is blind, and cannot see far off, and hath forgotten that he was purged from his old sins.
10 Wherefore, brethren, give rather diligence to make your calling and election sure: for if ye do these things, ye shall never fall.
11 For by this means an entering shall be ministered unto you abundantly into the everlasting kingdom of our Lord and Savior Jesus Christ.
12 Wherefore, I will not be negligent to put you always in remembrance of these things, though that ye have knowledge, and be established in the present truth.
13 For I think it meet as long as I am in this tabernacle, to stir you up by putting you in remembrance.
14 Seeing I know that the time is at hand that I must lay down this my tabernacle, even as our Lord Jesus Christ hath showed me.
15 I will endeavor therefore always, that ye also may be able to have remembrance of these things after my departing.
16 For we followed not deceivable fables when we opened unto you the power, and coming of our Lord Jesus Christ, but with our eyes we saw his majesty:
17 For he received of God the Father honor and glory, when there came such a voice to him from the excellent glory. This is my beloved Son, in whom I am well pleased.
18 And this voice we heard when it came from heaven, being with him in the Holy mount.
19 We have also a most sure word of the Prophets, to the which ye do well that ye take heed, as unto a light that shineth in a dark place, until the day dawn, and the daystar arise in your hearts.
20 So that ye first know this, that no prophecy of the Scripture is of any private motion.
21 For the prophecy came not in old time by the will of man: but holy men of God spake as they were moved by the Holy Ghost.

2 Peter Chapter 2

1 But there were false prophets also among the people, even as there shall be false teachers among you: which privily shall bring in damnable heresies, even denying the Lord, that hath bought them, and bring upon themselves swift damnation.

2 And many shall follow their damnable ways, by whom the way of truth shall be evil spoken of,

3 And through covetousness shall they with feigned words make merchandise of you, whose judgment long ago is not far off, and their damnation sleepeth not.

4 For if God spared not the Angels, that had sinned, but cast them down into hell and delivered them into chains of darkness, to be kept unto damnation:

5 Neither hath spared the old world, but saved Noah the eight person a preacher of righteousness, and brought in the flood upon the world of the ungodly,

6 And turned the cities of Sodom and Gomorrah into ashes, condemned them and overthrew them, and made them an ensample unto them that after should live ungodly,

7 And delivered just Lot vexed with the uncleanly conversation of the wicked,

8 (For he being righteous, and dwelling among them, in seeing and hearing, vexed his righteous soul from day to day with their unlawful deeds.)

9 The Lord knoweth to deliver the godly out of temptation, and to reserve the unjust unto the day of judgment to be punished:

10 And chiefly them that walk after the flesh, in the lust of uncleanness, and despise the government, which are presumptuous, and stand in their own conceit, and fear not to speak evil of them that are in dignity.

11 Whereas the Angels which are greater both in power and might, give not railing judgment against them before the Lord.

12 But these, as brute beasts, led with sensuality and made to be taken, and destroyed, speak evil of those things which they know not, and shall perish through their own corruption.

13 And shall receive the wages of unrighteousness, as they which count it pleasure to live deliciously for a season. Spots they are and blots, delighting themselves in their deceivings, in feasting with you,

14 Having eyes full of adultery, and that cannot cease to sin, beguiling unstable souls: they have hearts exercised with covetousness , cursed children,

15 Which forsaking the right way, have gone astray, following the way of Balaam, the son of Bosor, which loved the wages of unrighteousness.

16 But he was rebuked for his iniquity: for the dumb ass speaking with man's voice, forbade the foolishness of the Prophet.

17 These are wells without water, and clouds carried about with a tempest, to whom the black darkness is reserved forever.

18 For in speaking swelling words of vanity, they beguile with wantonness through the lusts of the flesh them that were clean escaped from them which are wrapped in error,

19 Promising unto them liberty, and are themselves the servants of corruption: for of whomsoever a man is overcome, even unto the same is he in bondage.

20 For if they, after they have escaped from the filthiness of the world, through the knowledge of the Lord, and of the Savior Jesus Christ, are yet tangled again therein, and overcome, the latter end is worse with them than the beginning.

21 For it had been better for them, not to have known the way of righteousness, than after they have known it, to turn from the holy commandment given unto them.

22 But it is come unto them, according to the true Proverb, The dog is returned to his own vomit: and, The sow that was washed, to the wallowing in the mire.

2 Peter Chapter 3

1 This second Epistle I now write unto you, beloved, wherewith I stir up, and warn your pure minds,

2 To call to remembrance the words, which were told before of the holy Prophets, and also the commandment of us the Apostles of the Lord and Savior.

3 This first understand, that there shall come in the last days, mockers, which will walk after their lusts,

4 And say, Where is the promise of his coming? for since the fathers died, all things continue alike from the beginning of the creation.

5 For this they willingly know not, that the heavens were of old, and the earth that was of the water and by the water, by the word of God.

6 Wherefore the world that then was, perished, overflowed with the water.

7 But the heavens and earth, which are now, are kept by the same word in store, and reserved unto fire against the day of judgment, and of the destruction of ungodly men.

8 Dearly beloved, be not ignorant of this one thing, that one day is with the Lord, as a thousand years, and a thousand year, as one day.

9 The Lord is not slack concerning his promise (as some men count slackness) but is patient toward us, and would have no man to perish, but would all men to come to repentance.

10 But the day of the Lord will come as a thief in the night, in the which the heavens shall pass away with a noise, and the elements shall melt with heat, and the earth with the works, that are therein, shall be burned up.

11 Seeing therefore that all these things must be dissolved, what manner persons ought ye to be in holy conversation and godliness,

12 Looking for, and hasting unto the coming of the day of God, by the which the heavens being on fire, shall be dissolved, and the elements shall melt with heat?

13 But we look for new heavens, and a new earth, according to his promise, wherein dwelleth righteousness.

14 Wherefore, beloved, seeing that ye look for such things, be diligent that ye may be found of him in peace, without spot and blameless.

15 And suppose that the long suffering of our Lord is salvation, even as our beloved brother Paul according to the wisdom given unto him wrote to you,

16 As one, that in all his Epistles speaketh of these things: among the which some things are hard to be understand, which they that are unlearned and unstable, pervert, as they do also other Scriptures unto their own destruction.

17 Ye therefore beloved, seeing ye know these things before, beware, lest ye be also plucked away with the error of the wicked, and fall from your own steadfastness.

18 But grow in grace, and in the knowledge of our Lord and Savior Jesus Christ: to him be glory both now and forevermore. Amen.

THE FIRST EPISTLE GENERAL OF JOHN

1 John Chapter 1

1 That which was from the beginning, which we have heard, which we have seen with our eyes, which we have looked upon, and our hands have handled of the Word of life,

2 (For the life appeared, and we have seen it, and bear witness, and show unto you the eternal life, which was with the Father, and appeared unto us)

3 That, I say, which we have seen and heard, declare we unto you, that ye may also have fellowship with us, and that our fellowship also may be with the Father and with his Son Jesus Christ.

4 And these things write we unto you, that your joy may be full.

5 This then is the message which we have heard of him, and declare unto you, that God is light, and in him is no darkness.

6 If we say that we have fellowship with him, and walk in darkness, we lie, and do not truly.

7 But if we walk in the light as he is in the light, we have fellowship one with another, and the blood of Jesus Christ his Son cleanseth us from all sin.

8 If we say that we have no sin, we deceive ourselves, and truth is not in us.

9 If we acknowledge our sins, he is faithful and just, to forgive us our sins, and to cleanse us from all unrighteousness.

10 If we say we have not sinned, we make him a liar, and his word is not in us.

1 John Chapter 2

1 My babes, these things write I unto you, that ye sin not: and if any man sin, we have an Advocate with the Father, Jesus Christ, the Just.

2 And he is the reconciliation for our sins: and not for ours only, but also for the sins of the whole world.

3 And hereby we are sure that we know him, if we keep his commandments. 4 He that saith, I know him, and keepeth not his commandments, is a liar, and the truth is not in him.

5 But he that keepeth his word, in him is the love of God perfect indeed: hereby we know that we are in him.

6 He that saith he remaineth in him, ought even so to walk, as he hath walked.

7 Brethren, I write no new commandment unto you: but an old commandment, which ye have had from the beginning: the old commandment is the word, which ye have heard from the beginning.

8 Again, a new commandment I write unto you, that which is true in him, and also in you: for the darkness is past, and the true light now shineth. 9 He that saith that he is in the light, and hateth his brother, is in darkness until this time.

10 He that loveth his brother, abideth in the light, and there is none occasion of evil in him.

11 But he that hateth his brother, is in darkness, and walketh in darkness, and knoweth not whither he goeth, because that darkness hath blinded his eyes.

12 Little children, I write unto you, because your sins are forgiven you for his Name's sake.

13 I write unto you, fathers, because ye have known him that is from the beginning. I write unto you, young men, because ye have overcome the wicked.

14 I write unto you, babes, because ye have known the Father. I have written unto you, fathers, because ye have known him, that is from the beginning. I have written unto you,

young men, because ye are strong, and the word of God abideth in you, and ye have overcome the wicked.

15 Love not the world, neither the things that are in the world. If any man love the world, the love of the Father is not in him.

16 For all that is in this world (as the lust of the flesh, the lust of the eyes, and the pride of life) is not of the Father, but is of the world.

17 And the world passeth away, and the lust thereof: but he that fulfilleth the will of God, abideth ever.

18 Babes, it is the last time, and as ye have heard that Antichrist shall come, even now are there many Antichrists: whereby we know that it is the last time. 19 They went out from us, but they were not of us: for if they had been of us, they would have continued with us. But this cometh to pass, that it might appear, that they are not all of us.

20 But ye have an anointment from him, that is Holy, and ye have known all things.

21 I have not written unto you, because ye know not the truth: but because ye know it, and that no lie is of the truth.

22 Who is a liar, but he that denieth that Jesus is Christ? the same is the Antichrist that denieth the Father and the Son.

23 Whosoever denieth the Son, the same hath not the Father.

24 Let therefore abide in you that same which ye have heard from the beginning. If that which ye have heard from the beginning, shall remain in you, ye also shall continue in the Son, and in the Father.

25 And this is the promise that he hath promised us, even eternal life.

26 These things have I written unto you, concerning them that deceive you.

27 But that anointing which ye received of him, dwelleth in you: and ye need not that any man teach you: but as the same Anointing teacheth you of all things, and it is true, and is not lying, and as it taught you, ye shall abide in him.

28 And now, little children, abide in him, that when he shall appear, we may be bold, and not be ashamed before him at his coming.

29 If ye know that he is righteous, know ye that he which doeth righteously, is born of him.

1 John Chapter 3

1 Behold, what love the Father hath showed on us, that we should be called the sons of God: for this cause the world knoweth you not, because it knoweth not him.

2 Dearly beloved, now are we the sons of God, but yet it doth not appear what we shall be: and we know that when he shall appear, we shall be like him: for we shall see him as he is.

3 And every man that hath this hope in him, purgeth himself, even as he is pure.

4 Whosoever committeth sin, transgresseth also the Law: for sin is the transgression of the Law.

5 And ye know that he appeared that he might take away our sins, and in him is no sin.

6 Whosoever abideth in him, sinneth not: whosoever sinneth, hath not seen him, neither hath known him.

7 Little children, let no man deceive you: he that doeth righteousness, is righteous, as he is righteous.

8 He that committeth sin, is of the devil: for the devil sinneth from the beginning: for this purpose appeared the Son of God, that he might loose the works of the devil.

9 Whosoever is born of God, sinneth not: for his seed remaineth in him, neither can he sin, because he is born of God.

10 In this are the children of God known, and the children of the devil: whosoever doeth not righteousness, is not of God, neither he that loveth not his brother.

11 For this is the message, that ye heard from the beginning, that we should love one another,

12 Not as Cain which was of the wicked, and slew his brother: and wherefore slew he him? because his own works were evil, and his brother's good.

13 Marvel not, my brethren, though the world hate you.

14 We know that we are translated from death unto life, because we love the brethren: he that loveth not his brother, abideth in death.

15 Whosoever hateth his brother, is a manslayer: and ye know that no manslayer hath eternal life abiding in him.

16 Hereby have we perceived love, that he laid down his life for us: therefore we ought also to lay down our lives for the brethren.

17 And whosoever hath this world's good, and seeth his brother have need, and shutteth up his compassion from him, how dwelleth the love of God in him?

18 My little children, let us not love in word, neither in tongue only, but in deed and in truth.

19 For thereby we know that we are of the truth and shall before him assure our hearts.

20 For if our heart condemn us, God is greater than our heart, and knoweth all things.

21 Beloved, if our heart condemn us not, then have we boldness toward God.

22 And whatsoever we ask, we receive of him, because we keep his commandments, and do those things which are pleasing in his sight.

23 This is then his commandment, That we believe in the Name of his Son Jesus Christ, and love one another, as he gave commandment.

24 For he that keepeth his commandments, dwelleth in him, and he in him: and hereby we know that he abideth in us, even by the Spirit which he hath given us.

1 John Chapter 4

1 Dearly beloved, believe not every spirit, but try the spirits whether they are of God: for many false prophets are gone out into the world.

2 Hereby shall ye know the Spirit of God, Every spirit that confesseth that Jesus Christ is come in the flesh, is of God.

3 And every spirit that confesseth not that Jesus Christ is come in the flesh, is not of God: but this is the spirit of Antichrist, of whom ye have heard, how that he should come and now already he is in the world.

4 Little children, ye are of God, and have overcome them: for greater is he that is in you, than he that is in the world.

5 They are of the world, therefore speak they of the world, and the world heareth them.

6 We are of God, he that knoweth God, heareth us: he that is not of God, heareth us not. Hereby know we the spirit of truth, and the spirit of error.

7 Beloved, let us love one another: for love cometh of God, and every one that loveth, is born of God, and knoweth God.

8 He that loveth not, knoweth not God: for God is love.

9 In this appeared the love of God toward us, because God sent his only begotten Son into the world, that we might live through him.

10 Herein is love, not that we loved God, but that he loved us, and sent his Son to be a reconciliation for our sins.

11 Beloved, if God so loved us, we ought also to love one another.

12 No man hath seen God at any time. If we love one another, God dwelleth in us, and his love is perfect in us.

13 Hereby know we, that we dwell in him, and he in us: because he hath given us of his Spirit.

14 And we have seen, and do testify, that the Father sent the Son to be the Savior of the world.

15 Whosoever confesseth that Jesus is the Son of God, in him dwelleth God, and he in God.

16 And we have known, and believed the love that God hath in us. God is love, and he that dwelleth in love, dwelleth in God, and God in him.

17 Herein is the love perfect in us, that we should have boldness in the day of judgment: for as he is, even so are we in this world.

18 There is no fear in love, but perfect love casteth out fear: for fear hath painfulness: and he that feareth, is not perfect in love.

19 We love him, because he loved us first.

20 If any man say, I love God, and hate his brother, he is a liar: for how can he that loveth not his brother whom he hath seen, love God whom he hath not seen?

21 And this commandment have we of him, that he which loveth God, should love his brother also.

1 John Chapter 5

1 Whosoever believeth that Jesus is the Christ, is born of God, and every one that loveth him, which begat, loveth him also which is begotten of him.

2 In this we know that we love the children of God, when we love God, and keep his commandments.

3 For this is the love of God that we keep his commandments: and his commandments are not grievous..

4 For all that is born of God, overcometh the world: and this is the victory that overcometh the world, even our faith.

5 Who is it that overcometh the world, but he which believeth that Jesus is the Son of God?

6 This is that Jesus Christ that came by water and blood, not by water only, but by water and blood: and it is the Spirit, that beareth witness: for the Spirit is truth.

7 For there are three, which bear record in heaven, the Father, the Word, and the Holy Ghost: and these three are one.

8 And there are three, which bear record in the earth, the spirit and the water and the blood: and these three agree in one.

9 If we receive the witness of men, the witness of God is greater: for this is the witness of God, which he testified of his Son.

10 He that believeth in the Son of God, hath the witness in himself: he that believeth not God, hath made him a liar, because he believed not the record, that God witnessed of his Son.

11 And this is the record, that God hath given unto us eternal life, and this life is in his Son.

12 He that hath the Son, hath life: and he that hath not the Son of God, hath not life.

13 These things have I written unto you, that believe in the Name of the Son of God, that ye may know that ye have eternal life, and that ye may believe in the Name of the Son of God.

14 And this is the assurance, that we have in him, that if we ask anything according to his will, he heareth us.

15 And if we know that he heareth us, whatsoever we ask, we know that we have the petitions that we have desired of him.

16 If any man see his brother sin a sin, that is not unto death, let him ask, and he shall give him life for them that sin not unto death. There is a sin unto death: I say not that thou shouldest pray for it.

17 All unrighteousness is sin, but there is a sin not unto death.

18 We know that whosoever is born of God, sinneth not: but he that is begotten of God, keepeth himself, and the wicked toucheth him not.

19 We know that we are of God, and the whole world lieth in wickedness.

20 But we know that the Son of God is come, and hath given us a mind to know him, which is true: and we are in him that is true, that is, in his Son Jesus Christ: this same is very God, and eternal life.

21 Babes, keep yourselves from idols, Amen.

THE SECOND EPISTLE OF JOHN

1 The Elder to the elect Lady, and her children, whom I love in the truth: and not I only, but also all that have known the truth,

2 For the truth's sake which dwelleth in us, and shall be with us forever:

3 Grace be with you, mercy and peace from God the Father, and from the Lord Jesus Christ the Son of the Father, with truth and love.

4 I rejoiced greatly, that I found of thy children walking in truth, as we have received a commandment of the Father.

5 And now beseech I thee, Lady, (not as writing a new commandment unto thee, but that same which we had from the beginning) that we love one another.

6 And this is the love, that we should walk after his commandements. This commandment is, that as ye have heard from the beginning, ye should walk in it.

7 For many deceivers are entered into the world, which confess not that Jesus Christ is come in the flesh. He that is such one, is a deceiver and an Antichrist.

8 Look to yourselves, that we lose not the things, which we have done, but that we may receive a full reward.

9 Whosoever transgresseth, and abideth not in the doctrine of Christ, hath not God. He that continueth in the doctrine of Christ, he hath both the Father and the Son.

10 If there come any unto you, and bring not this doctrine, receive him not to house, neither bid him, God speed.

11 For he that bideth him God speed, is partaker of his evil deeds. Although I had many things to write unto you, yet I would not write with paper and ink: but I trust to come unto you, and speak mouth to mouth, that our joy may be full.

12 The sons of thine elect sister greet thee, Amen.

THE THIRD EPISTLE OF JOHN

1 The Elder unto the beloved Gaius, whom I love in the truth.

2 Beloved, I wish chiefly that thou prosperest and fairest well as thy soul prospereth.

3 For I rejoiced greatly when the brethren came, and testified of the truth that is in thee, how thou walkest in the truth.

4 I have no greater joy than this, that is, to hear that my sons walk in varity.

5 Beloved, thou doest faithfully whatsoever thou doest to the brethren, and to strangers,

6 Which bare witness of thy love before the Churches. Whom if thou bringest of their journey as it beseemeth according to God, thou shalt do well,

7 Because that for his Name's sake they went forth, and took nothing of the Gentiles.

8 We therefore ought to receive such, that we might be helpers to the truth.

9 I wrote unto the Church: but Diotrephes which loveth to have the preeminence among them, receiveth us not.

10 Wherefore if I come, I will declare his deeds which he doeth, pratling against us with malicious words, and not therewith content, neither he himself receiveth the brethren, but forbiddeth them that would, and thrusteth them out of the Church.

11 Beloved, follow not that which is evil, but that which is good: he that doeth well, is of God: but he that doeth evil, hath not seen God.

12 Demetrius hath good report of all men, and of the truth itself: yea, and we ourselves bear record, and ye know that our record is true.

13 I have many things to write: but I will not with ink and pen write unto thee.

14 For I trust I shall shortly see thee, and we shall speak mouth to mouth. Peace be with thee. The friends salute thee. Greet the friends by name.

THE GENERAL EPISTLE OF JUDE

1 Jude a servant of JESUS CHRIST, and brother of James, to them which are called and sanctified of God the Father, and reserved to Jesus Christ:
2 Mercy unto you, and peace and love be multiplied.
3 Beloved, when I gave all diligence to write unto you of the common salvation, it was needful for me to write unto you to exhort you, that ye should earnestly contend for the maintenance of the faith, which was once given unto the Saints.
4 For there are certain men crept in which were before of old ordained to this condemnation: ungodly men they are which turn the grace of our God into wantonness, and deny God the only Lord, and our Lord Jesus Christ.
5 I will therefore put you in remembrance, forasmuch as ye once knew this, how that the Lord, after that he had delivered the people out of Egypt, destroyed them afterward which believed not.
6 The Angels also which kept not their first estate, but left their own habitation, he hath reserved in everlasting chains under darkness unto the judgment of the great day.
7 As Sodom and Gomorrah, and the cities about them, which in like manner as they did, committed fornication, and followed strange flesh, are set forth for an ensample, and suffer the vengeance of eternal fire.
8 Likewise notwithstanding these dreamers also defile the flesh, and despise government, and speak evil of them that are in authority.
9 Yet Michael the Archangel, when he strove against the devil, and disputed about the body of Moses, durst not blame him with cursed speaking, but saith, The Lord rebuke thee.
10 But these speak evil of those things, which they know not: and whatsoever things they know naturally, as beasts, which are without reason, in those things they corrupt themselves.
11 Woe be unto them: for they have followed the way of Cain, and are cast away by the deceit of Balaam's wages, and perish in the gainsaying of Core.
12 These are spots in your feasts of charity when they feast with you, without all fear, feeding themselves: clouds they are without water, carried about of winds, corrupt trees and without fruit, twice dead, and plucked up by the roots.
13 They are the raging waves of the sea, foaming out their own shame: they are wandering stars, to whom is reserved the blackness of darkness forever.
14 And Enoch also the seventh from Adam, prophesied of such, saying, Behold, the Lord cometh with thousands of his Saints,
15 To give judgment against all men, and to rebuke all the ungodly among them of all their wicked deeds, which they have ungodly committed, and of all their cruel speakings, which wicked sinners have spoken against him.
16 These are murmurers, complainers, walking after their own lusts: whose mouths speak proud things, having men's persons in admiration, because of advantage.
17 But, ye beloved, remember the words which were spoken before of the Apostles of our Lord Jesus Christ,
18 How that they told you that there should be mockers in the last time, which should walk after their own ungodly lusts.
19 These are makers of sects, fleshly, having not the Spirit.
20 But, ye beloved, edify yourselves in your most holy faith, praying in the Holy Ghost,
21 And keep yourselves in the love of God, looking for the mercy of our Lord Jesus Christ, unto eternal life.
22 And have compassion of some, in putting difference:

23 And other save with fear, pulling them out of the fire, and hate even the garment spotted by the flesh.

24 Now unto him that is able to keep you, that ye fall not, and to present you faultless before the presence of his glory with joy,

25 That is, to God only wise, our Savior, be glory, and majesty, and dominion, and power, both now and forever, Amen.

THE REVELATION OF JOHN THE DIVINE

Revelation Chapter 1

1 The revelation of JESUS CHRIST, which God gave unto him, to show unto his servants things which must shortly be done: which he sent, and showed by his Angel unto his servant John,

2 Who bare record of the word of God, and of the testimony of Jesus Christ, and of all things that he saw.

3 Blessed is he that readeth, and they that hear the words of this prophecy, and keep those things which are written therein: for the time is at hand.

4 John, to the seven Churches which are in Asia, Grace be with you and peace from him, Which is, and Which was, and Which is to come, and from the seven Spirits which are before his Throne,

5 And from Jesus Christ, which is a faithful witness, and the first begotten of the dead, and the Prince of the Kings of the earth, unto him that loved us, and washed us from our sins in his blood,

6 And made us Kings and Priests unto God even his Father, to him be glory, and dominion forevermore, Amen.

7 Behold, he cometh with clouds, and every eye shall see him: yea, even they which pierced him through: and all kindreds of the earth shall wail before him, Even so, Amen.

8 I am Alpha and Omega, the beginning and the ending, saith the Lord, Which is, and Which was, and Which is to come, even the Almighty.

9 I John, even your brother, and companion in tribulation, and in the kingdom and patience of Jesus Christ, was in the isle called Patmos, for the word of God, and for the witnessing of Jesus Christ.

10 And I was ravished in spirit on the Lord's day, and heard behind me a great voice, as it had been of a trumpet,

11 Saying, I am Alpha and Omega, the first and the last: and that which you seest, write in a book, and send it unto the seven Churches which are in Asia, unto Ephesus, and unto Smyrna, and unto Pergamus, and unto Thyatira, and unto Sardis, and unto Philadelphia, and unto Laodicea.

12 Then I turned back to see the voice, that spake with me: and when I was turned, I saw seven golden candlesticks,

13 And in the midst of the seven candlesticks, one like unto the Son of man, clothed with a garment down to the feet, and girde about the paps with a golden girdle.

14 His head, and hairs were white as white wool, and as snow, and his eyes were as a flame of fire,

15 And his feet like unto fine brass, burning as in a furnace: and his voice as the sound of many waters.

16 And he had in his right hand seven stars: and out of his mouth went a sharp two edged sword: and his face shone as the sun shineth in his strength.

17 And when I saw him, I fell at his feet as dead: then he laid his right hand upon me, saying unto me, Fear not: I am the first and the last,

18 And am alive, but I was dead: and behold, I am alive forevermore, Amen: and I have the keys of hell and of death.

19 Write the things which thou hast seen, and the things which are, and the things which shall come hereafter.

20 The mystery of the seven stars which thou sawest in my right hand, and the seven golden candlesticks, is this, The seven stars are the Angels of the seven Churches: and the seven candlesticks which thou sawest, are the seven Churches.

Revelation Chapter 2

1 Unto the Angel of the Church of Ephesus write, These things saith he that holdeth the seven stars in his right hand, and walketh in the midst of the seven golden candlesticks.

2 I know thy works, and thy labor, and thy patience, and how thou canst not forbear them which are evil, and hast examined them which say they are Apostles, and are not, and hast found them liars.

3 And thou hast suffered, and hast patience, and for my Name's sake hast labored, and hast not fainted.

4 Nevertheless, I have somewhat against thee, because thou hast left thy first love.

5 Remember therefore from whence thou art fallen, and repent, and do the first works: or else I will come against thee shortly, and will remove thy candlestick out of his place, except thou amend.

6 But this thou hast, that thou hatest the works of the Nicolaitans, which I also hate.

7 Let him that hath an ear, hear, what the Spirit saith unto the Churches, To him that overcometh, will I give to eat of the tree of life which is in the midst of the Paradise of God.

8 And unto the Angel of the Church of the Smyrnians write, These things saith he that is first, and last, Which was dead and is alive.

9 I know thy works and tribulation, and poverty (but thou art rich) and I know the blasphemy of them, which say they are Jews, and are not, but are the Synagogue of Satan.

10 Fear none of those things, which thou shalt suffer: behold, it shall come to pass, that the devil shall cast some of you into prison, that ye may be tried, and ye shall have tribulation ten days: be thou faithful unto the death, and I will give thee the crown of life.

11 Let him that hath an ear, hear what the Spirit saith to the Churches. He that overcometh, shall not be hurt of the second death.

12 And to the Angel of the Church which is at Pergamus write, This saith he which hath the sharp sword with two edges.

13 I know thy works and where thou dwellest, even where Satan's throne is, and thou keepest my Name, and hast not denied my faith, even in those days when Antipas my faithful martyr was slain among you, where Satan dwelleth.

14 But I have a few things against thee, because thou hast there them that maintain the doctrine of Balaam, which taught Balac, to put a stumblingblock before the children of Israel, that they should eat of things sacrificed unto Idols, and commit fornication.

15 Even so hast thou them, that maintain the doctrine of the Nicolaitans, which thing I hate.

16 Repent thyself, or else I will come unto thee shortly, and will fight against them with the sword of my mouth.

17 Let him that hath an ear, hear what the Spirit saith unto the Churches, To him that overcometh, will I give to eat of the Manna that is hid, and will give him a white stone, and in the stone a new name written, which no man knoweth saving he that receiveth it.

18 And unto the Angel of the Church which is at Thyatira write, These things saith the Son of God, which hath his eyes like unto a flame of fire, and his feet like fine brass.

19 I know thy works and thy love, and service, and faith, and thy patience, and thy works, and that they are more at the last, than at the first.

20 Notwithstanding, I have a few things against thee, that thou sufferest the woman Jezebel, which calleth herself a prophetess, to teach and to deceive my servants to make them commit fornication, and to eat meats sacrificed unto idols.

21 And I gave her space to repent of her fornication, and she repented not.

22 Behold, I will cast her into a bed, and them that commit fornication with her, into great affliction, except they repent them of their works.

23 And I will kill her children with death: and all the Churches shall know that I am he which search the reins and hearts: and I will give unto every one of you according unto your works.

24 And unto you I say, the rest of them of Thyatira, As many as have not this learning, neither have known the deepness of Satan (as they speak) I will put upon you none other burden.

25 But that which ye have already, hold fast till I come.

26 For he that overcometh and keepeth my works unto the end, to him will I give power over nations,

27 And he shall rule them with a rod of iron: and as the vessels of a potter, shall they be broken.

28 Even as I received of my Father, so will I give him the morning star.

29 Let him that hath an ear, hear what the Spirit saith to the Churches.

Revelation Chapter 3

1 And write unto the Angel of the Church which is at Sardis, These things saith he that hath the seven Spirits of God, and the seven stars, I know thy works: for thou hast a name that thou livest, but thou art dead.

2 Be awake and strengthen the things which remain, that are ready to die: for I have not found thy works perfect before God.

3 Remember therefore, how thou hast received and heard, and hold fast, and repent. If therefore thou wilt not watch, I will come on thee as a thief, and thou shalt not know what hour I will come upon thee.

4 Notwithstanding thou hast a few names yet in Sardis, which have not defiled their garments: and they shall walk with me in white: for they are worthy.

5 He that overcometh, shall be clothed in white array, and I will not put out his name out of the book of life, but I will confess his name before my Father, and before his Angels.

6 Let him that hath an ear, hear, what the Spirit saith unto the Churches.

7 And write unto the Angel of the Church which is of Philadelphia, These things saith he that is Holy and True, which hath the key of David, which openeth and no man shutteth, and shutteth and no man openeth.

8 I know thy works: behold, I have set before thee an open door, and no man can shut it: for thou hast a little strength and hast kept my word, and hast not denied my Name.

9 Behold, I will make them of the Synagogue of Satan,which call themselves Jews and are not, but do lie: behold, I say, I will make them, that they shall come and worship before my feet, and shall know that I have loved thee.

10 Because thou hast kept the word of my patience, therefore I will deliver thee from the hour of temptation, which will come upon all the world, to try them that dwell upon the earth.

11 Behold, I come shortly: hold that which thou hast, that no man take thy crown.

12 Him that overcometh, will I make a pillar in the Temple of my God, and he shall go no more out: and I will write upon him the Name of my God, and the name of the city of my God, which is the new Jerusalem, which cometh down out of heaven from my God, and I will write upon him my new Name.

13 Let him that hath an ear, hear what the Spirit saith unto the Churches.

14 And unto the Angel of the Church of the Laodiceans write, These things saith Amen, the faithful and true witness, the beginning of the creatures of God.

15 I know thy works, that thou art neither cold nor hot: I would thou werest cold or hot.

16 Therefore, because thou art lukewarm, and neither cold nor hot, it will come to pass, that I shall spew thee out of my mouth.

17 For thou sayest, I am rich and increased with goods, and have need of nothing, and knowest not how thou art wretched and miserable, and poor, and blind, and naked.

18 I counsel thee to buy of me gold tried by the fire, that thou mayest be made rich, and white raiment, that thou mayest be clothed and that thy filthy nakedness do not appear: and anoint thine eyes, with eye salve, that thou mayest see.

19 As many as I love, I rebuke and chasten: be zealous therefore and amend.

20 Behold, I stand at the door, and knock. If any man hear my voice and open the door, I will come in unto him, and will sup with him, and he with me.

21 To him that overcometh, will I grant to sit with me in my throne, even as I overcame, and sit with my Father in his throne.

22 Let him that hath an ear, hear what the Spirit saith unto the Churches.

Revelation Chapter 4

1 After this I looked, and behold, a door was open in heaven, and the first voice which I heard, was as it were of a trumpet talking with me, saying, Come up hither, and I will show thee things which must be done hereafter.

2 And immediately I was ravished in the spirit, and behold, a throne was set in heaven, and one sat upon the throne.

3 And he that sat, was to look upon, like unto a jasper stone, and a sardine, and there was a rainbow round about the throne in sight like to an emerald.

4 And round about the throne were four and twenty seats, and upon the seats I saw four and twenty Elders sitting, clothed in white raiment, and had on their heads crowns of gold.

5 And out of the throne proceeded lightnings, and thunderings, and voices, and there were seven lamps of fire, burning before the throne, which are the seven spirits of God.

6 And before the throne there was a sea of glass like unto crystal: and in the midst of the throne, and round about the throne were four beasts full of eyes before and behind.

7 And the first beast was like a lion, and the second beast like a calf, and the third beast had a face as a man, and the fourth beast was like a flying Eagle.

8 And the four beasts had each one of them six wings about him, and they were full of eyes within, and they ceased not day nor night, saying, Holy, holy, holy Lord God almighty, Which Was, and Which Is, and Which Is to come.

9 And when those beasts gave glory, and honor, and thanks to him that sat on the throne, which liveth forever and ever,

10 The four and twenty Elders fell down before him that sat on the throne and worshipped him, that liveth forevermore, and cast their crowns before the throne, saying,

11 Thou art worthy, O Lord, to receive glory and honor, and power: for thou hast created all things, and for thy will's sake they are, and have been created.

Revelation Chapter 5

1 And I saw in the right hand of him that sat upon the throne, a Book written within, and on the back side, sealed with seven seals.

2 And I saw a strong Angel which preached with a loud voice, Who is worthy to open the book, and to loose the seals thereof?

3 And no man in heaven, nor in earth, neither under the earth, was able to open the Book, neither to look thereon.

4 Then I wept much, because no man was found worthy to open, and to read the Book, neither to look thereon.

5 And one of the Elders said unto me, Weep not: behold, the Lion which is of the tribe of Judah, the root of David, hath obtained to open the Book, and to loose the seven seals thereof.

6 Then I beheld, and lo, in the midst of the throne, and of the four beasts, and in the midst of the Elders, stood a Lamb as though he had been killed, which had seven horns, and seven eyes, which are the seven spirits of God, sent into all the world.

7 And he came, and took the Book out of the right hand of him that sat upon the throne.

8 And when he had taken the Book, the four beasts and the four and twenty Elders fell down before the Lamb, having every one harps and golden vials full of odors, which are the prayers of the Saints,

9 And they sang a new song, saying, Thou art worthy to take the Book, and to open the seals thereof, because thou wast killed, and hast redeemed us to God by thy blood out of every kindred, and tongue, and people, and nation,

10 And hast made us unto our God Kings and Priests, and we shall reign on the earth.

11 Then I beheld, and I heard the voice of many Angels round about the throne and about the beasts and the Elders, and there were thousand thousands,

12 Saying with a loud voice, Worthy is the Lamb that was killed to receive power and riches, and wisdom, and strength, and honor, and glory, and praise.

13 And all the creatures which are in heaven, and on the earth, and under the earth, and in the sea, and all that are in them, heard I, saying, Praise and honor, and glory, and power be unto him, that sitteth upon the throne, and unto the Lamb forevermore.

14 And the four beasts said, Amen, and the four and twenty Elders fell down, and worshipped him that liveth forevermore.

Revelation Chapter 6

1 After, I beheld when the Lamb had opened one of the seals, and I heard one of the four beasts say, as it were the noise of thunder, Come and see.

2 Therefore I beheld, and lo, there was a white horse, and he that sat on him, had a bow, and a crown was given unto him, and he went forth conquering that he might overcome.

3 And when he had opened the second seal, I heard the second beast say, Come and see.

4 And there went out another horse, that was red, and power was given to him that sat thereon, to take peace from the earth and that they should kill one another, and there was given unto him a great sword.

5 And when he had opened the third seal, I heard the third beast say, Come and see. Then I beheld, and lo, a black horse, and he that sat on him, had balances in his hand.

6 And I heard a voice in the midst of the four beasts say, A measure of wheat for a penny, and three measures of barley for a penny, and oil, and wine hurt thou not.

7 And when he had opened the fourth seal, I heard the voice of the fourth beast say, Come and see.

8 And I looked, and behold, a pale horse, and his name that sat on him was Death, and Hell followed after him, and power was given unto them over the fourth part of the earth, to kill with sword, and with hunger, and with death, and with the beasts of the earth.

9 And when he had opened the fifth seal, I saw under the altar the souls of them, that were killed for the word of God, and for the testimony which they maintained.

10 And they cried with a loud voice, saying, How long, Lord, holy and true! Dost not thou judge and avenge our blood on them that dwell on the earth?

11 And long white robes were given unto every one, and it was said unto them, that they should rest for a little season until their fellow servants, and their brethren that should be killed even as they were, were fulfilled.

12 And I beheld when he had opened the sixth seal, and lo, there was a great earthquake, and the sun was as black as sackcloth of hair, and the moon was like blood.

13 And the stars of heaven fell unto the earth, as a fig tree casteth her green figs when it is shaken of a mighty wind.

14 And heaven departed away, as a scroll when it is rolled, and every mountain and isle were moved out of their places.

15 And the Kings of the earth, and the great men, and the rich men, and the chief captains, and the mighty men, and every bondman, and every free man, hid themselves in dens, and among the rocks of the mountains,

16 And said to the mountains and rocks, Fall on us, and hide us from the presence of him that sitteth on the throne, and from the wrath of the Lamb. 17 For the great day of his wrath is come, and who can stand?

Revelation Chapter 7

1 And after that, I saw four Angels stand on the four corners of the earth, holding the four winds of the earth, that the winds should not blow on the earth, neither on the sea, neither on any tree.

2 And I saw another Angel come up from the East, which had the seal of the living God, and he cried with a loud voice to the four Angels to whom power was given to hurt the earth, and the sea, saying,

3 Hurt ye not the earth, neither the sea, neither the trees, till we have sealed the servants of our God in their foreheads.

4 And I heard the number of them, which were sealed, and there were sealed an hundred and four and forty thousand of all the tribes of the children of Israel.

5 Of the tribe of Juda were sealed twelve thousand. Of the tribe of Ruben were sealed twelve thousand. Of the tribe of Gad were sealed twelve thousand.

6 Of the tribe of Aser were sealed twelve thousand. Of the tribe of Nephthali were sealed twelve thousand. Of the tribe of Manasses were sealed twelve thousand.

7 Of the tribe of Simeon were sealed twelve thousand. Of the tribe of Levi were sealed twelve thousand. Of the tribe of Issachar were sealed twelve thousand. Of the tribe of Zabulon were sealed twelve thousand.

8 Of the tribe of Joseph were sealed twelve thousand. Of the tribe of Benjamin were sealed twelve thousand.

9 After these things I beheld, and lo, a great multitude, which no man could number, of all nations and kindreds, and people, and tongues, stood before the throne, and before the Lamb, clothed with long white robes, and palms in their hands.

10 And they cried with a loud voice, saying, Salvation cometh of our God, that sitteth upon the throne, and of the Lamb.

11 And all the Angels stood round about the throne, and about the Elders, and the four beasts, and they fell before the throne on their faces, and worshipped God,

12 Saying, Amen. Praise and glory, and wisdom, and thanks, and honor, and power, and might, be unto our God forevermore, Amen.

13 And one of the Elders spake, saying unto me, What are these which are arrayed in long white robes? And whence came they?

14 And I said unto him, Lord, thou knowest. And he said to me, These are they, which came out of great tribulation, and have washed their long robes and have made their long robes white in the blood of the Lamb.

15 Therefore are they in the presence of the throne of God, and serve him day and night in his Temple, and he that sitteth on the throne, will dwell among them.

16 They shall hunger no more, neither thirst any more, neither shall the sun light on them, neither any heat.

17 For the Lamb, which is in the midst of the throne, shall govern them, and shall lead them unto the lively fountains of waters, and God shall wipe away all tears from their eyes.

Revelation Chapter 8

1 And when he had opened the seventh seal, there was silence in heaven about half an hour.
2 And I saw the seven Angels, which stood before God, and to them were given seven trumpets.
3 Then another Angel came and stood before the altar having a golden censer, and much odors was given unto him, that he should offer with the prayers of all Saints upon the golden altar, which is before the throne.
4 And the smoke of the odors with the prayers of the Saints, went up before God, out of the Angel's hand.
5 And the Angel took the censer, and filled it with fire of the altar, and cast it into the earth, and there were voices, and thunderings, and lightnings, and earthquake.
6 Then the seven Angels, which had the seven trumpets, prepared themselves to blow the trumpets.
7 So the first Angel blew the trumpet, and there was hail and fire, mingled with blood, and they were cast into the earth, and the third part of trees was burned, and all green grass was burned.
8 And the second Angel blew the trumpet, and as it were a great mountain, burning with fire, was cast into the sea, and the third part of the sea became blood.
9 And the third part of the creatures, which were in the sea, and had life, died, and the third part of ships were destroyed.
10 Then the third Angel blew the trumpet, and there fell a great star from heaven burning like a torch, and it fell into the third part of the rivers, and into the fountains of waters.
11 And the name of the star is called wormwood: therefore the third part of the waters became wormwood, and many men died of the waters, because they were made bitter.
12 And the fourth Angel blew the trumpet, and the third part of the sun was smitten, and the third part of the moon, and the third part of the stars, so that the third part of them was darkened: and the day was smitten, that the third part of it could not shine, and likewise the night.
13 And I beheld, and heard one Angel flying through the midst of heaven, saying with a loud voice, Woe, woe, woe to the inhabitants of the earth, because of the sounds to come of the trumpet of the three Angels, which were yet to blow the trumpets.

Revelation Chapter 9

1 And the fifth Angel blew the trumpet, and I saw a star fall from heaven unto the earth, and to him was given the key of the bottomless pit.
2 And he opened the bottomless pit, and there arose the smoke of the pit, as the smoke of a great furnace, and the sun, and the air were darkened by the smoke of the pit.
3 And there came out of the smoke locusts upon the earth, and unto them was given power, as the scorpions of the earth have power.
4 And it was commanded them, that they should not hurt the grass of the earth, neither any green thing, neither any tree: but only those men which have not the seal of God in their foreheads.
5 And to them was commanded that they should not kill them, but that they should be vexed five months, and that their pain should be as the pain that cometh of a scorpion, when he hath stung a man.

6 Therefore in those days shall men seek death, and shall not find it, and shall desire to die, and death shall flee from them.

7 And the form of the locusts was like unto horses prepared unto battle, and on their heads were as it were crowns, like unto gold, and their faces were like the faces of men.

8 And they had hair as the hair of women, and their teeth were as the teeth of lions.

9 And they had habergeons, like to habergeons of iron: and the sound of their wings was like the sound of chariots when many horses run unto battle.

10 And they had tails like unto scorpions, and there were stings in their tails, and their power was to hurt men five months.

11 And they have a King over them, which is the Angel of the bottomless pit, whose name in Hebrew is Abaddon, and in Greek he is named Apollyon.

12 One woe is past, and behold, yet two woes come after this.

13 Then the sixth Angel blew the trumpet, and I heard a voice from the four horns of the golden altar, which is before God,

14 Saying to the sixth Angel, which had the trumpet, Loose the four Angels, which are bound in the great river Euphrates.

15 And the four Angels were loosed, which were prepared at an hour, at a day, at a month, and at a year, to slay the third part of men.

16 And the number of horsemen of war were twenty thousand times ten thousand: for I heard the number of them.

17 And thus I saw the horses in a vision, and them that sat on them, having fiery habergeons, and of jacinth, and of brimstone, and the heads of the horses were as the heads of lions: and out of their mouths went forth fire and smoke and brimstone.

18 Of these three was the third part of men killed, that is, of the fire and of the smoke, and of the brimstone, which came out of their mouths.

19 For their power is in their mouths, and in their tails: for their tails were like unto serpents, and had heads, wherewith they hurt.

20 And the remnant of the men which were not killed by these plagues, repented not of the works of their hands that they should not worship devils, and idols of gold and of silver, and of brass, and of stone, and of wood, which neither can see, neither hear nor go.

21 Also they repented not of their murder, and of their sorcery, neither of their fornication, nor of their theft.

Revelation Chapter 10

1 And I saw another mighty Angel come down from heaven, clothed with a cloud, and the rainbow upon his head, and his face was as the sun, and his feet as pillars of fire.

2 And he had in his hand a little book open, and he put his right foot upon the sea, and his left on the earth,

3 And cried with a loud voice, as when a lion roareth: and when he had cried, seven thunders uttered their voices.

4 And when the seven thunders had uttered their voices, I was about to write: but I heard a voice from heaven saying unto me, Seal up those things which the seven thunders have spoken, and write them not.

5 And the Angel which I saw stand upon the sea and upon the earth, lift up his hand to heaven,

6 And sware by him that liveth for evermore, which created heaven, and the things that therein are, and the earth and the things that therein are, and the sea and the things which therein are, that time should be no more.

7 But in the days of the voice of the seventh Angel, when he shall begin to blow the trumpet, even the mystery of God shall be finished, as he hath declared to his servants the Prophets.

8 And the voice which I heard from heaven, spake unto me again and said, Go and take the little book which is open in the hand of the Angel, which standeth upon the sea and upon the earth.

9 So I went unto the Angel, and said to him, Give me the little book. And he said unto me, Take it, and eat it up, and it shall make thy belly bitter, but it shall be in thy mouth as sweet as honey.

10 Then I took the little book out of the Angel's hand, and ate it up, and it was in my mouth as sweet as honey: but when I had eaten it, my belly was bitter.

11 And he said unto me, Thou must prophesy again among the people and nations, and tongues, and to many Kings.

Revelation Chapter 11

1 Then was given me a reed, like unto a rod, and the Angel stood by, saying, Rise and mete the Temple of God, and the altar, and them that worship therein.

2 But the court which is without the temple cast out, and mete it not: for it is given unto the Gentiles, and the holy city shall they tread under foot two and forty months.

3 But I will give power unto my two witnesses, and they shall prophesy a thousand, two hundred, and threescore days, clothed in sackcloth.

4 These are two olive trees, and two candlesticks, standing before the God of the earth.

5 And if any man will hurt them, fire proceedeth out of their mouths, and devoureth their enemies: for if any man would hurt them, thus must he be killed.

6 These have power to shut heaven, that it rain not in the days of their prophesying, and have power over waters to turn them into blood, and to smite the earth with all manner plagues, as often as they will.

7 And when they have finished their testimony, the beast that cometh out of the bottomless pit, shall make war against them, and shall overcome them, and kill them.

8 And their corpses shall lie in the streets of the great city, which spiritually is called Sodom and Egypt, where our Lord also was crucified.

9 And they of the people and kindreds, and tongues, and Gentiles shall see their corpses three days and an half, and shall not suffer their carcasses to be put in graves.

10 And they that dwell upon the earth, shall rejoice over them and be glad, and shall send gifts one to another: for these two Prophets vexed them that dwelt on the earth.

11 But after three days and an half, the spirit of life coming from God, shall enter into them, and they shall stand up upon their feet: and great fear shall come upon them which saw them.

12 And they shall hear a great voice from heaven, saying unto them, Come up hither. And they shall ascend up to heaven in a cloud, and their enemies shall see them.

13 And the same hour shall there be a great earthquake, and the tenth part of the city shall fall, and in the earthquake shall be slain in number seven thousand: and the remnant shall be afraid, and give glory to the God of heaven.

14 The second woe is past, and behold the third woe will come anon.

15 And the seventh Angel blew the trumpet and there were great voices in heaven, saying, The kingdoms of this world are our Lord's, and his Christ's, and he shall reign forevermore.

16 Then the four and twenty Elders, which sat before God on their seats, fell upon their faces, and worshipped God,

17 Saying, We give thee thanks, Lord God almighty, Which art, and Which wast, and Which art to come: for thou hast received thy great might, and hast obtained thy kingdom.

18 And the Gentiles were angry, and thy wrath is come, and the time of the dead, that they should be judged, and that thou shouldest give reward unto thy servants the

Prophets, and to the Saints, and to them that fear thy Name, to small, and great, and shouldest destroy them, which destroy the earth.
19 Then the Temple of God was opened in heaven, and there was seen in his Temple the Ark of his covenant: and there were lightnings, and voices, and thunderings, and earthquake, and much hail.

Revelation Chapter 12

1 And there appeared a great wonder in heaven: A woman clothed with the sun, and the moon was under her feet, and upon her head a crown of twelve stars.
2 And she was with child and cried travailing in birth, and was pained ready to be delivered.
3 And there appeared another wonder in heaven: for behold, a great red dragon having seven heads, and ten horns, and seven crowns upon his heads:
4 And his tail drew the third part of the stars of heaven, and cast them to the earth. And the dragon stood before the woman, which was ready to be delivered, to devour her child when she had brought it forth.
5 So she brought forth a man child, which should rule all nations with a rod of iron: and that her son was taken up unto God and to his throne.
6 And the woman fled into wilderness where she hath a place prepared of God, that they should feed her there a thousand, two hundred, and three score days.
7 And there was a battle in heaven. Michael and his Angels fought against the dragon, and the dragon fought and his angels.
8 But they prevailed not, neither was their place found any more in heaven.
9 And the great dragon, that old serpent, called the devil and Satan, was cast out, which deceiveth all the world: he was even cast into the earth, and his angels were cast out with him.
10 Then I heard a loud voice, saying, Now is salvation in heaven, and strength and the kingdom of our God, and the power of his Christ: for the accuser of our brethren is cast down, which accused them before our God day and night.
11 But they overcame him by the blood of the Lamb, and by the word of their testimony, and they loved not their lives unto the death.
12 Therefore rejoice, ye heavens, and ye that dwell in them. Woe to the inhabitants of the earth, and of the sea: for the devil is come down unto you which hath great wrath, knowing that he hath but a short time.
13 And when the dragon saw that he was cast unto the earth, he persecuted the woman which had brought forth the man child.
14 But to the woman were given two wings of a great eagle, that she might fly into the wilderness, into her place, where she is nourished for a time, and times, and half a time, from the presence of the serpent.
15 And the serpent cast out of his mouth water after the woman like a flood, that he might cause her to be carried away of the flood.
16 But the earth help the woman, and the earth opened her mouth, and swallowed up the flood, which the dragon had cast out of his mouth.
17 Then the dragon was wroth with the woman, and went and made war with the remnant of her seed, which keep the commandments of God, and have the testimony of Jesus Christ.
18 And I stood on the sea sand.

Revelation Chapter 13

1 And I saw a beast rise out of the sea, having seven heads, and ten horns, and upon his horns were ten crowns, and upon his heads the name of blasphemy.

2 And the beast which I saw, was like a Leopard, and his feet like a bear's, and his mouth as the mouth of a lion: and the dragon gave him his power and his throne, and great authority.

3 And I saw one of his heads as it were wounded to death, but his deadly wound was healed, and all the world wondered and followed the beast.

4 And they worshipped the dragon which gave power unto the beast, and they worshipped the beast, saying, Who is like unto the beast! who is able to war with him!

5 And there was given unto him a mouth, that spake great things and blasphemies, and power was given unto him, to do two and forty months. 6 And he opened his mouth unto blasphemy against God, to blaspheme his Name and his tabernacle, and them that dwell in heaven.

7 And it was given unto him to make war with the Saints, and to overcome them, and power was given him over every kindred and tongue, and nation.

8 Therefore all that dwell upon the earth, shall worship him, whose names are not written in the book of life of the Lamb, which was slain from the beginning of the world.

9 If any man have an ear, let him hear.

10 If any lead into captivity, he shall go into captivity: if any kill with a sword, he must be killed by a sword: here is the patience, and the faith of the Saints.

11 And I beheld another beast coming up out of the earth, which had two horns like the Lamb, but he spake like the dragon.

12 And he did all that the first beast could do before him, and he caused the earth, and them which dwell therein, to worship the first beast, whose deadly wound was healed.

13 And he did great wonders, so that he made fire to come down from heaven on the earth, in the sight of men,

14 And deceived them that dwell on the earth by the signs, which were permitted to him to do in the sight of the beast, saying to them that dwell on the earth, that they should make the image of the beast, which had the wound of a sword, and did live.

15 And it was permitted to him to give a spirit unto the image of the beast, so that the image of the beast should speak, and should cause that as many as would not worship the image of the beast, should be killed.

16 And he made all, both small and great, rich and poor, free and bond, to receive a mark in their right hand or in their foreheads.

17 And that no man might buy or sell, save he that had the mark, or the name of the beast, or the number of his name.

18 Here is wisdom. Let him that hath wit, count the number of the beast: for it is the number of a man, and his number is six hundred threescore and six.

Revelation Chapter 14

1 Then I looked, and lo, a Lamb stood on mount Zion, and with him an hundred, forty and four thousand, having his Father's Name written in their foreheads.

2 And I heard a voice from heaven, as the sound of many waters, and as the sound of a great thunder: and I heard the voice of harpers harping with their harps.

3 And they sung as it were a new song before the throne, and before the four beasts, and the Elders, and no man could learn that song, but the hundred, forty and four thousand, which were bought from the earth.

4 These are they, which are not defiled with women: for they are virgins: these follow the Lamb whithersoever he goeth: these are bought from men, being the first fruits unto God, and to the Lamb.

5 And in their mouths was found no guile: for they are without spot before the throne of God.

6 Then I saw another Angel flee in the midst of heaven, having an everlasting Gospel, to preach unto them, that dwell on the earth, and to every nation, and kindred, and tongue, and people,

7 Saying with a loud voice, Fear God, and give glory to him: for the hour of his judgment is come: and worship him that made heaven and earth, and the sea, and the fountains of waters.

8 And there followed another Angel, saying, It is fallen, it is fallen, Babylon the great city: for she made all nations to drink of the wine of the wrath of her fornication.

9 And the third Angel followed them, saying with a loud voice, If any man worship the beast and his image, and receive his mark in his forehead, or on his hand,

10 The same shall drink of the wine of the wrath of God, yea, of the pure wine, which is poured into the cup of his wrath, and he shall be tormented in fire and brimstone before the holy Angels, and before the Lamb.

11 And the smoke of their torment shall ascend evermore: and they shall have no rest day nor night, which worship the beast and his image, and whosoever receiveth the print of his name.

12 Here is the patience of Saints: here are they that keep the commandments of God, and the faith of Jesus.

13 Then I heard a voice from heaven, saying unto me, Write, Blessed are the dead, which hereafter die in the Lord. Even so saith the Spirit: for they rest from their labors, and their works follow them.

14 And I looked, and behold, a white cloud, and upon the cloud one sitting like unto the Son of man, having on his head a golden crown, and in his hand a sharp sickle.

15 And another Angel came out of the Temple, crying with a loud voice to him that sat on the cloud, Thrust in thy sickle and reap: for the time is come to reap: for the harvest of the earth is ripe.

16 And he that sat on the cloud, thrust in his sickle on the earth, and the earth was reaped.

17 Then another Angel came out of the Temple, which is in heaven, having also a sharp sickle.

18 And another Angel came out from the altar, which had power over fire, and cried with a loud cry to him that had the sharp sickle, and said, Thrust in thy sharp sickle, and gather the clusters of the vineyard of the earth: for her grapes are ripe.

19 And the Angel thrust in his sharp sickle on the earth, and cut down the vines of the vineyard of the earth, and cast them into the great winepress of the wrath of God.

20 And the winepress was trodden without the city, and blood came out of the wine press, unto the horse bridles by the space of a thousand and six hundred furlongs.

Revelation Chapter 15

1 And I saw another sign in heaven great and marvelous, seven Angels having the seven last plagues: for by them is fulfilled the wrath of God.

2 And I saw as it were a glassy sea, mingled with fire, and them that had gotten victory of the beast, and of his image, and of his mark, and of the number of his name, stand at the glassy sea, having the harps of God,

3 And they sang the song of Moses the servant of God, and the song of the Lamb, saying, Great and marvelous are thy works, Lord God almighty: just and true are thy ways, King of Saints.

4 Who shall not fear thee, O Lord, and glorify thy Name! For thou only art holy, and all nations shall come and worship before thee: for thy judgments are made manifest.

5 And after that I looked, and behold, the Temple of the tabernacle of testimony was open in heaven.

6 And the seven Angels came out of the Temple, which had the seven plagues, clothed in pure and bright linen, and having their breasts girded with golden girdles.

7 And one of the four beasts gave unto the seven Angels seven golden vials full of the wrath of God, which liveth forevermore.

8 And the Temple was full of the smoke of the glory of God and of his power, and no man was able to enter into the Temple, till the seven plagues of the seven Angels were fulfilled.

Revelation Chapter 16

1 And I heard a great voice out of the Temple, saying to the seven Angels, Go your ways, and pour out the seven vials of the wrath of God upon the earth.

2 And the first went, and poured out his vial upon the earth: and there fell a noisome, and a grievous sore upon the men, which had the mark of the beast, and upon them which worshipped his image.

3 And the second Angel poured out his vial upon the sea, and it became as the blood of a dead man: and every living thing died in the sea.

4 And the third Angel poured out his vial upon the rivers and fountains of waters, and they became blood.

5 And I heard the Angel of the waters say, Lord, thou art just, Which are, and Which wast: and Holy, because thou hast judged these things.

6 For they shed the blood of the Saints, and Prophets, and therefore hast thou given them blood to drink: for they are worthy.

7 And I heard another out of the Sanctuary say, Even so, Lord God almighty, true and righteous are thy judgments.

8 And the fourth Angel poured out his vial on the sun, and it was given unto him to torment men with heat of fire,

9 And men boiled in great heat, and blasphemed the Name of God, which hath power over these plagues, and they repented not, to give him glory.

10 And the fifth Angel poured out his vial upon the throne of the beast, and his kingdom waxed dark, and they gnawed their tongues for sorrow,

11 And blasphemed the God of heaven for their pains, and for their sores, and repented not of their works.

12 And the sixth Angel poured out his vial upon the great river Euphrates, and the water thereof dried up, that the way of the Kings of the East should be prepared.

13 And I saw three unclean spirits like frogs come out of the mouth of the dragon, and out of the mouth of the beast, and out of the mouth of the false prophet.

14 For they are the spirits of devils, working miracles, to go unto the Kings of the earth, and of the whole world, to gather them to the battle of that great day of God Almighty.

15 (Behold, I come as a thief. Blessed is he that watcheth and keepeth his garments, lest he walk naked, and men see his filthiness)

16 And they gathered them together into a place called in Hebrew Armagedon.

17 And the seventh Angel poured out his vial into the air: and there came a loud voice out of the Temple of heaven from the throne, saying, It is done.

18 And there were voices, and thunderings, and lightnings, and there was a great earthquake, such as was not since men were upon the earth, even so mighty an earthquake.

19 And the great city was divided into three parts, and the cities of the nations fell: and the great Babylon came in remembrance before God, to give unto her the cup of the wine of the fierceness of his wrath.

20 And every isle fled away, and the mountains were not found.

21 And there fell a great hail, like talents, out of heaven upon the men, and men blasphemed God, because of the plague of the hail: for the plague thereof was exceeding great.

Revelation Chapter 17

1 Then there came one of the seven Angels, which had the seven vials, and talked with me, saying unto me, Come: I will show thee the damnation of the great whore that sitteth upon many waters,

2 With whom have committed fornication the Kings of the earth, and the inhabitants of the earth are drunken with the wine of her fornication.

3 So he carried me away into the wilderness in the Spirit, and I saw a woman sit upon a scarlet colored beast, full of names of blasphemy, which had seven heads, and ten horns.

4 And the woman was arrayed in purple and scarlet, and gilded with gold, and precious stones, and pearls, and had a cup of gold in her hand, full of abominations, and filthiness of her fornication.

5 And in her forehead was a name written, A Mystery, great Babylon, the mother of whoredoms, and abominations of the earth.

6 And I saw the woman drunken with the blood of Saints, and with the blood of the Martyrs of Jesus: and when I saw her, I wondered with great marvel.

7 Then the Angel said unto me, Wherefore marvelest thou? I will show thee the mystery of the woman, and of the beast, that beareth her, which hath seven heads, and ten horns.

8 The beast that thou hast seen, was, and is not, and shall ascend out of the bottomles pit, and shall go into perdition, and they that dwell on the earth, shall wonder (whose names are not written in the book of life from the foundation of the world) when they behold the beast that was, and is not, and yet is.

9 Here is the mind that hath wisdom. The seven heads are seven mountains, whereon the woman sitteth: they are also seven Kings.

10 Five are fallen, and one is, and another is not yet come: and when he cometh, he must continue a short space.

11 And the beast that was, and is not, is even the eight, and is one of the seven, and shall go into destruction.

12 And the ten horns which thou sawest, are ten Kings, which yet have not received a kingdom, but shall receive power, as Kings at one hour with the beast.

13 These have one mind, and shall give their power, and authority unto the beast.

14 These shall fight with the Lamb, and the Lamb shall overcome them: for he is Lord of Lords, and King of Kings: and they that are on his side, called, and chosen, and faithful.

15 And he said unto me, The waters which thou sawest, where the whore sitteth, are people, and multitudes, and nations, and tongues.

16 And the ten horns which thou sawest upon the beast, are they that shall hate the whore, and shall make her desolate and naked, and shall eat her flesh, and burn her with fire.

17 For God hath put in their hearts to fulfill his will, and to do with one consent for to give their kingdom unto the beast, until the words of God be fulfilled.

18 And the woman which thou sawest, is the great city, which reigneth over the kings of the earth.

Revelation Chapter 18

1 And after these things, I saw another Angel come down from heaven, having great power, so that the earth was lightened with his glory.

2 And he cried out mightily with a loud voice, saying, It is fallen, it is fallen, Babylon the great city, and is become the habitation of devils, and the hold of all foul spirits, and a cage of every unclean and hateful bird.

3 For all nations have drunken of the wine of the wrath of her fornication, and the Kings of the earth have committed fornication with her, and the merchants of the earth are waxed rich of the abundance of her pleasures.

4 And I heard another voice from heaven say, Go out of her, my people, that ye be not partakers of her sins, and that ye receive not of her plagues.

5 For her sins are come up into heaven, and God hath remembered her iniquities.

6 Reward her, even as she hath rewarded you, and give her double according to her works: and in the cup that she hath filled to you, fill her the double.

7 Inasmuch as she glorified herself, and lived in pleasure, so much give ye to her torment and sorrow: for she saith in her heart, I sit being a queen, and am no widow, and shall see no mourning.

8 Therefore shall her plagues come at one day, death, and sorrow, and famine, and she shall be burned with fire: for strong is the Lord God which will condemn her.

9 And the kings of the earth shall bewail her, and lament for her, which have committed fornication, and lived in pleasure with her, when they shall see the smoke of her burning,

10 And shall stand afar off for fear of her torment, saying, Alas, alas, the great city Babylon, the mighty city: for in one hour is thy judgment come.

11 And the merchants of the earth shall weep and wail over her: for no man buyeth their ware any more.

12 The ware of gold and silver, and of precious stone, and of pearls, and of fine linen, and of purple, and of silk, and of scarlet, and of all manner of Thyne wood, and of all vessels of ivory, and of all vessels of most precious wood, and of brass, and of iron, and of marble,

13 And of cinnamon, and odors, and ointments, and frankincense, and wine, and oil, and fine flour, and wheat, and beasts, and sheep, and horses, and chariots, and servants, and souls of men.

14 (And the apples that thy soul lusted after, are departed from thee, and all things which were fat and excellent, are departed from thee, and thou shalt find them no more.)

15 The merchants of these things which were waxed rich, shall stand afar off from her, for fear of her torment, weeping and wailing,

16 And saying, Alas, alas, the great city, that was clothed in fine linen and purple, and scarlet, and gilded with gold, and precious stone, and pearls.

17 For in one hour so great riches are come to desolation. And every shipmaster, and all the people that occupy ships, and shipmen, and whosoever travail on the sea, shall stand afar off,

18 And cry, when they see the smoke of her burning, saying, What city was like unto this great city?

19 And they shall cast dust on their heads, and cry weeping, and wailing, and say, Alas, alas, the great city, wherein were made rich all that had ships on the sea by her costliness: for in one hour she is made desolate.

20 O heaven, rejoice of her, and ye holy Apostles and Prophets: for God hath given your judgment on her.

21 Then a mighty Angel took up a stone like a great millstone, and cast it into the sea, saying, With such violence shall the great city Babylon be cast, and shall be found no more.

22 And the voice of harpers, and musicians, and of pipers, and trumpeters shall be heard no more in thee, and no craftsman, of whatsoever craft he be, shall be found any more in thee: and the sound of a millstone shall be heard no more in thee.

23 And the light of a candle shall shine no more in thee: and the voice of the bridegroom and of the bride shall be heard no more in thee: for thy merchants were the great men of the earth: and with thine enchantments were deceived all nations.

24 And in her was found the blood of the Prophets, and of the Saints, and of all that were slain upon the earth.

Revelation Chapter 19

1 And after these things I heard a great voice of a great multitude in heaven, saying, Hallelujah, salvation and glory, and honor, and power be to the Lord our God.

2 For true and righteous are his judgments: for he hath condemned the great whore, which did corrupt the earth with her fornication, and hath avenged the blood of his servants shed by her hand.

3 And again they said, Hallelujah: and her smoke rose up forevermore.

4 And the four and twenty Elders, and the four beasts fell down, and worshipped God that sat on the throne, saying, Amen, Hallelujah.

5 Then a voice came out of the throne, saying, Praise our God, all ye his servants, and ye that fear him, both small and great.

6 And I heard like a voice of a great multitude, and as the voice of many waters, and as the voice of strong thunderings, saying, Hallelujah: for our Lord God almighty hath reigned.

7 Let us be glad and rejoice, and give glory to him: for the marriage of the Lamb is come, and his wife hath made her self ready.

8 And to her was granted, that she should be arrayed with pure fine linen and shining, for the fine linen is the righteousness of Saints.

9 Then he said unto me, Write, Blessed are they which are called unto the Lamb's supper. And he said unto me, These words of God are true.

10 And I fell before his feet, to worship him: but he said unto me, See thou do it not: I am thy fellow servant, and one of thy brethren, which have the testimony of Jesus. Worship God: for the testimony of Jesus, is the Spirit of prophecy.

11 And I saw heaven open, and behold a white horse, and he that sat upon him, was called, Faithful and true, and he judgeth and fighteth righteously.

12 And his eyes were as a flame of fire, and on his head were many crowns: and he had a name written, that no man knew but himself.

13 And he was clothed with a garment dipped in blood, and his name is called, THE WORD OF GOD.

14 And the warrior's which were in heaven, followed him upon white horses, clothed with fine linen white and pure.

15 And out of his mouth went out a sharp sword, that with it he should smite the heathen: for he shall rule them with a rod of iron: for he it is that treadeth the wine press of the fierceness and wrath of almighty God.

16 And he hath upon his garment, and upon his thigh a name written, THE KING OF KINGS, AND LORD OF LORDS.

17 And I saw an Angel stand in the sun, who cried with a loud voice, saying to all the fowls that did fly by the midst of heaven, Come, and gather yourselves together unto the supper of the great God,

18 That ye may eat the flesh of Kings, and the flesh of high Captains, and the flesh of mighty men, and the flesh of horses, and of them that sit on them, and the flesh of all freemen and bondmen, and of small and great.

19 And I saw the beast, and the Kings of the earth, and their warrior's gathered together to make battle against him, that sat on the horse and against his soldiers.

20 But the beast was taken, and with him that false prophet that wrought miracles before him, whereby he deceived them that received the beast's mark, and them that worshipped his image. These both were alive cast into a lake of fire, burning with brimstone.

21 And the remnant were slain with the sword of him that sitteth upon the horse, which cometh out of his mouth, and all the fowls were filled full with their flesh.

Revelation Chapter 20

1 And I saw an Angel come down from heaven, having the key of the bottomless pit, and a great chain in his hand.

2 And he took the dragon that old serpent, which is the devil and Satan, and he bound him a thousand years,

3 And cast him into the bottomless pit, and he shut him up, and sealed the door upon him, that he should deceive the people no more, till the thousand years were fulfilled: for after that he must be loosed for a little season.

4 And I saw seats: and they sat upon them, and judgment was given unto them, and I saw the souls of them, that were beheaded for the witness of Jesus, and for the word of God, and which did not worship the beast, neither his image, neither had taken his mark upon their foreheads, or on their hands: and they lived, and reigned with Christ a thousand year.

5 But the rest of the dead men shall not live again, until the thousand years be finished: this is the first resurrection.

6 Blessed and holy is he, that hath part in the first resurrection: for on such the second death hath no power: but they shall be the Priests of God and of Christ, and shall reign with him a thousand year.

7 And when the thousand years are expired, Satan shall be loosed out of his prison,

8 And shall go out to deceive the people, which are in the four quarters of the earth: even Gog and Magog, to gather them together to battle, whose number is, as the sand of the sea.

9 And they went up into the plain of the earth, which compassed the tents of the Saints about, and the beloved city: but fire came down from God out of heaven, and devoured them.

10 And the devil that deceived them, was cast into a lake of fire and brimstone, where the beast and the false prophet shall be tormented even day and night forevermore.

11 And I saw a great white throne, and one that sat on it, from whose face fled away both the earth and heaven, and their place was no more found.

12 And I saw the dead, both great and small stand before God: and the books were opened, and another book was opened, which is the book of life, and the dead were judged of those things, which were written in the books, according to their works.

13 And the sea gave up her dead, which were in her, and death and hell delivered up the dead, which were in them: and they were judged every man according to their works.

14 And death and hell were cast into the lake of fire: this is the second death.

15 And whosoever was not found written in the book of life, was cast into the lake of fire.

Revelation Chapter 21

1 And I saw a new heaven, and a new earth: for the first heaven, and the first earth were passed away, and there was no more sea.

2 And I John saw the holy city new Jerusalem come down from God out of heaven, prepared as a bride trimmed for her husband.

3 And I heard a great voice out of heaven, saying, Behold, the Tabernacle of God is with men, and he will dwell with them: and they shall be his people, and God himself shall be their God with them.

4 And God shall wipe away all tears from their eyes: and there shall be no more death, neither sorrow, neither crying, neither shall there be any more pain: for the first things are passed.

5 And he that sat upon the throne, said, Behold, I make all things new: and he said unto me, Write: for these words are faithful and true.

6 And he said unto me, It is done, I am Alpha and Omega, the beginning and the end. I will give to him that is athirst, of the well of the water of life freely.

7 He that overcometh, shall inherit all things, and I will be his God, and he shall be my son.

8 But the fearful and unbelieving, and the abominable and murderers, and whoremongers, and sorcerers, and idolaters, and all liars shall have their part in the lake, which burneth with fire and brimstone, which is the second death.

9 And there came unto me one of the seven Angels, which had the seven vials full of the seven last plagues, and talked with me, saying, Come: I will show thee the bride, the Lamb's wife.

10 And he carried me away in the spirit to a great and an high mountain, and he showed me the great city, holy Jerusalem, descending out of heaven from God,

11 Having the glory of God: and her shining was like unto a stone most precious, as a Jasper stone clear as crystal,

12 And had a great wall and high, and had twelve gates, and at the gates twelve Angels, and the names written, which are the twelve tribes of the children of Israel.

13 On the East part there were three gates, and on the North side three gates, on the South side three gates, and on the West side three gates.

14 And the wall of the city had twelve foundations, and in them the Names of the Lamb's twelve Apostles.

15 And he that talked with me, had a golden reed to measure the city withal, and the gates thereof, and the wall thereof.

16 And the city lay four-square, and the length is as large as the breadth of it, and he measured the city with the reed, twelve thousand furlongs: and the length, and the breadth, and the height of it are equal.

17 And he measured the wall thereof, an hundred, forty and four cubits, by the measure of man, that is, of the Angel.

18 And the building of the wall of it was of Jasper: and the city was pure gold like unto clear glass.

19 And the foundations of the wall of the city were garnished with all manner of precious stones: the first foundation was Jasper: the second of Sapphire: the third of a Chalcedony: the fourth of an Emerald:

20 The fifth of a Sardonyx: the sixth of a Sardius: the seventh of a Chrysolyte: the eighth of a Beryl: the ninth of a Topaz: the tenth of a Chrysoprasus: the eleventh of a Jacinth: the twelfth an Amethyst.

21 And the twelve gates were twelve pearls, and every gate is of one pearl, and the street of the city is pure gold, as shining glass.

22 And I saw no Temple therein: for the Lord God almighty and the Lamb are the Temple of it.

23 And this city hath no need of the sun, neither of the moon to shine in it: for the glory of God did light it: and the Lamb is the light of it,

24 And the people which are saved, shall walk in the light of it: and the Kings of the earth shall bring their glory and honor unto it.

25 And the gates of it shall not be shut by day: for there shall be no night there.

26 And the glory, and honor of the Gentiles shall be brought unto it.

27 And there shall enter into it none unclean thing, neither whatsoever worketh abomination or lies: but they which are written in the Lamb's book of life.

Revelation Chapter 22

1 And he showed me a pure river of water of life, clear as crystal, proceeding out of the throne of God, and of the Lamb.

2 In the midst of the street of it, and of either side of the river, was the tree of life, which bare twelve manner of fruits, and gave fruit every month: and the leaves of the tree served to heal the nations with.

3 And there shall be no more curse, but the throne of God and of the Lamb shall be in it, and his servants shall serve him.

4 And they shall see his face, and his Name shall be in their foreheads.

5 And there shall be no night there, and they need no candle, neither light of the sun: for the Lord God giveth them light, and they shall reign forevermore.

6 And he said unto me, These words are faithful and true: and the Lord God of the holy Prophets sent his Angel to show unto his servants the things which must shortly be fulfilled.

7 Behold, I come shortly. Blessed is he that keepeth the words of the prophecy of this book.

8 And I am John, which saw and heard these things: and when I had heard and seen, I fell down to worship before the feet of the Angel, which showed me these things.

9 But he said unto me, See thou do it not: for I am thy fellow servant, and of thy brethren the Prophets, and of them which keep the words of this book: worship God.

10 And he said unto me, Seal not the words of the prophecy of this book: for the time is at hand.

11 He that is unjust, let him be unjust still: and he which is filthy, let him be filthy still: and he that is righteous, let him be righteous still: and he that is holy, let him be holy still.

12 And behold, I come shortly, and my reward is with me, to give every man according as his work shall be.

13 I am Alpha and Omega, the beginning and the end, the first and the last.

14 Blessed are they, that do his commandments, that their right may be in the tree of life, and may enter in through the gates into the city.

15 For without shall be dogs and enchanters, and whoremongers, and murderers, and idolaters, and whosoever loveth or maketh lies.

16 I Jesus have sent mine Angel, to testify unto you these things in the Churches: I am the root and the generation of David, and the bright morning star.

17 And the Spirit and the bride say, Come. And let him that heareth, say, Come: and let him that is a thirst, come: and let whosoever will, take of the water of life freely.

18 For I protest unto every man that heareth the words of the prophecy of this book, if any man shall add unto these things, God shall add unto him the plagues, that are written in this book.

19 And if any man shall diminish of the words of the book of this prophecy, God shall take away his part out of the Book of life, and out of the holy city, and from those things which are written in this book.

20 He which testifieth these things, saith, Surely, I come quickly. Amen. Even so come, Lord Jesus.

21 The grace of our Lord Jesus Christ be with you all, Amen.